Praise for *Lean Integration*

"What the authors have set out here is a philosophy built on best practices from both the fields of manufacturing and software development, but they do so with examples that bring the material alive, come from real life, and offer specific, measurable actions and practical alternatives. This work is fantastic, not just from a technical standpoint; it has a maturity that's vacant from other works, an understanding of internal business politics and human resources concerns, all the while wrapped in solid management principles and practices."

Kevin P. Davis, Senior Technical Architect

"Technology is a key enabler within any industry and a key success measure is the 'alignment' between business and information technology. Schmidt and Lyle provide practical advice for a fundamental shift in thinking, from IT as an internal services function to IT as an integral part of a company's strategy, creating value for customers. IT internal and external service providers have to operate as one management team. *Lean Integration* presents compelling examples of how integration teams play a role in leadership, strategic planning, and IT governance as some of the critical factors in achieving organizational alignment."

Zahid Afzal, Executive Vice President/Chief Information Officer,
Huntington National Bank

"In today's world, enterprises struggle with increasing global competition, the need for speed to market, and the ability for IT to enable the strategic intent of the business. One of the core tenets of lean that many integration professionals lose sight of is the need to put the customer first. This book serves as a reminder to our fiduciary responsibility to leverage IT as a competitive tool for planning and execution."

James McGovern, Enterprise Architect, The Hartford

"This book should help the IT executive and practitioner, alike, align on goals and objectives that drive long-term value to their enterprise. The Integration Competency Center can drive as much or more value for the IT department than any other capital investment it will make in the next decade."

Clark T. Becker, Former SVP and CTO, Best Buy Co., Inc.

"In this highly communicative world, one filled with a high degree of turbulence and uncertainty, the one key that will separate successful businesses from the rest is their ability to be agile and wield just-in-time, focused, trustworthy information. I am extremely pleased to see that John and David have written on such an important topic."

Mark Albala, President, InfoSight Partners, LLC

"John Schmidt and David Lyle have written an important book with a new perspective on lean thinking in the software development world. This is a must-read for leaders in all functional areas."

Arthur V. Hill, Lindahl Professor and Professor of Operations and M͟_____ ͟nt Science,
Carlson S͟_____ _____Minnesota

"At OMG we have always believed that integration, repeatable processes and methodology, and high-quality, widely available standards were the missing links in the software world. Given the huge number of lessons to learn from other engineering and management sciences, it's natural to apply the lessons of *Lean Manufacturing* to software production. John Schmidt has recognized the challenges and fought to integrate hard-won knowledge from other disciplines, and this book is a great example of what solid, clear, everyday lessons we can learn to make our organizations agile and innovative. Bravo!"

Richard Mark Soley, Chairman and CEO, Object Management Group, Inc.

"*Lean Integration* is invaluable to any business that relies on technological integration with its customers to expand. This book utilizes lean manufacturing principles to create successful software development projects in a replicable and measurable approach. By successful projects, I mean high quality, quick to production, maintainable for the long term, and under budget for both implementation and ongoing support. As an executive and a Six Sigma Black Belt of an expanding business process outsourcing company that relies on the integration of disparate customer systems for its growth and success, I believe the lean approach outlined in this book is the roadmap to follow."

Howard L. Latham, Executive Vice President, API Outsourcing, Inc.

"*Lean Integration* is an excellent resource for anyone struggling with the challenges of performing integration for a complex enterprise. The authors have combined their experience to provide a practical roadmap for applying lean principles to the integration problem. If you are looking for an approach to tackle the integration chaos that exists in your environment, this book should be at the top of your reading list."

Steve J. Dennis, Integration Competency Center Director, Nike

"As costs of raw technology decline, superior practice will dominate IT value. Increasingly, it's not enough to be clever: it's essential to be efficient, and that's what John Schmidt and David Lyle will help IT practitioners do with their new book, *Lean Integration*. Point-to-point connections grow with (roughly) the square of the number of connected things, but Schmidt and Lyle offer a better way. Rising above the spaghetti bowl to treat integration as a scalable process, they make it practical for enterprise IT to make the most of complementary services in the cloud—promising the attentive reader huge improvements in IT economics."

Peter Coffee, Director of Platform Research, Salesforce.com, Inc.

"*Lean Integration* is a practical discovery not an invention. For this reason everyone will eventually be doing it."

Erwin Dral, Principal Product Manager, Informatica

"John Schmidt and David Lyle's new book, *Lean Integration: An Integration Factory Approach to Business Agility,* is bound to shake up the software development industry. The authors show how to reduce costs and risks of software by applying lean management principles that force developers to focus on real customer/knowledge worker requirements to design quality into software the first time, from requirements definition to implementation and production operations. This is required reading for all information systems personnel who want to be on the cutting edge of quality management applied to software and systems engineering."

Larry P. English, author, Information Quality Applied: Best Practices for Business Information, Processes and Systems

Lean Integration

Lean Integration

*An Integration Factory Approach
to Business Agility*

John G. Schmidt

David Lyle

✦✦Addison-Wesley

Upper Saddle River, NJ • Boston • Indianapolis • San Francisco
New York • Toronto • Montreal • London • Munich • Paris • Madrid
Capetown • Sydney • Tokyo • Singapore • Mexico City

Many of the designations used by manufacturers and sellers to distinguish their products are claimed as trademarks. Where those designations appear in this book, and the publisher was aware of a trademark claim, the designations have been printed with initial capital letters or in all capitals.

The authors and publisher have taken care in the preparation of this book, but make no expressed or implied warranty of any kind and assume no responsibility for errors or omissions. No liability is assumed for incidental or consequential damages in connection with or arising out of the use of the information or programs contained herein.

The publisher offers excellent discounts on this book when ordered in quantity for bulk purchases or special sales, which may include electronic versions and/or custom covers and content particular to your business, training goals, marketing focus, and branding interests. For more information, please contact:

U.S. Corporate and Government Sales
(800) 382-3419
corpsales@pearsontechgroup.com

For sales outside the United States, please contact:

International Sales
international@pearsoned.com

Visit us on the Web: informit.com/aw

Library of Congress Cataloging-in-Publication Data

Schmidt, John G.
 Lean integration : an integration factory approach to business agility
/ John G. Schmidt, David Lyle.
    p.   cm.
Includes index.
ISBN 978-0-321-71231-8 (pbk. : alk. paper)
1. Factory management. 2. Production management. 3. Business
logistics. I. Lyle, David, 1964- II. Title.
TS155.S3234 2010
658.5—dc22

                                               2010007196

ISBN-13: 978-0-321-71231-8
ISBN-10:   0-321-71231-5
Text printed in the United States on recycled paper at Courier in Stoughton, Massachusetts.
Second printing, August 2010

To our loving and understanding families.

Contents

Figures and Tables

Foreword

More than ten years ago I wrote what many call the "definitive book on integration" entitled *Enterprise Application Integration*. The idea for the book was simple, really. Put some time and energy around planning how various enterprise systems communicate with each other, and leverage some sophisticated technology to make integration work in reliable and changeable ways.

Until then, and what is still sometimes the case today, many looked upon integration as a one-off development project, coding to interfaces between two or more systems. It was always cheaper, it always worked at first, but it always hit a brick wall at some point. This was a hack-after-hack approach that quickly led to a dysfunctional state of architecture where changes are difficult if not impossible to make. We needed a better approach and some good thinking around how integration is done.

While I often get credit for kicking off integration as an architectural discipline, the reality is that many smart people worked on the integration problem prior to my book, and they are still working on it today—for instance, the authors of this book, John and David. I remember meeting John for breakfast in 1998 when he was working for AMS and talking about what was next for integration. Even then John's thinking was highly innovative and forward-looking. John's most profound ideas placed discipline around integration, something that was not the case then and is still lacking today.

So, what is needed today? First and foremost is the importance of data in this generation of cloud computing and SOA. Data has always been, and always will be, the foundation of all sound architecture, no matter if you leverage SOA as an approach to architecture, or cloud computing as an option for platform deployment. Understanding the importance of data means that you'll create more efficient and agile architectures that can accommodate any required changes to the business.

In the last ten years, we've gone from hand-coding interfaces between source and target systems to EAI as a better approach to integration. Now we move on to SOA as a way to create architectures that address most behaviors and information as sets of services, and to data-oriented SOAs that are "Lean Integration and Integration Factories." In many respects we are returning to our roots, but doing so with better technology and refined approaches, such as Lean Integration. The benefits will be a reduction in system costs and a huge increase in efficiencies.

The fact of the matter is that integration is an architectural pattern. Like any architectural pattern, you can improve and refine integration into something more productive and more innovative. That is exactly what the authors have done here. In short, John and David have written the right book, at the right time, for the right reasons. John and David present concepts that take integration to the next level, making integration more accessible, efficient, and cost-effective. I jumped at the chance to promote this book to my publisher, as well as the chance to write the foreword. *Lean Integration* should be read by anyone involved with an integration project.

"Lean Integration" is a management system that emphasizes continuous improvements, meaning you don't complete the links and call it done. Integration requires an ongoing interest in the way integration is carried out and the mechanisms required. This means consistently reevaluating and improving the approaches we leverage for integration, as well as the technology employed. Integration is a journey, not a project.

The end results of leveraging Lean Integration go right to the bottom line, including as much as a 50 percent labor productivity improvement via value stream mapping. This is the use of constant improvement to locate and eliminate non-value-added activities, in short, things that are not needed and don't add value to the ultimate customer.

Moreover, Lean Integration provides the value of agility. This means you create an integration infrastructure that is able to change around a changing business or mission. You're able to quickly adjust around these changes, and thus you have the value of quickly altering the business to get into new markets, get out of old markets, and outmaneuver your competition. The strategic advantages of agility are huge.

The approach of addressing data quality within Lean Integration means that you can finally treat data as what it is: an asset. Not addressing data quality means not taking care of that asset, and thus the diminished value of the data results in the diminished value of the business. Data quality also addresses the use of data governance, which is required to adhere to regulations but needed more to protect our data assets no matter what systems are currently managing the data.

Core to this concept is the ability to promote and manage innovation, allowing those in the organization to create and test their own ideas for improving integration. This provides a feeling of empowerment, which is a benefit to the employee, as well as the actions around good ideas, which is a benefit to the company.

What is most profound about *Lean Integration* is that many of the ideas in this book are obvious, but not leveraged. In reading this book you find many things that seem to be simple but good ideas, and you find yourself asking, "Why did I not think of that?" over and over again. However, while the ideas are important, having a framework of understanding is vital as well. You have to place these disciplines into context and make them part of a repeatable process, which is another core feature of this book.

Lean Integration marks the end of chaotic integration practices and the beginning of continuous improvement, which enhances the value of integration. As the number of systems increases within enterprises, so does the need for integration. You can do integration the right way, which is the Lean way. Or you can struggle with it for years to come. I recommend the former.

David S. Linthicum

Preface

By John Schmidt

I have been practicing Lean Integration for over 15 years. I just didn't know it.

Over the past 30 years I've learned various Lean practices such as *kaizen* (continuous improvement) and closely related methods such as Six Sigma and agile software development. But I didn't fully understand Lean as a system until I studied it more thoroughly in 2008. The surprising discovery was that I had in fact been applying Lean principles for many years without formally identifying them as such.

The reality is that Lean principles such as customer intimacy, continuous improvement, seeking quality perfection, and developing effective teams are common sense. David and I don't have a monopoly on common sense, so we expect that as you read this book you will see examples of Lean principles in your own life. We hope that this book does at least two things for you: first, that it enriches your own experiences with more examples, case studies, and practical advice so that you can improve your level of competence; and second, that it provides a more complete management "system" that makes all these commonsense ideas teachable so that you can improve the level of competence of your team and throughout your value chain.

Contrary to common practices I have always viewed integration as a repeatable ongoing process rather than as a custom one-off project effort. While an integration point between any two systems always looks unique from the perspective of the two systems, if you step back and look at all the information exchanges between systems in an enterprise, what you find is a relatively small number of patterns that are repeated over and over again. The details are different for every instance (at a minimum the data itself that is being exchanged is unique) but the patterns are not.

I have been fortunate over the years in my work at the Integration Consortium, Wells Fargo Bank, Bank of America, Best Buy, American Management Systems, and Digital Equipment Corporation to have the opportunity to help hundreds of companies implement integration practices. The first successful Integration Factory I implemented (several prior attempts didn't quite take off) was an exercise in mass customization—building customized message adapters on top of vendor platforms with reusable components based on a service delivery model that focused on customer needs. The next successful Integration Factory encompassed not only real-time application-to-application integration, but also high-volume batch-oriented database-to-database integration, external business-to-business (B2B) managed file transfer, and business process integration. The factory also included an internal Web application that allowed users (customers of the integration team) to interact with the factory through a series of role-based user interfaces.

Through these and hundreds of other experiences over the years I have a developed a perspective on what it takes to implement sustainable integration practices. The first book on which David and I collaborated, *Integration Competency Center: An Implementation Methodology*,[1] articulated the concepts that make the difference between a successful and an unsuccessful integration strategy. This book takes Integration Competency Centers (ICCs) to the next level by adding more specific best practices and a rich collection of case studies, and by leveraging the vast body of knowledge that has developed over the past 50 years on Lean practices. The net result is sustainable integration that begins to turn an art into a science by making it teachable and repeatable.

By David Lyle

One of the most rewarding professional periods of my life was leading a remarkable team of developers who put together packaged analytic applications to sell as software products about ten years ago. Little did I realize that our team, at the high-water mark numbering over 80 people, was employing all of the Lean Integration principles discussed in this book while

---

1. John G. Schmidt and David Lyle, *Integration Competency Center: An Implementation Methodology* (Informatica Corporation, 2005).

putting together what John and I now describe as an Integration Factory. Like John, I didn't realize we were employing Lean thinking; I just thought we were continually benefiting from people's innovative ideas to work smarter, not harder.

Our development team made the realization that the integration logic in those analytic applications followed a relatively small number of integration or processing patterns. Because the time spent on the design, implementation, and testing of integration was such a large proportion of the total development costs, the team realized we became significantly more effective if we thought in terms of developing assembly lines around these integration patterns rather than crafting all integration logic as "unique works of art." By changing our entire approach over the course of four years, we became far more efficient as a development organization, but most important, we developed higher-quality, more maintainable products for our customers.

Over the past several years, John and I have worked at or talked with numerous companies around the world about how to develop and grow their ICCs. We found several ICCs achieving great success by automating certain processes, using mass customization techniques, or adopting agile development approaches. Several we call out explicitly as case studies in this book, but many of the ideas in this book are the products of conversations and achievements of numerous integration professionals we've spoken with over the years. In other words, besides our own experiences, John and I have seen others be successful with many of the ideas we're pulling together in this book.

That being said, we don't mean to ever imply that adopting these ideas is easy. Integration is an especially complex, challenging problem, both technically and organizationally. All companies have had to spend significant time continually convincing executive management of the benefits of attacking integration as a discipline that is part of the overall enterprise architecture, rather than as a temporary exercise that is unique to each project. Most IT executives are less aware of the detailed costs of integration or benefits of ICCs.

Lean Integration and the Integration Factory are neither destinations nor vendor products; implementing them is a journey that takes many years. Despite the fact that John and I both now work for Informatica, we worked hard to make this book vendor-neutral. We wanted the book to be broadly useful to integration professionals rather than to be based on a specific vendor's software offering. Successful ICCs are a product of the synergy of good people, effective processes, and appropriate technology. This book represents what we've learned over the years from so many people about how Lean thinking can make ICCs significantly more efficient and effective for their customers.

Acknowledgments

This book is itself an example of Lean practices. For starters, it was produced by a *value stream*. Over the years there have been countless individuals in many roles and functions who have contributed what we hope meets the expectations of our customers—you. The book demonstrates *pull* in the sense that we wouldn't have written it if we hadn't received numerous requests from readers of our first book asking for more detailed and prescriptive techniques. It demonstrates *just-in-time* in that Lean thinking is on a rapid growth curve for adoption across many nonmanufacturing business processes; two years ago the book would have been premature for broad-based adoption, and two years from now there will likely be many books on how to apply Lean to IT processes. It also demonstrates *continuous improvement*; many ideas in this book were first written as blog articles that resulted in reader feedback, which has improved the quality of the final result.

To fully acknowledge all the individuals and organizations that have contributed to the culmination of Lean Integration could double the length of this book but would not add value to our readers. So we apologize in advance for not mentioning all of the support and contributions we have received over the years. We would, however, like to mention a few noteworthy contributions that we hope will add some value.

The detailed practical examples from real-world situations add a level of depth to the book, and value to our readers, for which we are profoundly grateful. Many thanks go out to the following people for their case study contributions:

- Todd Soller for his support as well as the many people who accomplished the impressive results: Lucas Anderson, Anil Atri, Clark Becker, Charles Betz, Michael Frank, Greg Friesen, Arul James Suneela Kanuri, Mark

Karger, Todd Lauinger, Radhika Menon, Lelanie Moll, Balaji Ramaswamy, Rick Sorenson, Bob Steel, and Raghu Venkateshwar

- Michael Levine for the Wells Fargo Post-Closing case study, an amazing example of cycle-time reduction and quality improvement through effective flow-through processes
- Barbara Latullipe for her leadership and insights in applying Lean practices to data quality and master data management at Smith & Nephew
- Gary Kamath and Manish Varma for providing valuable contributions to the case studies
- Patrick Kirkes for his skills in mass customizing integration logic
- Steve Morgan for his persistence in implementing domain models; in conjunction with his organization's integration hub, the approach provided an impressive ability to mass-customize data in support of organizational agility

Many thanks, in no particular order, also go out to

- Dr. Art Hill, professor at the Carlson School of Management at the University of Minnesota, for his lessons in Lean and for giving us the idea for the title
- Paul Husby, author of Chapter 2 and most of the terminology in Appendix A, for helping us paint a rich picture of the Lean system as well as providing a history of Lean
- Sohaib Abbasi, CEO at Informatica, for constantly nagging us to write a sequel to the original ICC book
- Brian Hodges, Chris Boorman, Paul Hoffman, and James Markarian, senior executives at Informatica, for their strong support and for giving us the company time, resources, and creative freedom to develop a compelling message
- Kevin Davis, Stephen Dulzer, Jill Dyche, and Tom Poppendieck, for their detailed reviews and comments on the draft manuscript; the book is 100 percent better because of their constructive feedback
- David Linthicum, for encouraging us to write the book and introducing us to the publisher
- Tiffany Gumfory, Jeremy Phelps, and Alison Spong, for handling many of the logistical details associated with simply "getting it done"
- Michael Kuhbock and Leanne MacDonald, for their feedback and providing the support of the Integration Consortium to help make it happen

About the Authors

 John Schmidt's integration career began over 30 years ago when he was a hardware technician at Digital Equipment Corporation. He tells the story about plugging a PDP-11 cable into the wrong socket, which put 30 volts rather than 5 volts on the bus and fried every chip connected to it. Hence the first lesson in integration: While the plug might fit in the socket, hidden incompatibilities in behavior that are not readily visible can be disastrous.

John went on to work as a software engineer, project manager, sales representative, professional services manager, program manager, and enterprise architect. He has practiced and honed his integration expertise in half a dozen industries (banking, retail, telecommunications, education, government, and utilities) and in just as many countries. John was director and chairman of the Integration Consortium for eight years, has written numerous articles on systems integration and enterprise architecture, developed program management practices, and is a frequent speaker at industry conferences.

John's current role is vice president of Global Integration Services at Informatica. He advises clients on the business potential of emerging technologies; leads in the creation of strategies for enterprise initiatives; and plans, directs, and supervises Informatica's Integration Competency Center Practice. He graduated from Red River College and holds a master's degree in business administration from the Carlson School of Management at the University of Minnesota.

David Lyle's career has traveled from the hardware world of computer design to the software world of product development, and along the way he developed early massively parallel (MPP) UNIX systems and associated parallel RDBMS systems for Unisys. While working on the field implementations of these large-scale data warehousing systems, he began noticing consistent, recurring patterns.

From these experiences, David helped found Influence Software, one of the early packaged analytic applications companies. Informatica bought Influence Software at the end of 1999, and for three years David led the R&D organization that built the packaged business intelligence content, the data models, and the preconfigured data integration logic for extracting data out of the most common ERP and CRM systems. After Informatica divested itself of these packaged applications to focus on its core business of data integration, David turned his attention to guiding Informatica's product direction, based upon the "after-market" tools and utilities his earlier organization had used to automate common integration patterns or solve many of the challenges they faced. These ideas culminated in Informatica's Metadata Manager, automated generation of integration logic following configurable architecture patterns, and patents on using canonical data virtualization techniques within integration architectures to move toward elimination of point-to-point integration approaches.

David is currently vice president of Product Strategy, where he continues to guide the longer-term vision for how the Informatica platform assists organizations in integrating and managing their data more efficiently and effectively. He graduated from Stanford University with a bachelor's of science in electrical engineering.

Introduction

Knowledge is power.
Sir Francis Bacon[1]

Lean Integration is a management system that emphasizes continuous improvement and the elimination of waste in end-to-end data integration and process integration activities. Lean practices are well established in other disciplines such as manufacturing, supply chain management, and software development to name just a few, but the application of Lean to the integration discipline is new.

Lean manufacturing is a management system that emphasizes creating value for end customers and eliminating activities that are not value-added (waste). Its principles were derived from the Toyota Production System (TPS), which was developed over 50 years ago but since the 1990s has simply been referred to as Lean. While Lean is rooted in product manufacturing, it is now widely regarded as a management approach that can be applied effectively to a wide range of product and service industries. Lean is closely related to, and borrows from, other methodologies, including Value Network, Theory of Constraints, Six Sigma, and Statistical Process Control (including the work of W. Edwards Deming).

Lean software development is an agile approach that translates Lean manufacturing principles and practices for the software development domain. It was adapted from the TPS and introduced by Mary and Tom Poppendieck in their book *Lean Software Development* and expanded in

---

1. Sir Francis Bacon, *Relegious Meditations of Heresies,* 1597.

Implementing Lean Software Development, followed by *Leading Lean Software Development* in 2009.[2]

Lean Integration builds on these prior works by applying their principles to the process of integration. The definition of *integration* used in this book is "the practice of making independent applications work together as a cohesive system on an ongoing basis." While there are myriad integration technologies and information exchange patterns, broadly speaking, integration solutions typically fall into one of two styles:

1. **Process integration:** automation of processes that cut across functional or application boundaries where process state needs to be maintained independently of the underlying application systems or where multiple data consumers or data providers need to be orchestrated as part of a business transaction
2. **Data integration:** accessing data and functions from disparate systems to create a combined and consistent view of core information for use across the organization to improve business decisions and operations

Another integration style that some practitioners call out as a separate category is service integration as part of a service-oriented architecture (SOA), where application functions are separated into distinct units, or services, that are directly accessible over a network in a loosely coupled manner and may be orchestrated with stateless interactions. The contrary argument is that service integration and the associated infrastructure of an enterprise service bus (ESB) are simply characteristics of a given process integration or data integration design.

Regardless of how many integration categories there are, Lean Integration applies to all of them. Software systems are, by their very nature, flexible and will change over time (legacy systems are often an exception). Interfaces and information exchanges between systems are never built just once. Integration therefore is not a one-time activity; it is ongoing. In summary, therefore, Lean Integration is the application of Lean principles and methods to the challenges of process and data integration on a sustainable basis.

---

2. Mary and Tom Poppendieck, *Lean Software Development: An Agile Toolkit* (Addison-Wesley, 2003); *Implementing Lean Software Development: From Concept to Cash* (Addison-Wesley, 2007); *Leading Lean Software Development: Results Are Not the Point* (Addison-Wesley, 2009).

This book builds on the first book that we wrote in 2005, *Integration Competency Center: An Implementation Methodology*.[3] Integration Competency Centers (ICCs) continue to be a key ingredient of efficient and sustainable integration, and the core concepts in the 2005 book remain applicable to a Lean Integration practice. It is not necessary to read the ICC book first, but it still serves as an effective primer. This book adds depth to ICC principles and methods and extends the concepts to a broader view of the value chain.

One of the things we have learned since writing the first book is that an ICC by any other name is still an ICC. For example, some groups have names such as

- Integration Solutions Group (ISG)
- Center of Excellence or Center of Expertise (COE)
- Business Intelligence Competency Center (BICC)
- Data Quality COE
- Enterprise Data Warehouse (EDW)
- SOA COE
- Center of Competency (CoC)

And the list goes on. The point is that the principles and methods presented here are management practices that apply to all of them. Of course, the subject area expertise is different for each one, as are the scope, the technical skills needed by the staff, the specific tools and technologies that are used, and the internal and external customers that are served by it. In any event, we need to have a name for the organizational unit and need to call it something in this book, so we will continue to use Integration Competency Center, or ICC for short, as the umbrella term for all varieties. For the record, our definition of *Integration Competency Center* is as follows:

> A permanent cross-functional team operating as a shared-services function supporting multiple organizational units and sustaining integration solutions in a coordinated manner

This book is divided into three parts. Part I serves as a summary for executives of Lean Integration and therefore provides an overview for a broad

---

3. John G. Schmidt and David Lyle, *Integration Competency Center: An Implementation Methodology* (Informatica Corporation, 2005).

audience from senior IT executives to front-line operations staff. It provides an overview of and justification for Lean by answering questions like these:

- "Why Lean?" and "So what?"
- "As a business executive, what problems will it help me solve?"
- "As an IT leader or line-of-business owner, why am I going to make a considerable investment in Lean Integration?"
- "How is this different from other methods, approaches, and frameworks?"
- "Why am I as an IT professional going to embrace and sell Lean Integration internally?"

This first part also provides an overview of Lean practices, where they come from, and how they have evolved. It includes insightful research and current trends in how Lean is being adapted to different industries and management disciplines.

Part I concludes with an overview of the Integration Factory—the next-generation integration technology that adds a high degree of automation to the flow of materials and information in the process of building and sustaining integration points. Examples of automation include requirements definition, code generation, testing, and migration of code objects from development to test to production environments. The Integration Factory, we believe, will be the dominant new "wave" of middleware for the next decade (2010s). It views the thousands of information exchanges between applications in an enterprise as mass customizations of a relatively small number of patterns.

The management practice that optimizes the benefits of the Integration Factory is Lean Integration—the use of *Lean principles* and *tools* in the process of making independent applications work together as a cohesive system. The combination of factory technologies and Lean practices results in significant and sustainable *business benefits*.

Part II introduces the seven Lean Integration principles that optimize the Integration Factory and shows how they can be applied to the challenges of system, data, and application integration in a sustainable fashion. This section of the book is targeted at business and IT leaders who are implementing, or considering implementing, a Lean Integration program. Each chapter in this part focuses on one of the seven core principles:

1. **Focus on the customer and eliminate waste:** Maintain a spotlight on customer value and use customer input as the primary driver for the

development of services and integration solutions. Waste elimination is related to this principle, since waste consists of activities that don't add value from the customer's perspective rather than from the supplier's perspective. Related concepts include optimizing the entire value stream in the interest of things that customers care about and just-in-time delivery to meet customer demands.

2. **Continuously improve:** Use a data-driven cycle of hypothesis-validation-implementation to drive innovation and continuously improve the end-to-end process. Related concepts include how to amplify learning, institutionalizing lessons learned, and sustaining integration knowledge.

3. **Empower the team:** Share commitments across individuals and multi-functional teams and provide the support they need to innovate and try new ideas without fear of failure. Empowered teams and individuals have a clear picture of their role in the value chain, know exactly who their customers and suppliers are, and have the information necessary to make day-by-day and even minute-by-minute adjustments.

4. **Optimize the whole:** Make trade-offs on individual steps or activities in the interest of maximizing customer value and bottom-line results for the enterprise. Optimizing the whole requires a big-picture perspective of the end-to-end process and how the customer and enterprise value can be maximized even if it requires sub-optimizing individual steps or activities.

5. **Plan for change:** Apply mass customization techniques to reduce the cost and time in both the build and run stages of the integration life cycle. The development stage is optimized by focusing on reusable and parameter-driven integration elements to rapidly build new solutions. The operations stage is optimized by leveraging automated tools and structured processes to efficiently monitor, control, tune, upgrade, and fix the operational integration systems.

6. **Automate processes:** Judiciously use investments to automate common manual tasks and provide an integrated service delivery experience to customers. In mature environments, this leads to the elimination of scale factors, the ability to respond to large integration projects as rapidly and cost-effectively as small changes, and the removal of integration dependencies from the critical implementation path.

7. **Build quality in:** Emphasize process excellence and building quality in rather than trying to inspect it in. Related concepts include error-proofing the process and reducing recovery time and costs.

Part III is intended for those who have direct responsibility for implementing an integration strategy or are members of an integration team and are interested in improving their ICC or Lean skills. It provides detailed best practices, grouped into seven competency areas. These competencies are ongoing capabilities that an organization needs in order to provide a sustainable approach to integration.

1. **Financial management:** Financial management is a vital competency of a Lean practice that is operating a shared-services group; it takes more than technical activities to create and sustain an effective shared-services group. By showing how to articulate the business value of technology, we are seeking to ensure that the team does not become isolated from the business environment that sustains it. Credibility is established not only by operating a successful competency team, but also by being perceived by business leaders as doing so.

2. **Integration methodology:** An integration methodology defines the life cycle of dependencies that are involved in building a Lean Integration team to the point that it becomes an ongoing governing body, able to sustain the integration achieved from specific projects. The integration methodology is concerned with not just building quality solutions, but more important with setting up the processes to sustain solutions indefinitely in a production environment.

3. **Metadata management:** The ability to manage metadata is essential for managing data as an asset, and it is an enabler for a broad range of process and data integration programs such as straight-through processing, master data management, and data governance. Metadata is conceptually simple but challenging to implement in large, complex organizations. Essentially it is documentation and business rules about data in terms of what it means; where it is located; how it is accessed, moved, and secured; who is responsible for it; and who is allowed to use it.

4. **Information architecture:** Information architecture is an element of a broader enterprise architecture capability. Architecture and integration are complementary enterprise practices that intersect most significantly in the information domain. Architecture is about differentiating the whole and transforming the business, whereas integration is about assembling the parts into a cohesive, holistic system. One discipline takes a top-down approach while the other is bottom-up; both are essential.

5. **Business process management:** Business process management (BPM) is a method of efficiently aligning an enterprise with the needs of its customers. It is a holistic management approach that promotes business effectiveness and efficiency while striving for innovation, flexibility, and integration with technology. Business processes are a prime integration point since this is often where disparate functions come together and interact to share data in the interests of maximizing customer satisfaction and enterprise effectiveness.

6. **Modeling management:** Modeling management is the discipline for defining, using, and maintaining a variety of views (simplified abstractions) of the enterprise and its data in support of integration strategies. One of the critical needs within all large corporations is to achieve efficient information exchanges in a heterogeneous environment. The typical enterprise has hundreds of applications that serve as systems of record for information that, although developed independently and based on incompatible data models, must share information efficiently and accurately in order to effectively support the business and create positive customer experiences.

7. **Integration systems:** This competency addresses the need for managing the life cycle of integration technology and systems as a distinct class of application that provides a sustainable operating infrastructure to support the free flow of information in an organization in an integrated manner.

PART I

Executive Summary

> *Alice: Would you tell me, please, which way I ought to go from here?*
> *The Cat: That depends a good deal on where you want to get to.*
> *Alice: I don't much care where.*
> *The Cat: Then it doesn't much matter which way you go.*
> Lewis Carroll, *Alice's Adventures in Wonderland*

As the cat in Lewis Carroll's story so clearly advises, if you don't know your destination, it doesn't matter which path you take. This executive overview is intended to paint a picture of the destination for an enterprise integration strategy. Parts II and III of the book then illuminate the path.

The size of this book may be daunting to some readers, but Part I shouldn't be. We structured the book in three parts specifically to make the subject of Lean Integration more approachable for different audiences. Part I is designed to be read by anyone, not just executives. Front-line staff should read Part I to understand the big-picture context, and senior executives too should read it to appreciate the role they play in this new approach and to internalize the strategic framework.

This executive overview can be read as a stand-alone publication. It provides a solid overview of the business justification for Lean Integration, the history of Lean and how it has evolved to this point, and how its principles can be applied in the context of an Integration Factory. Readers who are primarily interested in understanding the concepts and strategic framework and will be relying on others to execute the strategy can stop after Chapter 3 and not feel as if they are missing anything. That said, Parts II and III contain some excellent real-life case studies that also can be read as stand-alone stories. We therefore encourage everyone to thumb through the book and select topics or cases that are of greatest interest.

CHAPTER ONE

What Is Lean and Why Is It Important?

Lean creates value. And it does that by creating competitive advantages that better satisfy the customer.

Joe Stenzel [1]

Lean Integration is not a one-time effort; you can't just flip a switch and proclaim to be done. It is a long-term strategy for how an organization approaches the challenges of process and data integration. Lean can and does deliver early benefits, but it doesn't end there. Lean principles such as waste elimination are never-ending activities that result in ongoing benefits. Furthermore, some Lean objectives such as becoming a team-based learning organization with a sustainable culture of continuous improvement may require years to change entrenched bad habits.

Before you start on the Lean journey, therefore, you should be clear about why you are doing so. This chapter, and the rest of the book, will elaborate on the technical merits and business value of Lean Integration and how to

---

1. Joe Stenzel, *Lean Accounting: Best Practices for Sustainable Integration* (John Wiley & Sons, 2007), Kindle loc. 1317–18.

implement a program that delivers on the promise. Here is a summary of why you would want to:

- **Efficiency:** Lean Integration teams typically realize 50 percent labor productivity improvements and 90 percent lead-time reduction through value stream mapping and continuous efforts to eliminate non-value-added activities. The continuous improvement case study (Chapter 5) is an excellent example.
- **Agility:** Take integration off the critical path on projects by using highly automated processes, reusable components, and self-service delivery models. The mass customization case study (Chapter 8) demonstrates key elements of this benefit.
- **Data quality:** Establish one version of the truth by treating data as an asset, establishing effective information models, and engaging business leaders and front-line staff to accept accountability for data quality. The Smith & Nephew case study (Chapter 6) shows how this is possible.
- **Governance:** Measure the business value of integration by establishing metrics that drive continuous improvement, enable benchmarking against market prices, and support regulatory and compliance enforcement. The integration hub case study (Chapter 10) is an excellent example of effective data governance.
- **Innovation:** Enable staff to innovate and test new ideas by using fact-based problem solving and automating "routine" integration tasks to give staff more time for value-added activities. The Wells Fargo business process automation case study (Chapter 9) is a compelling example of automation enabling innovation.
- **Staff morale:** Increase the engagement and motivation of IT staff by empowering cross-functional teams to drive bottom-up improvements. The decentralized enterprise case study (Chapter 12) shows how staff can be engaged and work together across highly independent business units.

Achieving all these benefits will take time, but we hope that after you have finished reading this book, you will agree with us that these benefits are real and achievable. Most important, we hope that you will have learned enough to start the Lean journey with confidence.

Let's start by exploring one of the major challenges in most non-Lean IT organizations: the rapid pace of change and surviving at the edge of chaos.

Constant Rapid Change and Organizational Agility

Much has been written about the accelerating pace of change in the global business environment and the exponential growth in IT systems and data. While rapid change is the modern enterprise reality, the question is how organizations can manage the changes. At one end of the spectrum we find agile data-driven organizations that are able to quickly adapt to market opportunities and regulatory demands, leverage business intelligence for competitive advantage, and regularly invest in simplification to stay ahead of the IT complexity wave. At the other end of the spectrum we find organizations that operate at the edge of chaos, constantly fighting fires and barely in control of a constantly changing environment. You may be somewhere in the middle, but on balance we find more organizations at the edge of chaos rather than at the agile data-driven end of the spectrum.

Here is a quick test you can perform to determine if your IT organization is at the edge of chaos. Look up a few of the major production incidents that have occurred in the past year and that have been closely analyzed and well documented. If there haven't been any, that might be a sign that you are *not* on the edge of chaos (unless your organization has a culture of firefighting without postmortems). Assuming you have a few, how many findings are documented for each production incident? Are there one or two issues that contributed to the outage, or are there dozens of findings and follow-up action items?

We're not talking about the root cause of the incident. As a general rule, an analysis of most production incidents results in identifying a single, and often very simple, failure that caused a chain reaction of events resulting in a major outage. But we also find that for virtually all major outages there is a host of contributing factors that delayed the recovery process or amplified the impact.

Here is a typical example: An air conditioner fails, the backup air conditioner fails as well, the room overheats, the lights-out data center sends an automatic page to the night operator, the pager battery is dead, a disk controller fails when it overheats, the failure shuts down a batch update application, a dependent application is put on hold waiting for the first one to complete, an automatic page to the application owner is sent out once the service level agreement (SLA) for the required completion is missed, the application owner quit a month ago and the new owner's pager has not been updated in the phone list, the chain reaction sets off dozens of alarms, and a major outage is declared which triggers 30 staff members to dial into the recovery bridge line, the volume of alarms creates conflicting information about the cause of the problem which delays problem analysis for several hours, and so on and so on.

Based on our experience with hundreds of similar incidents in banks, retail organizations, manufacturers, telecommunications companies, health care providers, utilities, and government agencies, we have made two key observations: (1) There is never just one thing that contributes to a major outage, and (2) the exact same combination of factors never happens twice. The pattern is that there is no pattern—which is a good definition of chaos. Our conclusion is that at any given point in time, every large IT organization has hundreds or thousands of undiscovered defects, and all it takes is just the right one to begin a chain reaction that results in a severity 1 outage.

So what does this have to do with Lean? Production failures are examples of the necessity of detecting and dealing with every small problem because it is impossible to predict how they line up to create a catastrophe. Three Mile Island is a classic example. Lean organizations relentlessly improve in numerous small steps. A metaphor for how Lean organizations uncover their problems is to imagine a lake with a rocky bottom, where the rocks represent the many quality and process problems affecting their ability to build the best products for their customers. Metaphorically, they "lower the water level" (reduce their inventories, reduce their batch sizes, and speed up reconfiguring their assembly lines, among other techniques) in order to expose the rocks on the bottom of the lake. Once the "rocks" are exposed, they can focus on continually improving themselves by fixing these problems. Integration systems benefit from "lowering the water level" as well. Every failure of a system uncovers a lack of knowledge about the process or its connections. Problem solving is learning more deeply about our processes, infrastructure, and information domains.

We are of the opinion that the edge of chaos is the normal state of affairs and cannot be mitigated purely by technology. The very nature of systems-of-systems is that they emerge and evolve without a complete (100 percent) understanding of all dependencies and behaviors. There are literally billions of permutations and combinations of the internal states of each software component in a large enterprise, and they are constantly changing. It is virtually impossible to test all of them or to build systems that can guard against all possible failures. The challenge is stated best in remarks by Fred Brooks in *The Mythical Man-Month*: "Software entities are more complex for their size than perhaps any other human construct, because no two parts are alike. . . . If they are, we make the two similar parts into one, a subroutine." And "Software systems have orders of magnitude more states than computers do."[2]

So what *is* the solution? The solution is to perform IT practices such as integration, change management, enterprise architecture, and project management in a disciplined fashion. Note that discipline is not simply a matter of people doing what they are supposed to do. Lack of discipline is not their problem; it is the problem of their managers who have not ensured that the work process makes failure obvious or who have not trained people to respond to revealed failures first with immediate containment and then with effective countermeasures using PDCA (Plan, Do, Check, and Act).

To effectively counter the effects of chaos, you need to approach integration as an enterprise strategy and not as an ad hoc or project activity. If you view integration as a series of discrete and separate activities that are not connected, you won't buy into the Lean concept. By virtue of the fact that you are reading this book, the chances are you are among the majority of IT professionals who understand the need for efficiency and the value of reuse and repeatability. After all, we know what happens when you execute project after project without a standard platform and without an integration strategy; 100 percent of the time the result is an integration hairball. There are no counterexamples. When you allow independent project teams to choose their own tools and to apply their own coding, naming, and documentation standards, you eventually end up with a hairball—every time. The hairball is characterized by an overly complex collection of dependencies between application components that is hard to change, expensive to maintain, and unpredictable in operation.

If for whatever reason you remain fixed in the paradigm that integration is a project process as opposed to an ongoing process, there are many methodologies to choose from. Virtually all large consulting firms have a proprietary methodology that they would be happy to share with you if you hire them,

---

2. Frederick P. Brooks, Jr., *The Mythical Man-Month: Essays on Software Engineering, Anniversary Edition* (Addison-Wesley, 2004), pp. 182, 183.

and some of them will even sell it to you. Some integration platform suppliers make their integration methodology available to customers at no cost.

But if you perceive the integration challenge to be more than a project activity—in other words, an ongoing, sustainable discipline—you need another approach. Some alternatives that you may consider are IT service management practices such as ITIL (Information Technology Infrastructure Library), IT governance practices such as COBIT (Control Objectives for Information and Technology), IT architecture practices such as TOGAF (The Open Group Architecture Framework), software engineering practices such as CMM (Capability Maturity Model), or generalized quality management practices such as Six Sigma. All of these are well-established management systems that inherently, because of their holistic enterprise-wide perspective, provide a measure of sustainable integration. That said, none of them provides detailed practices for sustaining solutions to data quality or integration issues that emerge from information exchanges between independently managed applications, with incompatible data models that evolve independently. In short, these "off the shelf" methods aren't sustainable since they are not your own. Different business contexts, service sets, products, and corporate cultures need different practices. Every enterprise ultimately needs to grow its own methods and practices, drawing from the principles of Lean Integration.

Another alternative to fixing the hairball issue that is often considered is the enterprise resource planning (ERP) architecture, a monolithic integrated application. The rationale for this argument is that you can make the integration problem go away by simply buying all the software from one vendor. In practice this approach doesn't work except in very unique situations such as in an organization that has a narrow business scope and a rigid operating model, is prepared to accept the trade-off of simply "doing without" if the chosen software package doesn't offer a solution, and is resigned to not growing or getting involved in any mergers or acquisitions. This combination of circumstances is rare in the modern business economy. The reality is that the complexity of most enterprises, and the variation in business processes, simply cannot be handled by one software application.

A final alternative that some organizations consider is to outsource the entire IT department. This doesn't actually solve the integration challenges; it simply transfers them to someone else. In some respects outsourcing can make the problem worse since integration is not simply an IT problem; it is a problem of alignment across business functions. In an outsourced business model, the formality of the arrangement between the company and the supplier may handcuff the mutual collaboration that is generally necessary for a sustainable integration scenario. On the other hand, if you outsource your IT function, you may insist (contractually) that the supplier provide a sustainable approach to integration. In this case you may want to ask your supplier to read this book and then write the principles of Lean Integration into the contract.

In summary, Lean transforms integration from an art into a science, a repeatable and teachable methodology that shifts the focus from integration as a point-in-time activity to integration as a sustainable activity that enables organizational agility. This is perhaps the greatest value of Lean Integration—the ability of the business to change rapidly without compromising on IT risk or quality, in other words, transforming the organization from one on the edge of chaos into an agile data-driven enterprise.

The Case for Lean Integration

The edge of chaos discussion makes the case for Lean Integration from a practitioner's perspective, that is, that technology alone cannot solve the problem of complexity and that other disciplines are required. But that is more of an intellectual response to the challenge and still leaves the five questions we posed in the Introduction unanswered. Let's address them now.

"Why Lean?" and "So What?"

In financial terms, the value of Lean comes from two sources: economies of scale and reduction in variation. Development of data and process integration points is a manufacturing process. We know from years of research in manufacturing that every time you double volume, costs drop by 15 to 25 percent.[3] There is a point of diminishing returns since it becomes harder and harder to double volume, but it doesn't take too many doublings to realize an order-of-magnitude reduction in cost. Second, we also know that manufacturing production costs increase from 25 to 35 percent each time variation doubles. The degree of integration variation today in many organizations is staggering in terms of both the variety of tools that are used and the variety of

---

3. George Stalk, "Time—The Next Source of Competitive Advantage," *Harvard Business Review*, no. 4 (July–August 1988).

standards that are applied to their implementation. That is why most organizations have a hairball—thousands of integrations that are "works of art."

Some studies by various analyst firms have pegged the cost of integration at 50 to 70 percent of the IT budget. This is huge! Lean Integration achieves both economies of scale and reduction in variation to reduce integration costs by 25 percent or more. This book explores some specific case studies that we hope will convince you that not only are these cost savings real, but you can realize them in your organization as well.

"As a Business Executive, What Problems Will It Help Me Solve?"

The answer is different for various stakeholders. For IT professionals, the biggest reason is to do more with less. Budgets are constantly being cut while expectations of what IT can deliver are rising; Lean is a great way to respond because it embodies continuous improvement principles so that you can keep cutting your costs every year. By doing so, you get to keep your job and not be outsourced or displaced by a third party.

For a line-of-business owner, the big problems Lean addresses are time to market and top-line revenue growth by acquiring and keeping customers. A Lean organization can deliver solutions faster (just in time) because of automated processes and mass customization methods that are supported by the technology of an Integration Factory. And an integrated environment drives revenue growth through more effective use of holistic information, better management decisions, and improved customer experiences.

For an enterprise owner, the biggest reasons for a Lean Integration strategy include alignment, governance, regulatory compliance, and risk reduction. All of these are powerful incentives, but alignment across functions and business units may be the strongest contributor to sustained competitive advantage. By simply stopping the disagreement across teams, organizations can solve problems faster than the competition.

In summary, Lean Integration helps to reduce costs, shorten time to market, increase revenue, strengthen governance, and provide a sustainable competitive advantage. If this sounds too good to be true, we ask you to reserve judgment until you finish reading all the case studies and detailed "how-to" practices. One word of caution about the case studies: They convey how example organizations solved their problems in their context. The same practices may not apply to your organization in exactly the same way, but the thinking that went into them and the patterns may well do so.

"As an IT Leader or Line-of-Business Owner, Why Am I Going to Make a Considerable Investment in Lean Integration?"

Get results faster—and be able to sustain them in operation. Lean is about lead-time reduction, quality improvements, and cost reduction. Lean delivers results faster because it focuses heavily on techniques that deliver only what the customer needs (no "gold-plating"): process automation and mass customization. In terms of ongoing operations, Lean is a data-driven, fact-based methodology that relies heavily on metrics to ensure that quality and performance remain at a high level.

"How Is This Different from Other Methods, Approaches, and Frameworks?"

Two words: *sustainable* and *holistic*. Other integration approaches either tackle only a part of the problem or tackle the problem only for the short term at a point in time. The predominant integration strategy, even today, is customized hand-coded solutions on a project-by-project basis without a master plan. The result is many "works of art" in production that are expensive to maintain, require a long time to change, and are brittle in operation.

Note that Chapter 12, Integration Methodology, includes a section that explicitly compares agile and Lean methodologies.

"Why Am I as an IT Professional Going to Embrace and Sell Lean Integration Internally?"

Because it will advance your career. Time and time again we have seen successful integration teams grow from a handful of staff to 100 or more, not because of a power grab, but because of scope increases at the direction of senior management. Successful team members become managers, and managers become directors or move into other functions in the enterprise in order to address other cross-functional business needs. In short, Lean Integration is about effective execution, which is a highly valued business skill.

What Is Integration?

This seems like a simple question, but what exactly is integration? Here are a couple of examples of how others have answered this question:

- "The extent to which various information systems are formally linked for sharing of consistent information within an enterprise"[4]
- "Seamless integration of all information flowing through a company"[5]

A careful review of these and other definitions reveals a number of common themes that describe the essence of integration:

- **Formally linked**: Communication between systems is standardized.
- **Seamless**: Complexities are invisible to end users.
- **Coordinated manner**: Communication is disciplined.
- **Synergy**: Value is added to the enterprise.
- **Single transactions that spawn multiple updates**: There is master management of data.
- **Fewer number of systems**: The cost of ownership is lower.
- **Non-duplicated data**: The focus is on eliminating redundancy and reducing costs of management.

The most comprehensive definition of integration we have come across is in Lester Singletary's doctoral dissertation.[6] It provides a rich definition by examining the domain of integration from four perspectives: (1) what integration is in terms of its attributes or operational characteristics, (2) the benefits or resultant outcomes of effective integration efforts, (3) the risks or challenges that arise from integrations, and (4) the metrics that provide a measure of objectivity concerning the integrated environment. Figure 1.1 has been adapted from Singletary's paper and serves as a foundation for our view of integration in this book.

To put all this together, our definition of integration, therefore, is as follows:

Integration: An **infrastructure** for enabling **efficient data sharing** across **incompatible applications** that **evolve independently** in a coordinated manner to serve the needs of the **enterprise** and its **stakeholders**.

---

4. G. Bhatt, "Enterprise Information Systems Integration and Business Process Improvement Initiative: An Empirical Study," *Proceedings of the First Conference of the Association for Information Systems (AIS)*, 1995.

5. T. H. Davenport, "Putting the Enterprise into the Enterprise System," *Harvard Business Review* 16, no. 4 (July–August 1998), pp. 121–31.

6. Lester A. Singletary, "Empirical Study of Attributed and Perceived Benefits of Applications Integration for Enterprise Systems" (PhD dissertation, Louisiana State University, 2003).

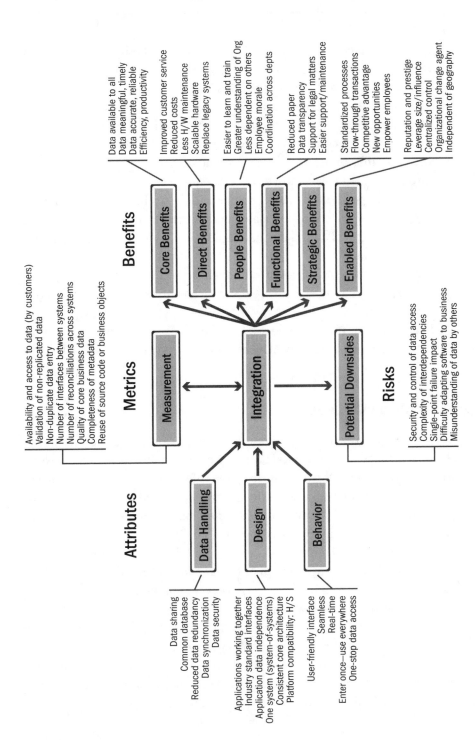

Figure 1.1 Definition of integration

13

- **Infrastructure:** a combination of people, process, policy, and technology elements that work together (e.g., highway transportation infrastructure)
- **Efficient data sharing:** accessing data and functions from disparate systems without appreciable delay to create a combined and consistent view of core information for use across the organization to improve business decisions and operations
- **Incompatible applications:** systems that are based on different architectures, technology platforms, or data models
- **Evolve independently:** management decisions to change applications (or parts of an application) are made by different organizational groups or external suppliers on independent timelines that are not controlled by a master schedule
- **Enterprise:** the organization unit that is the focus of the integration effort; it could be a department, division, an entire company, or part of a supply chain
- **Stakeholders:** the customers of the enterprise, its owners, and its employees, including management, end users, and IT professionals

Integration Maturity Levels

Another way to look at integration is to examine how integration technologies and management practices have evolved and matured over the past 50 years. Figure 1.2 summarizes four stages of evolution that have contributed to increasingly higher levels of operational efficiency. Hand coding was the only technology available until around 1990 and is still a common practice today, but it is gradually being replaced by modern methods. The movement to standard tools, more commonly known as middleware, began in the 1990s, followed by industry consolidation of tool vendors during the first decade of the 2000s, resulting in more "suites" of tools that provide the foundation for an enterprise integration platform.

As we look to the future, we see the emergence of the Integration Factory as the next wave of integration technology in combination with formal management disciplines. This wave stems from the realization that of the thousands of integration points that are created in an enterprise, the vast majority are incredibly similar to each other in terms of their structure and processing approach. In effect, most integration logic falls into one of a couple of dozen

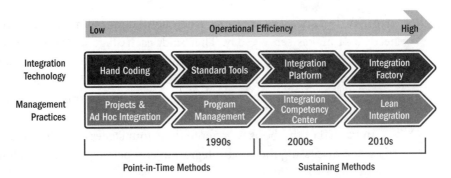

Figure 1.2 Evolution of integration technology and management practices

different "patterns" or "templates," where the exact data being moved and transformed may be different, but the general flow and error-handling approach are the same. An Integration Factory adds a high degree of automation to the process of building and sustaining integration points. We believe the Integration Factory, described in detail in Chapter 3, will be the dominant new "wave" of middleware for the next decade (2010s).

Management practices have also evolved from ad hoc or point-in-time projects, to broad-based programs (projects of projects), to Integration Competency Centers (ICCs), and now to Lean Integration. A major paradigm shift began early in the current century around the view of integration as a sustaining practice. The first wave of sustainable management practices is encapsulated by the ICC. It focused primarily on standardizing projects, tools, processes, and technology across the enterprise and addressing organizational issues related to shared services and staff competencies. The second wave of sustainable practices is the subject of this book: the application of Lean principles and techniques to eliminate waste, optimize the entire value chain, and continuously improve. The management practice that optimizes the benefits of the Integration Factory is Lean Integration. The combination of factory technologies and Lean practices results in significant and sustainable business benefits.

The timeline shown on the bottom of Figure 1.2 represents the period when the technology and management practices achieved broad-based acceptance. We didn't put a date on the first evolutionary state since it has been with us since the beginning of the computer software era. The earlier stages of evolution don't die off with the introduction of a new level of maturity. In fact, there are times when hand coding for ad hoc integration needs still makes sense today. That said, each stage of evolution borrows lessons from prior stages to improve its efficacy. We predict that Lean practices, in combination with past experiences in project, program, and ICC practices, will become the dominant leading practice around the globe during the 2010s.

In Part III of this book we refer to these four stages of evolutionary maturity when discussing the eight integration competency areas. The shorthand labels we use are as follows:

1. **Project:** disciplines that optimize integration solutions around time and scope boundaries related to a single initiative
2. **Program:** disciplines that optimize integration of specific cross-functional business collaborations, usually through a related collection of projects
3. **Sustaining:** disciplines that optimize information access and controls at the enterprise level and view integration as an ongoing activity independent of projects
4. **Lean:** disciplines that optimize the entire information delivery value chain through continuous improvement driven by all participants in the process

We think of this last level of maturity as self-sustaining once it becomes broadly entrenched in the organization.

We don't spend much time in this book discussing project or program methods since these are mature practices for which a large body of knowledge is available. Our focus is primarily on sustaining practices and how Lean thinking can be applied to achieve the highest levels of efficiency, performance, and effectiveness.

Economies of Scale (the Integration Market)

As stated earlier, the benefits of Lean are economies of scale and reduction in variation. As a general rule, doubling volume reduces costs by 15 to 25 percent, and doubling variation increases costs by 25 to 35 percent. The ideal low-cost model, therefore, is maximum standardization and maximum volume. But how exactly is this accomplished in a Lean Integration context?

A core concept is to view the collection of information exchanges between business applications in an enterprise as a "market" rather than as a bunch of private point-to-point relationships. The predominant integration approach over the past 20 years has been point-to-point integration. In other words, if two business systems need to exchange information, the owners and subject matter experts (SMEs) of the two systems would get together and agree on what information needed to be exchanged, the definition and meaning of the data, the business rules associated with any transformations or filters, the interface specifications, and the transport protocol. If anything needed to change once it was in operation, they would meet again and repeat the same process.

For a small number of systems and a small number of information exchanges, this process is adequate and manageable. The problem with a hand-coded or manual method is that it doesn't scale, just as manual methods for other processes don't scale well. Certainly if a second integration point is added to the same two systems, and the same two SMEs work together and use the same protocols, documentation conventions, and so on, the time and cost to build and sustain the integrations will indeed follow the economy of scale cost curve. But in a large enterprise with hundreds or thousands of applications, if each exchange is viewed as strictly an agreement between the immediate two parties, diseconomies begin to creep into the equation from several perspectives.

Imagine trying to follow a flow of financial information from a retail point-of-sale application, to the sales management system (which reconciles sales transactions with refunds, returns, exchanges, and other adjustments), to the inventory management system, to the general ledger system, to the financial reporting system. In a simple scenario, this involves four information exchanges among five systems. If each system uses different development languages, protocols, documentation conventions, interface specifications, and monitoring tools and was developed by different individuals, not only will we *not* receive the benefits from quadrupling volume from one integration to four, but we will in fact increase costs.

This example reflects the two largest factors that drive diseconomies: the cost of communication between teams and duplication of effort. Additional factors can drive further diseconomies, such as the following:

- **Top-heavy organizations:** As organizations get larger and add more layers of management, more and more effort needs to be expended on integrated solutions that require collaboration and agreement across teams that each play a narrow functional role.

- **Office politics:** Disagreements across teams are a result of different motivations and agendas, usually a result of conflicting goals and metrics but also sometimes caused by the "not invented here" syndrome.
- **Isolation** of decision makers from the results of their decisions: Senior managers may need to make decisions, such as how much of a budget to allocate to a given group, without a clear picture of what the group does and what value it brings to the organization.
- **Slow response time:** Delays are caused by multiple handoffs between teams or by queuing requests for information or support from other groups.
- **Inertia:** People are unwilling to change or are opposed to standards.
- **Cannibalization:** Limited resources (such as SMEs in specific business domains) are consumed for project B, slowing down progress on project A.

The degree of integration variation in many organizations is staggering in terms of both the variety of technology that is used and the variety of standards that are applied to their implementation. That is why most organizations have a hairball—hundreds or thousands of integrations that are "works of art."

The alternative is to view the need for information exchanges across applications as a market economy, and to serve the market with an efficient shared-services delivery model in order to gain economies of scale. For example, multiple groups within an organization may perform similar activities but do so with varying degrees of efficiency and consistency. Centralizing the activities makes it much easier to standardize and streamline the work, thereby reducing the cost per unit of work while improving the quality and consistency.

The two graphs in Figure 1.3 are borrowed from the field of economics and show the relationships between costs and volumes. These graphs reflect the well-understood laws of diminishing returns and economies of scale. The chart on the left reflects a manual or low-tech operation, such as when information exchanges are developed using custom hand-coded integration solutions. In this scenario, there are few (if any) capital costs since existing enterprise tools such as COBOL, Java, or SQL are used to build the integration. The overall average cost per integration initially falls as the individuals doing the work gain experience and are able to share some of their experience and knowledge, but then at some point it starts to increase as diseconomies

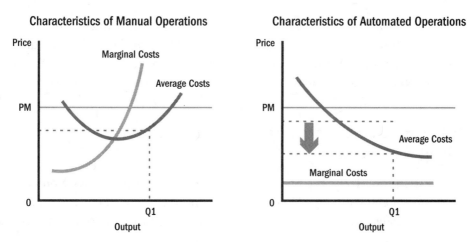

Figure 1.3 Diminishing returns and economies of scale

emerge. In terms of the marginal costs (i.e., the incremental cost for each additional integration), initially the curve is somewhat flat since the first integration developer can develop a second or third integration with a similar effort. The average cost also falls initially since the fixed costs of the developer (hiring costs, office space, desktop PC, etc.) are amortized over more than one integration. As the volume of integrations increases, however, the marginal costs increase on an exponential basis, and the average costs begin to increase as more and more diseconomies emerge from the increasing complexity and number of unique integration points.

The chart on the right of the figure shows the cost curve as a result of a capital investment in tools and infrastructure (such as an Integration Factory) to largely automate and standardize the development effort. Note that in this scenario, the marginal costs are small and constant. For example, it might cost Microsoft $5 billion to develop a new version of Windows, but once developed, it costs just pennies to make another electronic copy. The marginal cost per copy of Windows is essentially the same whether 1 copy or 1,000 copies are made, but the average cost drops significantly and continuously in this scenario as volume increases and as the up-front fixed costs are amortized over more and more units.

The key challenge for organizations is to determine at what level of integration complexity do diminishing returns begin to emerge from manual hand-coded solutions, and how much capital investment is warranted to achieve the time and cost advantages of a high-volume Integration Factory. The answer to this will become clearer in Parts II and III, where we discuss the Lean principles related to continuous improvement, mass customization, and process automation, and the financial management competency area.

Getting Started: Incremental Integration without "Boiling the Ocean"

Parts II and III of the book provide detailed and specific advice on how to implement a sustainable Lean Integration practice, but before you dig into the details, it is important to understand the approach options and related prerequisites.

There are two fundamental implementation styles for Lean Integration: top-down and bottom-up. The top-down style starts with an explicit strategy with clearly defined (and measurable) outcomes and is led by top-level executives. The bottom-up style, which is sometimes referred to as a "grassroots" movement, is primarily driven by front-line staff or managers with leadership qualities. The top-down approach generally delivers results more quickly but may be more disruptive. You can think of these styles as revolutionary versus evolutionary. Both are viable.

While Lean Integration is relevant to all large organizations that use information to run their business, there are several prerequisites for a successful Lean journey. The following five questions provide a checklist to see if Lean Integration is appropriate to your organization and which style may be most suitable:

1. **Do you have senior executive support for improving how integration problems are solved for the business?**
   Support from a senior executive in the organization is necessary for getting change started and critical for sustaining continuous improvement initiatives. Ideally the support should come from more than one executive, at a senior level such as the CXO, and it should be "active" support. You want the senior executives to be leading the effort by example, pulling the desired behaviors and patterns of thought from the rest of the organization.
   It might be sufficient if the support is from only one executive, and if that person is one level down from C-level, but it gets harder and harder to drive the investments and necessary changes as you water down the

top-level support. The level of executive support should be as big as the opportunity. Even with a bottom-up implementation style, you need some level of executive support or awareness. At some point, if you don't have the support, you are simply not ready to formally tackle a Lean Integration strategy. Instead, just keep doing your assigned job and continue lobbying for top-level support.

2. **Do you have a committed practice leader?**
   The second prerequisite is a committed practice leader. By "committed" we don't mean that the leader needs to be an expert in all the principles and competencies on day one, but the person does need to have the capability to become an expert and should be determined to do so through sustained personal effort. Furthermore, it is ideal if this individual is somewhat entrepreneurial, has a thick skin, is customer-oriented, and has the characteristics of a change agent (see Chapter 6 on team empowerment for more details).
   If you don't have top leadership support or a committed practice leader, there is little chance of success. This is not to suggest that a grassroots movement isn't a viable way to get the ball rolling, but at some point the bottom-up movement needs to build support from the top in order to institutionalize the changes that will be necessary to sustain the shift from siloed operations to integrated value chains.

3. **Is your "Lean director" an effective change agent?**
   Having a Lean director who is an effective change agent is slightly different from having one who is "committed." The Lean champion for an organization may indeed have all the right motivations and intentions but simply have the wrong talents. For example, an integrator needs to be able to check his or her ego at the door when going into a meeting to facilitate a resolution between individuals, who have their own egos. Furthermore, a Lean perspective requires one to think outside the box—in fact, to not even see a box and to think of his or her responsibilities in the broadest possible terms. Refer to the section on Change Agent Leadership in Chapter 6 for a description of essential leadership capabilities.

4. **Is your corporate culture receptive to cross-organizational collaboration and cooperation?**
   Many (maybe even most) organizations have entrenched views of independent functional groups, which is not a showstopper for a Lean program. But

if the culture is one where independence is seen as the source of the organization's success and creativity, and variation is a core element of its strategy, a Lean approach will likely be a futile effort since Lean requires cooperation and collaboration across functional lines. A corporate culture of autonomous functional groups with a strong emphasis on innovation and variation typically has problems implementing Lean thinking.

5. **Can your organization take a longer-term view of the business?**
   A Lean strategy is a long-term strategy. This is not to say that a Lean program can't deliver benefits quickly in the short term—it certainly can. But Lean is ultimately about long-term sustainable practices. Some decisions and investments that will be required need to be made with a long-term payback in mind. If the organization is strictly focused on surviving quarter by quarter and does little or no planning beyond the current fiscal year, a Lean program won't achieve its potential.

If you are in an organizational environment where you answered no to one or more of these questions, and you feel compelled to implement a Lean program, you could try to start a grassroots movement and continue lobbying senior leadership until you find a strong champion. Or you could move to another organization. There are indeed some organizational contexts in which starting a Lean program is the equivalent of banging your head against the wall. We hope this checklist will help you to avoid unnecessary headaches.

Lean requires a holistic implementation strategy or vision, but it can be implemented in incremental steps. In fact, it is virtually impossible to implement it all at once, unless for some reason the CEO decides to assign an entire team with a big budget to fast-track the implementation. The idea is to make Lean Integration a long-term sustainable process. When we say "long-term" we are talking about 10 to 20 years, not just the next few years. When you take a long-term view, your approach changes. It certainly is necessary to have a long-term vision and plan, but it is absolutely acceptable, and in many respects necessary, to implement it incrementally in order to enable organizational learning. In the same way, an ICC can start with a small team and a narrow scope and grow it over time to a broad-based Lean Integration practice through excellent execution and positive business results.

CHAPTER TWO

A Brief History of Lean

The Toyota Production System, however, is not just a production system. I am confident it will reveal its strength as a management system adapted to today's era of global markets and high-level computerized information systems.

Taiichi Ohno[1]

Since World War II, rapid increases in global market access have brought ever-accelerating changes to the global competitive environment. These competitive market forces have also quickened the pace of change in manufacturing management thinking and practices. Every generation for more than 200 years has made contributions to manufacturing technology and the evolution of management systems. These contributions include 14 major management systems and technology innovations and eight enabling technologies (see Figure 2.1) that led to the development of the Lean Enterprise Management System.

1. The first major contribution to Lean manufacturing practice was the innovation of Eli Whitney (1765–1825). An American inventor, pioneer, mechanical engineer, and manufacturer, Whitney is best remembered for his cotton gin invention. He also affected U.S. industrial development by

1. Taiichi Ohno, *Toyota Production System: Beyond Large-Scale Production* (Productivity Press, 1988), p. xv.

manufacturing government muskets in 1799. Whitney developed a musket design with interchangeable parts after taking a U.S. Army contract to manufacture 10,000 muskets at a price of under $14 each. He translated interchangeable parts concepts into a manufacturing system, giving birth to American mass production systems.

2. Over the next 100 years, manufacturers primarily focused on specific engineering conventions, practices, and process technologies. During this time our engineering drawing system, modern machine tools, and large-scale processes, such as the Bessemer process for making steel, were all developed.

Few people concerned themselves with the movement of products from one discrete process to another or with logistics systems from suppliers within factories and to customers. No one was asking questions such as these:

- What happens between processes?
- How should multiple processes be arranged within the factory?
- How does the chain of processes function as a system?
- How does each worker's task relate to the tasks of other workers?

This began to change in the late 1890s, when industrial engineering was developing as an important technology discipline.

3. The first and best-known industrial engineer was Frederick Winslow Taylor, the father of scientific management. He closely watched how work was done in steel factories and measured production output to find the most efficient way to perform specific tasks. Taylor believed that finding the right challenge for people and paying them well for increased output were important to improved productivity. At the steel mills, he used time studies to set daily production quotas. Incentives would be paid to those who reached their daily goal. Those who didn't reach their goal received differential and much lower pay rates. Taylor doubled productivity by using time study, systematic controls and tools, functional foremanship, and the new wage scheme. His significant contribution was applying science to management, but his success was limited because he never recognized the importance of human factors and behavioral sciences to productivity.

4. Frank Bunker Gilbreth Sr. worked at construction sites and noticed that no two bricklayers used identical methods or sets of motions. He improved existing methods by eliminating all wasted motions and raised

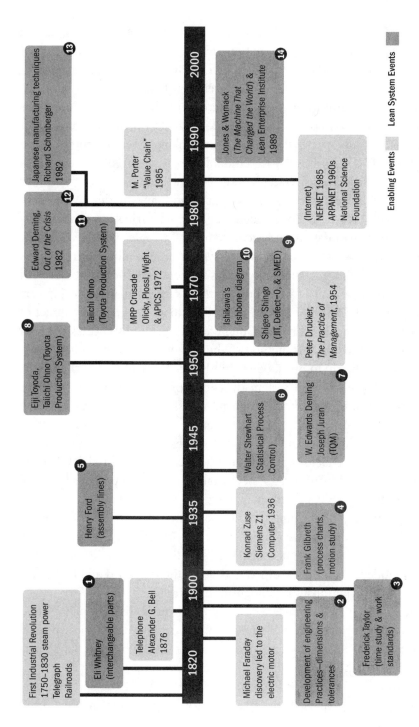

Figure 2.1 Manufacturing management system chronology

output from 1,000 to 2,700 bricks per day. From these studies Gilbreth developed laws of human motion, which evolved into principles of motion economy. Frank and his wife, Lillian, both highly educated, coined the phrase *motion study* to cover their field of research, thus differentiating it from *time study*. The second method they developed was process charts, which focus on all work elements—including non-value-added elements—with the goal of optimizing operator motion and method. The Gilbreths' two methodologies were important contributions to industrial engineering's body of knowledge.

5. Around 1908 Henry Ford and his right-hand man, Charles E. Sorensen, fashioned the first comprehensive manufacturing strategy. They arranged all manufacturing system elements—people, machines, tooling, and products—into a continuous system for manufacturing Ford's Model T automobile. This strategy was so incredibly successful that Ford quickly became one of the world's richest men by manufacturing cars everyone could afford. Many consider Ford to be the first practitioner of just-in-time and synchronized manufacturing. Ford's success inspired many others to copy his methods. When the world began to change, the Ford system began to break down, but Henry Ford refused to change the system. His production system depended on laborers working at jobs without meaningful content, causing a loss of dignity and decreased morale. In addition, annual model changes and product proliferation due to multiple colors and options put strains on the system and did not fit well in Ford factories. This became clear when Alfred P. Sloan at General Motors introduced a new strategy. He developed business and manufacturing strategies for managing very large enterprises while dealing with variety. By the mid-1930s General Motors had surpassed Ford to dominate the automotive market, yet many elements of Ford production were sound, even in the new age. Ford's methods were a deciding factor in the Allied victory of World War II. After the war, Ford and his system were studied rigorously and much admired by Taiichi Ohno.

6. Process and quality engineers have used rigorous statistical analysis tools in manufacturing since Walter Shewhart introduced statistical process control in the 1930s at AT&T. His work formed the basis of Six Sigma's statistical methodology and PDCA problem solving.

7. W. Edwards Deming and Joseph Juran introduced the thinking and practices that gave birth to Total Quality Management (TQM). Their

approaches were embraced by Japanese manufacturing after World War II, and the highest prize for quality in Japan is now the Deming Prize. Three decades later, American manufacturers began to accept and apply Deming's and Juran's thinking and methods.

8. At the Toyota Motor Corporation, Taiichi Ohno and his colleagues studied Ford's production system and American supermarket replenishment methods. These processes inspired Toyota's synchronized manufacturing and just-in-time techniques. Ohno was the founder of Toyota's production system and the creator of the most powerful enterprise management system known today.

The Toyota Production System evolved out of need. Certain marketplace restrictions required production of small quantities of many varieties under conditions of low demand, a fate the Japanese automobile industry had faced in the postwar period. The most important objective has been to increase production efficiency by consistently and thoroughly eliminating waste. This concept and the equally important respect for humanity are the foundation of the Toyota Production System.

Taiichi Ohno[2]

The Toyota people recognized the Ford system's contradictions and shortcomings, particularly with respect to employees. With General Douglas MacArthur actively promoting labor unions in the occupation years, Ford's harsh attitudes and demeaning job structures were unworkable in postwar Japan. They were workable in America only because of the "Greatest Generation"—people who had Great Depression attitudes that made the system work in spite of its defects. Toyota soon discovered that factory workers had far more to contribute than just muscle power, as they are the only value-adding positions in the business. This belief led to many practices such as quality circles, team development, and cellular manufacturing.

9. Shigeo Shingo, one of Taiichi Ohno's consultants, made numerous contributions to Lean through teaching, consulting, and writing books about Lean. By 1959 Dr. Shingo had gained notable fame as an "engineering genius" from his work in developing just-in-time (JIT) manufacturing,

2. Ibid., p. xiii.

Single Minute Exchange of Die (SMED), and consequently the Toyota Production System. In addition, by focusing on production rather than management alone, he was able to establish himself as the world's industrial engineering thought leader. In 1961 Dr. Shingo incorporated his knowledge of quality control to develop the "Defects = 0" concept, commonly known as *poka-yoke* or mistake-proofing. When Japanese productivity and quality gains became evident to the outside world, American executives sent industrial engineers to Japan to study them. They brought back mostly superficial aspects like *kanban* cards and quality circles. Most early attempts to emulate Toyota failed because they were not integrated into a complete system, as few understood its underlying principles.

10. Kaoru Ishikawa developed fishbone diagrams as he pioneered quality management processes at Kawasaki shipyards and, in the process, became one of the founding fathers of modern quality management. Fishbone diagrams were first used in the 1960s and are considered one of the seven basic tools of quality management, along with the histogram, Pareto chart, check sheet, control chart, flowchart, and scatter diagram.

11. Toyota's production system is the most significant advance since Henry Ford's fully integrated system paced by a moving assembly line. Taiichi Ohno began developing the Toyota Production System (TPS) in 1949. He and his colleagues worked tirelessly for more than 20 years to fully develop and deploy the system's processes and practices across the company and its key suppliers.

12. After great success in Japan, W. Edwards Deming returned to the United States and spent some years in obscurity before the publication of his book *Out of the Crisis* in 1982. In this book Deming set out 14 principles which he believed would save the United States from industrial doom at the hands of the Japanese. Although Deming did not use the term *Total Quality Management* in his book, he is credited with launching the movement. Most of the central ideas of TQM are contained in *Out of the Crisis*, and his 14 points are critical to understanding Deming's thinking on eliminating variation. The more variation—in the length of parts, in delivery times, in prices, in work practices—the more waste.

13. During the 1980s, North America learned about Toyota's use of JIT manufacturing and *kanban* from Richard Schonberger's book *Japanese Manufacturing Techniques*. Schonberger traveled to Japan and studied many of the Toyota Production System practices. He was a true pioneer in getting American companies to begin using these practices.

14. Lean manufacturing gained implementation traction in 1989 with the publication of James Womack and Daniel Jones's book *The Machine That Changed the World*, a five-year study of the global automobile industry. Their major finding was Toyota's significant competitive advantage over all other competitors based on the Toyota Production System. This was the most important contribution to Lean adaptation in America, where the improvement results from Lean practices were well documented and analyzed.

The Lean System

In his book *Toyota Production System*, Taiichi Ohno describes how the TPS began. Toyoda Kiichiro, the founder of Toyota Motor Company, was challenged by his father, Toyoda Sakichi, to start an automobile manufacturing company. When World War II ended, Toyoda Kiichiro discovered that American automobile manufacturers were nine times more productive than Toyota. He, in turn, challenged Taiichi Ohno, then a Toyota engineer and manager, and later executive vice president of Toyota Motor Company, to catch up with America in three years. The Japanese auto market was much smaller than the U.S. market, making this challenge even greater. This meant that Ford's inflexible production system would not be practical for producing Japan's high-variety, low-volume market requirements. These three leaders recognized that becoming competitive would require eliminating all waste. This stimulated their radical thinking, which led to Toyota Production System values, principles, and practices to eliminate all waste in pursuit of perfection.

> *Improving efficiency only makes sense when it is tied to cost reduction. Look at the efficiency of each operator and of each line. Then look at the operators as a group, and then at the efficiency of the entire plant (all the lines). Efficiency must be improved at each step and at the same time, for the plant as a whole.*
>
> *Taiichi Ohno*[3]

By 2009, Toyota was the world's largest car company and generated more profit than all other carmakers combined. The Toyota Production System (Lean) is now part of Toyota's DNA, but it has taken decades to

---

3. Ibid., p. 18.

mature. The more one understands about Lean, the more one marvels at Ohno's TPS. It is difficult to understand how the company knows "the footsteps of every operator every day," yet the employee relations environment has been positive enough for Toyota-built plants to remain union-free in the United States. This is one of the many counterintuitive lessons to be learned from a serious study of the Lean system. The TPS is often represented by the Toyota House (see Figure 2.2), which illustrates some of its core principles, practices, and end purpose.

Taiichi Ohno correctly believed that improving an integrated value stream was the best approach to delivering value to customers and other supply chain participants. Lean has proven its timelessness by delivering results for more than 50 years and remains the best practice yet known for manufacturing plant and supply chain operations.

TPS's purpose is achieved by the elimination of seven specific forms of waste:

1. Overproduction—making more than is needed
2. Transport—excessive movement of materials
3. Motion—inefficient movement of people
4. Waiting—underutilization of people
5. Inventory—material lying around unused
6. Overprocessing—manufacturing to a higher quality standard than the customer expects
7. Defect correction—The cost of fixing defects, including the part that gets thrown away and the time it takes to make the product correctly

A revolution in consciousness is indispensable. There is no waste in business more terrible than overproduction. Why does it occur? Industrial society must develop the courage, or rather the common sense, to procure only what is needed when it is needed and in the amount needed. This requires what I call a revolution in consciousness, a change of attitude and viewpoint by business people. Holding a large inventory causes the waste of over production. It also leads to an inventory of defects, which is a serious business loss. We must understand these situations in-depth before we can achieve a revolution in consciousness.

Taiichi Ohno[4]

---

4. Ibid., p. 15.

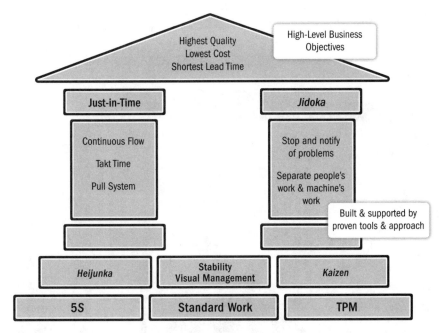

Figure 2.2 Toyota "House" of Lean

The Toyota House and the seven wastes provide important basic information about the TPS, but they do not provide a complete model to assist in understanding the entire system. In addition, the name *Toyota Production System* could be interpreted as implying that it has application only to producing products. This was clearly not Taiichi Ohno's intent; he describes TPS as a business management system well suited to success in global markets. This system we call Lean is intended as a complete enterprise management system, starting from the founders' values and principles to its processes and detailed tools and practices. The Lean Enterprise Management System is represented by Figure 2.3.

This model is a good total system representation, but total understanding of Lean in all of its dimensions is a lifelong pursuit. This is the way it should be for those of us who are committed to practicing Lean just as the curiosity, pursuit of perfection, and a better way were practiced and preached by Taiichi Ohno: "It is the duty of those working with *kanban* to keep improving it with creativity and resourcefulness without allowing it to become fixed at any stage."

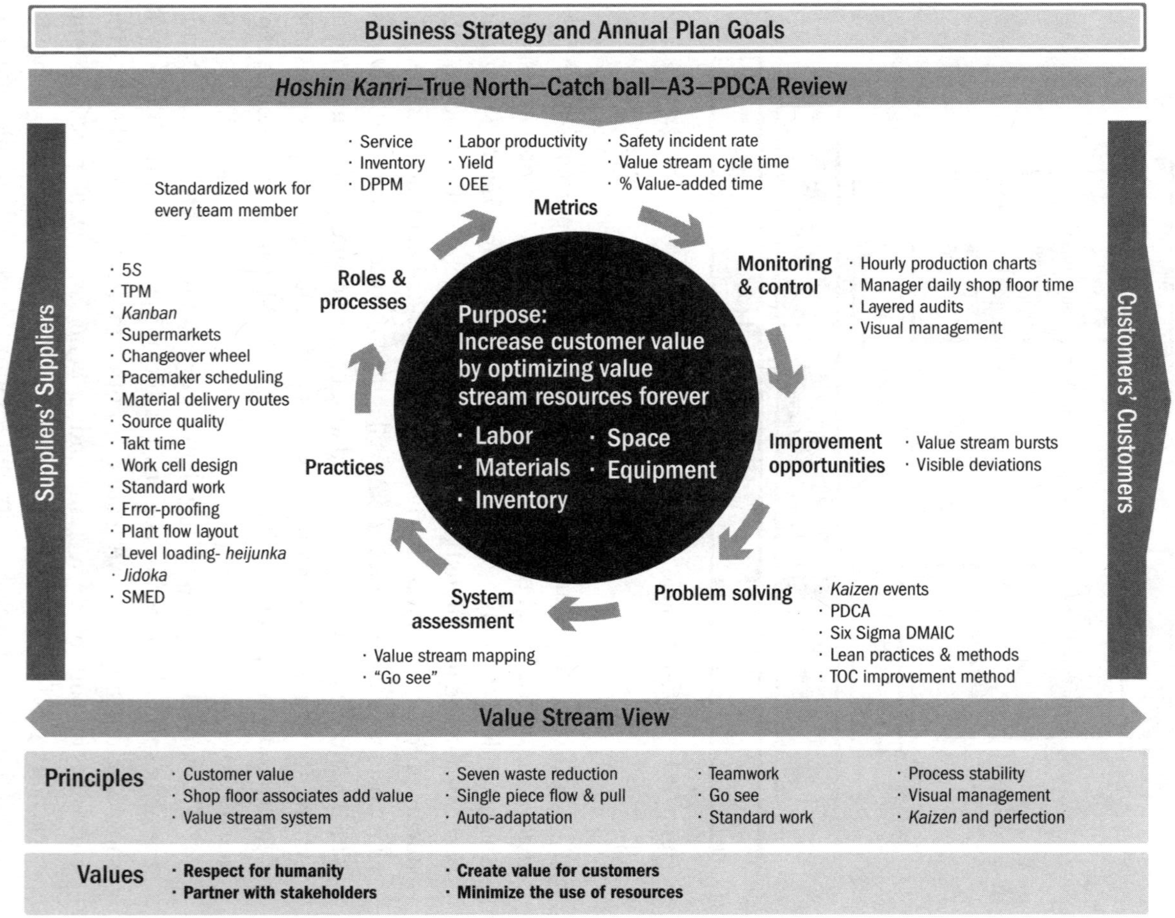

Business Strategy and Annual Plan Goals

Supplpliers' Suppliers

Customers' Customers

Hoshin Kanri–True North–Catch ball–A3–PDCA Review

Metrics

- Service
- Inventory
- DPPM

- Labor productivity
- Yield
- OEE

- Safety incident rate
- Value stream cycle time
- % Value-added time

Roles & processes

Monitoring & control
- Hourly production charts
- Manager daily shop floor time
- Layered audits
- Visual management

Improvement opportunities
- Value stream bursts
- Visible deviations

Problem solving
- *Kaizen* events
- PDCA
- Six Sigma DMAIC
- Lean practices & methods
- TOC improvement method

Purpose:
Increase customer value by optimizing value stream resources forever

- Labor
- Materials
- Inventory
- Space
- Equipment

System assessment
- Value stream mapping
- "Go see"

Practices

Standardized work for every team member

- 5S
- TPM
- *Kanban*
- Supermarkets
- Changeover wheel
- Pacemaker scheduling
- Material delivery routes
- Source quality
- Takt time
- Work cell design
- Standard work
- Error-proofing
- Plant flow layout
- Level loading- *heijunka*
- *Jidoka*
- SMED

Value Stream View

Principles
- Customer value
- Shop floor associates add value
- Value stream system

- Seven waste reduction
- Single piece flow & pull
- Auto-adaptation

- Teamwork
- Go see
- Standard work

- Process stability
- Visual management
- *Kaizen* and perfection

Values
- **Respect for humanity**
- **Partner with stakeholders**

- **Create value for customers**
- **Minimize the use of resources**

Figure 2.3 Lean Enterprise Management System

Lean Values and Principles

Lean's values and principles are foundational to the understanding and successful application of the Lean Enterprise Management System. There have been six decades of validation based on the success of companies that have adapted and internalized Lean. They provide a philosophical "true north" and boundaries within which Lean's purpose, practices, and tools have been successfully applied.

Lean has four core values discoverable from Taiichi Ohno's book *Toyota Production System*, forming the system's philosophical beliefs or tenets. Lean's four core values are these:

1. Create value for customers
2. Stakeholder partnerships
3. Respect for humanity
4. Minimize resource use

Lean's values, its foundational base, guided Ohno's thinking and development of nine identifiable Lean principles. These principles provide clear rules of the road for understanding the Lean way of working:

1. **Customer value** is the criterion applied to all enterprise activities to determine if they are value-adding or non-value-adding. A Lean enterprise focuses on increasing value to customers while reducing cost, resulting in improved profitability. It does this by improving the skills, knowledge, and processes of all its people.
2. **Only shop floor associates add value** directly to products and services supplied to customers. This implies that a Lean organization's role is to focus on making direct shop floor associate jobs easier, more productive, safer, and more satisfying, thus ensuring that customer value is continually increased.
3. **Value streams** are defined as materials and information flow from suppliers of suppliers to end-user customers. Value streams are systems that must be continually improved by reducing waste. Decisions on improvement are made based on optimizing system performance, not individual activity performance.
4. **The seven wastes** provide assistance in seeing system waste and making it easy to find value stream improvement opportunities.
5. **Single-piece flow and pull** define a value stream's ideal flow state, including what should trigger flow. If only one unit is being worked on at each

process with no other inventory and nothing is made until customers consume a unit, value streams are operating at perfection. This results in value streams with the shortest cycle time and zero waste, the ultimate goal for every Lean value stream.

6. **"Go see"** means to spend time observing value stream processes rather than making assumptions and creating theories sitting in conference rooms or offices. Reality is on the shop floor; it is where waste can be seen and ideas for system improvement are born.

7. **Visual management** is a powerful principle with connections to many Lean system dimensions. Lean system operations are to be transparent so that everyone involved can see and understand what is actually happening. Visual management and control empower shop floor associates. For example, *kanban* signals authorize making more product; having inventory below standard signals that an operation is behind and tells other operators to help it catch up; *andon* lights signal flow disruptions requiring support resources and managers to respond.

8. **Teamwork** is essential to Lean success. Teamwork with suppliers, shop floor associates, team leaders, managers, and support resources is an essential organizational attribute. Lean excellence depends on continual closed-loop communications across, up, and down value stream organizations.

9. *Kaizen* **and perfection** are the Lean system's improvement engines and catalysts. Relentless continual system improvement powers Lean systems and stimulates creative problem solving in pursuit of perfection.

These values and principles provide a foundation within which Lean's practices are applied in pursuit of increasing customer value by optimizing value stream resources through elimination of all waste.

The Lean Practices

Over a 20-year period, the TPS developed myriad practices to expose and solve problems, resulting in elimination of waste and improvement of flow. These practices include *hoshin kanri* for ensuring tight organizational alignment to key business goals. Other practices continually improve value stream design and eliminate deviations. Lean also employs an operational planning approach, ensuring deployment of only those resources required to support the rate of customer demand. Customer demand rate is established by a method called *Takt time*. Takt time defines cycle times required to produce a unit of product at a rate sufficient to meet average customer demand. It is the drumbeat synchronizing all operations and resources. Just enough resources are supplied to meet Takt time, optimizing system resource consumption. Operations are designed to produce at a cycle time slightly lower than Takt time and are synchronized by customer-demand pull signals. Lean standardized practices (see Figure 2.3) allow for quick reaction to value stream defects. This array of practices is applied to the value stream as appropriate through each continuous improvement cycle. Lean tools are the means to building, sustaining, and improving the Lean system.

Aligning the Organization to Strategy and Goals

Three conditions related to alignment typically exist in companies:

1. No organization vision
2. Organization vision without departmental and individual alignment
3. Organization vision with departmental and individual alignment

Each of these conditions has consequences for organizational effectiveness and productivity. Without a compelling vision, organizations have no clarity about the company's source of competitive advantage and value proposition. Functional leaders with good intentions create metrics, goals, and programs based on how they interpret their organization's contribution to enterprise success. Since there is no compelling direction, functions optimize their own area but not total enterprise customer value. A majority of companies are in either condition 1 or condition 2; a very small percentage fully meet condition 3. Well-aligned metrics are fundamental to effective business strategy implementation, as they drive program and project priorities, improving goal achievement probability.

Lean's *hoshin kanri*, or policy deployment, is a tool for effective organizational alignment to strategic and operational metrics and programs. This process starts with the identification of the vital few business goals ("true north"). A tool called an X-matrix is applied to ensure tight integration of long-term objectives and programs with annual improvement goals. "Catch ball" is a second process used to ensure organizational understanding and commitment throughout all organizational functions and levels. Key programs are defined and monitored using Lean's A3 process, a single page

(A3-size paper) summarizing projects and their status. The final element of *hoshin kanri* is regular reviews to keep programs on track to meet annual goals and to take any needed corrective action.

Value Stream Mapping and Planning Improvement

Value stream mapping (VSM) is the Lean system's assessment and planning tool. VSM includes a standard set of icons and instructions for completing value stream maps. Step 1 is current-state map completion, documenting material and information flows based on actual shop floor observation (Figure 2.4). As an example, building a plant value stream map starts with shipping, the process closest to the customer, and follows upstream, step by step, through raw materials receiving. Observers note product flow through work centers, key data about each process operation, non-value-added operator activities, utilization of material handling associates, and other signs of waste.

Second, a future state is constructed by redesigning value streams using appropriate Lean tools, methodologies, and practices to create an end-state vision conforming more closely to Lean ideals and principles. Third, future-state and current-state maps are compared to define improvement projects, which will move the enterprise toward future-state achievement. Projects are noted on a current-state map with a starburst at the point in the process where the project would be done. Fourth, 90- and 180-day implementation plans are developed for projects most important to improving the value stream and generating business results. Because a first priority in Lean implementation is gaining value stream stability, likely initial projects might include quick changeover, work cell design for flow, inventory supermarkets, and visual management tools. There are many possible options when constructing future-state maps, so experience is helpful to making good judgments about what projects to tackle and in what sequence.

This continuous improvement cycle is repeated every 90 to 180 days by going deeper into the value stream system to standardize, level load, stabilize, and improve flow to a new level. Each succeeding cycle of improving flow raises a new series of barriers that must be addressed, thus creating continual improvement. This involves taking some level of risk, which can potentially disrupt short-term product flow. A fundamental Lean implementation rule is "Always protect the customer." This means that when risk exists, sufficient backup should be available to ensure that any problems can be contained. If

1 Create current-state map

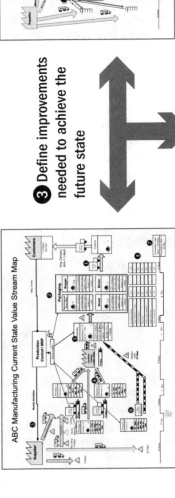

ABC Manufacturing Current State Value Stream Map

2 Create future-state map

Twin City future state value stream

3 Define improvements needed to achieve the future state

4 Prioritize improvement projects and define 90- to 180-day improvement project plans

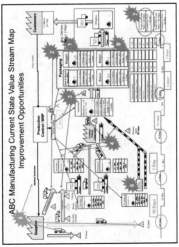

ABC Manufacturing Current State Value Stream Map
Improvement Opportunities

Figure 2.4 Value stream mapping

issues cannot be immediately resolved, additional resources are used to work around problems until they can be resolved.

Improvement Opportunity Identification and Problem Solving

Lean tools for identifying improvement opportunities are value stream mapping and visual management. VSM is applied at the Lean system level, where management is responsible for defining and implementing improvements. Shop floor visual management drives long-term continuous improvement. Daily deviations are exposed through visual management, and shop floor teams must identify root causes of problems so that permanent solutions can be implemented.

A Lean practice for identifying root causes is called the *five whys*. The first step is to ask why a problem is occurring. The response is then met with a second "Why is this occurring?" The process continues, and each successive response is met with another "why" until root causes are determined (Figure 2.5).

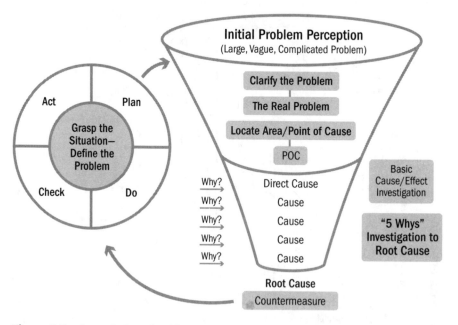

Figure 2.5 Lean Enterprise Management System problem-solving process

The Toyota Production System has been built on the practice and evolution of this scientific approach. By asking why five times and answering it each time, we can get to the real cause of the problem, which is often hidden behind more obvious symptoms. In a production operation data is highly regarded, but I consider facts to be even more important.

Taiichi Ohno[5]

Through experience, practitioners have learned that it normally takes five or more cycles to locate the root cause. After the root cause is identified, the four-step PDCA improvement process is applied.

The improvement cycle applying value stream mapping is led by management, focused on building and improving Lean value streams. Continuous operational improvement is made daily to eliminate waste caused by deviations from standards. These deviations include not achieving daily production goals, operations not consistently achieving cycle time, inventory levels that are not in compliance with standards, shop floor improvement suggestions, and many others. Team leaders and shop floor associates use PDCA and the five whys (Figure 2.5) to

- Identify the real problem
- Determine its root causes
- Define a countermeasure to eliminate or control the root causes
- Implement the countermeasure
- Check countermeasure effectiveness
- Repeat the problem-solving cycle if the original problem still exists

Top-down value stream system improvements and bottom-up waste elimination make two overlapping improvement cycles, which continue to drive value stream performance toward perfection. The end result is a powerful continuous improvement process focused on improving a company's competitive position.

Roles and Processes

Lean standardized work defines Lean system roles for every person in the organization, including management. Implementation normally starts on

---

5. Ibid., pp. 17–18.

the shop floor. Shop floor job activities are classified in three categories: value-added, non-value-added (waste), and non-value-added but required. For example, if product assembly is analyzed, handling of parts is waste, actual assembly is value-added, and quality checks are non-value-added but required. Work is organized in cells when possible, and tasks are balanced among the cell operators to ensure minimization of operator non-value-added activity. Each job is analyzed to eliminate non-value-added work, minimize non-value-added but necessary work, and optimize worker safety.

> *Standard work sheets are posted prominently at each workstation. They are a means of visual control, which is how the Toyota Production System is managed. High production efficiency has also been maintained by preventing the recurrence of defective products, operational mistakes, and accidents, and by incorporating workers' ideas. All this has been possible because of the inconspicuous standard work sheet. Standard work sheet combines materials, workers and machines to produce efficiently. It clearly lists the three elements of the standard work procedure as operation cycle time, work sequence and standard inventory.*
>
> Taiichi Ohno[6]

Metrics

Lean uses metrics to measure results and process effectiveness. Figure 2.3 contains representative high-level metrics. *Hoshin* planning ensures the selection of the most important metrics in alignment with key customer and business priorities. Metric improvement versus operational plan targets is the focus of regular operational reviews at every organizational level.

Monitoring and Control

Lean is a people-based system, so monitoring and control rely on everyone being present on the shop floor. Visual management is the Lean system's sensing mechanism, providing transparency of operational reality and data related to improvement. It also highlights deviations from detailed standards of performance, work procedures, scheduling, inventory, and scrap, among many other factors.

---

6. Ibid., pp. 21–22.

Lean Application Trends

Although Lean practices have most commonly been applied to manufacturing and supply chain operations, they are equally applicable to all processes and functions in a business. In fact, Taiichi Ohno repeatedly described the TPS as a management system that would work in every type of business. He clearly saw the goal as the elimination of waste everywhere it exists in an organization. As understanding of Lean practices and principles has grown, they are being applied to all functions and industries.

From the Shop Floor to Across the Enterprise

The first big trend was to extend Lean practices from product processes to enterprise processes and customer-facing processes as shown in Figure 2.6. Every function, from product development to marketing and IT, has processes for getting work done. This means that value stream mapping system design and PDCA problem solving can be used to continuously improve these processes. A good way to initiate Lean with technical, sales, marketing, and administrative processes is by starting a dialogue to identify current waste. Once participants see there are opportunities, they will want to take the next step and begin value stream mapping to redesign and improve their process.

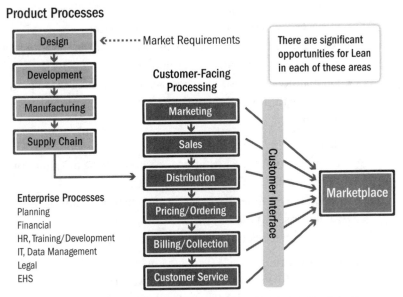

Figure 2.6 Applying Lean to nonmanufacturing business functions

The application of Lean to the enterprise in many respects has been restrained by Lean's great success in manufacturing, creating a perception that Lean is to be applied only to shop floor operations. As previously discussed, this was not the founders' intention, and only now are we seeing broader adaptation of Lean as an enterprise management system.

The following are representative questions that can be used to initiate a dialogue about waste in various functions:

- **Product design and development**
  - Are product development cycle times too long?
  - Are launch deadlines missed?
  - Is the commercialization process inefficient?

- **IT**
  - Do managers have access to the data they need to run their business, or do they need to fund a project to get the data?
  - Can customers get the information they need directly, or do they need to contact a sales/service office to get it?
  - Is there one version of the truth for critical enterprise data (such as financials, product sales, customer accounts, etc.)?
  - Is there a defined system of record for each data subject, or do users have to hunt for it?
  - Is it easy to determine in advance what systems/processes will be impacted by a planned change to a database?
  - Are different tools or standards used by different teams within the enterprise to perform similar data integration work?
  - Do maintenance costs increase each time an integration point is added?
  - Are integration activities the constraint (or critical path) in most projects?

- **Finance**
  - Do inefficient forecasting processes result in multiple forecast revisions?
  - Is excessive time spent creating custom reports (for which the requesters wait too long)?
  - Do disputed customer invoices delay payment?

- **Human resources**
  - Does the hiring process have long cycle times?
  - Do associates receive timely feedback and direction?

- **Customer service**
  - Are customers confused about whom to contact for help?
  - Do customers have to wait a long time to get help?
  - Do customers get timely responses to complaints?

- **Marketing**
  - Are marketing campaigns always effective?
  - Are communications with the sales team late, too frequent, too infrequent?
  - Does the sales team get timely new product knowledge/expertise to effectively sell the product?
  - Are there delays in communicating price increases to the sales force and customers?
  - Do pricing errors and price discrepancies exist?

- **Sales**
  - How much time do sales associates spend on administrative tasks instead of being in the field selling?
  - Are sales associates able to follow up on leads in a timely manner?
  - How much time do sales associates spend following up on orders to make sure they are right and delivered on time?

From Manufacturing to Services Industries

The second big trend in Lean adoption is from manufacturing to service industries. Many industries have published examples of adopting Lean; software development and health care are two examples.

Julia Hanna wrote about applying Lean at Wipro, the Indian software development company, in her article "Bringing 'Lean' Principles to Service Industries."[7] The initial Wipro effort grew to 603 lean projects within two years, producing improved productivity and empowered work teams. The company's research illustrated five examples of Lean practice application:

1. Using *kaizen* has altered software development approaches from sequential methods, where work moved from one developer to another, to iterative approaches, where teams complete logical software functionality collaboratively.

7. Julia Hanna, "Bringing 'Lean' Principles to Service Industries," Harvard Business School Working Knowledge, October 22, 2007.

2. Sharing mistakes across development teams enabled them to learn from each other and to apply these experiences to future projects.

3. Wipro used tools such as the system complexity estimator, which compared actual architectures to ideal-state architectures, helping teams understand where additional people would be needed during a project.

4. Value stream mapping was applied to projects, identifying waste of time and effort, leading to increased speed and productivity.

5. Engagement and empowerment energized the organization as all team members, regardless of organizational level, were seeing the bigger picture. This resulted in thousands of software engineers contributing to innovation through problem solving, creating an energized work environment while increasing productivity and quality.

Case Study: The Value of Lean in Service Industries

Another industry where Lean has been applied is health care. Doctors, nurses, and technicians at Park Nicollet Health Services (St. Louis Park, Minnesota) applied standard Lean analysis tools and practices to analyze and radically improve their operations. These included the use of stopwatches, spaghetti diagrams, standard work, 5S, level loading, and rapid changeovers, to name a few. The first clinic studied was Endoscopy, resulting in doubling the number of patients served each day. This success was replicated in the Cancer Center, Heart Center, Urgent Care, and Wound Clinic. The use of standard work applied to surgery resulted in 40,000 fewer instruments being used each month; this simplification also meant fewer errors because the right instrument was always available during surgery. In 2004 Park Nicollet completed 85 Rapid Process Improvement workshops, resulting in $7.5 million in savings. The results are transforming Park Nicollet Health Services.

Practicing Lean leads to seeing and understanding more about its organic nature as a system. It is a journey, and only through practice and study are new opportunities for understanding and improvement discovered and applied. Lean's life cycle, as practiced in a majority of organizations, is still in its embryonic phase, which speaks to future contributions of Lean to radically improving the competitiveness of businesses and government services.

CHAPTER THREE

The Integration Factory

Very simply, a flexible factory enjoys more variety with lower total costs than traditional factories, which are still forced to make the trade-off between scale and variety.

George Stalk[1]

Lean is a management system that originated in a factory setting. It has since been applied to many other types of production processes and also more recently to a wide range of nonmanufacturing business processes such as supply chain management, health care delivery, order management, and others. Perhaps one of the most interesting and innovative applications of Lean is the use of factory concepts for common integration activities. How can one apply Lean concepts such as mass customization, just-in-time delivery, mistake-proofing (*poka-yoke*), pace (Takt time), production leveling (*heijunka*), and work cells to the virtual world of process and data integration?

In this chapter we will explore the use of the factory model to answer these questions and explain how they can help you achieve improved customer satisfaction, greater efficiencies, and business agility.

---

1. George Stalk, "Time—The Next Source of Competitive Advantage," *Harvard Business Review*, no. 4 (July–August 1988).

What Is an Integration Factory?

An Integration Factory is a cohesive integration technology platform that automates the flow of materials and information in the process of building and sustaining integration points. The reason this approach has proven to be highly successful is the incredibly high degree of similarity among integration points. In a manner similar to automobiles, which can be classed as sedans, pickup trucks, coupes, and so on, integration "code" also falls into different classes. Whether the class is a "slowly changing dimension" class, a "change-data-captured event stream" class, or a "publish-and-subscribe" class, the exact makeup of the data being integrated may be different for each instance, but the general processing pattern and structure are the same for each class.

Not only do integration points fit into a relatively small number of classes similar to cars, but the life cycle of discovery, development, and deployment of these integration points also follows a similar pattern, and factory-oriented paradigms assist in the life-cycle process as well. Examples of automation include automating requirements definition by leveraging a business glossary, canonical models, and metadata repositories for source and target data models; automating code generation using pattern-based wizards; automating testing using script-driven testing frameworks; and automating migration of code objects from development to test to production environments using metadata-driven scripts and workflows.

The Integration Factory, we believe, will be the dominant new "wave" of middleware for the next decade (2010s). It views the thousands of information exchanges between applications in an enterprise as mass customizations of a relatively small number of patterns. The integrations are managed collectively as a system, independently of the applications they serve. The management practice that optimizes the benefits of the Integration Factory is Lean Integration—the use of *Lean principles* and *tools* in the process of making independent applications work together as a cohesive system. The combination of factory technologies and Lean practices results in significant and sustainable *business benefits*.

How does an Integration Factory compare with a traditional factory? The *Merriam-Webster Dictionary* defines *factory* as a "facility for manufacturing" and defines *manufacturing* as "the process of making wares by hand or machinery, especially when carried on systematically with division of labor." The term *factory* may, however, conjure up negative images of pollution or low-cost labor and poor working conditions. These older factories did indeed offer efficiencies in comparison to prior methods, but they also introduced downsides. Standardized work can be very mundane (boring), and working conditions may be less than ideal. The term *sweatshop* comes from a working environment where conditions are considered to be difficult and where the workers have few opportunities to address their situation.

Modern factories with a high degree of automation (*jidoka*) and emphasis on cleanliness look very different. There are still workers in these factories, but their roles are more related to maintaining the machines that do most of the work, supervising workflow, performing the manual activities that are difficult (or expensive) to automate, and dealing with exceptions.

The traditional view of a factory, and the images that come to mind for most people, relates to the *flow of materials* and the process that results in an end product—in other words, the assembly line. There is, however, another flow that is just as critical for an effective and efficient factory: the *flow of information* both among factory workers and to and from external customers, suppliers, and stakeholders.

Prior to the computer age, the information flow was largely verbal or paper-based. Lean organizations improve the information flow among workers with *andon* lights, *kanban* cards, and other visual signaling mechanisms. Computers, industry standards (such as EDI—Electronic Document Interchange), and supply chain integration methods have enabled suppliers to be more directly connected to the factory information flow. The age of the Internet has enabled customers, regulators, and other stakeholders to interact directly with the factory. Dell is a good example of a personal-computer factory that has largely automated the flow of information. The Dell Web site allows users to customize the configuration of a personal computer and return to the Web site later to change the configuration or track progress. These self-service portals coupled with mass customization techniques allow individuals to customize and purchase products and even monitor production status in some cases.

How Is the Integration Factory Different from Traditional Integration Approaches?

The Integration Factory is a unique innovation in the integration industry. It views the thousands or tens of thousands of information exchanges between application components in an enterprise or supply chain as a relatively small number of patterns that can be mass-customized. It combines the concepts of reusable component frameworks, a highly optimized process, the ability to perform specific integration activities anywhere in the world, a shared meta-data repository, and industry standards to produce low-cost, high-quality interfaces that can connect anything to anything.

Another way to think of the Integration Factory is that it produces *products of one, delivered as a service,* and it does so inexpensively and fast. It is based on the premise that the utopian vision of a universal interface doesn't exist and won't exist in the foreseeable future. Rapidly advancing technologies, a proliferation of standards, and vendor proprietary interests ensure that the software industry will continue to create new waves of interface protocols for years to come. The conclusion? Interfaces are not built once; they are built dozens or even hundreds of times over the life of the application as the various dependent platforms, tools, technologies, or business processes change.

The Integration Factory breaks the traditional paradigm of custom point-to-point interfaces with a new paradigm that challenges the traditional product model. The factory output is indeed a "product": a fully deployable and executable program (or set of components) that connects applications or consolidates data from two or more applications. Yet each "product" is unique in that it is constructed to meet a specific business need and to interface with a specific application, handle specific data, on a specific operating system platform, with a specific protocol. But the factory is also a "service." Interfaces are built on demand and to specification, they are maintained and supported in operation, and they are quickly regenerated whenever any of the dependent components or technology is changed.

A key difference between the Integration Factory and the traditional view of a widget assembly line is the operational aspect of the deployed integration components. In other words, we have both a development factory that builds or modifies integration components and an integration hub or bus that operationalizes the components to perform the day-to-day or second-to-second exchanges and transformations of data between applications. To put yet another spin on this, the *development factory* produces the machines (software components) for the *operational factory.*

Furthermore, both of these factories, the development factory and the operations factory, contain both types of flows: material flow and information flow. The net result is an Integration Factory that may provide both development and operational services, as summarized graphically in Figure 3.1.

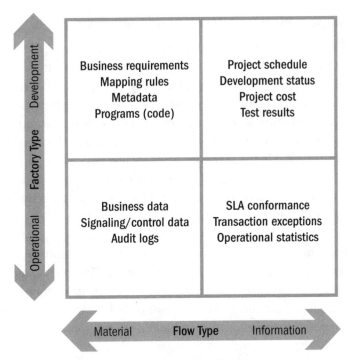

Figure 3.1   Four flow types in an Integration Factory

As we discussed in Chapter 1, the Integration Factory is a logical next step in the evolution of integration technology. It takes the integration platform to the next stage of maturity by adding automation to the flow of materials and the flow of information. In this regard it is difficult to separate the technology elements from the people and process elements because of the interplay between them.

Can an Integration Competency Center (ICC) run a factory without applying Lean practices? The answer is yes—at least to some degree. The ICC provides the necessary organizational focus, which is one of the prerequisites for effectively leveraging a factory. An ICC also brings to bear a number of competencies that are essential for sustaining factory operations. That said, it is the Lean practices that really begin to leverage the power of the factory infrastructure. The disciplines associated with continuous improvement, value stream mapping, pull, flow, and waste elimination (to name a few) will result in even greater benefits than ICC competencies alone.

What Problem Is the Integration Factory Trying to Solve?

The core objective of the factory is to provide an efficient and effective way to build and sustain information dependencies in a highly complex application environment that is constantly changing. The Integration Factory improves the quality and performance of the integration solutions by using reusable components, standard processes, and continuous improvement processes to build quality in. The factory also enables organizational agility by delivering integration solutions rapidly as needed (just in time). In short, the purpose of an Integration Factory is to design, build, and support integration solutions better, faster, and more cheaply than traditional custom or ad hoc integrations.

To put the Integration Factory approach into perspective, it is worth restating the fundamental reason why integration is needed and what approaches have been attempted in the past. In order to meet the computing needs of a typical enterprise, it is necessary to operate numerous distinct computing platforms simultaneously. On each platform, separate software applications work together to handle the data-processing needs of the enterprise. These computer applications are designed first and foremost to operate as stand-alone autonomous units and second to interoperate with other applications.

In the 1970s and 1980s, individual project teams handled intersystem communication on a case-by-case basis; interfaces were seen as simple "appendages" to applications. In the 1990s, in response to the rapidly growing number of interfaces, a new class of software emerged called *middleware*. Its express purpose was to provide a common reusable integration layer between independent applications with the goals of reducing the number of point-to-point interfaces, increasing reuse, and reducing costs. The vision was to provide a service to applications that would permit them to be tightly integrated while remaining loosely coupled; although dependent on each other, applications should be allowed to evolve independently. The middleware strategy worked extremely well—so much so, that the number of interfaces exploded in response to increasing business demands to link systems and automate business processes.

Despite all the progress, however, a major challenge remained. The industry failed to achieve a universal interface standard that would allow any given application to communicate with any given middleware tool. Several industry standards have been proposed and some are promising, but none is dominant, and any given large enterprise likely has many flavors. Furthermore, many middleware vendors and application vendors promote various proprietary protocols in the interest of promoting their product strengths or other marketing-related motivations. The interface variations are further complicated by the constant evolution of new proposed standards and new technology waves. Since it is rarely justifiable to rewrite all the legacy interfaces for every new technology wave, most organizations have a variety of legacy and new interfaces that all must be supported. The end result is that a typical large enterprise has a hodgepodge collection of interfaces and high maintenance costs. Estimates for building and maintaining interfaces between applications range from 30 percent to 70 percent for typical large, complex IT environments.

When *Not* to Use a Factory Approach

There are indeed some circumstances when an Integration Factory is *not* the best approach for data and process integration. If we go back to the car manufacturing comparison, the first Model T rolled off the Ford assembly line in 1908 and ushered in an era of affordable automobiles. Yet even now, over 100 years later, while the vast majority of cars are built in highly efficient factories, there are still times when it is appropriate to build a car by hand. The most common reasons for custom-built cars are to meet special high-performance requirements such as for racing cars, prototypes to test new ideas, or simply for aesthetic and artistic motivations.

There are similar justifications for custom-built integrations in the software world. The first time an enterprise has requirements for extremely high-performance response, massive scalable throughput, special security controls, or other innovations, a custom solution is often the only way to achieve the desired results. If the solution requires a truly innovative approach, it may indeed warrant building a prototype or two to test the ideas and find out which way works best before building the production implementation.

The point is that factories are most effective when there is a clear pattern. Architecture and integration teams should be prepared to build custom solutions when required, but they should also always be on the lookout for new patterns that can be standardized and addressed with reusable components and efficient processes.

Is there a place in the integration world for creative approaches strictly for aesthetic reasons? It's hard to imagine a business sponsor funding such an initiative, but in any event, we will leave it to you to answer this question.

The Integration Factory as an Element of an ICC

In Chapter 1 we wrote about how the Integration Competency Center needs to be viewed as a business serving an internal market. At the highest level, this unit governs itself by measuring the value it provides to the enterprise from the perspective of the internal customers. There are several practices that can be established for how the ICC initiates engagements so that customer *pull* triggers factory *flow*. Or, as stated in *Lean Thinking*, "It is because the ability to design, schedule, and make exactly what the customer wants just when the customer wants it means you can throw away the sales forecast and simply make what the customers actually tell you they need. That is, you can let the customer pull the product from you as needed rather than pushing products, often unwanted, onto the customer."[2]

The ICC must have a way to initiate integration projects in a repeatable, structured way. This can involve creating a structured project document that outlines who the primary contact is, who the business sponsor is, what the primary objective of the initiative is, and a preliminary idea of what the scope might look like at a very high level. The document should specify only *what* the business is looking for, *who* the key people are on the business side, *what* the important systems are, *when* the business needs this, *what* some of the basic business requirements are for integration (real-time synchronization or not), and a rough estimate of whether the effort required is easy, medium, or difficult. The speed and effectiveness with which the ICC responds to the business requirements will be measured from the perspective of the customer. For that reason, it is useful to understand *why* the customer needs the problem solved. From that, it is usually possible to find a customer-driven metric that can galvanize the ICC effort and allow measurement of the end-to-end value chain from the end-customer perspective rather than the internal factory/ICC perspective.

2. James P. Womack and Daniel T. Jones, *Lean Thinking: Banish Waste and Create Wealth in Your Corporation* (Simon & Schuster, 1996), p. 24.

The resulting project initiation document is stored in a structured document (either an online form or a structured document that can be loaded into the metadata repository). Ultimately, all of the documents that describe the activities within the factory will be tied together, from the requirements documents to the design documents to the implementation artifacts to the testing plans and test code to the deployment scripts, history, and change management history. This requires a metadata repository to house and relate this information, which serves as the live documentation describing all information sources and exchanges.

Automating processes is not just the use of computers to do things automatically for people. Ultimately, it is the ability to tie together related information in a way that allows humans to quickly and efficiently grasp tremendous complexity. Our goal is to transform the integration hairball into a flexible integration system that quickly adapts to the needs of the business and technical dependencies as they change.

At this point, no decisions have been made about how the project should get done, which team is appropriate, or what the priority is. Effectively, the customer has stated what type of vehicle is wanted: a "small blue truck" or a "red four-door sedan." This describes a car style and the basics that can get passed to the appropriate "factory" within the ICC business for manufacturing.

Integration Factory Variants

The ICC and its factory processes can be designed to execute one or more styles of integration projects. Examples of these projects include

- Data warehousing
- Master data management
- Straight-through process integration
- Application retirement
- Data migration
- Business-to-business (B2B) or supply chain integration

Each of these project styles (this is not an exhaustive list and your terminology may be different) has a unique methodology. Once the ICC has identified a particular project and the people are mobilized to execute on this project, the factory for that project kicks into gear.

For each project style, particular life-cycle stages, roles, and artifacts are mobilized. While at the highest level traditional projects go through requirements, design, implementation, testing, deployment, and change control processes, the details of the roles, the way they interact, and the detailed artifacts that get produced are specific to the style of "vehicle" being produced. Furthermore, some projects may use agile methods, which involve less formal documentation and multiple iterations before the final solution emerges. Therefore, each factory, while having a similar shape and construction, must be uniquely styled to the type of products it is producing and the process for handling material and information flows.

Let's take one factory as an example. A leading mortgage company, prior to the subprime mortgage meltdown, had a data migration factory that had eliminated waste in the process of merging acquired companies' data into its systems. The company was purchasing small mortgage companies at a rate of approximately two per month between 2005 and 2007. When a company got purchased, the data migration factory kicked into gear. The factory had a detailed methodology and trained personnel who followed well-documented steps to achieve virtually waste-free integration of the purchased company's data with that of the parent company.

The mortgage company defined specific target models for each of the different critical data subject areas it required. It mapped the purchased company's source data to these target models, kept the target model definitions constant, and transformed and cleansed the source data where necessary. Business people were directly involved in the resolution of data issues in the process. And because the processes were so explicitly defined, multiple migrations could be in motion simultaneously, all working efficiently toward completion.

While this example leaves room for further automation, the company was indeed taking advantage of specialization and was using some factory concepts to increase the speed and efficiency with which acquired businesses could be integrated. It had purchased specific tools and developed people for the purpose of eliminating waste from the data migration process. Migrations were not seen as one-off projects that appeared and disappeared as if the current merger were the last one the company would ever go through. The company recognized that it had a "growth through acquisition" strategy and adjusted and invested in its IT model to meet that business strategy.

To generalize this further, it may be easier to think about these Integration Factories as operating in a hierarchy. The top level in this example is the data migration factory that applies Lean concepts to the repeatable process of rationalizing applications in acquired companies. This factory in turn takes advantage of lower-level factories that apply Lean concepts to repeatable processes such as data mapping, data cleansing, data replication, and application retirement.

Taking this approach provides several benefits. Quality is built into the integration logic because the logic follows patterns that have been proven to work best over time. Change management is easier because the integration logic looks familiar to developers. Productivity is improved because a great deal of manual labor is eliminated. An Integration Factory that takes automation down to the level of maintaining assembly lines for mass-customizing common integration patterns is taking one of the most effective Lean approaches to reducing waste and delivering better, faster, and cheaper to the customer.

How Does the Integration Factory Work?

There are several perspectives from which the factory workings could be described. In this section we will describe the factory in three ways: a project workflow scenario, work-group interactions, and a factory tools perspective.

Project Workflow Scenario

Figure 3.2 shows an overview of a process for creating middleware interfaces in support of an IT project. Note that the workflow steps and activities will change for different styles of integration, but nonetheless this should be a helpful representation of a typical process.

In step 1, a customer (which may be a project team that requires services from the factory) requests one or more integrations during the initiation stage of a project, which generally includes the scoping and business justification activities—in short, before the full project funding is approved. At this stage in the project life cycle, the requirements are high-level functional in nature; the low-level detailed requirements and technical specifications are determined in subsequent stages. Note that even in this very early, often exploratory, stage of a project, the team interacts with the Integration Factory

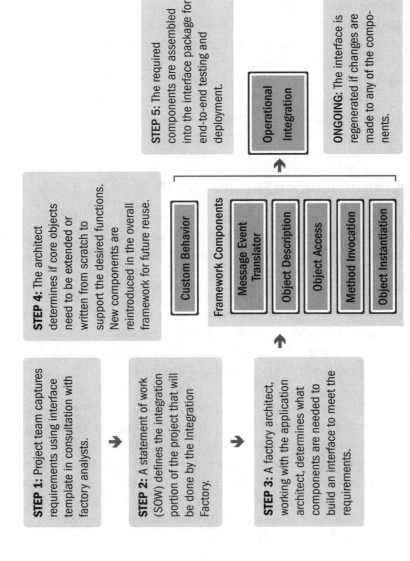

STEP 1: Project team captures requirements using interface template in consultation with factory analysts.

STEP 2: A statement of work (SOW) defines the integration portion of the project that will be done by the Integration Factory.

STEP 3: A factory architect, working with the application architect, determines what components are needed to build an interface to meet the requirements.

STEP 4: The architect determines if core objects need to be extended or written from scratch to support the desired functions. New components are reintroduced in the overall framework for future reuse.

STEP 5: The required components are assembled into the interface package for end-to-end testing and deployment.

ONGOING: The interface is regenerated if changes are made to any of the components.

Custom Behavior

Framework Components

Message Event Translator

Object Description

Object Access

Method Invocation

Object Instantiation

Operational Integration

Figure 3.2 Example factory process

using standardized tools and templates. This facilitates clear communication and sets the stage to initiate the flow of information between teams.

Step 2 formalizes the integration scope in the form of a statement of work (SOW) or equivalent. In short, this document represents the promise the Integration Factory makes to the customer. It is hard to overestimate the importance of this step since much of the credibility, and the ultimate success, of the factory arises from effectively making and keeping promises to customers. Chapter 11, Financial Management, discusses techniques for scoping the effort and cost of integrations based only on a high-level understanding of requirements.

Step 3 involves developing detailed (low-level) functional requirements for the integration and also determining nonfunctional requirements related to specific technology platforms and physical constraints.

Step 4 is where the integration effort transitions from problem-solving activities to assembly and construction activities. For routine integrations, this process may be very quick since it involves simply configuring existing reusable objects or infrastructure elements. However, if the requirements cannot be met by the current portfolio of reusable parts, the integration team will need to either construct the new elements or purchase them from a supplier. The components shown in the figure are representative of the types that may be involved in assembling a real-time integration. A mature Integration Factory may have hundreds of reusable components.

Step 5 comprises the final stages of assembly, quality assurance, and deployment activities. Once the integration elements become operational in a production environment, the factory teams may be called upon to address defects or to create a new variant of the integration components in response to changes.

Large-scale factories may have separate assembly lines for new integrations and modifications to existing interfaces. If the requested interface is new, the interface is designed, developed, and tested. Design and development typically occur at the factory site, which may be remote from the customer site. Testing can occur either at the factory or at the customer's location, but in any event quality control is governed by the factory processes. If the requested integration is a modification to an existing interface, the related code is extracted from a version control tool, changed, and regression-tested to compare the results to those of the original tests.

Work-Group Integrations

The factory (people, tools, and materials) for a given enterprise can be at one physical location, or it can be virtual with different activities and process steps performed anywhere in the world. This high degree of flexibility is enabled by modern network technology, structured repositories, and integrated workflow tools.

Figure 3.3 shows the primary flow of materials (large block arrows), beginning with requirements and the flow of information (thin lines) between teams inside and outside the Integration Factory. Note that this is a generalization and abstraction of a real-world factory for the purpose of making several key points related to how Integration Factories work. An actual factory may have more or fewer teams, subject to its scope of integration services and volume of work.

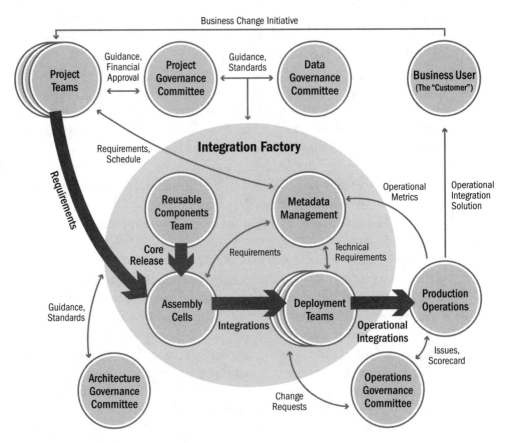

Figure 3.3 Integration team interactions

Furthermore, a "team" may be represented by a group of people, one person, or, in small factories, even a fraction of a person who fulfills several roles. Nonetheless, the key roles and their interactions are instructional.

Reusable Components Team

The flow of material in an Integration Factory begins with the concept of mass customization, that is, standardized components that can be configured or assembled with other standard components to meet the unique needs of a given set of integration requirements. It is critical that this team be separate from the project or deployment teams so that it can retain a long-term rather than point-in-time perspective on requirements. It is also critical that this team synthesize and integrate the needs of different projects to create components that are standard where appropriate and configurable as needed.

Reusable objects are made available to the factory assembly line through a formal release process. Versioning of objects is essential, since reusable objects are often refactored to accommodate new functions. Releases may come in large batches in situations where a collection of objects that are dependent on each other all need to change at the same time. In general, however, the recommendation is to apply the Lean concept of small incremental batches to the release process, ideally, batches of one.

Assembly Cells

The distinction between "assembly" and "development" is fuzzy at best. As software development tools have continued to mature and morph over the years, the line where development stops and configuration begins has continued to move. In any event, the intent with the factory is to truly achieve a metadata-driven assembly process rather than a custom development process. The output of this group in terms of the flow of materials is the collection of objects and code elements that represent the integration points as required by a given project effort.

A factory assembly process may have only one cell, but as the scope and scale of a factory increase, the Lean concept of work cells all operating according to a defined pace (Takt time) begins to pay off. Some of the major sub-activities associated with the core factory line are given below. Depending on the scale and workload associated with each activity, these activities should be grouped to optimize staff skills, workload, and cycle time for each cell.

- Source-to-target mapping
- Canonical mapping
- Message schema definition
- Integration design
- Component assembly and configuration
- Unit testing
- Performance testing
- As-built metadata documentation

Deployment Teams

Figure 3.3 shows multiple deployment teams—typically in a one-to-one alignment with the external project teams. In effect, the deployment teams are part of the project teams but are shown as separate entities since they operate within the factory context. One of the key responsibilities of these teams in the information flows is to supplement the functional requirements (*what*) from the project teams with technical requirements (*how*) related to physical implementation details.

The level of effort for managing the integration elements of a project is generally less demanding than the management effort for the overall project. For this reason we often find that one integration project manager can manage several deployment teams at the same time.

To continue the flow of materials, the deployment teams accept assembled integration elements from the assembly team and deliver high-quality tested integration elements to the project teams.

Project Teams

The project teams in this model are exactly what you would expect—cross-functional teams led by a project manager who is focused on business process changes and application system implementations. These project teams are in effect the key customers of the development Integration Factory. The integration requirements are the *pull* signal from the customer that signals demand for integration elements and begins the factory *flow*.

Production Operations

The production operations teams are the final step in the flow of materials. The operations function may be performed by one team or multiple teams.

Common scenarios for multiple operational groups include enterprises with separate operations for different countries, supply chain integration, or cloud integration, which includes externally hosted applications.

Furthermore, depending on how the ICC is organized, the factory itself may have operational responsibility for selected portions of the IT infrastructure—typically the middleware systems such as data integration hubs or enterprise service buses (ESBs). In any event, the factory staff may be called upon to support production operations for incident management and problem resolution.

Finally, the production groups provide operational metrics, which are captured in a metadata repository.

Metadata Management

The metadata management team's role is crucial in the information flows between all teams; hence this team is an enabler for the efficient operation of the overall factory processes. If we accept the old adage that "knowledge is power," the metadata team has the most power and influence in a factory operation.

The metadata team responsibilities generally include defining the information metamodel, developing interfaces/integrations between various metadata sources and repositories, optimizing the processes to maintain a high level of data quality in the repositories, enabling access to the repositories by different users through a user interface, and developing standard or custom reports.

Finally, this team may go by different names. The term *metadata* is somewhat techie and may not resonate with customers of the factory or with business managers. Alternative names for this could be the "Data Exchange Administration Team" or "Knowledge Base Management."

Governance Committees

Governance committees play an essential role in the processes, policies, standards, organization, and technologies required for a sustainable and Lean factory. Figure 3.3 lists four distinct domains that typically require a formal level of management control:

1. **Data governance**, to ensure the availability, accessibility, quality, consistency, auditability, and security of data in a company or institution

2. **Project governance**, to evaluate, prioritize, approve, enable, control, monitor, and steer business and IT initiatives

3. **Architecture governance**, to provide a comprehensive picture of the business (functions, processes, systems, technology, etc.) and its transformation from the current state to a defined future state

4. **Operations governance**, to control the pace of changes to the production environment and monitor the quality of the changes

Whether an enterprise has one or many committees, they are an essential ingredient of a sustainable integration strategy, and the ICC or Integration Factory must be an active participant, or even a leader, in them.

Factory Tools

We all have images of what tools and machines in a traditional widget factory look like: looms for weaving cloth, boilers for brewing beer, robots for assembling cars, saws for milling wood, and so on. An Integration Factory also needs tools, although they may be harder to visualize since we are talking about machines that exist in the virtual world of software.

Factory tools may be purchased from a number of suppliers or custom-developed in-house. As we have stated previously, developing and maintaining tools is a big part of the job that factory staff need to perform. Even when one buys integration tools, there is almost always an opportunity to improve efficiency by enhancing them. Factories that produce physical products do this all the time. For example, they might buy one machine that molds pieces of wood to a particular shape, buy another machine that cuts them to specified lengths, and then custom-build a conveyer system to automatically feed the materials from one to the other. By the same token, Integration Factory staff should be prepared to build custom harnesses or interfaces between factory tools, for example, to move metadata from a data quality assessment tool to a data-cleansing or workflow tool, or to automatically move code objects from development to test to production.

Figure 3.4 is a block diagram showing a factory knowledge base. The knowledge base includes a repository and a collection of tools to facilitate the information flows in the development factory. The knowledge base functions as a repository of information gathered throughout the development life cycle. For example, information gathered in the engagement tool is provided to and stored in the repository. This information is typically the high-level requirements of the interface provided to the factory by the customer. It can include such high-level requests as when the interface is needed, how many interfaces are required, and the like. Information from the engagement tool is provided to the designer, as is further information provided via the requirements tool. The requirements tool asks for more detailed and technical information about the interface requirements than the engagement tool and is also captured and stored in the repository.

The repository can also generate a set of reports for insight into the factory process in connection with a tool having information related to the factory process. The reports in the set are customized to the intended audience and can include a support view, a test team view, a build team view, a design team view, and a customer view. These reports provide audience-specific information to aid in the creation of the integration.

Note that there are two central elements to the factory tools: the repository (or metadata repository), which is the permanent knowledge base for the factory information and material flows; and the scheduler tool, which controls the workflow according to customer pull demands and factory *Takt* time. Not only does the scheduler tool provide factory management with a picture of what is happening in the factory at any given moment (which, if you recall, may be distributed to all corners of the world), but it also provides

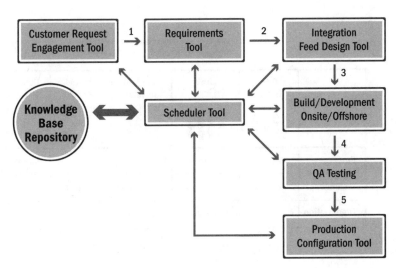

Figure 3.4 Development factory information flow tools and repository

information about upcoming activities. For example, the scheduler tool can provide a projection of how many data-mapping analysts will be needed next week or how many integration testers will be required next month on a given day. This forward-looking perspective is essential in order to scale factory cells (teams) up or down in support of production leveling and to maintain factory *flow*.

Integration Factories as Self-Service ICCs

When we wrote our first book on Integration Competency Centers, we created a graphic that showed a progression of models or approaches into which ICCs generally fell, shown in Figure 3.5.

At the far right of this figure we describe a "self-service" ICC model, where highly mature teams automate many of their processes and dynamically generate (or mass-customize) a great deal of their integration logic, and the customers of the ICC are able to self-serve many of their integration needs without concern for the detailed behind-the-scenes operations. This effectively describes what we now call an Integration Factory.

Several examples of Integration Factories, or self-service ICCs, are well established. Some vendors have created integration-as-a-service offerings in

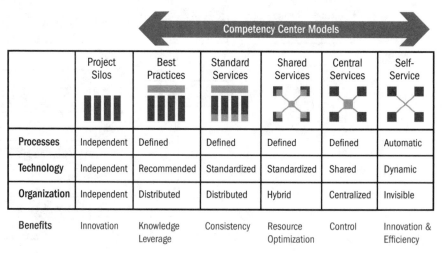

	Project Silos	Best Practices	Standard Services	Shared Services	Central Services	Self-Service
Processes	Independent	Defined	Defined	Defined	Defined	Automatic
Technology	Independent	Recommended	Standardized	Standardized	Shared	Dynamic
Organization	Independent	Distributed	Distributed	Hybrid	Centralized	Invisible
Benefits	Innovation	Knowledge Leverage	Consistency	Resource Optimization	Control	Innovation & Efficiency

Figure 3.5   ICC organizational models

the cloud that provide perfect examples of Integration Factories. These services allow a customer to directly select an assembly line (data replication of Salesforce.com data, for example, or data synchronization between heterogeneous relational databases) and walk through the process of selecting the data to be integrated, defining any special transformation logic that the data requires, scheduling when the integration should happen, and so on. The patterns behind the assembly line take the high-level definition of *what* the customer wants and translate that into *how* the integration gets executed. These services allow the self-service of standard integrations directly by business users.

Some ICCs today are using the "data synchronization between relational databases" service for two different use cases. The first use case is where the ICC "publishes" data as sources for the business, allowing the business to define its own extracts or pulls from this data. At many organizations, the requests for data from the ICC exceed the ICC's capacity to deliver to the business fast enough, thereby creating large (and wasteful) backlogs of work. The self-service capability for the business provides an elegant resolution to the problem.

Sometimes this self-service capability raises concerns among IT leaders. "The users are coming in and doing integration by themselves? What about governance? What about best practices?" Ironically, self-service capabilities provide better governance and adherence to best practices since in the absence of an easy-to-use tool that provides users with what they need, the users will generally resort to creative desktop-based solutions that have few controls. The integration-as-a-service approach, on the other hand, audits and logs absolutely all aspects of what the customers did, when they did it, where they moved the data, when the data was moved, and so on. And all generated integrations followed patterns optimally generated based on best practices.

The second use case allows data analysts to prototype the source-to-target mapping and transformation specifications, as well as execute those specifications to test whether they work as expected. At many organizations, analysts specify an integration using an Excel spreadsheet, which is then handed off to developers as a document. This use case allows a similar capability but with the added ability to test the results. Once the analyst is satisfied, he or she passes the specification to the ICC developers to augment and prepare the integration for production, collaborating with the original data analyst. In both use cases, significant waste is eliminated from existing processes.

In summary, Integration Factories are emerging faster than most people realize. While these integration services in the cloud today (at the time of this writing) may handle rudimentary integration problems, they add value and provide a model for what is possible in the future. Real-world complexity that deals with the unique realities of complex enterprises requires a more challenging journey toward on-premises Integration Factories. The next part of this book is devoted to helping organizations learn about Lean principles in taking this journey.

PART II

Applying Lean Principles

Policies are many; principles are few. Policies will change; principles never do.
John C. Maxwell[1]

There are seven Lean principles—that's it. They are

1. Focus on the customer and eliminate waste.
2. Automate processes.
3. Continuously improve.
4. Empower the team.
5. Build quality in.
6. Plan for change.
7. Optimize the whole.

Whether we are applying Lean principles to manufacturing, financial services, government, or integration, the principles remain the same and have been proven to work. To a large degree, they are common sense, which makes Lean a simple idea and is the essence of its effectiveness. Lean works because the concepts are easily understood. And in the world of integration, where a wide variety of individuals, business

---

1. John C. Maxwell, *Developing the Leader Within You* (Thomas Nelson, 2005), p. 79.

functions, and organizations need to work together to achieve optimal outcomes despite constant changes, it is essential to have an anchor around a small number of memorable principles.

Part II of this book explains these principles in the context of data and process integration. In this part we explain the importance and relevance of each principle, provide examples of how to apply them, and then bring them to life in the context of real-world case studies.

CHAPTER FOUR

Focus on the Customer and Eliminate Waste

The most significant source of waste is overproduction. . . . [which]
results in shortages, because processes are busy making the wrong
things. . . . you need extra capacity because you are using some of your
labor and equipment to produce parts that are not yet needed.
Mike Rother and John Shook[1]

In Rother and Shook's *Learning to See*, they seek to teach how to recognize sources of waste. As humans, we become so conditioned to our environment and the way things have always been done that we are often blind to opportunities for improvement. For example, producing large quantities of products in batches in order to optimize the efficiency of a particular plant doesn't appear wasteful from the perspective of the plant manager. But if the products then sit in inventory for months until they are needed by downstream processes to satisfy customer demand, it is tremendously wasteful. Waste in the world of integration can be hard to see because of past conditioning, because of our narrow perspective, and because we are dealing with "virtual" computer software products. For example, gold-plating, or building software functionality before it is needed, is an example of overproduction. As you progress through this chapter and the rest of the book, we hope that you will learn to see more opportunities to eliminate waste.

---

1. Mike Rother and John Shook, *Learning to See: Value-Stream Mapping to Create Value and Eliminate Muda* (The Lean Enterprise Institute, 2003), p. 43.

Lean Integration starts by focusing on the customer, that is, the people who demand, and usually pay for, the integrated capabilities in an enterprise. This requires that integration be defined as a service in order to establish a customer-supplier relationship. The Integration Competency Center acts as an internal services business, providing a variety of integration services to functional groups and disparate application teams across the enterprise.

This contrasts with the traditional approach where integration is performed as ad hoc point-to-point information exchanges or is controlled by a project with a finite life. When the project is over, ongoing management of the integration elements is dispersed to various teams, none of which sees the total picture, and the focus on the end customer rapidly fades. Enough has been said about the inevitable emergence of the integration hairball and its negative effects under this approach. In order to implement a Lean Integration strategy, you must break out of the old pattern where integration elements are static extensions of business systems and accept a new paradigm where integration components collectively are a system with their own life cycle.

This chapter presents the concepts and core principles of what it means to focus on the customer, eliminate *muda* from the customer's perspective, and map the value chain of end-to-end activities that produce value. To amplify the concepts, we include case studies from a retail company that we shall call Clicks-and-Bricks, and a large bank that we call Big Bank, to provide concrete examples of waste elimination and value stream mapping.

Focus on the Customer

The critical element in the Lean paradigm is to view integration as a service and to understand the value that integration provides in the eyes of the customer. Value is a customer perspective, not a supplier perspective. For example, most business users don't care about data quality; they care about reducing the order-to-cash cycle, increasing market campaign effectiveness, approving more loans without increasing risk, reducing average resolution time in the call center, and getting accurate and timely financial reports. Of course, data that is complete and consistent across multiple operational systems facilitates these business results, but it is the outcomes that business leaders care about and not the methods and tools that produced them.

The first step in the Lean Integration journey, therefore, is to identify who the internal customer is, understand the customer's needs, define the services that the ICC will provide, and develop a clear picture of the value the customer expects. This is easier said than done. Chapter 12, Integration Methodology, delves into specific techniques for defining the mission of an ICC, its scope of operations, the activities it performs, the customers it serves, and the services it provides. But first it is essential to understand the concept.

Once you have defined the customer, the services that are provided, and the value that is expected, you can map out the value stream. Womack and Jones in *Lean Thinking* define the value stream this way: "The *value stream* is the set of all the specific actions required to bring a specific product (whether a good, a service, or, increasingly, a combination of the two) through three critical management tasks of any business: the *problem-solving task* running from concept through detailed design and engineering to production launch, the *information management task* running from order-taking through detailed scheduling to delivery, and the *physical transformation task* proceeding from raw materials to a finished product in the hands of the customer."[2]

A restaurant experience, for example, involves *finding out what the customer wants to order*, *processing the order* and related transactions including payment, and actually *producing and delivering the meal*. An integrated and optimized implementation of these tasks provides superior customer experiences. In a data integration example, the three management tasks are

1. **Clarifying the business problem** by figuring out the specific data that needs to be combined, cleansed, synchronized, or migrated
2. **Transacting the project activities**, such as initiation, planning, execution, tracking, and deployment
3. **Building the integration infrastructure**, such as installing middleware platforms, codifying business transformation rules, optimizing performance, and capturing operational metadata

Each of these three management tasks (problem solving, information management, and physical transformation) contains activities and steps that the

---

2. James P. Womack and Daniel T. Jones, *Lean Thinking: Banish Waste and Create Wealth in Your Corporation* (Free Press, 2003), p. 19.

customer will value, as well as some that from the customer's perspective are non-value-adding. From a Lean perspective, non-value-added activities are *muda* and must be eliminated. The percentage of waste in a value stream is a good measure of the maturity of a Lean Integration practice. As Womack and Jones wrote, "Based on years of benchmarking and observation in organizations around the world, we have developed the following simple rules of thumb: Converting a classic production system . . . will double labor productivity all the way through the system while cutting production throughput times by 90 percent and reducing inventories in the system by 90 percent as well."[3]

In other words, if you have not yet implemented a Lean Integration practice, a detailed value-stream-mapping exercise will likely show that 50 percent of the labor and 90 percent of the delivery time in the end-to-end process is waste. By applying Lean practices, you should expect, over time, to produce twice as much work with the same staff, reduce lead time by 90 percent, and reduce work in progress and integration dependencies ("inventories" in the integration domain) by 90 percent. Do these claims sound fantastic and unbelievable? If so, it may be that you have become locked into the perspective, driven by years of fragmented silo thinking, that integrations are being built as efficiently as they can be. Time and time again we have come across managers and technical leaders in organizations who insist they are highly efficient. One manager told us he needed 90 days to build and deploy a new integration feed to the enterprise data warehouse. When we challenged that perspective and suggested it should take no more than 5 days, the response was "That would never work here." An analysis of the manager's operation showed that the value stream consisted of 1 day of value-added work and 89 days of waste. Here are a few of the specifics that contributed to the high percentage of waste:

■ Problem-solving activities were slow because there were no documented data standards. Each integration problem required meetings (usually several of them) with multiple SMEs. Once the right people were in the room, the requirements were quickly identified, but simply finding a time to schedule the meeting when everyone was available typically added 20 to 30 days to the process. Furthermore, the time to schedule,

---

3. Ibid., p. 27.

and reschedule, meetings was non-value-added, as were the delays in waiting for meetings. The actual time spent solving problems in the meeting was also waste, but this may have been unavoidable in the short term until documentation, metadata, and processes improved.

- Process execution activities included a great deal of waiting time because multiple teams were involved and the communication between teams was inconsistent and slow because of a traditional batch and queue system. For example, a given project might involve staff from multiple teams such as project management, systems engineering, network security, multiple application teams, database administration, testing, change management, and operations management. Any time a team needed support from another team, someone would request it through either an email or an internal Web application that captured the details. The SLA for each team was typically 2 days (i.e., a request for support would typically result in a response within 2 days), which sounds relatively quick. Sometimes teams responded more quickly, and other times the response after 2 days was to ask the submitter to resend the request because of missing or inaccurate information. In any event, even a simple integration project required on the order of ten or more inter-team service requests, which added up to an average of 20 days of delay waiting for responses.

- Manual reviews of the changes to authorize movement of integration code from development to test and then from test to production added another 20 days to the process. The standard process in this case was that each time code was to be migrated, it required signoff by a change control committee that consisted of 10 to 15 staff members from different departments (the number varied based on the nature of the change). This process had been established over a period of years in response to production incidents and outages as a result of deploying changes where the dependencies between components were not well understood. Of course, the customer values changes that don't disrupt current operations when deployed, but the fact that 10 or more people needed to review each change (twice) before moving it to production was a waste. Once again this waste may have been unavoidable in the short term until quality improved and change controls could be automated, but nonetheless it was still waste from the customer perspective.

- Other wasted activities included excessive project ramp-up time because of disagreements about what tools or project standards to use, delays in gaining access to test environments that were shared by multiple project teams, rework in the integration cycle once data quality issues were identified, and other factors.

When we added up all the wasted time, we found that the amount of actual value-added work was only 1 day out of 90. This ratio of value-added work to non-value-added work is not unusual for organizations looking at their end-to-end processes from the customer's point of view for the first time. Changing processes to eliminate this waste will not happen overnight. As anyone who has worked in this sort of complex, federated organizational environment knows, gaining agreement across the organization for the necessary process changes to eliminate the waste is neither easy nor quick. But nonetheless, it is possible to do so, and the rewards when you are successful are huge from the customer's perspective.

Integration Wastes

The seven wastes (*muda*) that were targeted in manufacturing and production lines are

1. Transportation (unnecessary movement of materials)
2. Inventory (excess inventory including work in progress)
3. Motion (extra steps by people to perform the work)
4. Waiting (periods of inactivity)
5. Overproduction (production ahead of demand)
6. Overprocessing (rework and reprocessing)
7. Defects (effort involved in inspecting for and fixing defects)

Developing software has many parallels with the production of physical goods, and Mary and Tom Poppendieck have a done an excellent job in *Implementing Lean Software Development* to translate these wastes into the world of software development. Many of these are fairly obvious, of course, such as wasted effort fixing defects rather than developing defect-free code in the first place. Overproduction in the software world is the equivalent of adding features to a software component that were not requested or are not immediately required (sometimes referred to as "gold-plating"). As the

Poppendiecks say, "Wise software development organizations place top priority on keeping the code base simple, clean, and small."[4] We can reexpress the seven wastes in terms of their software corollaries:

1. Transportation (unnecessary people or data handoffs)
2. Inventory (work not deployed)
3. Motion (task switching)
4. Waiting (delays)
5. Overproduction (extra features)
6. Overprocessing (revisiting decisions or excessive quality)
7. Defects (data *and* code defects)

Other parallels between the physical product world and the virtual software world are less obvious, such as transportation waste being the equivalent of loss of information in handoffs between designers, coders, testers, and implementers, or motion waste being the equivalent of task switching in an interrupt-driven work environment. We don't need to repeat here what the Poppendiecks say about waste in software development, but their book does not address all the integration sub-disciplines, and there are several areas where we often see a tremendous amount of wasted time, effort, and money.

The following sections describe five integration wastes, but the list is not complete or exhaustive. We include these to highlight some areas that are often overlooked as waste and to change your perspective so that you can begin to identify waste in your own environment.

Waste 1: Gold-Plating

Building functional integration capabilities or extra features before they are needed is a waste. There is a strong desire among integration teams to anticipate organizational needs and build interfaces, data marts, canonical messages, or service-oriented architecture (SOA) services with the needs of the entire enterprise in mind. This is an admirable objective indeed, but the integration teams often don't have the resources and funding to build the common capability, and so they run into trouble when the first project that could use the capability is saddled with the full cost to build the enterprise-wide

---

4. Mary and Tom Poppendieck, *Implementing Lean Software Development: From Concept to Cash* (Addison-Wesley, 2006), p. 69.

solution. This practice is referred to as "the first person on the bus pays for the bus" or a similar metaphor. Business leaders whose project budgets are impacted by this practice hate it. The business units are given a budget to optimize their function and they become frustrated, and even angry, when told that the implementation will take longer and cost more money because it must be built as a generic reusable capability for other future users. This may indeed be the policy of the organization, but in the end it pits the integration team against the project sponsor rather than fostering alignment.

Developing functionality before it is needed is a waste of time and money for the initial development and a waste of the resources that are then required to maintain and support the increased complexity resulting from the unused functionality. The rationale for eliminating this category of waste includes these factors:

- There is an imperfect understanding of requirements for future projects if they are built in advance, so it is possible that the wrong thing will be developed.
- The additional code or data will cost money to develop and maintain without any benefits until the next project comes along to use it.
- The business benefits from the first project are delayed while the supposedly "ideal" solution that will meet future needs is being built.
- The business sponsor for the first project will be dissatisfied with the implementation team (which is a good way to chase away your customer).

We suggest another approach: Build only the features/functions that the first project requires, and do so in such a way that they can be extended in the future when the second project comes along. And if the nature of change is such that the second project requires refactoring of the solution that was developed for the first project, so be it. This approach is more desirable because of the risks and *muda* of building functionality prematurely.

Organizations would be much better off adding the cost of refactoring to the second project when (and if) it comes along rather than burdening the first project. Under this scenario, the needs of the second project are clear, as are the needs of the first project (since of course it is already in operation), so there is no ambiguity about what to build. Furthermore, the benefits of the first project will be realized sooner, which can in essence help to fund the cost of the second project (silo accounting practices may still make this difficult in many organizations, but nonetheless the advantage is clear). Our bottom-line advice is "Refactor integrations constantly so that they don't become legacy."

Michael K. Levine adds another perspective to the waste of gold-plating in *A Tale of Two Systems* when explaining how requirements specifications are like work-in-process inventory and excessive requirements can be a drag on change: "That requirements document is inventory, just as piles of work in process in a factory are inventory. If you have a smaller inventory of ideas to change, change can be positive, instead of a threat. Think of unimplemented tested code, untested code, designs not yet coded, and requirements not yet designed as inventory waste, like computer parts when the industry moves so fast the probability of obsolescence is high."[5]

If there really is a solid need within the organization for a generic reusable interface or integration object, the cost of building it should be borne by the integration function (the ICC) rather than the first project team. For example, if a contractor told you that building your house will cost an extra $50,000 and take a few months longer to finish because he needs to develop an automated process for constructing modular cabinets so that all future houses can be built more quickly and at a lower cost, you simply wouldn't hire that contractor. You would expect this sort of investment to be borne by the contractor in the interests of being faster, cheaper, and better than his/her competitors.

In summary, then, the recommended policy in a Lean Integration organization is to deliver solutions only to meet project needs and to build general-purpose reusable components either by refactoring existing components as new projects come along or by funding the reusable components as separate initiatives not tied to the business project. We will come back to the topic of how to address the "first person on the bus pays for the bus" in Chapter 11 on Financial Management.

Waste 2: Using Middleware like Peanut Butter

Applying middleware technology everywhere is a waste. This may sound like heresy to integration specialists; after all, a host of benefits emerges from implementing an abstraction layer between applications, such as facilitating

---

5. Michael K. Levine, A Tale of Two Systems: Lean and Agile Software Development for Business Leaders (CRC Press, 2009), p. 292.

loose coupling between applications, orchestrating flow-through processes, extending the life of legacy business applications, and many more. No debate on that front. But the reality is that while each middleware layer adds a potential benefit, it also adds a cost, so this is really a cost/benefit trade-off decision.

As integration professionals, we often deride point-to-point integrations as "evil" since they tightly couple components and, if applied without standards, over time will result in an integration hairball. True enough. But that doesn't mean that point-to-point interfaces for specific high-volume data exchanges with stringent performance requirements aren't the best solution when used as part of an integration system. Each middleware layer bears a cost in terms of technology, people development, organizational change, and complexity on an ongoing basis, so the abstraction layers should be added only when the benefits outweigh the cost of sustaining them.

Another example of a middleware abstraction layer is canonical models or common data definitions. It is hard to argue against the principle of having a common definition of data across systems with incompatible data models, but nonetheless common data models are not static objects that are created at a point in time; they evolve constantly and need to be maintained. Unless you can justify the incremental staff to maintain the canonical model, don't add this layer since it will surely become stale and irrelevant within just a few short years, which is yet another example of waste. That said, if you are implementing a metadata strategy along with a Lean Integration strategy, you may not need to add any staff at all since the labor productivity savings from the elimination of *muda*, along with the appropriate metadata tools, will more than compensate for the labor required to maintain the abstraction layer.

Waste 3: Reinventing the Wheel

Not taking advantage of economies of scale and instead reinventing the wheel is a waste. The reality is that there is a relatively small number of integration patterns that can satisfy the integration needs of even the largest corporations. While the total number of integrations may be large (thousands or tens of thousands), the number of patterns is quite small—probably no more than a handful for 90 percent or more of the data exchanges. If each project team treats the integration development work as a unique effort, the result over time will be thousands of "works of art."

We know from years of experience in manufacturing lines that cost savings of 15 to 25 percent accrue every time volume doubles[6] in a repeatable process. But if you are like Rembrandt producing an original oil painting, the second, third, and hundredth paintings will still take as long as the first. However, our experience in software development tells us that these savings are real, because of two factors: the benefits of the learning curve (the more times you do something, the better you get at it) and visibility into reuse opportunities (the more integrations one does, the more obvious the patterns become).

Waste 4: Unnecessary Complexity

Unnecessary variation in tools and standards is a waste. We have also learned from the world of manufacturing that costs increase 20 to 35 percent every time variation doubles.[7] Variation in the integration arena arises from different middleware platforms, development tools, interchange protocols, data formats, interface specifications, and metadata standards, to name a few. In the absence of governance around these and other sources of variation, the variety of integrations could be huge.

If we combine the effects of not reinventing the wheel and stopping unnecessary variation, the cost and quality implications are an order of magnitude different. To take a simple example, consider an organization with eight divisions where each develops one integration per year with its own preferred set of tools, techniques, and standards. It is fairly obvious that if they were to combine efforts and have one team build eight integrations, there would be cost savings from a reduced learning curve, reuse of tools, and common components.

Using this simple example and the rule-of-thumb savings, if the cost of building an integration for each of the eight divisions was $10,000, the cost for a central team would be $3,144 or less—a 70 percent reduction! This result comes from doubling volumes three times with savings of 15 percent each time and cutting variation in half three times with a 20 percent savings each time. Real-world case studies have shown that this kind of dramatic improvement in integration development savings is very achievable.

---

6. George Stalk, "Time—The Next Source of Competitive Advantage," *Harvard Business Review*, no. 4 (July–August 1988).

7. Ibid.

The basic idea is that a team that builds multiple integrations per year will see more opportunities for reuse and will get much faster simply by doing similar work with similar tools on a repeated basis. A centralized team that is producing higher volumes sees the patterns and can take advantage of them.

Waste 5: Not Planning for Retirement

Everything has a life cycle—people, products, software, even data and ideas. The typical life-cycle phases are birth, growth, change, and death. Traditional ad hoc or project-based integration practices deal effectively with the birth phase but do a poor job supporting the rest. More mature practices such as ICCs typically address the growth phase (in terms of both growth in volume and reuse of common components) as well as the ongoing change phase needed to ensure that integration points don't disintegrate over time.

The phase that generally receives the least focus is the death phase—that is, determining in advance when and how integration points are no longer needed or adding value and should be eliminated. For example, when does a business no longer need a business intelligence report that is generated daily, weekly, or monthly from the data warehouse? Most of the organizations we have worked with have no systematic way of tracking whether business users are actually reading the reports that are generated or even care about them any longer. One organization that was producing 20,000 reports on a regular basis conducted a detailed survey and eventually reduced the number of reports to fewer than 1,000. Or what about data that is being replicated daily from operational systems to tables in a shared central repository—when is the shared data no longer needed? The case study of waste elimination at Clicks-and-Bricks (described later in this chapter) demonstrated with its real-time message queue system that 25 percent of the infrastructure was waste.

As a result of our experience in working with dozens of organizations across different industries around the globe, we have developed a rough rule of thumb about the amount of IT infrastructure waste. In any large organization (Global 2000) that has been in business for over 30 years and has not had a systematic enterprise-wide IT architecture with a clear rationalization (simplification) focus, 25 to 50 percent of the IT infrastructure is waste. Granted, this is not a scientific study, but it is based on dozens of real-life cases, and so far the rule of thumb is holding firm. Eliminating this waste is not easy because of the high degree of complexity and interdependency between many of the components, which of course is exactly why we wrote this book—to provide the structures, tools, and disciplines to systematically eliminate the waste and keep it from coming back.

Fortunately, one area of retirement planning that has been growing in many organizations in recent years is information life-cycle management (ILM). The proliferation of data and the massive size of databases have forced organizations to begin to establish formal policies and processes for the archiving or destruction of everything from emails, to Web site statistics, to outdated and inactive customer records. ILM is a relatively new class of middleware software that helps efficiently archive data that is not needed for company operations, but still makes it accessible if the need ever arises, and to systematically destroy it when it eventually has no further value or could even potentially become a liability.

For example, we spoke to the research director of a life sciences research organization who said the organization doesn't keep the data generated from its tests once a particular research project is over. The data for a single sample from a genome sequencer or an electron microscope can be hundreds of gigabytes. The director said that while there is value in keeping the data for potential future research efforts, there is also a cost to maintain it, and that overall it costs less to rerun the experiment than to keep the data indefinitely.

Planning for the retirement of integration points and integration infrastructure is an essential component of a Lean Integration strategy. Subsequent chapters provide further specifics on how to go about creating business cases to justify retiring legacy integrations and to establish effective metrics and monitoring techniques to determine when an integration point is no longer being used or valued.

Case Study: Waste Elimination at Clicks-and-Bricks

Clicks-and-Bricks is a North American retailer of office products and consumer electronics with both a network of stores (Bricks) and an e-commerce Web site (Clicks). In the retail industry, and especially for Clicks-and-Bricks, the holiday shopping season between Thanksgiving and year end is a very critical and busy time. The company does a large percentage of its business for the whole year during this time, most of it on just ten days. So the IT function must deal with huge spikes in volume on its systems and infrastructure. The most important thing is to make sure that on the day after Thanksgiving, the system does not go down!

At the time of this case study, one of Clicks-and-Bricks's critical infrastructures, the message queue (MQ) transport system that was used to shuttle real-time and near-real-time transactions between hundreds of business applications, was experiencing problems. The MQ system operated on a first-in first-out store-and-forward basis. Real-time transactions such as credit card authorizations, gift card balances, pricing updates, and so on were sent through high-performance queues and usually with sub-second response time. Other transactions, such as point-of-sale transactions, would result in a message containing line item details of the sale, customer information, and payment and promotional details and did not need to be processed instantly. These messages would be written to a queue in the store server, where they would wait until a central office computer got around to polling it on a round-robin basis (usually every 15 minutes), at which time the messages would be transferred to the input queue of the sales-reporting system for near-real-time consolidated updates of sales volumes. Other transactions such as refunds and exchanges also were sent through the MQ infrastructure and ultimately were reconciled by the sales system every night to produce the daily audited sales results. In short, the MQ system was an absolutely critical part of the IT infrastructure that could dramatically impact business performance if it didn't work perfectly.

In 2007, and in the years leading up to then, things had been quite bad on days with peak business volumes: Message queues were filling up, and as a result disk storage would overflow and servers would crash, and alarms and pagers would go off all over the place. The MQ system was having quite a serious impact on the company's business, slowing down sales in stores and lengthening customer queues at the checkouts, reducing performance on the Internet to the point where customers went elsewhere, and even losing some transactions when systems crashed.

To address the challenges, Clicks-and-Bricks launched an ICC. One of the first operational challenges for the team was dealing with the MQ infrastructure. Over a number of years various project teams had been building the infrastructure incrementally without a master plan. There was a general sense that the MQ operational run-time environment was quite extensive, but no one had an end-to-end picture of all the queue interactions or message flows.

The ICC strategy to solve the problem started by focusing on the internal customer, in this case the business application owners. They didn't care about queues or messages; they cared about rapid credit approval, correct pricing, accurate inventory counts, and timely shipping of orders, to name just a few items. In this context, the *value* that the ICC could provide would be to ensure accurate, safe, and rapid delivery of information between systems in a seamless, almost invisible manner. In order to deliver this value, the ICC needed to change a few things.

First, the team had to change the accountability for message queues. Message queues are software components that reside on various computer servers. In the pre-ICC context, the queues on the servers where the merchandising applications ran were managed by the merchandising team, while the queues on the sales or distribution servers were managed by those teams. Each team had control over its own queues, but no one had a clear understanding of the end-to-end flow of data. So the first change was a policy action to declare that henceforth, the responsibility for managing all queues, regardless of where they were physically implemented, was the responsibility of the ICC team.

Second, the ICC acquired a tool that had the ability to scan all the production computers to automatically discover queues. Furthermore, the team developed a central metadata repository to keep track of all the queue parameters and dependencies. The first time the tool ran, Clicks-and-Bricks discovered there were 80,000 queue objects on 800 computers—local queues, remote queues, dead-letter queues, channels, links, and so on—all of the things that made the MQ structure work. This was a huge number of elements and much more than anyone had imagined.

The ICC team then tracked performance data on all of the objects for 30 days to determine the workload on each of the objects. With this data they concluded that 25 percent of all production objects—20,000—were not being used. So the unused elements were eliminated, which simplified the environment significantly. This was the first level of *muda* (waste) elimination.

Third, the ICC team took a closer look at the information in the metadata repository and started organizing and analyzing it systematically in order to validate the configuration settings on all queue objects. They found that 60 percent of the objects in production had invalid or somehow incorrect settings. Some channel link time-outs were inappropriate, maximum queue size was too small for peak business volumes, the queue-low threshold was set higher than the queue-high threshold, monitoring was disabled, queue names were inconsistent—things that would create unpredictable behavior or make it difficult to manage. The team then cleaned up all of these problems, which resulted in a second wave of waste elimination in terms of fewer production outages, reduced maintenance costs, and more rapid deployment of changes to the infrastructure.

Next, the ICC team began to correlate performance data with usage patterns. As a result, they were able to see that many of the servers were underutilized, which set the stage for consolidation of workloads. Out of a total of 21 servers that processed the majority of MQ transactions, Clicks-and-Bricks was able to eliminate 9 (a 42 percent reduction). Based on just the physical costs of maintaining a server (approximately $30,000 per year), the ability to consolidate servers alone saved the company $300,000 annually.

Finally, the ICC team implemented rigorous governance processes to ensure that the problems wouldn't come back in the future. These consisted of a formal change approval process and a way to automatically audit it to make sure that all changes were preapproved. The audit mechanism involved scanning all production servers each evening and comparing 25 configuration parameters for each of the 60,000 queue objects in operation with the parameters that were stored in the metadata repository. If any differences were found that did not have a corresponding approved change ticket, the team would track down who made the change and make sure that person wouldn't do it again.

All of these activities took about six months. The impact from the 2007 peak shopping period to the 2008 peak shopping period couldn't have been more dramatic. The MQ infrastructure went from being literally the biggest technology problem the company had to being totally invisible. In fact, the pager for production outages didn't go off once! There were no outages or downed servers, and there were no complaints. In fact, everyone was thrilled and couldn't have been happier with the results. The high availability and reliability of the system easily saved the company millions in comparison to the problems that it had experienced in prior years.

One question people often ask is "OK, I understand and accept the benefits of this case, but what is the ongoing cost of the central team, all the scanning tools, metadata repositories, and governance processes?" The best way to answer may be to compare the Clicks-and-Bricks MQ operations costs with those of similar infrastructures in other companies. We have had the opportunity to review the team size and cost structure of other organizations that have large-scale MQ infrastructures. The Clicks-and-Bricks ICC team was managing 60,000 queues on 800 servers, including project support, design and development of changes, change management, production support, capacity planning, and performance optimization with a total of three staff members. We have yet to find any other organization handling these functions with the same number of people or fewer. In fact, one organization with a similar scale and scope of operations had 16 people performing the same work.

In summary, the key factors that allowed Clicks-and-Bricks to eliminate the waste in this mission-critical integration infrastructure included these:

- Start with a customer focus and understand the value proposition of the infrastructure.
- Take a holistic perspective and understand the entire value stream.
- Systematically eliminate waste—start with the most obvious wastes and use a fact-based approach to eliminate second- and third-level wastes.
- Implement controls to ensure continued operational efficiency.

Case Study: Waste Elimination at Big Bank

One of the trickier aspects of Lean Integration is mapping, and optimizing, the value chain. Let's take a simple example such as logging in to the Web site at Big Bank (a fictitious example based on real-world scenarios). We mapped the flow of transactions and data at Big Bank from the time the customer entered name and password to the time the first account summary page was displayed. For the scenario, we used a customer who had 6 accounts: savings, checking, credit card, line of credit, mortgage, and investment. Some Big Bank customers have 10 to 15 accounts, so 6 was a relatively small number and a very common pattern. The SLA for login was eight seconds, measured from the time the Enter key was pressed after password entry until the time the account summary screen began to display.

From the customer's perspective, logging in is one transaction. The data that needed to be displayed on the account summary screen for the six accounts was stored in ten different business applications, each with its own database. Why were there ten systems and not six—or even just one? The reason is that each of the business systems was implemented independently at different points in time by different business groups to address the specific functional needs for specific products. In other words, they were solving Big Bank's needs for optimal product-by-product management as opposed to the customer's need for a seamless experience. The account databases were further fragmented by years of mergers and acquisitions without fully rationalizing and shutting down redundant business applications.

At a simple level, the basic sequence of login steps behind the scenes is

1. Authenticate the customer.
2. Look up the customer's profile to find all relevant accounts.
3. Access the database of each of the account systems to get the core account summary data.
4. Access secondary applications to obtain supporting details or in-process transactions.
5. Compile all the data into a standard format.
6. Render and display the Web page.

As we mapped out the detailed steps in the login process, we found five integration systems involved in mediating and facilitating transactions in addition to the ten business systems. The integration systems played not just the data lookup and consolidation roles but also included some business rules and logic, such as "If the business application containing the intraday debit card transactions is unavailable or doesn't respond within two seconds, display the most recent end-of-day balance with a note stating that pending transactions are not included in the balance."

The total number of low-level intersystem transactions (that is, a message or data exchange between two systems) in this scenario was 48. If we relate this to the world of Lean manufacturing, we can think of these 48 transactions as transportation—the movement of data. In essence, Big Bank was picking data up and putting it down 48 times in order to display the account summary page for a customer with six accounts. What was even more amazing is that the ten business systems and the five integration systems were located in four internal data centers and three external data centers in widely distributed parts of the United States, from California, to New

England, to Florida and Texas. The 48 transactions physically traveled from 30,000 to 70,000 miles for a single login—and all within the eight-second SLA. Modern high-speed networks and high-performance commercial computers are truly amazing in their ability to transfer data at the speed of light. Since each low-level transaction is measured in milliseconds, it seems hardly worth it to spend any time trying to eliminate a few unnecessary transactions. Yet, at this low level of detail, Big Bank processes billions of transactions per hour, so even a relatively modest improvement in performance can have a noticeable impact on cost, response time, and quality.

From the customer's perspective, only the movement of the data from the six accounts is value-added, which translates into 12 low-level transactions (one message sent to each account system to request the data and one return message from each system). In Lean terms, this suggests that 36 of the transactions, or 75 percent, are waste. As stated previously, some of these additional transactions may be unavoidable in the short term because of the fragmentation of functions and data across independent business systems, but our analysis also found that the end-to-end flow had redundant integration systems with middleware calling middleware. The analysis showed that by consolidating the middleware systems, Big Bank could reduce the number of low-level transactions by 50 percent (24 rather than 48) with a corresponding significant reduction in operational cost, fewer production incidents, and improved response time.

Focus on the Integration Value Chain

The Big Bank case highlights an example of mapping data flows in the delivery of integrated data in an operational environment. Another category of mapping the value chain relates to how the integration team (the ICC or Integration Factory) works with other functional teams in an enterprise to deliver new integrated solutions.

We tend to think of the ICC as the "prime contractor" responsible for delivering a finished product to the customer and all the other dependent functional teams as subcontractors. In the Clicks-and-Bricks waste elimination case study, the ICC was responsible and accountable for the end-to-end operation of the MQ infrastructure, yet the ICC could do so only by relying on and working with other groups. For example, a separate team of systems engineers was responsible for configuring the actual computer systems on which the queue objects ran; it was therefore essential that the ICC work closely with the engineering team to ensure that the MQ objects operated as expected on the IBM mainframe, UNIX server, AIX server, and Wintel server in all the different versions of operating systems and a wide variety of software and security configurations. The ICC also needed to work with production operations to schedule changes, with network security to maintain security keys, and with business analysts to understand future business volume projections in order to perform capacity planning.

In a nutshell, the integration team must

- Know who their customers are
- Offer clearly defined services that provide value to the customers
- Maintain integrated processes that deliver the value-added services
- Establish and manage internal and external subcontractor relationships with other groups that are (usually) invisible to the customer

CHAPTER FIVE

Continuously Improve

Lean companies work to develop and establish value with continuous improvement of their value stream flow, not by cost reduction practices.

Joe Stenzel[1]

A core principle of Lean is continuous improvement through experimentation and learning. The general notion is that there isn't a "perfect" way to do something. Rather, seeking perfection is an ongoing process, since there are always opportunities for improvement that can be uncovered using scientific disciplines. As described by Mary and Tom Poppendieck, ". . . any development process that deals with a changing environment should be an empirical process, because it provides the best known approach for adapting to change."[2] The scientific method in general follows these steps:

1. Observe and describe a phenomenon or group of phenomena.
2. Formulate a hypothesis to explain the phenomena.
3. Use the hypothesis to predict something—the existence of other phenomena or the results of new observations.

---

1. Joe Stenzel, *Lean Accounting: Best Practices for Sustainable Integration* (John Wiley & Sons, 2007), Kindle loc. 981–82.

2. Mary and Tom Poppendieck, *Implementing Lean Software Development: From Concept to Cash* (Addison-Wesley, 2006), p. 21.

4. Perform experiments to see if the predictions hold up.

5. If the experiments bear out the hypothesis, it may be regarded as a theory or rule.

6. If the experiments do not bear out the hypothesis, it must be rejected or modified.

This breaks down to the more simplified four-step method prescribed by Deming: Plan, Do, Check, and Act.

Continuous Learning and Knowledge Management

Most Lean practices focus on building knowledge, but we prefer to put the emphasis on *sustaining* knowledge, which incorporates the idea of ongoing maintenance and institutionalization of insights that drive continuous improvement. There a number of ways the principle of continuous learning can be applied to integration activities.

First, standards should be challenged and improved. A corollary to this principle is Integration Law #3: "There are no universal standards."[3] Standards are in fact essential for Lean Integration, but it is a mistake to consider them to be fixed, static, unchangeable, and applicable in all situations. Industry standards such as COBOL, TCP/IP, and HTTP (to name just a few) have evolved significantly over the years. Enterprise integration standards also need to be sustained and to evolve over time. This principle is reinforced by Integration Law #2: "There is no end state."

Second, Lean practices put a strong emphasis on scientific methods. One of the reasons this is so important in the integration arena is that we are often faced with the challenge of achieving alignment across multiple independent teams or organizational functions. Gaining agreement across groups that don't usually work together is hard. In the absence of data, all you have are opinions, and gaining agreement between people with different opinions that are filtered by paradigm-colored glasses is virtually impossible without objective data. A particularly useful, and practical, technique for data-driven cross-team problem solving is management by fact (MBF).

Third, integration dependencies between components should be maintained in a structured, and searchable, repository rather than in static, unstructured formats. Your first reaction might be that this is unnecessary

---

3. John Schmidt, "The EAI Laws," *EAI Journal* (July 2002). Also see Appendix B.

since your organization already has a mandate that each project develop detailed documentation about all information exchanges between components. In that case ask yourself these questions:

1. Does the documentation reflect what was deployed to production, including changes made after the design was completed?
2. Would a typical business analyst, designer, or developer be able to find the documentation two years later? Five years later? What if the original author of the documents is no longer with the company?
3. If the documentation can be found, would it be understandable? In other words, are the graphical notation conventions the same for all documentation, and are they based on a common glossary and taxonomy for data objects?
4. If maintenance changes were made to production after the project was deployed, was the documentation updated to reflect the changes?

If you answered yes to all four questions, you already have the necessary discipline for this particular aspect of sustaining integration knowledge. If you answered no to one or more questions, you are wasting time every time you need to change something and need to re-create yet another version of a custom integration document.

The remainder of this chapter is a rather detailed case study. We felt the best way to reinforce the principle of continuous improvement would be through a demonstrable real-life example. The case study actually touches on many Lean principles, including focus on the customer, team empowerment, mass customization, and automation. As you read it, take note of how all these elements were brought together with the financial management competency and fact-based metrics to align the organization and establish a sustainable integration strategy.

Case Study: Continuous Improvement at Clicks-and-Bricks

In early 2005, the chief technology officer at Clicks-and-Bricks discussed one of his major concerns. Maintenance costs were high and increasing steadily, and the complexity of the information exchanges between applications was becoming increasingly worrisome because of the quantity of integration points and the high degree of variation in tools, protocols, and standards. In the words of the CTO, "There has to be a better way!"

The complexity of the Clicks-and-Bricks environment had started to come into focus a few years earlier. The company had undertaken a major effort to inventory all the application systems and integration points as part of a major business transformation. At the time there were no plans to sustain the inventory in a structured repository, but nonetheless the team that did the work produced a very comprehensive picture of the application landscape. Every organization has its own version of such a picture, which illustrates the "integration hairball"—the unmanaged complexity that results from years of independent efforts to implement point-to-point integrations.

In any event, the comments from the CTO launched the ICC on a path to develop a formal business case and gain broad-based management agreement to move forward with a solution. The integration challenges were not new, and efforts had started one year earlier to establish the ICC and build a reusable framework that would serve as a standard for real-time integrations between applications. Management's perception was that progress was slow, and there was great resistance from application groups and project teams to adopting the ICC standards, so the company brought in a new director to head up the group.

The first activity by the new director was to assess the capabilities of the ICC staff, their role in the organization, and how the group was perceived by internal stakeholders. The ten staff members on the ICC team at the time were very knowledgeable, competent, and committed individuals who worked well together. Furthermore, they had a deep understanding of the technical challenges that the company was struggling with, and they knew exactly how to solve them. In fact, the team had already architected and designed a reusable software framework as the basis of a standardized real-time integration infrastructure that would reduce costs, improve operations, and simplify maintenance.

While the ICC team had the right staff, an accurate analysis of the problem, and a well-designed solution, the group was running into a great deal of resistance from project teams that were accustomed to doing things their own way. The project architects and lead developers already had a set of tools and methods that they were comfortable with, and they were skeptical of a new approach. Project managers and project sponsors were afraid to rely on another team to perform some of the project deliverables; they felt the central team would slow down the project, add unnecessary bureaucracy, increase costs, and reduce quality. And across the IT organization, senior management support of the ICC concept was spotty; some executives strongly supported the approach while others were doubtful.

So while the ICC had the right staff and the right solution, it was missing a few things: It did not have strong leadership and management support for the ICC strategy; the group was using the "stick" rather than the "carrot" to gain adoption of standards; it did not have an effective approach to engaging project teams; and when the team did get involved in a project, the result was generally higher costs and slower implementation since the new integration framework was not fully developed. In short, the ICC was inwardly focused and trying to force a solution on others that was not yet better, faster, or cheaper than the alternatives.

The first step that the team took to turn things around was to build a business case to gain broad-based senior management support for a formal Integration Factory. An analysis of existing projects at Clicks-and-Bricks showed that the average cost of designing, building, testing, and deploying a new integration between two applications was $30,000 and took 30 to 40 days. This was the first time anyone had done the analysis, and management was shocked at the high cost. The factors contributing to the high cost included

- Poor or nonexistent documentation of existing interfaces; each new integration required a bottom-up analysis, discovery, and problem definition
- No coding or software standards, which prevented reuse of prior work and often led to disagreements among newly formed teams about what tools or standards to adopt
- Highly complex data and process interactions that could not be fully understood or specified in the analysis phase; these were left to the software engineers to figure out during the development phase, which usually resulted in a high degree of rework during integration testing.

In short, each integration point was a "work of art" that required lots of meetings, debate, and rework.

The business case showed that the variable cost per interface could be reduced from $30,000 to $10,000 if an investment was made to finish constructing the integration framework, install a metadata repository, and implement an integrated workflow management capability. The cost of the investment was $3 million, and at the time Clicks-and-Bricks was building

200 to 300 new integrations per year. Table 5.1 shows a five-year projection of low-end and high-end annual costs using the baseline analysis. Note that this is a very simple model that assumes no cost improvements due to efficiencies or any cost increases due to inflation or increasing complexity. There were valid arguments for both cases, so the team decided to simply project the status quo.

In a nutshell, the business case was to invest $3 million in order to save $4 to $6 million per year in development costs as well as reduce maintenance costs, improve quality, and accelerate implementation of new integrations. Table 5.2 shows the investment costs in year 1 and the annual low-end and high-end savings from the resultant reduced variable cost. The worst-case net present value based on a 10 percent discount rate was $12.4 million with a return on investment of 415 percent.

This business case is a very simple model that does not include any maintenance savings or quantified benefits from cycle-time reductions. These other areas were treated as "soft benefits" from the perspective of the business case since the business case was already strong based solely on development cost savings. If the ROI had been marginal, the team could have performed additional analysis to quantify the maintenance and cycle-time benefits.

The point of all this is that the business case provided a simple, clear, and unambiguous value proposition for centralizing and standardizing the integration development process. More important, it established the business metrics, including baseline measures and target goals, that served as the foundation for continuous improvement. In any event, the investment funding was secured, and the CIO, CTO, and other senior IT executives provided strong support to proceed with the plan.

The second step that the ICC team took was to improve the customer engagement process—specifically the *information management task* as described by Womack and Jones in *Lean Thinking*.[4] The "customers" in this case were the internal project teams that had specific requirements for new or modified interfaces between applications or databases. The project roles that the ICC focused on included project sponsor, project manager, project

---

4. James P. Womack and Daniel T. Jones, *Lean Thinking: Banish Waste and Create Wealth in Your Corporation* (Simon & Schuster, 1996).

Table 5.1 Integration Development Cost Projections Based on Custom Project Silo Approach

Baseline	Year 1	Year 2	Year 3	Year 4	Year 5
Number of Integrations (Low)	200	200	200	200	200
Number of Integrations (High)	300	300	300	300	300
Average cost/integration	$30,000	$30,000	$30,000	$30,000	$30,000
Projected Baseline Cost—Low Estimate	$6,000,000	$6,000,000	$6,000,000	$6,000,000	$6,000,000
Projected Baseline Cost—High Estimate	$9,000,000	$9,000,000	$9,000,000	$9,000,000	$9,000,000

Table 5.2 Integration Development Cost Projections Based on Integration Factory

ICC Business Case	Year 1	Year 2	Year 3	Year 4	Year 5	NPV	ROI
Investment	$3,000,000	$ –	$ –	$ –	$ –		
Average cost/integration	$10,000	$10,000	$10,000	$10,000	$10,000		
Total Cost—Low Estimate	$2,000,000	$2,000,000	$2,000,000	$2,000,000	$2,000,000		
Total Cost—High Estimate	$3,000,000	$3,000,000	$3,000,000	$3,000,000	$3,000,000		
Annual Savings—Low Estimate	$1,000,000	$4,000,000	$4,000,000	$4,000,000	$4,000,000	$12,435,874	415%
Annual Savings—High Estimate	$3,000,000	$6,000,000	$6,000,000	$6,000,000	$6,000,000	$20,017,448	667%

architect, lead developer, and tester. For the ICC to be successful, it would need a customer engagement process whereby the staff in these roles felt they were receiving value from the ICC and that they were in control of the process. The solution to achieve this was twofold.

First, the team developed a role-based Web application that project teams could use to initiate an integration project, specify requirements, and track progress. This represented a paradigm shift in how project teams interacted with central support groups. The process previously had been either informal (hallway discussions, a visit to a coworker's cubicle to request support, etc.) or formal (queue-based requests sent by email or a request form to the support group's generic mailbox). The traditional methods meant problems and frustrations for the customer—misunderstandings from informal communications, several days' delay waiting for a response to formal email requests, and no ability to track the progress or status of specific requests. This last point was often the most frustrating. For example, the project manager might call the support administrator after a two-day wait with no response and ask about the status of the request. The administrator would say, "Oh, yes, I got your request and forwarded it to Jane for review." The project manager would then call Jane and possibly after a rally of telephone tag get the response "Oh, yes, the request is fine. We can handle it but Frank needs to assign the staff resources so I forwarded your email to him." The project manager would track down Frank and might get a response like "What request? I don't recall seeing anything from you," which would send the project manager back to Jane. And the merry-go-round kept on spinning.

The Integration Factory approach, however, solved the problem by providing project team members with a customized user interface that allowed them to provide the necessary information to the ICC and to track the progress of their requests. For example, if a project team was relying on the ICC to design and build ten integrations for a given project, the project manager could log in to the Web application and review a dashboard that showed the status of each integration point, including current status and projected dates for subsequent phases. If there was an issue with any item, the project manager could quickly identify the right contact person and thereby clarify the issue with one phone call. In short, the customers of the ICC felt as if they had a direct and efficient communication mechanism by which to interact with the group.

The second element of the solution for an effective engagement process was to provide a simple pricing model that could be applied very early in the life of a project, before the high-level design was done and even before the budget was finalized. The solution the team came up with was to define five categories of interfaces (simple, standard, medium, complex, and custom) and to determine average costs for the first four. Custom interfaces, on the other hand, had unique characteristics and high variation in cost, and they represented less than 5 percent of the total new integration development; hence they needed to be sized and estimated on a case-by-case basis.

For example, a simple interface might cost $5,000 (costs changed over time, as we shall see in this case study) and was defined as one where the adapters for extracting and loading the data were similar to ones that had already been implemented, which meant they could easily be reused; data transformations were not required or the messages were already in an appropriate XML format; and the interchange paradigm was either a straightforward point-to-point or file transfer protocol. A standard interface, on the other hand, might cost $10,000 and include simple business rules for extracting and loading the data (such as filters, default values, etc.), routine data transformations (such as translation into standard formats, date validations, etc.), and an interchange paradigm that was either point-to-point or publish/subscribe with or without acknowledgment.

The value that this pricing model provided is that project teams could determine the cost of integration by themselves. There was no need to send a request to a central group, wait for several days, have extensive meetings, play telephone tag, and all the other *muda* activities that are so common in many centralized shared-services groups. Furthermore, the commitment from the ICC was that the prices were a "firm fixed cost"; in other words, regardless of whether or not the actual effort was greater or smaller than the estimated effort, the cost that was charged to the project was fixed. The business sponsors and project managers loved this aspect. In other words, a fixed-price commitment was a huge part of the value that the ICC provided, since it eliminated one of the major risks in project cost overruns. From the ICC perspective, some interfaces did indeed end up costing more than the project was charged and others less, but on average all of the integration costs were recovered from project chargebacks. This is yet another example of how value can be provided to customers by taking a holistic perspective.

As mentioned earlier, the ICC first tried to use the "stick" approach to gain adoption of standards. It didn't work. Clicks-and-Bricks is an organization with a dynamic, entrepreneurial culture where project teams and individuals are fiercely proud of their independence and relate the success of the enterprise to their personal innovations. When the ICC took the position that "you must do it our way because we have the mandate and this standard approach is in the best interests of the enterprise," it simply ran into brick walls of resistance. It took some time (over one year) to switch the team to a "carrot" approach, but in the end it was much more effective.

The carrot approach is based on the idea that you can get people to change and adopt a standard by making it *better*, *faster*, and *cheaper* rather than by mandate. Several items that have already been discussed in this case were key ingredients in enabling the change. The streamlined engagement process and the investment in a reusable framework were both essential elements, but they were not sufficient. The ICC team also needed to be pragmatic and not get locked into idealistic "my way or the highway" positions. Once again, the ICC team needed to keep in mind that it was serving the customer, and it needed to understand the customer's perspective when solving problems.

One of the best tools the ICC team used to avoid battles with architects and technical leads on project teams was to take a long-term perspective. For example, the ICC would always try to convince the project team to use the standard framework and integration protocols, but if the project architects dug in their heels because it would mean displacing their favorite technology or because they had a technical or risk concern, the ICC would look at it this way: "Fine. We'll do it your way on this project. And it's OK because we know this interface will need to be rebuilt again in a few years (because things are constantly changing), so we will apply the ICC standard next time around." It is amazing how many of the technology-war battles (*muda*) between technical staff simply disappear when you take a five- to ten-year perspective.

The final ingredient in transforming the Clicks-and-Bricks integration hairball into an efficient integration system was the Lean principle of continuous improvement. As the Integration Factory business case demonstrates, there was a compelling case for the investment to drive the variable cost per interface to $10,000. But if the team had stopped making improvements once this goal was reached, it would not take long for expectations to be reset around this new standard, and project teams (and management) would no longer see value in the ICC. After a year or two of steady-state costs of $10,000 per interface, it would be easy for management to rationalize that the ICC was no longer needed and the organization might be better off without the central team. Indeed, if the group stopped improving, disbanding it probably would be the best decision. In other words, a one-time improvement in productivity is not sustainable; you need to continuously improve.

In order to institutionalize the continuous improvement mind-set in the team, the ICC managers were given a challenge: Reduce the cost per interface by 50 percent each year for the next three years. Since the initial investment would result in a target cost per interface of $10,000, this meant that one year later the average should be $5,000, two years later it should be $2,500, and three years later it should be $1,250. This goal was radical, and everyone initially considered it to be impossible. But the team actually achieved the goal! How did they do it?

The key factors were to have a well-defined end-to-end process, to measure each step in the process in excruciating detail, and to regularly review the process (*kaizen*) to look for opportunities for efficiency gains. In particular, every manual activity was viewed as potential *muda* and therefore was a candidate for elimination through automation.

A key aspect of the detailed metrics tracking is that it was *not* used for individual incentives or rewards. For example, the team tracked the number of defects found in integration testing and the amount of resultant rework effort, but developers were not rewarded or punished if they missed or exceeded the targets. The metrics were used to bring management attention to problem areas or potential improvements so that the entire team could help solve them. The team was, however, rewarded for achieving the overall end-to-end goals for cost per interface and lead-time reductions.

The ICC team made a point of communicating the cost per interface to all project teams and senior IT management on a quarterly basis. These, and other key metrics, of the ICC were one of the ways the team was able to demonstrate very clearly the continuous improvement results and therefore create a sustainable business model. Table 5.3 shows the actual results of the business case three years after it was approved. Note that the ROI was now up to 934 percent, which was double that in the original plan!

Table 5.3 Business Case Results after Three Years of Integration Factory Operation

Actual Results after three years	Year 1 Actual	Year 2 Actual	Year 3 Actual	Year 4 Projected	Year 5 Projected	NPV	ROI
Number of Integrations	250	300	350	350	350		
Average cost per integration	$10,000	$5,000	$2,500	$2,000	$2,000		
Total cost of integration	$2,500,000	$1,500,000	$875,000	$700,000	$700,000		
Savings compared to baseline	$2,000,000	$7,500,000	$9,625,000	$9,800,000	$9,800,000	$28,026,495	934%

In terms of overall outcomes, the financial results from applying customer focus, mapping the end-to-end value chain, eliminating waste, and continuously improving the process are impressive. The net present value of positive cash flows over five years of the original $3 million investment was up to $28 million after three years. The average cost per interface went from $30,000 to $2,500 after three years, and over 50 percent of the interfaces fell into the "simple" category for which the cost was only $1,000 (which included costs for design, development, assembly, testing, deployment, and one month of warranty support in production). In addition, the average time to build an interface fell from 30 days to fewer than 5 days, and many of the simple interfaces were delivered within 1 day.

Furthermore, the size of the ICC team grew from the initial team of 10 to 180 after three years (approximately two-thirds of the staff were contractors and 60 percent of those were offshore). Despite the tremendous labor productivity improvements, no employees were laid off. Instead, the scope and responsibilities of the ICC group expanded in order to leverage the effective model in other integration areas. The original scope with 10 staff included only the real-time message-based integration for a subset of applications. After three years the ICC team was responsible for 100 percent of the real-time integration, all the database-to-database integration, most of the external business-to-business integration, all the database administrators, the LDAP security authentication system, and the metadata repository.

CHAPTER SIX

Empower the Team

Success is completely dependent on quality of people, culture, and learning. You cannot build a complex business system without building its development team simultaneously. Focus on both.

Michael K. Levine[1]

Please don't skip this chapter. Every business book emphasizes the importance of people to the extent that it is hard to imagine something new being said. We all agree that empowered teams are important, but how do you develop them? We will do our best to say something fresh in the hope that our ideas, combined with your ideas and the thinking of so many others, will provide the spark and initiative needed to make your organization a great example of energized, inspired people innovating together.

Team empowerment brings the most out of all employees, motivating their best efforts in working together toward a shared vision. The full participation of all team members in working toward innovative ideas and continuous improvement is what makes the other Lean principles possible. Empowered teams realize their creativity from the bottom up; individual contributors on the teams are motivated to apply their best thinking to problem solving and continuous improvement.

---

1. Michael K. Levine, *A Tale of Two Systems: Lean and Agile Software Development for Business Leaders* (CRC Press, 2009), p. 294.

People at Toyota say that if they had to choose the two most important principles, they would choose "respect for people" and "continuous improvement." Dennis Kinlaw, in his book *Developing Superior Work Teams*, said, "Teamwork is the fundamental requisite for continuous improvement."[2] All the other principles can logically grow from people working effectively together in an effort to continuously improve.

All of the other Lean Integration principles can be achieved through the commonsense efforts of totally engaged and continuously improving teams, without reading this book or knowing anything about the other principles. However, without empowerment, it is unlikely that teams can achieve the advantages of the other Lean principles. Furthermore, sustaining those advantages over long periods is unlikely.

In this chapter we will examine the characteristics of successful teams and the power that can result from these characteristics, then we'll tackle the challenge of setting up the environment in which empowered teams can thrive and grow.

We wrap up the chapter on team empowerment with a case study from Smith & Nephew, a multinational company in the health care industry. The study is based on a data governance program and illustrates a number of Lean principles, including effective use of metrics, visual controls, and value stream mapping, all in the interests of getting business executives and front-line staff engaged in the process of continuous improvement and sustainable data quality.

What Is a Team?

Rather than use sports analogies to describe effective teams, we have borrowed an analogy from the world of music. A jazz combo can be either a team or a group of talented individuals making music together. Even the untrained jazz listener can tell when a combo is a team. The music is tight, the musicians play off each other spontaneously, the music ebbs and flows between the rhythm section and the soloists in a way that stirs the emotions, and you can tell that the musicians are into the music and enjoy what they're doing.

---

2. Dennis Kinlaw, *Developing Superior Work Teams: Building Quality and the Competitive Edge* (Lexington Books, 1991), p. *xx*.

Certainly, the musicians themselves know when they are part of a team. When they are simply "phoning in the performance," going through the chord changes, and finishing at the same time, the jazz combo is more like a work group, each member competently playing his or her role but not putting in the energy to understand what the others are doing and what could be done to enhance the team. Perhaps they're tired, they feel disrespected or inferior to the others in the group, or perhaps they don't enjoy the music they're playing. For these or other reasons, magic is not created, and listeners can tell.

One of our favorite musical examples of an empowered team is the Bill Evans piano trio. He talked about the freedom he gave to the bass player and drummer, how they were free to stray beyond the traditional roles of bass and drummer if they felt the result would enhance the musical result. One of the seminal albums in jazz is *Sunday at the Village Vanguard*, which captures this magic in full flower with a bass player (Scott LaFaro) *not* laying down the traditional walking bass lines but effectively creating melodies that mesh beautifully with Bill Evans's piano, and a drummer (Paul Motian) who didn't lay down the traditional swing rhythms but literally created a percussive accompaniment that gels with the bass and piano. As a whole, by giving the freedom to everyone along with a shared vision of the objective, they created a style that changed the way that most piano trios play.

Work groups are not teams. If you think back on your experiences working on software projects, most "teams" might be best described as work groups—groups of highly competent individuals working on their separate responsibilities whose efforts were combined into the end result.

You know when you're working on an empowered team and not just a work group because the synergy and synchrony among the people are exhilarating. You can feel the energy, the progress, the excitement, and the expectation. It's fun to solve problems. Your combined efforts produce something beyond what was expected. You achieve something superb that you all are proud of. Think back through your own work experiences as we further break down the characteristics of successful, empowered teams, and think about ways that these characteristics can be fostered in your organization.

Characteristics of Empowered Teams

Whether discussing business, information technology, sports, or music, superior team experiences are described with remarkable similarity. Empowered teams differ from work groups in their consistency, intensity, and ceaseless striving.

For instance, when people describe their experiences on fantastic teams, they frequently use the extreme words *always* and *never*. "We always kept the feedback loop with our end users fresh—hearing what they had to say about how we were serving them." Or "We never allowed our training to fall below par; we kept our skills up-to-date and deep." People on these teams were consistent in their pursuit of excellence. They were driven by a vision of success that inspired them.

Intensity is strong in superior, empowered teams. The level of energy and commitment is high and can be described as a feeling of group impatience. And finally, there's a feeling of restless dissatisfaction that creates a natural push for continuous improvement. "If it ain't broke, improve it."

Dennis Kinlaw describes these elements in his model for superior team development and performance, which we've adapted here in Figure 6.1. The top-level elements of this model are

1. **Superior team results:** This is best seen by building enthusiastically positive customers. The team achieves beyond expectations and is energized about the process.
2. **Informal team processes:** Day-to-day communication and responsiveness are consistent and quick, and there's a feeling of safety and a lack of hierarchy in bringing up suggestions and issues.
3. **Positive team feelings:** This is best exemplified by feelings of inclusion, commitment, loyalty, pride, and trust.
4. **Developing leadership:** Team members are focused on development and performance.

If you think about your own experiences with strong teams, you might be able to add some other ways of describing them. The point of this chapter is to get you thinking about what engaged people working toward common goals could accomplish in your organization, then about how to get them there. Most people have at some point been a part of a superior team. Think of the reasons why those teams worked well. Why were people excited and motivated? How did they get that way? Why did it end? How can you be a part of making that experience a reality again, and how can the team sustain this principle?

For example, our experiences show that teams that operate in an environment of open communication, with access to the information they need

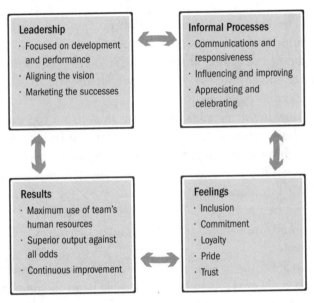

Figure 6.1   Model for team development and performance[3]

to get their work done, are both more effective and more creative. As Michael Levine wrote, "To make good decisions, team members need information and context."[4]

Examples of Empowered Teams in Software

The Open Source Community

The Open Source community starkly demonstrates a unique and interesting dynamic. Individuals, typically spread around the world, without any monetary compensation or managerial directive, successfully collaborate to create software "products" of substantial value, from Web browsers to operating systems to databases to thousands of other useful tools. When critical bugs surface, virtual teams collaborate around the clock to provide solutions, once

---

3. Adapted from ibid, p. 42.

4. Michael K. Levine, *A Tale of Two Systems: Lean and Agile Software Development for Business Leaders* (CRC Press, 2009), p. 294.

again without managerial direction or monetary reward. New features are developed relatively quickly in most Open Source software, without work breakdown structures and executive guidance. High software quality is maintained, and software is continually refactored so that continual change and consistent progress are possible.

How is this possible, given that there is no top-down traditional command-and-control structure? The Open Source community benefits from the highly motivating power of respect, trust, and commitment. Participating in the creation and continual evolution of something that others will use, benefit from, and enjoy, fosters a deep feeling of being part of something important among people who will likely never meet. Creating code and features and improvements that engender the respect of peers is a powerful motivator.

In a way that is similar to the "invisible hand" behind the behavior of free markets, there seems to be an "invisible hand" behind the behavior of these virtual software teams.

While Open Source provides a good example of what's possible through the power of respect, trust, and commitment, it would be simplistic to say that empowering an internal team in an IT department could achieve the same results easily. Often an internal team in an IT department has finite resources already stretched to the breaking point before a Lean Integration effort begins. How do we build a team and somehow establish the same kind of team-oriented "invisible hand" that energizes and motivates the people on Open Source teams?

Respect, Trust, and Commitment

Monetary compensation is not the driver behind successful Open Source teams. Nor are management directives driving the teams, handing down schedules, and monitoring progress. In a similar way that there is an invisible hand that drives market behavior in free markets, there is also an invisible hand that motivates individuals to work in these teams. It can be described in many ways, but we'll take one approach here.

The motivation for people to participate actively in these communities is somewhat similar to what drives people to contribute to Wikipedia. People seek to be part of something important, useful, and successful. They are looking for the respect of their peers and to work in an environment where they have the support they require and the freedom to grow and achieve.

People's motivations are no different today from what they were before the Internet. They have always existed, but modern examples like Open Source, Wikipedia, and any number of different social networking phenomena show them in exceptional relief.

Software Start-up Companies

Not everyone participates in Open Source, so here is another example that highlights the "invisible hand" behind exceptional empowered teams. You frequently find effective teams within start-up software companies. Typically, the level of passion and alignment is extremely high (commitment). Employees feel they are involved in the creation of something new and important. Because of funding issues, market situations, and a huge variety of other issues, many start-ups don't succeed, but frequently their innovative techniques live beyond the company's life span. From the people who participated in these endeavors, you will hear wistful recollections of the team they were a part of.

The challenge, and objective, is to create a similar feeling in the midst of much larger, traditional IT organizations.

How do we achieve this vision of being part of something important, especially when our topic, integration, has a history of being "underappreciated"? How do we create the environment for teams to grow using the "invisible hand" of respect, trust, and commitment? The most successful answer that we've seen is to treat the Integration Competency Center as a business, as if it were a software start-up company within a larger IT organization providing products and services to the internal market. This is not only beneficial to the customer (the business) but is equally important for fertilizing the soil to create effective, empowered teams.

Creating an Empowered Lean Integration Team

Launch "ICC, Inc." Like a Software Start-up Company

We ask people to think of the ICC as a business from several different perspectives in different chapters throughout this book. The ICC is an internal services business that provides software products and services to customers, the business community. You are creating "ICC, Inc." within your enterprise, and your objective is "customer delight" for your business customers. You do this by trying to create the best product of exactly the right specification supplied in the least time at the least cost for your customers.

The conventional wisdom is "Better, cheaper, and faster; pick any two." With Lean Integration and "ICC, Inc.," we're going to work toward delivering all three. Improving the ICC processes, people, and technology takes time, but setting this vision provides a foundation for developing the feeling of team empowerment necessary to make this happen.

We talk all the time about the pace of change in business, and particularly in the world of technology. But to be realistic, it usually takes three to five years to establish a top-notch "ICC, Inc.," which is also about how long it takes most start-ups to mature to a level where they are gaining market share and becoming entrenched in their markets.

Thinking in terms of a software start-up company has tremendous power in instilling a vision and synchronizing everyone's view of the customer. You are trying to create integration (or business intelligence) services and capabilities that will be highly sought after by the business. You will be able to meet their goals better, cheaper, and faster than any alternative.

Thinking of the ICC as a business has numerous benefits to the people working on the team:

1. It clarifies the view of who the customer is.
2. The view of what is valuable to the customer can therefore be clearer.
3. The objective of delighting the customer by providing integration solutions better, cheaper, *and* faster becomes the driver for the company.
4. Thinking in terms of "ICC, Inc." provides an identity and a group in which to be included. All aspects of what a start-up provides should be considered:

   a. Marketing the products, services, and successes of "ICC, Inc." to management and each other. Celebrate the successes of the team.
   b. Know the competition of "ICC, Inc." What other ways are projects being done that compete with the ICC? Are you happy to give away that business, or would you like to win it for yourselves?
   c. Measure and chart the growth and success of "ICC, Inc." (See the next chapter for ideas about how to do this.)

The objective is to paint a clear vision, get people excited about achieving it, and then discuss the roadblocks that can and should be removed to enable teams to innovate and continuously improve toward this vision. Even when this vision has been painted and people are excited, the next goal is equally critical to enabling empowered teams.

Ensure Sufficient Capacity for Continuous Improvement

The hardest nut to crack in making ICCs successful is getting enough spare bandwidth to make some of the changes that the team desires. Many use the analogy of trying to change the tires on a car while it is moving at 60 miles per hour. If teams are totally consumed year-round with just meeting day-to-day operational needs, progress toward the vision will be hampered and the feeling of empowerment toward the ultimate goals of Lean Integration will be distrusted as nothing more than verbiage. People need time and space to breathe and think. Time and again, it is during these moments of breathing that most true innovation takes place.

Google is famous for allowing 20 percent of its software developers' time to be set aside for thinking and innovation. Other organizations taking agile approaches leave a week between two- to four-week iterations for downtime, allowing developers to develop ideas without guidance or direction. Frequently, it is during these periods of "free" time that the most innovative ideas emerge. And more often than not, innovation breeds efficiency and further opportunity for more innovation.

We realize that there is a chicken-and-egg problem here. You need excess capacity to make the changes to improve processes that make you more efficient, but you don't have excess capacity because your current processes consume all resources. This is a difficult cycle to get out of, but truly, finding a small win in this area can do more to get the ball rolling with "ICC, Inc." than just about anything else. Excess capacity, when it exists within an empowered team that shares a Lean vision of the future, is the most powerful weapon available to make Lean Integration successful. Excess capacity and an empowered team lead to innovation and therefore more excess capacity and more innovation, and along the way customers are getting what they need, better, cheaper, and faster.

Excess capacity is so important to team empowerment that perhaps the two are almost equivalent. If a team never gets time or space to change or innovate, how can the team be truly empowered? Not addressing this important issue leads to ICC maturity stagnation at many organizations.

Leadership and Vision

In our first ICC book, we discussed the importance of people and change agents, but we didn't specifically address the role of leadership. Empowerment does *not* mean that leadership is either neglected or deemphasized. Leadership simply plays a different role.

Create a Sense of Safety

Change and flexibility are hallmarks of continuous improvement and Lean principles. One additional requirement that falls out from a continual quest to eliminate waste is to institutionalize the principle that staff won't eliminate their own jobs as a result of productivity improvements.

The leadership of "ICC, Inc." needs to create an environment where it's fun to solve problems and where significant improvements in productivity aren't going to end up costing people their jobs. This feeling of safety is foundational to making Lean thinking work. Lean does not mean layoffs. Lean means getting people involved and engaged in the process of creating *additional* customer value. A higher percentage of people's time is spent automating the common patterns, creating and maintaining the "assembly lines," rather than working as craftspeople on individual integration works of art.

Roles for Leaders

Besides helping to set the vision and promote "ICC, Inc." wherever that promotion is beneficial to the success of the ICC business, leaders need to understand their role as that of initiator, model, and coach.

Initiator

Leaders within Lean Integration teams initiate various actions and processes for building the teams' capabilities. They accomplish this by first initiating team development exercises for setting goals, and subsequently instituting exercises around working toward achieving those goals. All goals are team goals, not individual goals. Having a leader who is a change agent to make this happen is critical.

Model

Leaders must also model the behavior they expect other members of the team to follow. This is exemplified not only by the way they perform when they interact with the team and perform work within the team, but also when they interact with people outside the team (customers and other stakeholders) to accomplish the goals of the team. This means modeling the characteristics outlined in Figure 6.1: results, informal processes, and feelings.

Coach

Finally, leadership means providing coaching wherever it can be helpful to the team. This includes counseling, mentoring, tutoring, and improving performance. Just as important is to encourage people to take responsibility for driving bottom-up improvements. "The people with ideas, working with their teams, should be the implementers of their ideas. They should not be asked to drop their ideas into a suggestion system to be implemented by others."[5]

Empowering individual contributors does *not* mean abandoning management structures. Leadership plays a crucial role in Lean Integration that is different from its role in the traditional hierarchical, command-and-control world. Leadership is about creating the environment where team members are truly empowered to think and innovate, make decisions and mistakes, and question authority for the good of the vision. They have the resources they need, the time they need, the freedom they need, and the trust and respect they need to continuously work toward making the vision a reality.

Change Agent Leadership

One of the dangers of success is that it can breed complacency. One of the hardest things to do is to challenge the things that drove the current measure of success—but not to do so can lead to stagnation. It is for this reason that a sustainable integration strategy must drive change constantly.

Change is difficult and brings risks, so we must be careful to manage the tug-of-war between driving change rapidly and slowing it down. To facilitate this apparent paradox, a range of change leaders is required, including change agents, early adopters, late adopters, and change resisters. An empowered team needs all types. Change resisters ask the tough questions and put up roadblocks to ensure that change doesn't happen too fast; late adopters are the pragmatists who ensure that all the details of a new initiative are thoroughly

---

5. Mary and Tom Poppendieck, *Implementing Lean Software Development: From Concept to Cash* (Addison-Wesley, 2006), p. 236.

worked out; early adopters are the experimenters who fine-tune new ideas to fit the organizational dynamics; and change agents are the explorers with innovative ideas.

The appropriate diversity of change leaders is critical. In order to achieve a Lean Integration practice, particularly in light of continuous improvement, more change agents are needed than change resisters. Womack and Jones encourage us to look for change agents inside the organization: ". . . in the fifty firms we've looked at it was possible to find the right change agent, and generally after only a short search."[6]

But what exactly is a "change agent"? A change agent

- Is a voracious learner
- Does not wait for orders to take action on new ideas
- Expresses excitement freely concerning new ideas and change
- Demonstrates a sense of urgency to capitalize on innovations and opportunities
- Challenges the status quo
- Transcends silos to achieve enterprise results
- Skillfully influences peers and colleagues to promote and sell ideas
- Displays personal courage by taking a stand on controversial and challenging changes

A successful Lean Integration team is also a successful change management team. It would be a mistake to underestimate the difficulty in leading change in a large enterprise. Womack and Jones make this point in *Lean Thinking*: "The most difficult step is simply to get started by overcoming the inertia present in any brownfield organization. You'll need a change agent plus the core of lean knowledge, some type of crisis to serve as a lever for change, a map of your value streams, and a determination to kaikaku quickly to your value-creating activities in order to produce rapid results which your organization can't ignore."[7] (**Note:** In Lean terms there are two kinds of improvement. *Kaizen* refers to steady incremental improvement, and *kaikaku* means revolution, or radical improvement.)

---

6. James P. Womack and Daniel T. Jones, *Lean Thinking: Banish Waste and Create Wealth in Your Corporation* (Simon & Schuster, 1996), p. 248.
7. Ibid., p. 247.

Some of the more difficult challenges facing the Lean team include

- The "not invented here" syndrome and other similar behaviors
- Project funding by fine-grained silos that don't have the money for and aren't motivated to solve the "big picture"
- Emphasis on tactical short-term investment that doesn't appear to leave any room for strategic infrastructure investments
- Short-term, tactical time pressures that prevent solving the problems "the right way"
- Autonomous operating groups in distributed geographies that will not accept guidance from a central team
- Fear of change and a vested interest in the status quo, resulting in the belief that there is no compelling reason to change

The word *challenges* may be too moderate when referring to this list; these seem a lot more like immovable barriers. As insurmountable as these hurdles may appear to be, they are not unique to an integration team and have been conquered in the past. Joe Stenzel provides some encouragement: "It is generally accepted that people are afraid of change. In reality, people are afraid of the unknown. People are not afraid of change if they understand and believe that the change will benefit them. When this happens, they adopt change so fast that it can make one's head spin."[8]

While there is no simple "silver bullet" solution, there are a number of key concepts that have been proven over and over to be effective in driving changes. Here are seven of the best:

1. **Think strategically—act tactically:** Have a clear vision of the future, but be prepared to get there one step at a time. It is good to keep in mind that *there is no end state*. In other words, something is always changing, so if you miss a window of opportunity to establish, say, a new architectural standard on the latest project, don't worry. Another project will come along. If you are in it for the long run, individual projects, even big ones, are just blips on the radar screen.
2. **Credibility through delivery:** In order to be perceived as a leader by others in the enterprise, you need their trust and respect. It's not just about

---

8. Joe Stenzel, *Lean Accounting: Best Practices for Sustainable Integration* (John Wiley & Sons, 2007), Kindle loc. 1691–93.

being open, honest, and trustworthy; do people trust that you will actually get the job done? In the final analysis it comes down to your ability to execute. To organize your work, you should set appropriate priorities, assign the appropriate resources to the task, and maintain good communication with your customers. Above all, keep your promises.

3. **Sidestep resource issues:** In this global economy of outsourcing, offshoring, and contracting, there should never be a reason not to find the resources to get a particular job done. If you want to create a reputation as a "can do" customer-service-oriented team, there should never be a time when you need to say no to a service request because of lack of resources (but there may be other reasons to say no).

4. **Choose your battles:** Whenever you have the choice between a carrot and a stick approach, always use the carrot. You can, and should, carry a stick in terms of having the support of senior executives for any mandated processes or standards, but you should use the power as infrequently as possible. Sometimes this might even mean deviating from enterprise standards. One way to help you choose your battles is this exercise: Write down your integration standards on a piece of paper and stroke out one at a time, starting with the ones on which you would be willing to compromise if pushed into a corner, until you have only one left. That is the standard for which you should use your stick.

5. **Take out the garbage:** Accept responsibility for work that no one else wants. An interesting lesson learned is that many of the jobs that others don't want are those that don't serve a specific function but end up being ideal integration initiatives. Sometimes these also end up being difficult challenges, but generally management recognizes them as such, which opens the door to your asking for top-level support when needed.

6. **Leverage knowledge:** There is a well-known truism that states that "knowledge is power." In an integration team you are ideally positioned to talk with just about anyone in the organization. By asking a lot of questions and being a good listener, you can gain a lot of knowledge about the organization that narrowly focused project teams or groups don't have. This knowledge can come in very handy in terms of which projects get approved and where you shouldn't spend your time, where next year's budget will land, which groups are hiring and which aren't, and so on.

7. **Take it outside:** Another aspect of leadership is active participation in the broader community, specifically, participation in standards bodies or professional organizations. The external activities can be useful both for getting new ideas and insights and for polishing your own ideas though discussion and debate with others. In the end, these activities can make you stronger individually, which can only help you play a leadership role inside your enterprise.

Important Practices That Help Enable Empowered Teams

Rotate Team Members into the Customer's Shoes

One of the more difficult challenges for developers is to understand the business perspective. In other Lean business initiatives, people usually have an intuitive grasp of the customer and the products and services that customers need. Whether we're talking about cars, health care, homes, or other tangible, everyday items, understanding the customer is not much different from understanding ourselves. For instance, in the automobile industry, everyone on the assembly line has driven a car before. Everyone has gone through the process of opening a new bank account. For so many different "products," people have some sort of intuitive, commonsense grasp of what the customer might want, although this must never be completely substituted for constant interaction with and feedback from real customers.

In the IT world, however, "ICC, Inc." serves the business community. What the business community requires to do its job is frequently more abstract and difficult for a software developer to understand. What business professionals do in the different organizational departments is often completely foreign to people in the IT department. This makes it seem as if the business and IT speak different languages.

People in the IT department who have a firm grasp of the business as well as a strong technical competence are usually some of the most valuable people on integration or quality projects. In some cases, these people came from a business function, or they came from system integrators where they had much more interaction with the business community. In any case, working toward a goal where people have the opportunity to walk in the shoes of customers has a tremendous benefit in developing and clarifying the vision of what will create customer delight. Additionally, this can be a good motivator and can help to build bridges and improve communication between the IT community and the business community.

Conversely, making some business analysts honorary members of "ICC, Inc." has many of the same benefits. People pontificate about the importance of "business/IT alignment" to the point where nobody's listening anymore, but rotating business and IT team members in this way can help facilitate this alignment.

Grow the Skills of Team Members

Many ICCs already understand the importance of growing integration skills to make team members more effective. But to make Lean Integration more effective, growth in other skills is important as well. The Poppendiecks state this succinctly: "Deskilling workers creates interchangeable people while upskilling workers creates thinking people."[9]

Continuous improvement and problem-solving skills are the hallmarks of success with Lean thinking. Chapter 5 discussed *kaizen* methods for continuous improvement, but there are also other problem-solving methods that are important for teams to use.

Lean thinking and continuous improvement require the ability to get to the root cause of problems. Often, attempts are made to solve issues by treating the symptom rather than the root cause. In many cases, the symptom was mistaken for the root cause.

One useful method for ensuring that you arrive at the root cause is the "5 Whys" method, which we should learn from our children. Young children drive us crazy sometimes, asking us why the world is the way it is. After each answer we give, they continue to ask "why?" Time and again, why, why, why? Finally, despite our best efforts at patience, we answer, "Because I said so."

Lean thinking adopts this childlike approach to getting to the root of process problems. By continually asking "why?" to determine why a process works the way it does, at some point you reach the "because I said so" stage. At this point, back up one "why?" and you will find that the last answer is the root of the problem. With this root cause on the table, the team can begin to discuss alternatives for remedying it.

---

9. Poppendieck, *Implementing Lean Software Development*, p. 228.

Incentives, Compensation, and Rewards

One of the most important practices to ensure empowered teams is appreciating that metrics, rewards, and objectives should emphasize team objectives. Personal performance should be judged in reference to performance within the team and the team's success. Individual metrics around how many software objects someone created or how many bugs someone fixed should be avoided entirely. Group metrics are fine. Individual metrics are not.

The Poppendiecks add some advice to this discussion: "Eliminate annual performance ratings for salaried workers; do not undermine team cooperation by rewarding individual performance" and "If you have a [employee] ranking system in your company, a lean initiative will be hollow at best. The behaviors that ranking systems encourage are competition, hiding information so as to look good, and hiding problems so as not to look bad."[10] Stenzel reinforces this line of thinking: "Instead of motivating higher performance, extrinsic rewards actually put limits on what employees want to do and what they judge to be fair."[11]

Judge quality based on the bigger picture, and improve the process to make the creation of quality problems less likely, because quality issues are a result of the process, not of someone's personal performance. Individuals should be incented to help other members of the team, to coach and mentor others, and to participate in ways that benefit the bigger picture to support improving the value chain from the perspective of the customer. Individually oriented metrics and incentives can drive behavior that degrades positive team behavior.

We would do well to follow Stenzel's advice: "It has been known for a long time that people are not motivated by financial rewards or stretch goals and targets beyond fulfillment of the basic necessities of life. They are motivated by work that uses their inherent creative capacity. In his classic *Harvard Business Review* article 'One More Time, How Do You Motivate Employees?' Frederick Herzberg makes the point that people are not motivated by targets, rewards, or negative reinforcement. The article states, 'Forget praise. Forget punishment. Forget cash. You need to make their jobs more interesting.'"[12]

---

10. Ibid., pp. 141, 143.

11. Stenzel, *Lean Accounting: Best Practices for Sustainable Integration*, Kindle loc. 2300–2301.

12. Ibid., Kindle loc. 1863–67.

Global Teams

Some of the most effective teams we've seen are global teams. Whether these are Open Source teams, IT teams that use offshore partners, or simply extremely large IT teams that span numerous time zones, the best global teams sometimes operate better than teams operating within the same building.

How does this happen? This happens through practicing constant communication and continual checkpointing and synchronization, and ensuring that no team members are treated as second-class citizens.

In today's connected environments, the ability to share desktops and virtual whiteboard concepts is quite mature. Successful global teams don't happen by accident or naturally; it takes effort and good habits on the part of the team members to make them work. But we've seen many cases where time zone differences can result in great productivity as long as synchronization points take place either daily or several times a week. Tossing specifications over the wall and working at arm's length demonstrates the batch-and-queue mentality. With Lean Integration, remember our mantra is pull and flow. Using the 24-hour clock, some teams are seeing great advantages to working this way on bug fixes and other development initiatives.

Of all the Lean Integration principles, empowering the team may be the most important and the most difficult. Change takes time. While people may be motivated by the Lean Integration vision at first, sustaining and building toward true team empowerment and a learning organization takes years, not months. But getting started toward this objective can create a self-sustaining, self-improving trajectory, assuming it is nurtured and consistently emphasized along the way.

Organizing the Team: Thoughts on Organizational Structures

An organization's structure must support enough hierarchy to facilitate accountability and responsibility, but not so much structure that the bureaucracy introduces waste by serving itself rather than the customer. Being Lean means not "overorganizing": Division of work by specialization can lead to waste and a tendency to focus on maximizing individual resource utilization rather than minimizing customer lead times.

Typically, ICCs begin focusing on a particular class of integration, such as process integration, and grow the maturity of that capability before adding another class of integration, such as data integration. This is because the technologies and skill sets are a bit different. For an area such as application integration, ICCs frequently start by focusing on administration and operations of the integration environment, because these are the easiest places to start. In other words, for a fairly large organization, the ICC will install, upgrade, administer, and operate the integration environment while other project teams use the technology for their integration projects. This is a valuable improvement over the integration anarchy approach, where every project team chooses and administers its own technology (which is what makes the hairball grow so fast).

While providing administration and operations services for the integration environment does deliver significant value to large organizations, providing integration development and maintenance services with a Lean mind-set has a much higher payoff. The political barriers are higher, but the returns are higher as well. In some ways, this book is about applying Lean thinking to development and maintenance responsibilities in order to break out of the admin/operations rut where many ICCs find themselves stuck.

Once an organization has focused on improving its services for application integration, there are significant economies through skill and process sharing by taking on data integration as well.

Factors driving the organizational structure include the ICC model you select (shared services versus centralized services, for instance), the scope of responsibilities, geographic distribution of the team, strengths of the various team members, and corporate culture. If the team consists of fewer than a dozen people or so, you may not need any structure at all and simply have all the staff report directly to the ICC director. Figure 6.2 shows a typical structure for a medium-sized shared-services or central-services ICC, where the dotted lines around "Data Integration" and "Application Integration" suggest that the ICC may start with one or the other, rather than both, in the beginning.

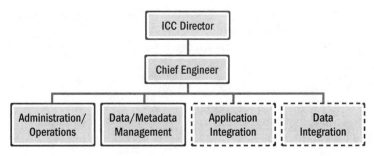

Figure 6.2 ICC organizational structure

One of the critical factors in making Lean Integration initiatives successful is to establish the role of the chief engineer. Sometimes, particularly in smaller organizations, this role may be owned by the person who is the ICC director, but the key is that this person has responsibility for delivery of solutions. Put another way, the chief engineer is the hands-on "chief integration architect"; people in this position roll up their sleeves and get their hands dirty in the trenches. This person has a deep understanding of the vendor integration tools in play and looks for the existence of patterns throughout the integration projects. Above all, the chief engineer is accountable for the success of the ICC's output from the customer's perspective.

Governance committees can be the bane of Lean Integration. The objective of any governance committee is important, but being Lean means finding ways where the process of achieving that objective doesn't interfere with the satisfaction of the customer. Having a chief engineer helps to ensure that governance committees are not used as an excuse for delays and waste because of distributed accountability.

In a larger ICC, the data/metadata management team is responsible for the development of shareable objects and services, as well as growing the capabilities of the metadata management system that in turn enables visual management capabilities. Administration/operations is responsible for the integration infrastructure components, and the one or more integration teams work on the development and maintenance of the different styles of integration projects.

Everyone on the different teams is involved in the constant, continuous improvement of the value streams associated with customer delivery. Organizational structures need to support and not hinder that primary imperative.

Case Study: Smith & Nephew—Integrating Lean Principles with Data Quality

Smith & Nephew is an industry leader in each of three main global business units (GBUs): Orthopedic Reconstruction and Trauma, Endoscopy, and Advanced Wound Management. These businesses jointly offer over 1,000 products.

The company operates in 32 countries and generates annual sales of $3.8 billion. S&N has a track record of bringing innovative new products to market that provide improved clinical outcomes for patients and save costs for health care providers.

But the company had a dilemma: It was almost impossible to obtain a clear, holistic version of the company's global data, including customer information, vendor partners, and SKUs (stock keeping units). The lack of synchronized data led to a high degree of manual input, obsolete or inaccurate data in the SAP systems, and data migration "collisions." Troubleshooting was an inexact science and involved multiple handoffs to different teams in each GBU.

In order to support the business demand for more sophisticated technology and help the organization get closer to customers and patients, in 2007 the CIO endorsed a plan to improve data quality and governance.

Vision

The first task was to secure executive sponsorship for the "Get Clean/Stay Clean" vision for data quality. S&N needed to stabilize operations as part of a "get clean" approach while at the same time building awareness of how to build data quality into day-to-day activities in order to "stay clean." Given that there were three major business units on different SAP applications, this was a challenge. The vision, therefore, was to empower business users to adopt continuous improvement practices in their operations.

C-level management of each business unit was engaged by the data quality team to understand pain points and strategic goals. Lean concepts and principles were applied in three main areas: supply chain, customer relationship management, and compliance. Executive buy-in and funding were secured for a four-year MDM (master data management) road map. The goal was to focus first on the operational back-end systems and then on the front-end point of data entry.

The first objective was to baseline data accuracy and enable business owners to capture and retain business process knowledge. The goal was to achieve greater than 95 percent data accuracy, which was expected to result in productivity savings by avoiding rework of sales orders and billings, minimizing lost time due to missing or incomplete data, improving the transportation of products, and decreasing the amount of returned correspondence.

It was generally accepted at S&N that data quality issues existed, but it was challenging to fix them as the extent of the impact was not quantified or documented. As the saying goes, "You cannot improve what you cannot measure." One of the first initiatives by the Data Governance Council, therefore, was to launch data quality scorecards, which were viewed by more than 100 users to help each business unit monitor and analyze its data quality performance against predefined key performance indicators (KPIs).

Materials and customers were among the first SAP data domains to benefit from these scorecards. Within a few short months, Smith & Nephew harmonized, standardized, and cleansed data; eliminated obsolete records; and achieved accurate customer master data. Putting these powerful capabilities in the hands of the business users allowed them to measure, monitor, analyze, and govern the accuracy and completeness of their data. The publicly visible scorecards also promoted healthy competition among business units—no unit wanted to be the last to clean up its data.

Data Governance Awareness and Infrastructure

In 2007 the strategy and road map were communicated via evangelism by the data quality team, a data dictionary, governance councils, and a worldwide SharePoint site, resulting in business support for building an MDM platform to address data quality profiling, audit, quality, and cleansing of business rules. The process helped the business gain visibility into disparate part-numbering conventions, duplicate customer records, missing data, and incorrect data relationships.

Evangelism involved delivering presentations that focused on each functional team with specific examples of how master data was impacting its ability to be Lean and efficient. The first three months involved a road show in each of the business process areas: Quote to Cash, Procure to Pay, Manufacturing to Distribution, and Finance.

The most important part of this activity was to listen to what the business wanted to achieve and to describe technical solutions in a strategic context. For instance, an SAP consolidation may be an IT strategy, but it should be articulated as standardization of vendor and part number descriptions, enabling the business to have cross-GBU visibility and management of vendor relationships.

The data quality goal during this period was to give business users a glimpse of what could be achieved over time in order to inspire their willingness to change and to identify the business champion. The business champion turned out to be the COO, who had the challenge of bringing Lean and Six Sigma changes to the manufacturing sites.

S&N adopted a four-tiered governance pyramid:

- **Executive:** the executive steering committee
- **Strategic:** a governance team with one representative from each GBU plus regional representatives
- **Tactical:** the lead data steward within each GBU and region
- **Operational:** the site business owner and data maintainer of the systems environment

The governance councils were formed by domain with one each for Finance, Supply Chain, and Customer. They met biweekly with formal agendas, presentations, and action steps. The data quality team developed policies, and the council typically voted on field usage and adoption.

S&N identified the need to invest in robust data quality tools that were scalable and could handle large volumes of data. The solution needed to encompass the ability to deliver data profiling, data quality, data integration, and point of entry. A comprehensive integration platform was acquired which formed the basis of a consolidated MDM solution, thereby enabling the business to obtain a clear, holistic picture of the company's global data, including customer information, vendor partners, and SKU/catalog management.

Leveraging Lean Concepts in Data Quality

While Smith & Nephew's long-term goal was to achieve consistent business processes sharing the same master data, the short-term goal was to help each business unit monitor and improve the quality of its data and measure its impact on operational efficiency.

The enterprise data quality team began by narrowing the data governance program down to 35 key item master fields that were impacting manufacturing production, sales order management, and product logistics in four major functional scorecards:

Scorecard	Operational Focus
Enterprise	Design, engineering, and rationalization of SKUs
Quality and risk classification	Compliance of key FDA fields
Sales and marketing	Sales and gross margin analysis
Manufacturing and warehousing	How products are stored and batch-managed

Each data field was assigned an owner who was ultimately accountable for the correct data content as measured by the scorecard metrics. A business semantic definition was created for each field, and an executive sponsor was identified to assist with business function alignment.

There are ten dimensions to profiling and data quality, as shown in Figure 6.3. S&N chose initially to adopt three of the major measurement criteria, focusing on aspects that business users could control and correct: completeness, conformity, and accuracy. By profiling key fields such as SKU, the data quality team could identify quality patterns and use them to facilitate discussions with the business, which resulted in many process reengineering efforts such as part-numbering conventions.

Two key Lean concepts were integral elements of the data quality program: waste elimination and continuous improvement. The team felt that the data quality initiative should result in lower data capture lead times, improved responsiveness, elimination of process breakdowns between organizations, and reduction in overall operating cost. Users were encouraged to use the results of data quality monitoring to drive fact-based analysis of problem areas and continuously drive incremental improvements.

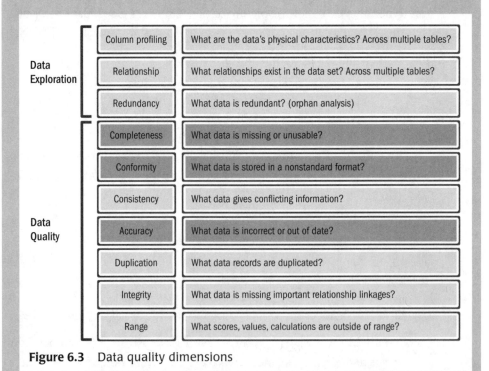

Data Exploration	Column profiling	What are the data's physical characteristics? Across multiple tables?
	Relationship	What relationships exist in the data set? Across multiple tables?
	Redundancy	What data is redundant? (orphan analysis)
Data Quality	Completeness	What data is missing or unusable?
	Conformity	What data is stored in a nonstandard format?
	Consistency	What data gives conflicting information?
	Accuracy	What data is incorrect or out of date?
	Duplication	What data records are duplicated?
	Integrity	What data is missing important relationship linkages?
	Range	What scores, values, calculations are outside of range?

Figure 6.3   Data quality dimensions

A value stream approach was used as part of the data quality project to assess the process flow in creating a material master and reviewing what were non-value-adding activities. Manual steps were critically examined to see if they could be automated or if handoffs between groups were really necessary and could be eliminated.

Process Steps in Data Quality

As an initial step, the team performed a six-week baseline audit and determined enterprise versus local fields. This was done by visiting each of the GBU sites for one week and meeting with SMEs to discuss and obtain business rules. The team partnered with the business leads to present the findings to the executive steering committee and trigger a full data quality initiative.

It was especially important to articulate the steps that would be needed in order to secure resources and funding to define quality and how to measure it. Following are the "Get Clean/Stay Clean" process steps:

1. Access the data.
2. Profile the data (gain insight).
3. Choose what to measure—record definitions and ownership, and identify critical fields that cause cross-organization or functional breakdowns.
4. Collect business rules—content knowledge about the business process.
5. Define enterprise standards.
6. Eliminate waste (remove old records and clean up active information).
7. Measure business processes and create a scorecard.
8. Enrich data with missing values.
9. Develop change management and integration load processes.
10. Cleanse, match, and merge data.
11. Enhance point of entry to build quality in at the source.

Data Quality Scorecards and Business Rules

Visual presentation via published scorecards was an important part of gaining attention and communicating the status of the data quality. The process of working with the business required the assignment of a data quality analyst. The business needed guidance on how to interpret the scorecards and identify different approaches to cleaning up problems. The data quality analyst was responsible for meeting with the functions on a regular basis and coordinating cleanup plans by working with technical teams.

As part of the data quality approach, one of the steps, and probably the most difficult, was capturing undocumented tacit knowledge from SMEs that represented business rules about data. A business rule is critical information since it represents a policy or standard practice. This step often required collecting information from various functional teams in order to develop a complete rule, since functions operated independently and were unaware that their determination impacted a downstream application or process. The accuracy of a good data quality system is dependent on how precise the business rules are. This turned out to be an iterative process since the first pass at developing scorecards generated questions from different functions that needed to be researched and often resulted in a more complete set of rules for a given data field.

As a result of collecting data and process dependencies, relationships, and exceptions, S&N was able to identify nonoptimal business processes with significant *muda*. Once a rule is defined, compliance with it can be verified. For example, by profiling part numbers against the defined business rule conventions, S&N found the following:

1. More part-numbering convention variations across the company than anticipated
2. Noncompliance of number ranges
3. Business process intelligence built into part number descriptions

These were key indicators of process gaps (a process that is not working as intended or poorly designed, which leads to inaccurate master data). This visibility enabled Smith & Nephew to take action and as a result identify a number of major improvement projects.

Measuring Success

Measurable objectives included achieving an initial target of 95 percent quality in vendor, customer, and SKU/item master followed by continuous improvements. Dashboard views displaying KPIs were used to communicate status and track progress, enabling business data owners to measure, monitor, and analyze the quality of their information on an ongoing basis. Placing these tools in the hands of business users was a huge advantage. Since tools were typically in IT hands prior to this program, business users traditionally had to wait for application development or new reports, which often fell to the bottom of the priority queue. But dashboards provided real production data at the tips of their fingers on a weekly basis. Some business users also were trained to develop their own dashboards.

Progress was measured and assessed by data governance councils and leadership team reviews. For example, indicative of the import placed on data quality, the business vision is owned by the president's council, which reviews data quality quarterly as an indicator of the information health of the enterprise.

Some Key Achievements

- Saved $1.4 million in the first six months because of improved customer master data quality (e.g., reduced postal costs from not sending mail to inaccurate addresses, improved safety notifications or recalls from having correct customer data)
- Increased confidence in the accuracy of data used for planning and forecasting
- Contributed to earnings by improving cross-sell of products to existing customers
- SKU reduction by 40 percent in one GBU of old/obsolete parts
- Deactivated more than 30 percent of old and inactive customer masters
- Ensured regulatory compliance by a validation check of all relevant fields
- Standardized, enriched, cleansed, and validated more than 5 million customer and material fields
- Avoided 20,000 part collisions in data migrations using a central repository
- Cross-business-unit visibility
- Achieved 85 percent data quality targets within 6 months with a clear path to achieve the 95 percent goal within 12 months

Recommendations

The success of the S&N data quality program owes much to the lessons the team leaders learned from prior experiences, as well as some new insights gained as a result of the project. Following is a summary of key elements that helped to ensure that the vision was realized:

- Present scorecards at the executive level.
- Visualization: Cross-GBU scorecards create competition to reach the goal.

- Hold "lunch and learn" sessions for functional teams; people want to do the right thing and need knowledge to be empowered.
- Assign dedicated data quality analysts to support business functions.
- Constant evangelism and perseverance and steady, small progress in improving data quality help build trust and confidence with the business.
- Establish no-blame, nonjudgmental reviews of data quality—focus on the future, not on how you got there.
- Manage by facts and details versus generalizations.
- Measure the cost of nonconformance with tangible examples.
- Implement in achievable milestones so the business has continuous improvement.
- Break down barriers between GBUs and functions by training collaborative teams.
- Empower users to fix data and expose the root causes of problems, enabling them to focus on the higher-value-adding deliverables.
- Communicate success.

Moving toward Proactive Governance

As Smith & Nephew's master data model has matured from minimal awareness of data quality to active data governance—the emphasis has shifted toward an integrated view of data. This in turn demands the use of an Integration Factory to automate the process of transforming and loading clean data back into SAP from the data quality repository. While the initial focus was to standardize, cleanse, and integrate master data, the data quality team and business stakeholders are quickly moving to the next stage of proactive data governance.

The data quality and governance project has been viewed as a huge success and is attracting visibility from senior executives, including the SVP of operations and the CFO, an indication of their commitment to the value of data and its significance as an asset of the company.

Twelve months ago, data governance was less than optimal at Smith & Nephew. Today, thanks to the data quality project and the IT/business collaboration, there is a revolution under way in how the company thinks about data and the way it is used for competitive advantage.

CHAPTER SEVEN

Optimize the Whole

There is an old saying in the systems field, "If you divide a cow in two, you do not get two small cows." Systems have integrity. While they are composed of elements, they are not defined by their elements but by how all these elements function as a whole.

Joe Stenzel[1]

"You get what you measure." This mantra has helped many organizations embark on metrics-driven management initiatives to improve themselves. Certainly measurement is an important part of Lean thinking, but it is just as critical not to choose the wrong measurements or use them in the wrong way since they can harm the overall objective. Stenzel provides a cautionary note: "In a mechanical system one-dimensional quantities can both describe results and enable one to control the linear process that produces those results. In a living system quantities can only describe results, but cannot explain or enable one to control the multidimensional interactions and feedback loops of the process that produces the results."[2]

Large, complex integrated environments behave more like living systems than mechanical systems, so we need to be thoughtful in choosing the right

---

1. Joe Stenzel, *Lean Accounting: Best Practices for Sustainable Integration* (John Wiley & Sons, 2007), Kindle loc. 171–73.
2. Ibid., Kindle loc. 628–30.

metrics and to use them in a way that optimizes the whole rather than the parts. In other words, we need to be careful not to read too much into certain metrics that may measure the composite impact of many activities by many individuals at different points in time. This chapter will explore these thoughts and suggest some ways to measure Lean progress to motivate and align an organization's journey toward successful Lean Integration.

Optimize the Whole Rather than Optimize the Parts

Mary and Tom Poppendieck, in their book *Lean Software Development*, use the analogy of the Tour de France to communicate the concept of "optimizing the whole by sub-optimizing the parts."[3] The objective of the Tour de France is to complete all 21 stages with the lowest cumulative time. In recent years, no one has done this more successfully than Lance Armstrong. He has never won more than 4 of the stages in any year and has usually won fewer. Yet he won the overall Tour de France with the lowest cumulative time seven times in a row. Certainly, one could win the Tour de France by winning all 21 stages of the race. Lance's strategy was not to go out and win each stage each day. Rather, with the objective of achieving the lowest cumulative time over 21 days, he chose to pick his spots, optimizing to push hardest when his performance relative to others would have the most benefit, and saving his energy at other times. He sub-optimized the stages with the objective of optimizing the overall race.

In the IT and business world, we have a tendency to functionally decompose problems into smaller pieces to make complex problems more solvable. Once these problems are decomposed to smaller sizes, we correctly attempt to solve them. The difficulty arises when we lose sight of the fact that we're trying to achieve the best cumulative score over all the problems. We're not trying to optimize to win a single stage, or to solve a single problem. We're trying to optimize the entire value chain.

Typically, piecemeal metrics do not necessarily cause irreparable harm to enterprises. There is often so much inefficiency in many business processes that shoring up a piece of the process has some value and can be done without harming the upstream or downstream steps in the larger process. But

---

3. Mary and Tom Poppendieck, *Lean Software Development: An Agile Toolkit* (Addison-Wesley, 2003), p. 155.

once you've handled the low-hanging fruit, what next? Doing harm is certainly possible.

Let's take a supply chain example and consider how optimizing a part of the process could impact other parts:

- **Optimize customer fill rate:** If optimizing how often we're able to deliver on time to our customers is our primary objective, what could happen to our inventory levels and to sales revenue?
- **Optimize revenue:** If we optimize revenue, costs could go up because "we get what we measure." For example, we might carry more inventory or use expedited delivery methods in order to increase sales, which would increase costs.
- **Optimize market share:** If we optimize for market share, what might happen to quality, costs, or longer-term customer satisfaction?
- **Optimize inventory:** And if we reduce inventory to the lowest levels possible, what might happen to our fill-rate metric and customer satisfaction levels?

Of course, businesses do not necessarily optimize only one metric to the exclusion of all others. But for all the work going on in mission-critical data warehouse environments, how many companies have analysts actually performing these kinds of cross-departmental analytics to see the effects of these different metrics on each other, and for different products and customers in different regions?

This is a powerful concept. It is especially powerful for those who have been steeped in business intelligence, whether on the business side or on the IT side. Years of metrics-driven management and focus on providing those metrics can lead to thinking in terms of the smaller picture rather than the bigger picture.

How do you avoid a strategy of trying to win all of the stages of the race? By keeping the overall objective in mind and ensuring that your continuous improvement efforts and measurements are for the greater good for the long term. You need to avoid getting mired down in localized optimization that frequently ends in internal efficiencies that do not add value from the customer's perspective. In other words, you need to understand the big picture of how value is delivered to the customer and work to optimize the overall process, not just one part.

Localized Measurements and Knowledge Workers

When we move out of the supply chain example and into dealing with knowledge workers within the Integration Competency Center, the problem gets more challenging. The actual number of parts of the process is extremely hard to pin down and measure. The amount of uncertainty and change is very high. Certainly, there are parts of the process that can be pinned down and measured, but therein lies the problem. We run the very real risk of sub-optimizing the whole by optimizing what we can actually measure. Frequently the parts we can easily measure are the internal efficiencies of the ICC, not the external successes of the ICC from the perspective of the end customer.

When we say "Optimize the whole by sub-optimizing the parts," some people misunderstand the word *sub-optimizing* to mean "make worse." That is not what we mean. The Nobel Prize winner Herbert Simon coined the word *satisficing*, which may actually be a better word to carry the intent of our meaning. *Satisficing* combines the words *satisfying* and *sufficing*, meaning that in a business environment with imperfect knowledge, incomplete information, yet lots of data and choices, rational decisions are bounded by time, cost, and available good information. So people possess only "bounded rationality" and use "satisficing" to choose the option that will work "well enough" but may not be optimal.[4]

What Is "the Whole"? An Introduction to Value Stream Mapping

The first problem, once the concept of "optimizing the whole" is accepted, is to work on defining what "the whole" is. Once again, it is helpful to see the ICC or Integration Factory as a small business within an enterprise that behaves like a market. "The whole" refers to the customer or, in the case of the ICC, the functions that require integration products and services.

One Lean technique that is widely used to assist this process was introduced in Chapter 2: value stream mapping (VSM). This technique helps analyze how material flows and information flows are used to deliver value to a

---

4. Herbert Simon, *The Sciences of the Artificial* (The MIT Press, 1996).

customer. Usually done on paper or a whiteboard, value stream maps begin when the customer makes a demand of the ICC. They end when the solution to that demand is satisfied, thereby addressing the customer's need. The value stream map is a timeline diagram of the steps that occur between initial request and final delivery.

The objective of Lean Integration is to reduce the lead time by removing non-value-adding activities. When you notice long delays and loop-backs in the flow, a clear picture of *muda* in the process appears. Creating a current-state value stream map and then a future-state value stream map where the non-value-adding activities in the process are incrementally reduced results in a road map for improvement of the ICC.

How to Create a Value Stream Map

A key advantage of value stream maps is that they can be done quickly and are remarkably effective at highlighting the opportunities for improvement. First, choose a process to map and identify the start and end times from the customer's perspective. As an example, if we choose to map the ICC's response to a customer request, we would start the map from when a request is submitted and stop the timeline when the feature is delivered. You would not start the timeline when a feature is approved, because you are looking at value from the customer's point of view, and customers do not care about other requests or how busy the ICC is.

Next, map the different steps in the process, including those performed by external groups or functions, leading to delivery of that feature. Once that is completed, look at how long it takes to get a feature developed or to fill a customer request. Then examine what percentage of that elapsed time is spent actually adding value.

The value of value stream maps is not in their details or their accuracy. The benefit of value stream maps is that they generate insightful discussions about identifying and eliminating waste in a simple and practical manner. Don't try to make the value stream map "perfect" since this is an iterative and continuous improvement process. As long as you end up with a picture that identifies opportunities for improvement by capturing data about each of the process steps, you have a useful diagram. Once you've made the improvements, redraw the value stream with more details to identify the next set of improvement opportunities.

Some Example Value Stream Maps

For this scenario, let's say that a call center manager wants to improve call resolution times and suspects that a small number of customers are generating most of the problem. In order to quantify the problem and identify specific high-volume callers, the manager needs to add "call duration" to the customer call history database in the data warehouse. The scenario starts with a business request to add a data element to a data warehouse, from which we can draw the simple value stream map in Figure 7.1. The map shows the steps from initial request by the business sponsor, approval and prioritization, analysis and design, build, test, and finally deployment. Below the diagram we show where and how the time is spent, noting the time spent performing value-added work and the time spent waiting or reworking issues that are not perceived as adding value from the customer's perspective. Making a calculation of the efficiency percentage of this value stream shows the proportion of value-adding activities to the time spent on non-value-adding activities.

Note the amount of waste that accumulates every time there is either a handoff to another person or team or a review is required before proceeding to the next step. The number in the triangle shows inventory of partially done work accumulating before the next step. Our goal with Lean is to minimize these queues to achieve single-piece flow, or just-in-time, development of value for the customer. The goal is not to achieve maximally efficient use of ICC resources, but rather to achieve the best performance from the customer's perspective, including delivering fast, high-quality solutions that meet the requirements. An efficiency of 1 percent from the customer's perspective is typical of organizations that have been optimizing around silo resource utilization rather than end-to-end overall delivery of value quickly.

As the handoffs and reviews create a lot of queuing, how then does the team eliminate queuing without compromising quality? Many reviews performed by internal groups are rubber-stamp approvals that add little value. A common pattern we have seen is that organizations implement a review step in response to a specific incident, which then becomes institutionalized and over time turns into a mechanical process that no longer adds value. Certainly, checks and balances are important, but they should be done within the flow of the activity rather than as batches. For example, developers may be able to work in pairs to solve problems or could be trained and empowered to make more design decisions. Altering the way handoffs and reviews are done is typically a fruitful way to eliminate waste.

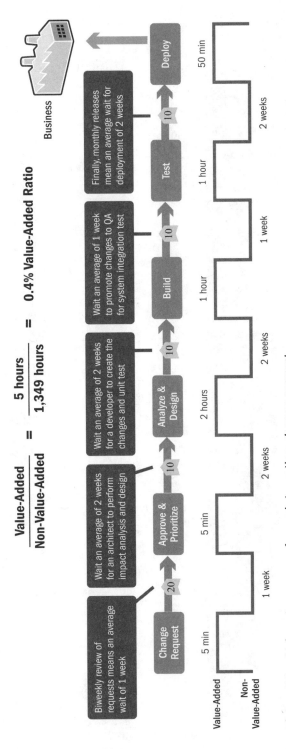

Figure 7.1 Value stream map for an integration change request

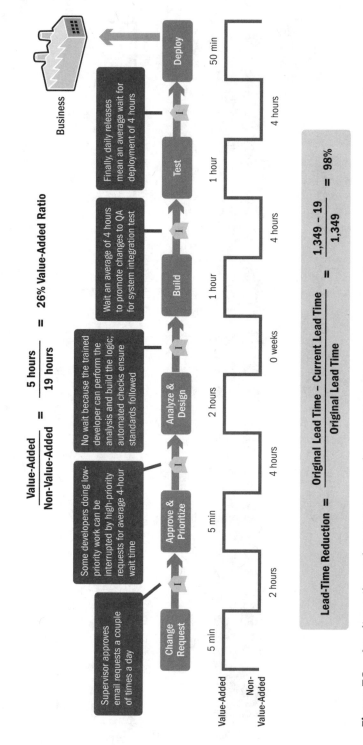

Figure 7.2 An alternative value stream map for an integration change request

Figure 7.2 shows an alternative value stream map for handling a change request without the queuing, work-in-process inventory, and delays that the previous example showed. Keeping a small number of developers interruptible by higher-priority business requests and enabling those developers to make design decisions (because they have been trained on the standards and best practices to an appropriate certification level) can remove some of the inefficiencies. Furthermore, increasing the frequency of deployments and integration testing at the systems level surfaces problems earlier and allows the release of changes for the business more frequently. This may not seem as efficient from the ICC's perspective, but this is where process improvements using automation around deployment and system testing (see Chapter 9) help to make this possible.

Value stream maps should be created for larger projects as well. Identify the most common products and services that you are delivering to your customers, and create value stream maps when you want to improve productivity or reduce lead times. These value stream maps force a focus on the end-to-end process, "the whole."

Selecting Metrics to Optimize the Whole

"The whole" must truly be defined from the customer's point of view. Unfortunately, in many Lean organizations, the definition of the value chain sometimes conceptually ends at the shipping dock rather than at acceptance and use by the customer. "The whole" includes everything from managing expectations through training, delivery, and effective communications throughout the process.

James Womack, in *Lean Solutions*, describes this *consumer*-oriented thinking as Lean Consumption.[5] Womack articulates six principles that describe Lean Consumption. Think of these principles as if you were a business person who requires products or services from the ICC:

1. Solve my problem completely.
2. Don't waste my time.
3. Provide exactly what I want.
4. Deliver value where I want it.

---

5. James P. Womack and Daniel T. Jones, *Lean Solutions: How Companies and Customers Can Create Value and Wealth Together* (Simon & Schuster UK Ltd., 2005).

5. Supply value when I want it.

6. Reduce the number of decisions I must make to solve my problems.

None of these principles describes the specific attributes or performance of the products themselves. Typically, the product is usually not the problem. We are trying to understand the consumer's total experience in order to understand the total cost of the situation (including waste) from the perspective of the customer.

If the ICC meets these requirements for the business, the ICC has won the Tour de France. On the other hand, the desires of the business can be at odds with the capabilities, resources, and temporary priorities of the ICC at a given point in time. Keep in mind that these Lean Consumption principles take years of work in the same way that Lean Integration principles are a process of continuous improvement over many years. Lance Armstrong didn't win the Tour de France when he was 11 years old. It took years of individual and team training and continuous improvement before he began even entertaining the possibility of winning the Tour de France. But from the age of 11, he held out that goal as the objective that drove and aligned his efforts.

In order to make progress toward "optimizing the whole," it is useful to look at "sub-optimizing the parts" that will have the highest returns. Continuing the Lance Armstrong analogy, where are the mountain stages where it is most useful to apply your efforts to win, because this will give the highest returns toward optimizing the whole?

If we describe our goal as creating products and services for our customers that are *better*, *faster*, and *cheaper* that the alternatives they have, we need some end-to-end customer and operational metrics. Following are a few of the key metrics that should be considered for a customer or operational scorecard.

Metrics for Getting Better (Improving Quality)

Customer survey question(s):	What percentage of my problem was solved? Did I get what I wanted?
Key customer metric:	Net Promoter Score
Internal ICC metrics:	First-time-through percentage Reuse of objects/data/services

We want to continually improve integration quality from the customer perspective as well as the ICC's perspective. The Net Promoter Score is a common measure of customer satisfaction; it could be an internal metric for an integration team that has multiple internal customers or could refer to the external customer of the enterprise. This measure was developed by Fred Reichheld in *The Ultimate Question*,[6] which describes a formula for subtracting the number of dissatisfied customers from delighted customers to end up with a net score. The beauty of this method is that you need to ask only one question on the customer survey, such as "On a scale of 1 to 10, to what degree would you be willing to recommend our product/service to your coworkers and friends?" Scores of 9 and 10 are considered promoters, a score of 6 to 8 is neutral, and 1 through 5 are detractors. The formula for calculating the Net Promoter Score over a given time period is

NPS = (Number of promoters − Number of detractors)/Total number of surveys

Achieving an NPS of more than 10 percent is quite difficult. World-class organizations are generally in the 30 to 40 percent range.

The ICC also needs to continually improve its internal processes to do things "better," and two of these metrics are "first-time-through percentage," which tracks the number of projects or requests that are completed successfully without rework, as well as a metric that tracks how successfully the ICC is reusing work to assist completing new work faster and with improved modularity. The team should note every time a defect is found in the integration test cycle that requires a bug fix and subsequent retest resulting in rework. Based on this definition, many ICCs will find a very low first-time-through percentage until their "build quality in" practices (Chapter 10) begin to mature.

Metrics for Getting Faster

Customer survey question:	Did I get my problem solved in a timely manner?
Key customer metric:	Lead time and lead-time reduction
	On-time delivery percentage
Internal ICC metrics:	Value-added ratio

Lead time tracks the elapsed time from the start of a project (usually defined as the time when it was requested by the customer) until its deployment or

---

6. Fred Reichheld, *The Ultimate Question: Driving Good Profits and True Growth* (Harvard Business School Press, 2006).

completion. Lead-time reduction is an improvement metric that could be used to show improvements over time on a trend-line chart. The formulas are

Value-added ratio = Value-added time/Lead time

Lead time = Value-added time + Non-value-added time

Lead-time reduction = (Original lead time − Current lead time)/Original lead time

Tracking how fast the ICC is delivering to its customers is obviously critical to keeping customers happy. If you are tracking the "promise date" of projects or requests, tracking the percentage of tasks that are completed on schedule is a great customer metric. Note that it is most important to deliver "on schedule," not early or late. Making promises and keeping promises are essential aspects of establishing credibility for the ICC.

Internally, operational metrics around how efficiently the ICC is operating from the perspective of "value-added" time to the "lead time" of the project or customer request helps to track the relative improvements in waste elimination. The value-added ratio is calculated as value-added time divided by lead time.

Metrics for Getting Cheaper (Lower Cost)

Customer survey question(s):	Did you waste my time?
	Did I get value for money?
Key customer metric:	Average cost/Unit of output
Internal ICC metrics:	Deliverables/Labor hour

Tracking monetary information on integration is difficult if you don't do a thorough job of keeping track of time or resource consumption for discrete activities. Adding this type of data collection typically imposes its own cost, but it is nonetheless essential in order to drive continuous improvements and to demonstrate the results to your customers. Detailed activity-based cost data is also critical feedback for job costing and estimating tools. It may seem counterintuitive, but the more detailed and specific your data is, the easier it becomes to create estimating tools that produce relatively high-level costs for generic classifications of integrations such as easy, medium, and complex. The end result of knowing how much integration processes cost is worth the time spent. Please refer to Chapter 11 on Financial Management for a more complete discussion of the concepts of chargeback models and on the financial aspects of thinking of the ICC as a business.

One could also take these metrics down to more specific, lower-level measures that are literally driven off of the metadata repository. For instance, it would be nice to tie the survey responses and project names or customer requests to the project names or object names in the actual metadata repository. This way, many of the aspects of the integration process can be tracked and analyzed over time and from multiple points of view, thereby providing a richer fact base for the development of business cases and continuous improvement.

To a certain extent, this chapter is the metrics-oriented chapter. In the Financial Management chapter, we'll talk about approaches to chargeback models and some more theory behind treating the ICC as a business. But in this chapter, we have focused on what it means to follow the Lean principle of keeping "the whole" in mind and sub-optimizing (or satisficing) the parts.

As with all of the concepts in this book, we are not dictating precise practices for you to follow. Rather, we are outlining core principles to help you understand how you might serve your customers better with the purpose of helping the business to be more successful. You determine your own practices by understanding your own organization and thoughtfully considering your best approach.

CHAPTER EIGHT

Plan for Change and Mass-Customize

Reality is merely an illusion, albeit a very persistent one.
Albert Einstein

Planning for change is a principle based on the underlying premise that it is impossible to precisely specify or control all requirements for an integrated enterprise information system. As this quote from Einstein suggests, when we think we have a clear specification for an application interface, it may not be reality. Factors that contribute to the hopelessness of realizing precise and complete specifications include

- Unpredictability of complex dependent software systems with millions of permutations and combinations of internal states
- Constantly evolving needs because of business, market, or technology changes
- Limits of human cognitive ability to translate qualitative needs and tacit knowledge into quantitative and codified requirements

In other words, while small, well-defined components can be precisely specified and engineered, the overall end-to-end integrated system must be viewed as an evolving system that is not entirely predictable and in a constant state of flux. In systems theory this is referred to as *emergence*, and it is the way complex systems arise out of many relatively simple interactions. In other words, the enterprise system-of-systems that emerges from years of individual integration efforts is considered a "complex" system that is continuously changing. It is for this reason that the principle of planning for change is critically important.

Most Lean practices refer to this principle as "defer commitment" or "decide as late as possible." The general idea is to wait as long as possible until you have the maximum amount of information before making a decision that would be hard (or expensive) to reverse. Agile software development makes effective use of the plan-for-change principle in the practice of constantly refactoring components as new requirements emerge. A concept that is closely tied to this idea is mass customization, which includes practices such as designing products that are based on standard components and are customized, assembled, or configured for specific users; reducing setup times to enable small batch sizes (even batches of one); and leveraging the supply chain to achieve just-in-time inventory management. In the realm of integration, it is more relevant to think of this principle as planning for change, and there are several key techniques that can be leveraged to enable it.

This chapter describes several methods for enabling constant change and how to apply the concept of mass customization in an integration context. We then describe how these concepts can be applied in an Integration Factory scenario to deliver increased business value.

The chapter closes with a case study of a company in the health industry that used integration design patterns so that it could quickly create, or re-create, integration points to meet the needs of a dynamic and constantly changing business and technical environment.

Techniques for Enabling Constant Change

This section describes three practices that help to turn the principle of planning for change into concrete actionable activities:

1. **Break dependencies** so that one element of the system or process can change without affecting others.
2. **Make decisions reversible** in order to adjust quickly when new requirements or dependencies emerge.
3. **Maintain "live" documentation** to facilitate reuse and streamline planning.

Break Dependencies

The concept of breaking dependencies between components to enable each component (or system) to change without impacting others is not new or difficult to grasp; an example would be upgrading to a larger flat-screen monitor or an ergonomic keyboard for your desktop PC without changing other components. In practice it is difficult to implement at the enterprise system-of-systems level and requires three complementary techniques.

The first technique is an architectural approach to **differentiating the whole**. By this we mean that you need to create a holistic picture, or model, of the enterprise and its system-of-systems, and to divide it into logical components that minimize information exchanges between components. To relate this to a simple example in the non-IT world, a car consists of a number of systems including the power-train, electrical, cooling, steering, and braking systems, to name a few. Each system in turn consists of multiple components, many of which have interchangeable parts. One of the reasons this works is because car designers have clearly separated the functions of each system to minimize the number of interaction points with other systems and to optimize the overall economy and efficiency of the vehicle. There is nothing physically preventing the cooling system from generating electrical power for its own use, but if each system did this, it would create inefficiencies due to redundant electrical systems as well as limit the flexibility of interchangeable parts.

A number of architectural methodologies can accomplish modeling the enterprise to identify logical components that minimize information exchanges between components. A detailed discussion of them is beyond the scope of this book, but we do have some general advice. The best approaches for integrating information systems are those that use a top-down, service-based orientation for modeling the enterprise at the operations level. From a business perspective, the relationships between external entities, such as suppliers, channels, or customers, are described based on the services that flow between them. Services include provision of goods, selling of goods, transport, installation, and repair. A service-oriented approach is useful at this level for identifying cross-enterprise collaboration opportunities, evaluating in-sourcing and outsourcing scenarios, and assessing integration synergies with merger and acquisition candidates.

Just as companies provide services to each other in a supply chain, so too do internal functions within a corporation provide services to each other.

Both the internal and external services can be modeled at a business level, independent of technology implementation details, including a description of the information exchanges associated with the flow of services. In other words, functional groups within an organization are linked by the services they provide to each other. This is a powerful way to view the internal capabilities of the enterprise, since the services focus on the purpose and results of the function. A service-oriented approach provides clean delineations for designing process interfaces, establishing meaningful performance metrics, and aligning functional accountability throughout the organization.

The end result of a good architectural approach is a model of the business that is ME&C—mutually exclusive and comprehensive. The model is comprehensive in that it describes the entire business entity, and it is mutually exclusive in that each of the elements of the model is maximally differentiated and nonoverlapping. Furthermore, the best models also map the functions to the data that is created and used by each function. This matrix of "service functions" mapped to "information subjects" provides a crisp and unambiguous definition of business services. This is essential for an architectural view that describes a hierarchy of systems that are maximally differentiated and minimally dependent.

While the *model* of the business may be ME&C, the underlying systems and data as implemented are not structured as nicely. Business processes and data are duplicated in different systems, and the lines of responsibility can be challenging to determine and relate across systems. While creating a model of the business is challenging, it is more challenging to take the next step of mapping that model to the underlying data as implemented.

It is important to use a logical abstraction layer for this mapping of data to the logical business model, because you do not want to have numerous groups independently reinventing the mapping on a continuous basis, which would be extremely wasteful and error-prone. Knowing the difficulty of the enterprise complexity of data and creating abstractions that can break traditional dependencies, and doing this in a governed, architected way that assumes continual change, means having an information or data service model layer that the business service layer uses for its operations.

The second technique for breaking dependencies is to implement **loose coupling** strategies between dependent components. Loose coupling is one of the most highly valued architectural properties—especially at the enterprise level—and is described more fully in Chapter 16, Modeling Management.

Despite the earlier caution about applying middleware blindly, middleware technologies are indeed one of the most effective ways to achieve loose coupling and thereby help to break dependencies between applications.

One of best examples of loosely coupled systems can be seen in the typical supply chain. B2B interactions are made possible by industry standard data definitions, common protocols, and tools that handle process orchestration as a separate layer from the business applications. In other words, B2B interactions often include at least three types of middleware abstractions: canonical data models, common transport, and an orchestration layer. Loose coupling within an enterprise between vendor-purchased applications can be achieved with similar middleware infrastructures.

The third technique for breaking dependencies is to implement a **modular integration process**. Lean manufacturing uses the concept of "cells," where each cell is a somewhat autonomous unit of work in an end-to-end manufacturing process. For example, some integration projects may require a data quality assessment while other projects may not. Furthermore, for some projects the data quality assessment might need to be performed during the requirements phase, whereas for other projects it might be needed during the design phase or the testing phase. To maintain this flexibility, the data quality assessment should be structured as an activity "cell" with similar inputs and outputs that can be applied at various points in a project process.

For this cell-like approach to work, it is critical that the information needs of the cell be well defined and that all the information be passed along when its work is initiated. If some information is missing, the cell will be blocked from completing its work or its output will be low quality. In traditional waterfall project methodologies this was referred to as "over the wall" and is often viewed as an antipattern because of the dysfunctions that are created if it is not done correctly, for example, when analysts pass their requirements over the wall to designers, who then pass designs over the wall to developers, who then pass coded software over the wall to testers.

A modular project process will fail if cells are forced to deliver their output on a fixed date or schedule even if they don't have sufficient resources or information to complete the work properly. The resultant deliverable that is passed over the wall is therefore of low quality. After several handoffs in succession, the quality of the output will have deteriorated to the point of total write-off. The key, therefore, to successful modularization is to pass *all* the information that is needed from one step in the process to another. Clear and consistent documentation standards and a shared metadata repository are key enablers. We will talk about this topic in more detail in Chapter 12, Integration Methodology.

Make Decisions Reversible

The core concept behind making integration decisions reversible is to automate changes as much as possible. First, make it easy to rebuild integrations at the "push of a button" by using metadata-driven automated processes. The reality is that you never build an integration just once. You build it many times—and in fact it is common practice to rebuild an integration a number of times even before the first production deployment since it sometimes isn't until system integration testing that the "real" data definitions and data quality issues appear. So if changing an integration is the norm, why not automate as much of the work as possible to the point where you can quickly re-create a production integration at the push of a button?

For example, let's say you made a design decision to use an EII (enterprise information integration) approach to create composite views of heterogeneous customer account data in real time, only to discover through volume testing that the response time does not meet requirements. The alternative approach is to use a data integration solution with some of the customer account data replicated or cached in order to achieve the performance requirements. Normally this would be a significant design change that would impact the overall project timeline if made late in the implementation cycle. However, if the logical model is location-transparent and the definition of the model hasn't changed, this technology change would be entirely transparent to consuming applications. Furthermore, if the systems of record and data-mapping rules are maintained in a metadata repository, and if the data transformation routines are reusable middleware components, it will be possible to quickly reverse the original design decision, if this is ever desired.

An additional capability is to use metadata-driven automated processes to migrate software changes between environments (development to test to production) and to reverse the changes at the "push of a button" if unintended consequences emerge. This technique provides the benefit of maintaining an audit trail of configuration changes for improved governance of the IT environment. It also enables the capability of implementation changes in production in small increments (small batch sizes).

Maintain "Live" Documentation

Our definition of *live documentation* in the integration domain is "a structured repository that contains current data about data and data processes." In other words, maintain a metadata repository that always shows the current configuration of data sources, data targets, business transformation rules, and information interchange processes. Methods for metadata management are discussed in more detail in Chapter 13, but what we want to address here is why it is important.

An analogy may help to make the point. Do you need the blueprints of a high-rise building after it has been constructed if you never plan to change the building? The short answer is no. Blueprints serve as design documents to help the builders construct a complex structure. Once construction is complete, the design documents are of little use and in fact may be wrong, since it is common for builders to modify the construction to resolve implementation details that the designer didn't think about or didn't specify. The reality for most buildings, however, is that they do change. The changes may be relatively simple, such as upgrading the heating and air-conditioning system, installing a security system, or wiring the building with fiber-optic cables. Or they may be major changes, such as knocking down a wall to create a larger room, adding a swimming pool to the roof, or rebuilding the sewer system that runs under the building. If you don't have blueprints that reflect an accurate model of the building, you have three options before making a significant change: invest the time, money, and expense to re-create the design documents "as built" so that engineers and designers can safely plan the change; make the change and see what happens; or demolish the building and construct a new one.

At the enterprise level, the system-of-systems is constantly changing. In most large enterprises, hardly a day goes by without one or more changes being made to production systems. The count of change tickets documenting production changes typically numbers in the thousands of changes per year for most Fortune 1000 companies. Demolishing and rebuilding are not options for large enterprises because of the massive cost and complexity, not to mention the resulting downtime. Therefore, without current and accurate metadata, organizations are faced with a trade-off: Either perform the expensive and time-consuming process of re-creating an adequate understanding of the current state each time a change needs to be made, or simply make the change and keep your fingers crossed.

There is a compelling business case to be made for maintaining a metadata repository in terms of reducing operational risk, reducing the cost of implementing changes, and increasing the speed with which changes can be made. It is not easy to build a business case for a metadata investment, and it is not easy to implement a metadata strategy. Nonetheless, both are achievable, as we will describe in Chapters 11 and 13, and organizations that have done so have realized tremendous benefits and sustained competitive advantages.

Mass Customization

Mass customization techniques facilitate planning for change in that a given integration becomes more of an assembly process than a custom development effort so it can be completed quickly in response to new or changed requirements.

The benefits of mass customization are all around us. You can order a PC online from Dell with a custom combination of CPU chip, memory capacity, graphics card, hard drive, DVD, and other components, and it shows up on your doorstep within a few days. You can lay out your Yahoo! Web page with whatever news, weather, stocks, and other information suits your needs. Or you can order customized food such as personalized M&M candies, cakes with your picture or logo on them, or custom cereal with just the right mix of ingredients to match your dietary needs.

At its core, mass customization enables a tremendous increase in variety and customization without a corresponding increase in costs. When mass customization is done well, it costs the consumer no more for a customized product than for a mass-produced standard product. Of course, the reason this trend is so strong is that everyone is different; if we can have something that meets our unique needs at a similar cost to a generic product, it becomes an easy decision.

To be clear, mass customization is different from mass production and from continuous improvement. Pine, Victor, and Boynton stated the differences well in their 1993 article:[1]

---

1. B. Joseph Pine II, Bart Victor, and Andrew C. Boynton, "Making Mass Customization Work," *Harvard Business Review* (September–October 1993).

Mass Production

The traditional mass-production company is bureaucratic and hierar-chical. Under close supervision, workers repeat narrowly defined, repe-titious tasks. Result: low-cost, standard goods and services.

Continuous Improvement

In continuous-improvement settings, empowered, cross-functional teams strive constantly to improve processes. Managers are coaches, cheering on communications and unceasing efforts to improve. Result: low-cost, high-quality, standard goods and services.

Mass Customization

Mass customization calls for flexibility and quick responsiveness. In an ever-changing environment, people, processes, units, and technology reconfigure to give customers exactly what they want. Managers coordi-nate independent, capable individuals, and an efficient linkage system is crucial. Result: low-cost, high-quality, customized goods and services.

Mass Customization of Data

Mass customization is a core concept behind SOA, but discipline is still required to execute it effectively. For example, most large IT shops have a common routine for doing customer address cleansing, but it is surprising how many teams within the enterprise don't use it and reinvent their own, which defeats the purpose of a common routine. Part of the solution is to establish an ICC or a central team that is responsible for maintaining and enhancing the shared business objects and reusable components on an ongoing basis.

Mass customization can be applied to the integration domain in two contexts: mass customization of integration components, or mass cus-tomization of data. Mass customization of integration components has many parallels with traditional product manufacturing. The basic idea is to build integration components (standard routines for data extract, data load, transformation, security, encryption, etc.) so that they can quickly be configured and assembled for a specific set of requirements rather than developed from scratch.

The idea of mass-customizing data may not be so intuitive. This may sound radical, but we suggest that organizations should strive to create more, not less, customized data. Actually, it's not that organizations *need* more customized data; what they need is the flexibility to adapt information to meet local needs (e.g., for different functions, divisions, or regions) while still maintaining consistency where it matters—in other words, to accept the reality of variation in data and, rather than fight it, adopt methods that effectively support it.

For example, at a high level of abstraction, the process and supporting data for authorizing a loan for a consumer are quite consistent. Whether you are applying for a credit card, car loan, mortgage, line of credit, or student loan, the types of data that is needed are similar. The lending organization needs information about the borrower, what the money is for, and the borrower's ability to repay the loan, and then the lender can make a calculated decision about whether or not to extend credit. The devil, of course, is in the details. Is the credit request for a large or small amount; for a high-net-worth customer or a minimum-wage worker living from paycheck to paycheck? Is there a secured asset that needs to be appraised? Is the application being processed on the Internet, at a call center, or at a retail outlet? What regulatory rules apply, and should the documents be printed in English, Spanish, or French? These and many other factors drive the need for tremendous variation. Rather than trying to eliminate the variation, we should embrace the natural diversity that exists in a typical complex business setting.

This is where the concept of mass customization comes in. We need a way to facilitate a huge, even limitless, variety of data without losing the ability to consolidate it or make sense of it. Having the appropriate metadata and modeling management capabilities is crucial for understanding the relationship between the enterprise model for data and the "customized for local needs" variants necessary to run the business.

The industry has been fighting variation in data for decades with efforts such as enterprise data models, which attempt to impose consistent definitions on data for the entire enterprise, or ERP solutions, which mandate a "one size fits all" strategy on business processes. The industry has also tried to standardize data through industry organizations that have worked hard to homogenize subject domains as diverse as financial transactions, shipping orders, invoices, health insurance claims, and credit ratings. The prevailing practice that is embedded in most IT methodologies is the notion that all data should be consistent. It is our view that this is a flawed premise that fights the natural order of things, and that instead we should find ways to efficiently customize data and effectively manage the inherent variations.

To visualize this, the first thing you need to do is step out of your silo and look at the big picture: the information needs of the enterprise where "one version of the truth" is the *product* that is being produced. The information needs at this level are relatively modest when compared to the information needs of the front-line operations of all functions combined. Most enterprises have in the order of 10 to 20 subject areas, and each subject area has around 50 to 100 business objects. Simple objects might only have 10 attributes, and complex objects could have 100 or more attributes. While it is a nontrivial effort to create an enterprise-level subject area model, it is an order of magnitude (10 times or 100 times) simpler than the detailed operational-level data model that captures all the as-built variations.

From an enterprise information perspective, what you should see is a relatively stable and consistent picture of the business, and the information to support the enterprise should also be correspondingly stable. From an operational perspective, what you should see is a highly customized and dynamic collection of data and processes that allows each function to adapt quickly to meet day-to-day needs and to do so without having to rely on complex coordination with other functions.

To achieve this apparent paradox between the stable enterprise view and the flexible operational view, we need four elements: an enterprise-level subject area model, an architectural approach that separates business functions into logical groups, a middleware layer that decouples the enterprise view from the operational view, and an integration function that sustains the links between operational functions and the enterprise view. We will come back to each of the elements in specific sections of Part III of the book, but for now we will stay at a high level with the following definition:

To mass-customize data: Implement a *consistent definition* of information that can be applied across all business functions *independent of the technology implementation* and based on a *sustainable integration infrastructure* that separates the *consolidated enterprise view* from the many departmental and functional systems in a *loosely coupled fashion*. This is quite a mouthful, so we will elaborate on the highlighted terms.

For a *consistent definition of the business* and its information needs you must start from a top-down perspective. This is hard work but it needs to be done. There may be a tendency to take a bottom-up approach since it seems easier to abstract away details from an existing system or data model, but this presents several problems. First, the existing systems may not be ideal implementations in terms of their support of the business operations and won't be consistent if they came from different vendors or were architected by different groups. A bottom-up approach tends to impose current-state implementation details on the business, which may limit future flexibility. As a result, you end up "paving the cow path" by institutionalizing an inappropriate implementation at the enterprise level. Furthermore, a bottom-up approach may be overwhelming and take on the characteristics of a "boiling the ocean" problem.

It is also critical to describe the business functions and data *independent of implementation details*, which also argues for a top-down approach. In other words, you need to describe *what* the business does and not *how* it does it. The *how* part of the picture is a black hole of implementation details; it is a never-ending job to try to model it all.

A *sustainable integration infrastructure* demands two key elements. First is the recognition that integration systems are distinct entities from business systems and should be viewed as applications in their own right and not simply as extensions or appendages of business applications. The second key point is that the infrastructure must be sustainable, which means it needs to be managed in a disciplined fashion with periodic investments to continuously optimize it.

The core purpose of the integration infrastructure is to maintain a *consolidated enterprise view* by collecting and synchronizing data across operational systems, and to do so in a *loosely coupled fashion* so that individual components can change with little or no impact on other components. This concept is not new, but it is not automatic or trivial. Mature ICC groups have demonstrated that it is both achievable and beneficial, but it does require an enterprise strategy and a dedicated organization to execute it.

Mass Customization of Integration Logic Using Assembly Lines

One of the most logical approaches to mass-customizing data is to use mass customization of integration logic to deliver that data. Within different types of process or data integration projects, there are different styles of data movement, transformation, and delivery. Assembly lines can create this integration logic, customized for the data in question, but following a relatively small number of identifiable patterns that are common to that type of project.

For instance, in a data warehousing project, many different pieces of integration (sometimes called "mappings" or "services") are necessary to keep the data warehouse populated with clean, current, and historically correct data. Some integration logic is necessary to update master data or dimension tables, and some integration logic is necessary to update transaction data or fact tables. For a dimension table, whether it is a product dimension or a customer dimension table, the integration logic follows a common pattern. The specifics of the field names and the particular field transformations may be unique, but the way that the keys are generated, the way that date fields are updated, and the way that history is maintained are common from one dimension table to another. For a typical warehouse project, there may be hundreds of mappings or services, but there are typically a dozen or so different patterns into which those mappings or services fall.

In specific data warehousing terms, patterns that are readily known in the industry include these:

- Slowly changing dimensions (SCDs)
- Audit dimensions
- Incremental fact tables
- Accumulating fact tables
- Bridge tables
- Staging area tables
- Aggregate tables
- Incrementally updating aggregate tables
- Change-data-captured real-time fact tables
- Change-data-captured real-time dimension tables

Other types of integration projects would introduce different patterns. For data warehousing, while this list is not exhaustive, it provides a representative idea of different patterns of integration logic.

An optimal approach to implementing patterns (or mass customization) in a factory context is to have the integration architect capture the pattern in a tool that allows the generation of many mappings that follow this pattern. In other words, once the template or pattern is defined, a wizard is automatically generated from it. Individual analysts or developers fill out this wizard or set of forms, specifying the unique characteristics of each mapping or service.

This pattern-oriented approach to integration represents a purpose-built instantiation of model-driven architecture, as applied specifically to the field of integration services, mappings, or flows. We cleanly separate *what* a mapping is supposed to do from *how* the mapping gets executed, so that we can more specifically tune the *how* based upon the style of integration we are building.

The big win comes with the second project of that type. In the new project, most if not all of the patterns may be reused. The first project benefited from the use of patterns, but subsequent projects benefit even more.

Several organizations have incorporated this approach. One of us (Lyle) and his ICC team, responsible for building the Informatica Analytic Applications in 2000–2003, built a tool set with about a dozen data warehousing mapping patterns. Once the data warehouse target data model was designed, an Excel spreadsheet for the appropriate pattern was identified. The developers would fill out the spreadsheet, defining how SAP or Oracle application fields mapped to the target fields within the data warehouse, and a proprietary tool would read the spreadsheet and generate a robust, real-world mapping that corresponded to the mapping logic specified by the spreadsheet.

The result was elimination of waste not only in the implementation process, but more important in the QA and change management cycles. The details of the different patterns of data warehouse mappings were generalized and hidden from the analysts and developers, so they didn't have to worry about concepts like how to handle SCDs, or how to resolve surrogate keys, or how to properly convert currencies to a global currency, or how to design mappings that took advantage of the best-known system performance approaches. The analysts and developers focused on the core business requirements, reducing wasted energy and variance in the output.

These same concepts are just as valuable when building other styles of integrations besides data warehousing. Master data management projects have their own integration patterns, as do process automation projects. Building and using these patterns so that developers are simply filling out forms or custom wizards is a way to use automation to effectively eliminate waste while still allowing customizations when necessary.

Using these patterns to generate integration logic (mappings, services, or what have you) allows for the automatic incorporation of the best-known approaches for that particular pattern. The person filling in the pattern does *not* have to be an expert in all of the intricacies of how to best build that integration artifact. He or she needs to focus only on the specific data and any unique business rules or cleansing that are unique to that data. Once the form is filled out, the generated object automatically incorporates the best approaches as defined by the continuously improved integration patterns produced by the team over time.

For many ICCs whose members have time to be responsible for only administration and operations, this assembly-line approach is the way to make the ICC, or any integration team, scale to create higher quality and more efficient integration. Quality will be built into the integration logic, reducing variance and defects. Deviation from those standards is both possible and allowed, but having some foundation to start from has tremendous benefits.

Case Study: Using Mass Customization

The integration problems experienced by a North American company in the health industry were typical of most companies in any industry over the past several decades. As the company grew through acquisition and the complexities of its systems became more difficult to manage, the cost of integration continued to grow. Over the years every piece of integration logic was designed and implemented separately by different developers and contractors using a wide variety of technologies, so the quality and maintainability of the integration hairball were costing the company in terms of both money and agility in meeting the needs of the business.

Investing in commercial data integration software was certainly beneficial in bringing these costs down and improving the company's agility, but management saw that there were still difficulties in getting everyone to use the software in the most efficient way. The diverse designs employed by developers and contractors in the ICC meant that not all integration logic was following best practices, and the speed with which projects were undertaken was making design reviews very difficult; in many cases design reviews were happening too late in the process to make proper corrections.

The integration architect for this company acutely felt the pain this was causing the organization in terms of performance, rework, and responsiveness to the business. Even though he and a couple of others had deep knowledge of the best way to solve various integration problems, getting everybody to follow their lead was a never-ending challenge because of the constant need to respond quickly to the needs of the business.

What Did the Company Do to Solve This Problem?

The integration architect realized that every integration project consisted of mappings or services whose logic followed one of several largely repeatable patterns. If the general mapping patterns were designed at the beginning of a project, and if there was a way to generate the "bones" of the mappings so that they established the structure and rules of the patterns, developers could flesh out the details within that best-practices mapping structure.

So he and his team used a commercial utility that allowed them to design a pattern in Visio and then generate different mappings that followed that pattern in the data integration software. These patterns could be discussed, reviewed, and understood by the architects and developers (and the business, when appropriate), and they served as useful documentation for all members of the project team. The developers used the utility to generate the starting points for the mappings they needed to implement the elements of the integration project. Finally, the developers customized these mappings with the specific data integration logic required for the integration task in question.

The trick was to identify and build the patterns in the early stages of the project, before developers dove into building integration logic. Then, because mappings could be regenerated, changes to designs could be implemented in a fraction of the time they would normally take without this approach.

What Were the Benefits of This Approach?

The benefits of automating the generation of mappings that follow best-practices patterns were many. The most obvious benefit was the speed of implementation and ability to respond to change. The integration architect said that the patterns usually took the developers about 80 percent of the way toward a completed mapping, greatly reducing the amount of time needed to implement the mappings. This saved hundreds of hours of labor over the course of a project.

But he pointed out that some of the other advantages were perhaps even more important than productivity improvements. The developers found that by consistently following their methodologies and processes as enforced by the automated mapping generator, they vastly improved the quality and performance of the integration logic they were constructing. Developers gained valuable architectural awareness and design experience about the best way to construct integration logic. And contractors, who come into ICC teams with a wide variety of previous experience and integration sophistication, were able to quickly conform to the best practices of the ICC team once they started following the automated approaches.

The ICC is now able to perform integration projects with a responsiveness and quality more like those of ICCs of a much greater size. Using patterns and process automation in this way maximizes the efficiency of the ICC, leverages the best knowledge of the right way to do things, and ensures that as much as possible those best practices are followed consistently. By focusing on the patterns, or assembly lines, the ICC changed its integration shop from a collection of individual craftspeople into a super example of Lean Integration at work.

CHAPTER NINE

Automate Processes and Deliver Fast

Don't make anything until it is needed; then make it very quickly.
James P. Womack and Daniel T. Jones[1]

In the previous chapter, Plan for Change and Mass-Customize, and in Chapter 3, The Integration Factory, we introduced process automation and fast delivery by showing how assembly lines can be used to mass-customize integration components, and how decoupling systems allows organizations to change and grow with more agility. Across the entire landscape and life cycle of integration, there are significant opportunities for eliminating much waste and delivering fast by using a mantra we'll describe as "Use the computer!"

What do we mean by this? Doesn't all integration, by definition, use the computer? While integration "code" certainly runs on computers to integrate data, applications, or systems, the design, development, testing, deployment, and change of this integration "code" are usually done manually by visually inspecting code, data, metadata, and documentation. Human

---

1. James P. Womack and Daniel T. Jones, *Lean Thinking: Banish Waste and Create Wealth in Your Corporation* (Simon & Schuster, 1996), p. 71.

eyeballs examine flat files, database tables, message structures, and interface definitions to understand the structure, content, and semantics of data. Knowledgeable developers laboriously trace the dependencies between data models, business processes, services, and applications to understand how integration solutions should be designed or changed. Administrators collect lists of objects that need to be moved from development to test to production, manually ensuring that these lists contain the proper dependent objects and that impact analysis was validated properly.

As the integration hairball grows in an enterprise, the complexity escalates beyond what humans can reasonably be expected to efficiently and effectively maintain. The vast majority of organizations are using computers simply as a code-editing interface, generating individual integration artifacts and thereby increasing the size of the hairball without improving their ability to manage it more effectively going forward.

So when we say, "Use the computer!" we mean harness computer power not just for business systems, but also for integration systems. And also not just to develop integration code, but to automate the flow of materials and flow of information in the development process. In its ultimate form this transforms manual custom development into rapid implementation of self-service integrated solutions.

The chapter closes with a case study from Wells Fargo Bank that illustrates how computers can be used to automate and speed up a business process that was traditionally viewed as manual and paper-intensive. The Lean principles that were used to generate the impressive benefits and continuous improvements for the bank are the same ones that can be applied to the integration process under the direction of an Integration Competency Center.

Pitfalls of Automation—Building "Stuff" Faster

Automation can be an extremely powerful tool, helping people accomplish repetitive tasks more quickly. However, an important Lean principle that we discussed in depth in Chapter 7 is to ensure that we are optimizing the whole end-to-end process, rather than optimizing individual parts of the process that may not add any value to the end-to-end process.

For instance, there is little or no benefit to making an activity that is not on the critical path of a project more efficient. To use a restaurant example, it would not make sense to invest in a handheld device for waiters to transmit orders wirelessly to the kitchen if the food preparation step is the bottleneck. In fact, this could make the problem worse by giving customers the expectation of rapid delivery while the electronic order simply sits in a queue. By the same token, providing software developers with tools to more rapidly generate Web service interfaces could make problems worse if the primary reason for slow implementation times is integration testing; more Web service interfaces could actually lengthen the integration testing time frame.

There are many examples of exciting software technologies that IT can use to more efficiently meet the needs of the business. These software solutions automate much of the work that IT departments have traditionally done using low-level tools, allowing people to quickly craft new solutions to a variety of different problems. Did you ever notice how most vendors demo their products? Most demos (and therefore most vendor tool requirements) seem to be driven by the creation of new things, not the maintenance of existing complex things in the context of their real-world environment. Do you need nice-looking reports with drill-down capabilities? Easy. Drag and drop using this nifty business intelligence tool, and within seconds you've got a good-looking report. Do you need a new service? Easy, use the service creation environment and at the push of a button craft another that meets the requirements.

It's so easy. Perhaps it's too easy.

The reality is that IT organizations spend five to ten times the cost of the original development effort on integrating and maintaining components, so the true objective should be to "build for change." Let's look at some of these examples in more detail.

SOA—Generating the Next-Generation Hairball More Rapidly?

Taking an SOA approach when creating composite applications or other business solutions solves a raft of historical problems. The holy grail of software engineering has been to compose applications out of easily reusable building blocks that can be modified, mixed, and matched quickly. "Business agility" is touted as the key benefit, and certainly SOA can be an enabler to achieving this goal, but it can also be a detractor.

Besides the oft-cited problem of difficulties in achieving business/IT alignment, early experiences of organizations that adopted SOA showed that a newer, more modern service-oriented hairball was growing, and the rate of growth was far faster than that of the original hairball that they hoped SOA would eradicate.

Furthermore, because one of the benefits of SOA is decoupling the services from the underlying applications, the hairball is more abstract and harder to detangle. The registries and tools in place have been constructed primarily to assist service consumers, the people seeing the SOA iceberg above the waterline. Tools to assist the service providers in maintaining the growing hairball below the waterline are mostly missing. For instance, if data semantics in a source application change, how do the service providers know what services are affected? The explosion in Java code development for data access within these services and the abstraction from the service interfaces result in more complex dependencies that are poorly understood and more difficult to detangle than before. Reducing point-to-point interfaces is a desirable goal, but it needs to be done with an understanding of the end-to-end problems over the long term; otherwise a new problem develops that marginalizes the benefits.

Were Business Intelligence Environments Better before Drag and Drop?

With business intelligence (BI) tools, all too quickly the user community creates an enormous bucket of reports with tremendous duplication and waste. This report morass makes it challenging for users to find what they need. Certainly some great examples with high information content and good layout exist, but it is hard for users to find the gems amid the rocks.

Making it easy to create reports should be a good thing. But there's something to be said for the days when it was so difficult to create an enterprise information management system that requirements and business thinking had to be deeply understood before solutions were constructed. In the most successful examples, actual "analytic applications" were built, rather than buckets of reports. Certainly, those analytic applications were difficult to construct and modify, but deep business understanding was built into them, effectively incorporating what was inside the heads of the most valuable SMEs, and they were constructed in such a way that other business users became nearly as knowledgeable. Commercial examples of these applications include budgeting and forecasting applications, anti-money-laundering applications, and fraud detection applications.

Industry Data Models—Too Much of a Good Thing?

Here's a different example where "building faster" may turn out to have short-term benefits but higher long-term costs. Some organizations buy industry data models to jump-start their enterprise data model initiative. The vendors of these models sell the inbuilt domain expertise and how they've considered so many details and industry vertical permutations through their vast experience. These vendors also humbly state that they can't fully know your business, so you should expect to have to change or extend perhaps 40 percent of the model.

What those vendors don't say is that their models actually contain perhaps 400 to 600 percent of the requirements that you need. In other words, you need to learn how to use the pieces of their models that are relevant to your business, modify things that they missed, and hide the rest. This means you need to navigate through and understand an overly complex model to find the components you need, strip away what is not of interest, and customize and extend the parts you do need.

Then comes the hard part. How do you actually use the model to meet the needs of your business? That is typically something that you have to discover for yourself, and it is where the majority of time is spent. Because you didn't go through the effort of understanding the requirements for the model in the first place, you're missing the understanding of how the business can and should use the model.

The point of this example is that automation or purchased content needs to be evaluated within the context of the big-picture end-to-end process and life cycle. Buying a solution to part of a problem may solve that problem but create a more expensive problem or not provide as much value as originally anticipated.

Once again, the point is *not* to optimize a part if it results in sub-optimizing the whole. The goal is to optimize the whole by having a clear understanding of the end-to-end value chain. We clearly want to achieve agile and iterative (small batch size) changes, and powerful tools can help, but they need to be harnessed and governed in a way that supports the entire value chain from the perspective of the end customer.

Delivering Fast

There is an old project manager saying that goes "Do you want it fast, good, or cheap? Pick any two." That trade-off may be true for custom point solutions, but it is not true for integration development if you approach it as a repeatable process. Some organizations have reduced their integration costs by a factor of ten while also delivering rapidly and with consistently high quality. The secret to achieving this amazing result is to focus on time.

A funny thing happens when you speed up the development of integrations using sustainable Lean thinking—costs drop and quality improves. This may seem counterintuitive since speed is often equated with throwing more people at a problem to get it done faster, which drives up cost. Another common misperception is that speed means rushing, which causes mistakes and reduces quality, thereby driving up cost because of errors and rework. If you are stuck in a paradigm where each integration is a custom solution and your processes are reliant on manual labor, the result will most likely be higher defects and increased downstream costs. Time-based competition—or using time to differentiate your capabilities—can fight the old paradigm.

Time-based competition[2] (TBC) is a time-compressing operational strategy. Time is emphasized throughout organizational processes as the main aspect of accomplishing and upholding a competitive edge. The goal is to compress time cycles. As they are reduced, productivity increases and resource potential is released.

The best way to speed up development of integrations is to eliminate wasted activities, reduce delays, and reuse common components. Here are few additional TBC techniques that can improve delivery times.

First, take integration development off the critical path for projects. Each project has a critical path or bottleneck that is the limiting factor in how quickly the end-to-end project can be completed. Integration activities are often on the critical path because of the complexities and uncertainties about how all the pieces work together. This doesn't need to be the case if you clearly understand the root cause of problems that tend to put integration activities on the critical path, and tackle them head-on. For example, data quality issues between disparate systems are a common cause of significant delays during integration testing. Not understanding the dependencies and relationships between systems leads to delays in the project. The next section will discuss some approaches to solving these issues, helping to take integration development off the critical path for projects.

Second, implement a variable staffing model and develop processes to rapidly ramp up new staff. Supply and demand mismatch is another common

---

2. George Stalk, "Time—The Next Source of Competitive Advantage," *Harvard Business Review*, no. 4 (July–August 1988).

root cause of delays. For example, if you have a fixed number of integration staff to support new project development, some of them may be idle at times when the demand is low, while at other times demand may peak at well above the planned staffing level. If you have 10 staff members and the demand jumps to 15 for a period of several months, there are only a few options available:

1. Get all the work done with 10 people by cutting some corners and reducing quality. This is not sustainable since reduced quality will come back to haunt you as increased maintenance costs or reduced future flexibility.
2. Make the 10 people work overtime and weekends. This is not sustainable since you could end up "burning out" the staff.
3. Delay some of the projects until demand drops. This is not sustainable since you are in fact chasing away your customers (telling them that you can help them in two months when they need help now is the same as not helping them).
4. Bring on additional staff. This is the only sustainable model, but only if you can ramp up the staff quickly and then ramp them down when the volume of work subsides. The keys to making this happen include having well-defined standard processes, good documentation, and a long-term relationship with consulting firms or some other pool of resources.

Third, focus on driving down end-to-end project cycle time and not on optimizing each activity. This may seem counterintuitive, but optimizing the whole requires sub-optimizing the parts. For example, the task of creating user documentation is most efficient when all the software is developed. However, this can significantly delay the overall project if the documentation is prepared in a sequential manner. The overall project timeline can be reduced if the documentation effort is started early (even in the requirements phase), despite the fact that some of it will need to be rewritten to reflect the changes that take place in the design and development phases. But if all functional groups that support a project are motivated to reduce the total cycle time rather than focusing on the efficiency of their teams, the overall improvements can be very significant.

Automating Processes—Using the Computer to Make Complexity Manageable

Rather than simply "build faster," you can harness the power of the computer to eliminate the real bottlenecks that slow projects up. Start by identifying the slowness and waste that result from excessive complexity, and use the computer to automate the tedious, error-prone, and laborious aspects of integration. Previous chapters discussed how mass customization and planning for change automate common development processes, creating assembly lines that leverage the patterns to eliminate development waste and variation in integrations.

But there are more opportunities for waste elimination. Our investigations into dozens of companies' different integration projects revealed that significant time is spent understanding and documenting data, applications, and systems, as well as understanding and documenting dependencies and version histories, because so many of these tasks are manual efforts. If ICCs had the full power of the computer to search, analyze, and drive integration life cycles to assist people in an automated fashion, developers, architects, and analysts could be significantly more productive in solving integration problems.

Using Data Profiling to Eliminate Project Waste

Integration project overruns frequently occur because data issues surface late in the project cycle. Rather than being uncovered as early as possible in the planning and estimation stages of integration projects, data issues usually surface once testing is performed in earnest, well down the project path. At this point, changes are expensive and project timelines are at risk.

In most integration projects, manual examination of data is done in order to understand the kinds of code and logic required to deliver or integrate the data. Frequently this kind of manual examination doesn't find many of the issues because the process is haphazard, looks only at sandbox data, or is dependent upon the experience and approach of the individual integration developer. Additionally, the developers performing these tests are not the analysts who are most knowledgeable about the data. In many cases, the integration developers would not notice a problem with the data if they saw one because they do not have the business and semantic knowledge of the data that a data analyst on the business side has.

Data profiling is a useful software utility that "uses the computer" to process vast quantities of data, finding and documenting the patterns and anomalies so that analysts and integration developers can work together to construct the best logic to deal with the data. It is good to understand where data is missing, inconsistent, or wrong as early in a project as possible in order to prevent rework and even longer delays later. Additionally, documenting the semantic meaning of data is helpful, not just for the task at hand, but for future analysts or developers who will need to make changes to integrations when the business changes down the road.

Understanding the characteristics of information in ERP systems, mainframes, message queues, database applications, complex flat files, and XML documents is a critical component of integrating this information with other information. Because of the incredibly vast quantity of information out there, cataloging this knowledge for current and future consumption is time well spent.

To really harness the power of data profiling, tagging and categorizing data are also important. Constructing a business glossary that provides a common language between business and IT can help to solve communication issues between these teams. This also helps search and find operations to organize and classify the data within the integration systems for better management and governance. Data-profiling attributes are simply additional metadata attached to data structures.

Testing Automation

The process of developing test plans and test cases is an area where QA developers have typically tested systems manually. The most mature ICCs create regression test harnesses and use the computer to test the before and after images of data to ensure that integration logic is operating as designed.

In scheduled or batch integration scenarios, tests are built that sum or analyze the target data and compare that to the source data to ensure that the number of records, the sum of the results, and other data characteristics tie together properly. Comparing large data sets and summing and aggregating large amounts of information are things that computers do really well. Unfortunately, we see developers doing all too much manual querying of source and target data during testing phases. These queries are typically not put into an automated test harness for continual testing, which is yet another waste.

Similarly, with real-time integration, testing typically doesn't cover all the different scenarios that can occur because data profiling wasn't used to uncover many of the different potential variants and outliers that can (and inevitably will) occur. Using the computer (through data profiling) to help identify and construct the test cases is a powerful way to ensure that test coverage is sufficient to deliver the desired integration quality.

Deployment and Change Management Automation

Other areas where automation can reduce manual activities are change management and integration deployment. Release management of changes to production systems often requires understanding a highly complex combination of dependencies that can be difficult to manage, slow, and error-prone if done manually. In particular, many times the person doing the deployment is different from the person doing the development or the testing, and therefore information often gets lost in translation.

The goal is actually to catch dependency problems long before deployments to other systems take place. For instance, in cases where a new integration requires a minor change to a shared object, it is optimal to know the impact of this change on all other places this shared object is used. You don't want to wait until the object is promoted to production to learn about the dependency and detailed impact of the change. If metadata is used properly, "the computer" can figure this out and visualize it for the developer and administrator early in the process.

Figure 9.1 shows the realities of change management in a retail organization. Some retailers generate over 50 percent of their sales volume during the last two months of the year, between Thanksgiving and Christmas. Yet this

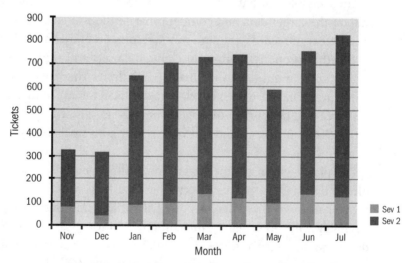

Figure 9.1   Integration problem tickets closed by month

graph shows that the organization's systems suffered half as many errors during November and December (the first two bars on the chart) as they did during the other ten months. The reason for this is that during times of system stress, end of year, or other critical business periods, changes to operational systems are drastically reduced. The fact that few changes were allowed from mid-October through the end of the year meant that the systems would run with far fewer outages than normal. Seemingly, the only good change is no change.

Certainly, outages are not just the result of problems with the deployment and change management processes. Many times they are caused by inadequate testing of code or other issues. Introducing a repeatable automated process that reduces the chances for the introduction of human error means that files or pieces of the release don't get lost in translation.

Life-Cycle Automation

One of the innovative uses of automation is noticing that what is usually thought to be unstructured information actually has a structure. For instance, design specifications and requirements documents typically follow a common structure or template. Tools are available that allow the relatively simple ability to translate .pdf, Word, Excel, email, and other "semistructured" documents into structured metamodels for import into a metadata repository. (In the Wells Fargo case study at the end of this chapter, similar automation was used to translate "unstructured" business documents into automatically consumable digital documents in an analogous fashion.) Bringing project documentation into the metadata repository and tying it to the actual integration implementation artifacts is a powerful way to create "live" documentation for your integration environment.

Normally, all of these unstructured documents are stored on file servers, in SharePoint, or somewhere away from the actual integration artifacts. Developers probably don't spend as much time as they should on documentation for this very reason—the documentation is disconnected from the actual artifacts, so the chances that someone will find and read the relevant document in a timely manner are pretty low. Developers know this. If documentation is directly connected with the artifacts of the integration system, more time would be spent on quality documentation, thereby cutting waste for the inevitable future changes to come.

Understanding the requirements, specifications, test plans, and other documentation that surrounds the integration artifacts greatly speeds the time to change those artifacts when the business changes. This is a critical aspect of the Integration Factory. Making the necessary changes to integration interfaces, services, mappings, and so on is a constant challenge because of the complexity of the logic, the usual lack of up-to-date documentation, and the lack of anything to link metadata across different vendor products to create an end-to-end view. Having an active metadata repository that links the data models, the integration logic, and the applications models to show the impact and lineage of integration points is a critical part of using the computer to change what is otherwise a wasteful, manual, error-prone process into a task that can be done quickly and accurately. We will talk more about this in Chapter 13 on Metadata Management.

Furthermore, being able to bring together the business and IT is critical for making integration projects of all types work more effectively. It is a truism to say that the business knows the data, but IT is responsible for the systems behind the data. They must work together to be successful and to truly support the concept of the Integration Factory.

Case Study: Automating Processes at Wells Fargo Home Mortgage

This case study concerns Wells Fargo Home Mortgage's Post Closing business group and how a new imaging and IT automation initiative implemented in 2002 improved processes.

The role of Post Closing is to make Wells Fargo Home Mortgage loans salable to investors, serviceable with high-quality data for customers, and insurable with risk partners. This is a critical aspect of the mortgage business and incredibly complex when considering the regulatory rules to be followed, management of financial risks, handling of paper, and sustained collaboration with multiple organizations. Of course, this all needs to happen while making the process look seamless to customers, keeping their loan and personal information secure, and retrieving it quickly when needed.

Take a moment to consider the processing of paper alone. In 2002 the Post Closing group was handling 2 million mortgages per year. Each case file contained dozens of documents, typically totaling 100 to 150 individual pieces of paper. If stacked one sheet on top of the next, one year's worth of the paper required in processing would stack 23 miles high or, laid end-to-end, reach around the world 1½ times, or fill 95 offices (wall to wall and floor to ceiling of a 160-square-foot room). Each year the required paperwork grew larger, and all the paper needed to be copied, distributed, inventoried, archived, and then remain retrievable for years.

The Business Challenge

In 2001 the Post Closing group identified a problem: Mortgage volume was increasing rapidly. While growing the business was desirable, the core processes were heavily paper-based and highly manual and did not scale well. The group consisted of around 1,300 staff, and it was not practical to continue expanding into new buildings each year to house all the people and paper resulting from acquisitions and the refinancing boom that was going on at the time.

The manual processes were also expensive and slow and had increased potential for human error. The average cost per loan (CPL) was not decreasing with increased volumes as would be expected, and the cycle times were too long. One of the key metrics related to processing efficiency and business risk is the number of uninsured loans after 60 days, that is, the number of loans that cannot be insured by FHA or packaged and sold as securities because a required closing document was missing or a post-closing activity was outstanding. At the end of 2001, there were more than 19,000 mortgages in the "Uninsured >60 days" category.

The Solution

A decision was made to invest in technology that would enable the elimination of paper and that would automate many of the manual loan review processes. From an architectural perspective, there were several key elements that enabled the outcome (see the second part of this case study in Chapter 15).

The first was to turn all the paper into information. It wasn't sufficient to simply make an electronic image of the paper documents; all the key information on the documents also needed to be converted to structured data that would allow a computer to process it. This not only required a large investment in imaging technology, but it was a paradigm shift in how people would have to work.

The decision to use a straight-through processing (STP) approach was contrary to the prevailing practice in the industry. The question was whether to make the workflow capability the heart of the system or make the process state engine the heart of the system and have it process everything that didn't require human attention. The common practice at the time was to mimic paper-handling processes and keep people in control of each step, gradually automating selected activities over time. The program leaders believed that STP would be more effective, but it was not an easy decision. In the end, the team moved forward with this approach and developed a customized process state engine.

Another key architectural principle was that each business process include a mechanism for handling exceptions. The Post Closing business was very focused on reducing costs and increasing throughput. The team identified the easiest and highest-volume transactions first. This meant that nonautomated steps still needed to be handled by a person in conjunction with performance support tools.

Having a manual work queue was also useful for handling unplanned exceptions. If a message or document arrived that the system couldn't process, rather than send an error message back, it would place it in a work queue for a person to review. This is a powerful technique in an environment of loosely coupled systems where it is virtually impossible to anticipate and/or test every possible permutation and combination of process states. Furthermore, in cases where the requirements or design was not complete, the exception messages tended to fill up the manual work queues quickly, making them visible and allowing the team to resolve the issues.

Perhaps surprisingly, there was little resistance from staff to the business process changes. As soon as people saw what was possible with the new solution, they embraced the changes and other innovations began to surface throughout the organization. The biggest factors that created an appetite for change included the frustrations of spending a great deal of time chasing paper files, managing a high ratio of temporary staff, and consistently feeling behind in the process.

The Results

The results were impressive. The new process

- Significantly reduced the cost of operations
- Lowered the business risks and the seasonal cycle time and inventory level variation
- Dramatically improved process cycle times, making them more consistent

- Thrilled customers with the rapid turnaround and responsive support
- Improved staff morale and the ability to perform more valued activities
- Built upon Wells Fargo's reputation among government groups as a leader in industry improvements

The CPL was reduced from $61 in early 2002 to $46 in early 2004, equating to a 25 percent reduction. This is extremely impressive for any organization that has the size, scale, and complexity of the Post Closing group. And if $15 per loan doesn't sound like a lot of money, just multiply it by 2 million loans per year.

An example of risk reduction and process improvement is the change in quality and cycle time of insuring government loans. FHA loans must be reviewed by HUD to ensure that they are complete and accurate and meet all requirements. Once all the paperwork for a government loan was complete, it was copied, printed, and sent as a case file to HUD for review. Under the paper-based process, the average time from "ready to send" to "insured by HUD" was 12 days for clean case files. Twenty percent of the case files were rejected because of errors or omissions; these loans required an average of 49 days to become insurable.

Table 9.1   Before and After Metrics for HUD Review of FHA-Insured Loans

	Cycle Time for Clear Loans	Cycle Time for Rejected Loans	Rejected Loans
Manual paper-based approach	12 days	49 days	20%
Image-enabled STP solution	Same day	< 5 days	1%

Once the new system was up and running, the reject rate dropped to 1 percent since the system could automatically check for completeness and accuracy of all the required information before it was sent to HUD. With the elimination of copying, printing, packaging, and mail delays, the cycle time for clean loans was virtually same-day. Many rejected loans could also be resolved as quickly as the same day, and nearly all resolved within five days.

It is important to note that these improvements did not happen overnight and were implemented in several phases. Phase 1 automated most of the New Loan Boarding processes by imaging the relevant loan documents, keying data from the images, and conducting the servicing system comparison from that data. This enabled the paper files to flow more directly to the Government Insuring team. Subsequent phases applied this same approach to the work to insure loans with HUD. The Post Closing group also changed the organizational structure from a caseworker approach to one that split the loan review and deficiency correction activities. Wells Fargo then began working with HUD on eInsuring, helping to implement the same philosophies around STP and EBP (exception-based processing) that had proven effective in the Post Closing operation. After detailed process and risk reviews, the group accepted data-only submissions with follow-up image submission on an exception basis (to support quality audits). This set the foundation for big improvements in insuring performance, which continued in subsequent implementations. The final phase resulted in the biggest drop in rejection rates, from 20 percent or so to less than 1 percent.

Customers also are being more rapidly serviced. For example, the Wells Fargo Home Mortgage group receives a wave of calls each year around income tax time from customers who need copies of their HUD-1 Settlement Statement or other documents that they simply cannot find. If the customers are able to accept email and print their own copies, they can have the documents instantly.

The staff is also happier as they have a better work environment. For example, the New Loan Management department went from a staff of 140 full-time members to 30. The reduction was achieved primarily by terminating contract staff, and the team members who remain are doing more value-added activities.

All of these improvements have combined to create a powerful capability for Wells Fargo.

The Key Lessons Learned

There were several key insights that the Post Closing project team gained:

- Turning paper documents into electronically usable data allowed process improvements to come from several dimensions. The obvious improvements came from the ability to store, search, and transfer documents instantly. However, this alone was not sufficient to justify the investment.
- A less obvious improvement came from the ability to process activities in parallel rather than serially. This benefit enabled Post Closing to drive down insuring risks.

- There were benefits from combining STP and EBP. One of the favorite sayings in the group is "The best image is the one no one ever sees." When an image does need to be seen, the ability to present it to users at the right time, with the right data, in an easy-to-view format, is a tremendous benefit.

An incremental and iterative "test and learn" approach is highly recommended. This project had high-quality people, technology, management support, and an urgent problem. Nevertheless, the team found significant errors in its business analysis and technical designs at several points, some of which in retrospect should have been obvious. The approach of having a broad, flexible architecture, and implementing partial solutions to reap business benefits as quickly as they could be deployed, avoided what could have been an indeterminately long integration test-and-fix period, and an awful lot of rework.

The question remains: Should servicers start with STP or workflow and migrate to the target state? If the end game is for staff to continue to touch most steps in the process and be the gating factor, starting with workflow is appropriate. But if the end game is to automate most of the process steps, making the process state engine the heart of the solution is the first step. This is a paradigm shift that requires a different state of mind, so research indicates it is ideal to begin with this step.

Maintaining the conceptual integrity of the architecture is essential. An initiative of this scale and complexity involves hundreds of people over the life of the program. The team members have their own experiences and knowledge bases, which drive their views of what the "right" technical solution is. As a result, a constant tug-of-war could emerge among project team members to apply different techniques. It is essential to keep the team aligned so that the program can be developed to include a coordinated set of architectural principles and an established delivery team that is responsible for both development and architecture, and to ensure that technical leaders see themselves as business leaders who are responsible for making decisions in the best interests of shareholders and customers.

CHAPTER TEN

Build Quality In

When things go wrong, the cause is almost always inherent in the system, and therefore it is a management problem. Managers who push harder on people to meet deadlines or reduce defects are ignoring the system problem and will usually make things worse. Instead, leaders must envision and institute fundamental changes that address the systemic causes of current problems.

Mary and Tom Poppendieck[1]

You've probably heard the story about the light bulb factory that stopped testing all the bulbs when they figured out how to improve quality to the point where they all worked. This story may be an urban myth, but it makes the point. In a perfect world, testing is waste; just build it right the first time. If all prior steps in a software development cycle were perfect, there wouldn't be a need for testing at all.

However, perfect knowledge, perfect requirements and design, perfect automation and mass customization, perfect team empowerment, and so on are outside the current capabilities and state of technology at the enterprise system-of-systems scale. So we will concede that short test cycles are not waste. The reason organizations perform long test cycles over several months is that they typically find a large number of defects. Most defects occur because of less-than-perfect quality in prior steps, particular requirements definition.

---

1. Mary and Tom Poppendieck, *Implementing Lean Software Development: From Concept to Cash* (Addison-Wesley, 2007), p. 123.

How do you strive for perfect requirements? One way is to simulate and execute the business process during development. If users are required to specify requirements to a level of precision and specificity needed for a business process simulator to function, most issues would be identified early. The problem with most requirements is that users/analysts throw up their hands when they don't know exactly what data or transformations are required, and in the interest of sticking to the project schedule, they write very general requirements and let the developers figure out the details. The developers, of course, don't have the in-depth business knowledge, so they make their best guess using whatever information they have. This ultimately leads to elongated testing cycles where the "real" requirements are discovered.

If every step in a process has high standards and strives to ensure that its output to the next step never has to backtrack to the previous step, we can envision a time when integration testing that today takes months can be reduced to days. This leads to small batch sizes. Large batch sizes and expensive integration testing feed on each other. If integration testing is expensive, the tendency is to make releases as big as possible. If batches are large, there are lots of defects, so organizations feel they need a lot of testing. And so on.

Building quality in is a journey that uses all six of the other Lean principles. The Lean approach to quality is to create a culture in which the objective is to identify problems as early as possible and immediately stop to fix those problems. Lean focuses on doing it right the first time. Rather than finding, accumulating, and fixing issues in batches downstream, Lean means building quality into the flow of development and fixing problems in small batches (ideally batches of one) as soon as they are identified.

With Lean Integration, data quality and integration quality are two distinct areas you should be working to improve. Initiatives to improve quality in these areas are somewhat different, involving different people and approaches. This chapter discusses both of these areas.

The chapter finishes with a case study from a utility company ICC showing how the team drove a data quality program to achieve "one version of the truth."

Two Areas of Quality: Data Quality and Integration Quality

Data quality is a broad umbrella term used to describe the accuracy, completeness, consistency, conformity, and timeliness of a particular piece or set of data.

Numerous books have been written about data quality, so we will only summarize thoughts on this topic in this chapter. We suggest checking out Larry English's book *Information Quality Applied*[2] and Jack E. Olson's book *Data Quality*[3] for more detailed information.

The gigabytes, terabytes, or even petabytes of data held by large organizations should be one of the most valuable assets those organizations have. However, examination of that data shows that its quality can be quite poor. Bad data results in loss of value and measurable business waste. This waste is measured in lost business, shrinking market share, process inefficiencies, or lost revenue from cross-sell or up-sell opportunities missed because of bad or missing customer data. Additionally, newspaper headlines announce the costs of bad data that lead to compliance issues in banking, insurance, health care, and just about every other industry. Incomplete, missing, or inconsistent data has monetary repercussions. Quantifying this cost is not always easy, but companies that do so are able to energize management and staff to improve data quality and thereby reduce risks, improve customer service, and drive bottom-line financial results.

Integration quality refers to the quality of the software services, workflows, processes, transformations, and other logic that control the movement and integration of data. The complexity of the integration dependencies in the system-of-systems and the need to modify them frequently because of the changing needs of the business make maintaining high-quality standards challenging and typically inefficient. Lean approaches that build quality into the integration construction process itself can eliminate a tremendous source of waste in the value stream.

The payload for integration is data. One of the most frequent reasons for cost overruns is finding data quality issues late in the project cycle. Other books have treated data and software or integration quality separately, but we bring these two topics together because if they are not attacked together, it is difficult to remove waste from your ICC.

Lean Integration aligns beautifully with the manufacturing metaphor. Imagine an automobile factory: We can view cars and their parts as being like data in our Integration Factory. Additionally, we can view the assembly lines

---

2. Larry P. English, *Information Quality Applied: Best Practices for Improving Business Information, Processes, and Systems* (Wiley Publishing, 2009).
3. Jack E. Olson, *Data Quality: The Accuracy Dimension* (Morgan Kaufmann, 2003).

as being like the integrations that transport and manipulate the data in the Integration Factory. Quality involves the continual improvement of identifying and fixing the root causes of problems in the cars/parts (the data) as well as the processes or assembly lines (the integration logic and metadata) that move and change these cars/parts.

Quality Evolution and Lean

Quality initiatives swept through the North American and European business communities starting in the late 1970s and 1980s when the superior quality of Japanese cars and electronics became recognized worldwide. At that point, North American and European businesses recognized the work of W. Edwards Deming, who had been working with Japanese industry starting in 1950. They began studying his thinking and adopting his principles and ideas in the quality revolution that followed. Quality initiatives took hold not only in the manufacturing world but in the service and retail industries as well. The benefits of high quality and the costs of poor quality were too great to ignore, and high quality became a business imperative in order to be more competitive.

Overall, one of Deming's most important innovations in management thinking is that mistakes are typically not the fault of the person making them. They are the fault of the system that fails to mistake-proof the places where mistakes can occur. The cause of problems is almost always inherent in the system, and therefore the problem is a management problem. Managers who pressure workers to work harder to produce more or meet deadlines or reduce defects are ignoring the system problem and are often making things worse.

Efforts to reduce the variance in data or integration quality by using the mass customization and automation-of-processes principles discussed in the previous chapters go a long way toward mistake-proofing data and integration systems. Discussions with organizations that use mass customization and automation show that quality benefits actually outweigh productivity benefits, which might come as a surprise to many.

One of the key tenets of Lean thinking is that it is less costly to fix problems immediately than it is to let problems build up and fix them in batches later.

Toyota implemented a system on its assembly lines that allowed individual workers to stop the line the moment that they identified any problem.

This visual and tactile system for immediately identifying problems as they occur and initiating action to do something about them is a completely novel way of attacking quality. At first glance, fixing problems every time they surface seems extremely inefficient. Traditional manufacturers, for instance, would pull bad-quality items out of the line into another area to be reprocessed later. The traditional approach to mass production is to keep the line moving at all times for maximum efficiency.

At Toyota, a worker would pull an "*andon* cord," which notified the team leader of the problem at that station. The team leader would look at the issue, identify the root cause, and decide whether to stop the line or not, depending on the size and severity of the problem. In either case, the objective was to fix the underlying problem as quickly as possible. Do not let problems fester or accumulate. Fix problems immediately. Letting problems linger means more items will be produced with the same problem. Fixing the underlying root cause will result in less waste and higher value for the customer.

As Toyota began implementing its Lean philosophy at plants in North America, an interesting dynamic occurred. North American plant managers who came to Toyota after working for years at American car companies were not stopping the lines when problems occurred. They had to unlearn the goal of keeping the line running at all times. It took time and repeated reinforcement to convince these new plant managers that management supported these stoppages and was willing to live with slightly slower output at first in order to achieve higher quality and higher output later.

The Lean (and agile) objective of working quickly in small batch sizes, fixing most problems as they are discovered, ultimately results in less waste from the perspective of the overall customer value stream.

Data Quality

Data is one of the most important assets in any organization. Data represents the customers, products, transactions, events, outcomes, and results of the enterprise. As data gets older, it usually degrades in quality and therefore depreciates in value. The reasons for data quality degradation are many, but principal causes include human error, process inconsistencies, and system changes that do not address all impacted data dependencies. There is so much data in organizations that most data problems are hidden. Here are some examples:

- A bank holding more in reserve because of concerns over the householding and identity-matching success of its algorithms
- Direct mailings being returned or duplicated because addresses are incomplete or incorrect
- Bad management decisions because analysis is made using incomplete or incorrect data
- Costs incurred because manufacturing processes are done improperly but are masked by incomplete or inconsistent data

Business Drivers and Objectives

Poor data quality costs businesses money and leads to breakdowns in the supply chain, poor business decisions, and inferior customer relationship management. Defective data also hampers efforts to meet regulatory compliance responsibilities. More subtly, inconsistent data quality implementations at different levels of the organization—even when individually the data quality is good—impose additional costs as organizational data is migrated to more centralized locations.

Data quality encompasses more than finding and fixing missing or inaccurate data. It means delivering comprehensive, consistent, relevant, fit-for-purpose, and timely data to the business, regardless of its application, use, or origin.

Ensuring data quality is a challenge for most organizations—partly because they may not be fully aware of their own data quality levels. Without this information, they cannot know the full business impact of poor or unknown data quality or how to begin addressing it. While moving this information to the enterprise level increases the challenge, it also greatly increases the potential return as duplication of effort may be reduced, the hidden costs of data inconsistencies may be avoided, and a holistic understanding of enterprise data quality issues may be realized.

The most common business drivers for data quality initiatives are

- Growing revenue
- Lowering costs
- Ensuring compliance
- Mergers and acquisitions (M&A)
- Partnering and outsourcing

Beyond data quality, we need to govern all aspects of data as an asset that requires the joint collaboration of IT and the business. We define *data governance* as "the processes, policies, standards, quality, consistency, auditability, and security of data in a company or institution." The following sections examine the business drivers in more detail to understand the integral role data governance can play in furthering these business drivers by "building quality in" as part of a sustainable practice rather than reacting to discrete events.

Growing Revenue

A top-priority goal for almost any business is to grow revenue, and one of the effective ways to do so is to increase cross-sell and up-sell rates and improve retention among existing customers. To do so, organizations require a broad and deep understanding of their existing customers. They need a "single view of the customer" in order to be able to provide superior service and to better target campaigns and offers based upon a specific customer's needs.

Customer data is often scattered across dozens or even hundreds of different business systems. To resolve these data issues, companies must address the underlying organizational, process, and technical issues related to the data. Data governance provides the framework for building quality in by addressing complex issues such as improving data quality and developing a single view of the customer at an enterprise level.

Lowering Costs

One of the important ways organizations can reduce costs and increase operational efficiency is to automate business processes. For example, organizations may automate their procurement processes to lower purchasing and administration costs. While business process automation increases efficiency, problems with enterprise data prevent companies from capitalizing on the full potential of operational efficiency initiatives. Streamlining business processes across multiple financial, human resource, sales, and other business systems requires that the structure and meaning of data be reconciled across those systems—a task that has often been an afterthought in operational efficiency initiatives.

The need to lower costs is driving projects such as supplier or product master data management that enable companies to streamline core business processes (e.g., inventory and supply chain management) by rationalizing, cleansing, and sharing key master data elements. Data governance plays a critical role in the success of such projects, providing a structure for addressing the organizational, policy, and process issues around data.

Ensuring Compliance

Virtually every business today is required to comply with a number of external regulations as well as with internal corporate governance policies designed to increase transparency and prevent corporate malfeasance and fraud. To ensure compliance with regulations such as Sarbanes-Oxley (SOX), Basel II, the U.S. Patriot Act, the U.S. Health Insurance Portability and Accountability Act (HIPAA), and with internal policies and controls, companies must streamline the collection of reporting data. For many regulations they must also document the sources of the data being reported, certify its accuracy, and implement specific governance policies. Complying with these regulations and policies can be a burden.

Data governance is an essential foundation for ensuring compliance. It establishes the rigorous data standards, policies, and processes that are required by regulations and corporate governance policies, and it helps to automate compliance-related tasks (while lowering costs). It also helps to ensure auditability and accountability for the data.

Mergers and Acquisitions

With M&A activity, organizations are faced with the need to rationalize and reconcile the IT environments from merged or acquired entities. Typically these IT environments have very different systems, data models, and business processes. Post-M&A, IT organizations are often pressed to meet very tight timelines for integration. The goal is to accelerate the promised synergies from the merger, in the form of both cost reductions from eliminating redundancies and revenue growth from increased cross-selling.

The process of migrating and consolidating the data after a merger or acquisition is a huge task—one that is often underestimated. IT organizations must deal with unknown systems, resolve quality issues, and provide detailed documentation of how the information has been merged. The task involves much more than technical integration. Not only must IT organizations reconcile different data definitions and models, but processes must be put in place to ensure alignment of the various entities. A data governance framework provides significant value in managing the organizational and technical complexities of M&A consolidation and accelerating positive business results.

Partnering and Outsourcing

Another broad market trend is the increasing use of partners and outsourcers to manage parts of the value chain. Organizations are focusing on core competencies and handing off non-core functions and processes to partners and outsourcing providers. Here are some examples:

- High-tech equipment companies rely on contract manufacturers for production.
- Manufacturers turn to UPS and FedEx for logistics and warehouse management.
- Pharmaceutical companies rely on third-party clinical trials management firms.
- IT departments outsource application development and network management.
- HR groups outsource administrative functions such as payroll or benefits management.

As business processes and IT systems shift to outside providers, the data associated with those processes and systems is relocated outside the boundaries of the organization. Organizations must ensure that the data is correctly migrated to the outside provider. The data must be complete and accurate, and it has to be restructured to work in the third-party system. It is important to note that although the data has been moved to a third party, it remains a core asset of the organization. Even though it sits outside the firewall, the organization cannot relinquish visibility into and control over that data. A data governance framework is critical to managing data that is fragmented across the extended value chain, especially when it comes to defining the standards and processes for interaction and collaboration with external partners and outsourcers.

Ideas for Where to Start and How to Prioritize

We just outlined some of the business drivers for institutionalizing data quality, but with the inventory of existing quality problems, how does one prioritize what data to correct and what to ignore?

First off, as we've already said, Lean thinking means fixing problems when they are identified. An organization may have many data quality problems that are not formally identified or may be covered up by manual processes so that they are not visible to senior management. Business priorities drive data quality priorities. Don't try to resolve data quality problems if you can't develop a fact-based justification to do so. While this seems obvious, it is important to keep in mind.

That being said, what can be done to be proactive about improving the quality of data that will benefit the business? One technique that many organizations have used is to identify, define, and track the quality of the "golden elements" that drive the business. These are the business terms, metrics, or database fields that the business feels are most critical for efficient operations and solid business decisions.

Typically, it is useful to limit the number of golden elements to 50 or so, and then group these elements into subject areas or categories. Obviously, there are tens of thousands of potentially important data elements, and different sectors of the business will have their own lists, but the key concept when getting started is to pare the list down to several dozen to keep this problem manageable, as we demonstrated in the Smith & Nephew case study in Chapter 6.

But even limiting the elements or subject areas typically does not help to prioritize the quality problems fully enough to make the problem manageable. There can be millions of customers, hundreds of thousands of SKUs, or tens of millions of orders. For that reason it is necessary to tie information about problem records to the importance of those records (How much business have we done with that customer? How many places do we use that part? Is that order information recent and sizable?) in order to focus on fixing the important records in the midst of the totality of records that have problems.

Stop the Line: Using Andon and Visual Management

At Lean manufacturing companies, *andon* lights are used to "stop the line" when problems are identified. Any individual on the line can "pull a cord" that causes that station's number to light up on a board. This immediately notifies the team leader, who helps to fix the root cause of the problem. This low-tech communication system is useful in a manufacturing environment to bring real-time attention to quality issues.

The corollary to this for integration is the data quality scorecard or dashboard. As data problems are identified by business rules against the data records of the golden elements, the magnitude of these problems is visually highlighted on a computerized data quality dashboard for business owners to see. On these scorecards, users can click into the dashboard to either fix the underlying problems or work with IT either to determine a root cause to be fixed or to validate the data upstream.

Creating a scorecard that highlights quality issues is extremely effective at involving the business in the data quality improvement process. This dashboard or scorecard of the golden elements not only engages business managers in the process of fixing the underlying data, but it also creates friendly competition in the process. No business unit wishes to have lower quality scores than other business units. Using friendly competition is helpful in motivating the business to get involved in playing its critical role in data quality improvement.

But the scorecard is not just for scoring and motivation; it is also intended to keep front-line staff and business users focused on what is most important. As we mentioned, the number of potential problems that the business could be asked to help fix is literally limitless. Therefore, having a scorecard helps keep IT and the business aligned and focused on the same things.

Identify Problems as Early as Possible

A common cause of cost overruns in integration projects is identifying data quality problems too late in the project cycle. The best way to resolve this is to profile the characteristics of the data early in the life cycle of every integration project. Dealing with data quality problems or with complex matching and joining problems is extremely time-consuming. Therefore, including this task early in the schedule will set expectations properly. Frequently, when we have seen projects run late because of data issues that were discovered in the integration testing phase or user acceptance testing phase, and we asked whether the data had been analyzed up front, the answer was "No, not really." Profiling data late in the project cycle results in a tremendous amount of rework and wasted time and effort.

As data is profiled, rules are uncovered, anomalies are discovered, and patterns emerge. Do not waste the profiling opportunity to begin documenting what is discovered during this early stage before the project gets under way.

Make Business Involvement Simple

For all the vast amounts of data that exist, computers can be brought to the rescue for only certain parts of the problem. For example, matching algorithms, address cleansing, and so forth can eliminate a tremendous amount of waste and do certain repetitive things more accurately than humans. Because these types of quality issues are so frequent and so time-consuming, it is important to bring automation to bear to improve quality.

On the other hand, fixing other quality issues requires a business analyst's eyes and insights. Frequently, data records that do not pass quality controls are copied to files that IT puts into spreadsheets for the business to fix. Manual approaches like this, while hardly ideal, can get the job done but are quite difficult to manage in complex projects with large amounts of bad data.

A leaner approach is to create a simple Web-based user interface where the business users can fix data problems and/or consolidate potentially matching records. Connected to the visual management or dashboard user interface, this approach is designed to get each business user to participate in the data quality improvement process simply and easily. Not only can the business user alter problem data directly in a staging area, but governance of this process is improved because IT and/or other business users have the ability to audit the changes prior to updating the production systems.

There are massive numbers of data issues in virtually all large enterprises. Priorities must be established, data must be examined, rules for determining good versus bad data must be set, and then the process of fixing the high-priority data records must be streamlined and made as easy as possible. The Lean approach to data quality means automating the collaboration between business and IT, using visual management, automating workflow, using automated algorithms, and identifying and fixing data quality problems as early as possible. Data quality has a tendency to degrade over time in a similar fashion to the natural tendency toward entropy in nature. Unless forces are brought to bear on improving data, data quality will get worse. Data quality does *not* improve on its own.

Integration Quality

Integration quality, as we have said, refers to the quality of the software services, workflows, processes, transformations, and other logic that control the movement and integration of data. While much has been written about improving quality in the software development life cycle, we will focus on approaches to building quality into integration code in ways that eliminate significant waste in the integration process.

When we discuss *code* in the integration space, we mean all software, business rules, and systems required to access, transform, cleanse, and move data to and from business applications and users. This includes Web services, integration mappings, SQL, Java, COBOL, stored procedures, and the plethora of other code that is written, either by hand or with graphical and metadata-driven integration platforms. This code represents the integration points between applications in the enterprise system-of-systems. Building quality into the development and continual change of this code goes a long way toward eliminating waste.

The Five *Ss*: Create a Workspace Suitable for Visual Control

When Japanese companies adopted Lean production, one of the tools they used was to clean up their environments so that problems would be more visually identifiable. They developed what they called "5S programs" that comprised activities for eliminating wastes that contribute to errors and injuries. Here are the five *Ss*:

1. **Sort** (*seiri*): Separate needed items from unneeded items. Throw away the unneeded items.
2. **Straighten** (*seiton*): Arrange and identify items for ease of use and visual accountability: "A place for everything and everything in its place."
3. **Shine** (*seiso*): Cleaning the environment is an effective form of inspection that reveals problems that could hurt quality or future failures.
4. **Standardize** (*seiketsu*): Create the processes to maintain and monitor the first three *Ss*.
5. **Sustain** (*shitsuke*): Make the previous four *Ss* a habit. Develop the discipline to make this an ongoing process of self-improvement.

What Japanese companies found was that without these cleanup procedures, waste accumulates over the years and covers up the underlying problems. The more these wastes accumulate, the more difficult they are to clean up in the future and the more likely they are to hide current or potential problems.

This is even more important in the integration environment. How much of the integration hairball is waste because of redundant and duplicate data or integration points, and how much is waste because no one is using the integration anymore? With the rapid growth in complexity of the IT environment, constantly cleaning and refactoring it is a crucial exercise that can promote higher quality in several ways. First, a clean virtual environment can increase pride in the workplace; developers and administrators are less likely to foul the system if they find an environment where visually all items have their place and everything looks tidy and understandable. Second, developers will be able to more quickly understand the environment, allowing them to learn and be productive more quickly. And most important, excess code bloat and complexity can be removed, making the entire environment more understandable and supportable over time.

The five *Ss* can be applied to the virtual world of software by making the integration environment clean and organized, stripping unnecessary complexity from systems, and allowing people to manage the environment more efficiently.

1. **Sort:** Sort through the services, business rules, mappings, workflows, adapters, queues, parameter files, and other objects to identify those that were never deployed or are no longer used. A general rule of thumb is that 25 to 50 percent of the integration infrastructure in most Global 2000 companies is waste (unless the organization has already applied a rigorous simplification initiative). As part of this process, create queries or reports that can be rerun in the future to continually maintain the freshness of the environment by identifying the deadwood easily.

2. **Straighten:** Are the items organized into projects, folders, or categories, or tagged in a way that will allow them to be easily found by the people who need them? In particular, in the integration space, it is highly useful to organize the same objects in multiple ways. For instance, sometimes it is useful to see objects organized by project. Other times it might be useful to see things organized by the system or subject that they access. And at still other times you may want to see code organized by the business function that is relevant to that code. In other words, some kind of tagging or flexible organization capability, as well as a powerful search and metadata reporting capability, is extremely useful in being able to flexibly organize objects so that they can be found and interpreted easily.

3. **Shine:** Shining the integration environment can mean resolving test case failures and improving the test coverage. Improving operational performance, resolving outstanding defects, and enhancing monitoring and

error-logging features of integration objects are further examples of shining.

4. **Standardize:** Create a series of reports that are run on a schedule to identify items that do not follow the standards or are the deadwood in your environment. Implement continuous improvement activities to refactor existing integration components that do not conform to standards.

5. **Sustain:** Create a process where users are excited to think of new reports or queries to ferret out other problems on a regular basis.

Defining and Enforcing Standards

Standardized work is one of the most powerful countermeasures to quality problems. By limiting variance and promoting best practices, standards help integration developers "get things right the first time." Standards help to improve predictability, in that different developers will solve similar problems in similar ways. Here are some examples of standards in an integration environment:

- Standard approach to tool choices for integration projects
- Standard processes for the integration development life cycle
- Naming conventions
- Canonical data models
- Object organizing standards (folder structures, categories, tags, etc.)
- Use of integration patterns and common data definitions wherever possible
- Deployment and configuration management processes
- Security standards

The recommended way to promote standards is to make them easy to find, understand, and use. To some degree it is possible to force (push) people to use standards, but a more effective and sustainable approach is to pull everyone to the standards by making them easy to follow. Many organizations maintain these standards prominently on the ICC Web site or make them available from the Help area of the different integration tools in order to keep the information close at hand for the people who need it, where they need it.

As part of defining standards, you must also define how to measure compliance. For example, you could create queries against the integration environment that deliver reports on the number of items that don't conform to the standards with the ability to drill into those numbers to find the offending items. Running these reports on a daily basis against the development metadata is an important part of monitoring whether people are adhering to the standards and limiting the variation, complexity, and waste of the integration environment.

Some developers see standards as rules that restrict their creativity. One of the best ways that organizations have found to overcome this concern is to keep these standards undergoing continuous improvement with the involvement and input of all the developers and architects. Most developers don't mind the concept of standards if they participated in their evolution, or if they know about the standards before they do their work. Usually, developers balk at following standards when the standards dictate a way of doing things that is different from either what they are used to or what they think is most efficient. Whatever the reason, going back to the team empowerment principles provides the best foundation for getting developers on board.

Code Reviews

One of the most common refrains we hear from ICC managers is that their team is always behind in reviewing the integration code of the different project groups. In other words, there is a huge inventory of yet-to-be-reviewed integration code. In order to fix this problem, think Lean. Think "flow" rather than "batch." Batching up lots of code for a seemingly more efficient review process creates the major obstacle of finding the time for team members to participate in heavyweight batch review sessions, causing review inventory to back up even further.

To change the approach from batch to flow, we suggest following a "pairing" approach throughout the development process. Pair developers so that they are learning, reviewing, and problem-solving each other's code. Building this into the flow of the integration development process is significantly more efficient and workable than the traditional code review approach. Even when a pair is geographically separated by distance and time zones, viewing review as a constant process rather than a periodic process helps to keep review inventories low and to keep developers on task.

Another benefit of mass customization and automation is the familiarity of the integration logic for review. Leveraging configurable reusable objects means that the core of the service or mapping or data flow will be familiar— only the specifics that deal with the data peculiarities will be different. This is where the time should be devoted in any event. The efficiency of the review process can be significantly enhanced by following other Lean principles as well. This improves quality and makes the review process smoother and more effective.

Automation of Quality Testing

Automation can provide tremendous efficiencies in the testing of integration code. Traditionally, this has been an extremely manual process, involving writing SQL or visually examining before and after data to ensure that the logic is working properly. In the Web services area, utilities for testing individual services with test messages have been in use for a number of years. When large, complex integrations involving data from multiple systems must be tested, the lack of testing automation makes validation extremely time-consuming and error-prone.

However, this situation has been changing, and we are entering a new era of software maturity. As we said in Chapter 9, this is a perfect time to "use the computer." Some start-up companies have begun to create products that address this area. These tools work by allowing the QA engineer to define the before and after data tests against the before and after data images and automatically highlight the anomalies. This approach is somewhat similar to data profiling, except that it compares the data sets in a way that uses the computer to mine lots of data rather than requiring a human to find the defects in the integration code.

For instance, keys can be compared across large data sets to ensure that they were either generated or resolved properly. Automated tests can identify orphan records, duplicate records, and missing records. Certainly, these are the kinds of checks that QA engineers have been manually creating for years, but the ability to automatically add these to a regression test harness as the tests are being developed, and then to re-execute these tests on periodic schedules in the future, takes the QA environment to the next level of maturity.

What frequently happens when integration projects fall behind is that testing becomes a manual process rather than a more automated process. To be Lean and to work both more efficiently and more effectively, turning human manual testing into automated testing early in the process enables flow. The breakthrough with these new software approaches is that it is faster to perform testing in this automated query-and-comparison environment, while automatically constructing the regression test suite. The end result is that you are able to make changes in small batch sizes and flow them to production with often up to 90 percent reduction in lead times.

Make Quality Issues Visual

In addition to the five Ss, another practice we can learn from the Lean principle of "building quality in" is visual control. Many integration environments have used dashboards to show the behavior of the *operational* integration environment. Earlier in this chapter we wrote about how many companies have used scorecards to track and improve data quality. Organizations should use the same *andon* approach to improving integration quality as well. Display the summary of the reports that track waste in integration artifacts on an integration quality dashboard. What objects are not following standards? What objects are performing most poorly? As with data quality, one of the best ways to get people involved in the continual improvement process is to make the important process metrics visible.

As has been demonstrated by many data warehousing projects, significant numbers of data quality problems don't surface until people actually look at large amounts of data. Similarly, metadata quality problems don't surface until metadata is made visible. In the same way, standards issues don't surface until nonstandard objects are made visible.

Visual controls are yet another action that organizations can take to tame the integration hairball and transform it into a well-managed and efficient integration system.

Case Study: Building Quality In at a Utility Company ICC

With over 18,000 employees across approximately eight states, Good Energy (our made-up name to disguise the source) is a large power company in the United States Midwest, offering a diverse mix of energy- and power-generating resources, including nuclear, coal-fired, oil- and natural-gas-fired, and hydroelectric power plants. The company supplies and delivers energy to 4 million U.S. customers and also has operations in South America.

Good Energy began considering a change in how to achieve "one version of the truth" in 2005. Up to that point, data was integrated across the company in a variety of ways without a consistent approach. The enterprise data integration challenges caused a number of issues for the company, including

- High cost of integration due to a lack of standardization on enterprise class tools
- High cost of IT maintenance due to project silos producing a high degree of variety
- Difficulty integrating systems from acquired organizations
- Inconsistent data models leading to a lack of a "single view" of transactional data
- Reporting models tied to source systems that made changes to such systems very difficult
- Poor data quality in terms of consistency and accuracy across functional areas

As a result of Good Energy's analysis of its data integration needs on an enterprise level, the organization launched an Integration Competency Center in order to establish policies and procedures that would encourage best practices and reuse of existing components across its enterprise data integration projects. The ICC also built an enterprise data hub to "untangle the integration hairball" with the following objectives:

- Reduce integration costs.
- Accelerate future acquisitions.
- Eliminate IT constraints in scaling business growth.
- Establish the Good Energy Data Model and Integration Hub.

Through the Good Energy ICC, best practices, standards, and policies were subsequently implemented.

A key element of the solution is the Good Energy Data Model and Integration Hub. This resulted in a consistent definition of information applied across all business functions independent of the technology implementation and based on a sustainable integration infrastructure that separates the consolidated enterprise view from the many departmental and functional systems in a loosely coupled fashion. The Good Energy Data Model consists of 11 subject areas, as shown in Figure 10.1. Each of the subject areas has a responsible data sponsor, data steward, and IT hub owner.

The strategy the ICC selected was to treat each of the subject areas as an "application" and implement them in a centralized integration hub. The

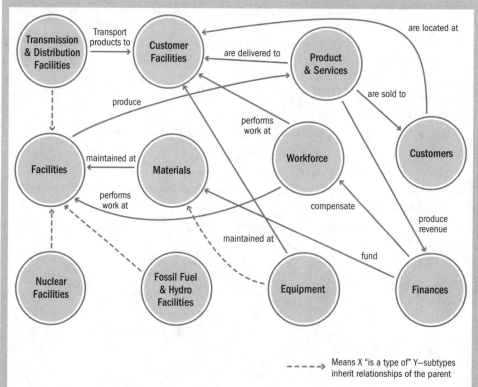

Figure 10.1 Good Energy enterprise subject area model

core purpose of the integration infrastructure was to maintain the consolidated enterprise view by collecting and synchronizing data across operational systems, and to do so in a loosely coupled fashion so that individual applications could change with little or no impact on other applications.

The ICC used a continuous improvement philosophy to build out the integration hubs. Specifically, several key governance touchpoints were established to ensure that as business-driven projects were executed, the necessary hub interfaces were developed.

The key process touchpoints included the following:

1. The project team modeled data for the hub environment:

   a. Identified data for the systems in scope for the project

b. Defined entity-level relationships and distinguishing attributes

c. Received approval of the model by the enterprise data architect

2. Entities were mapped to subject areas:

a. The project data architect reviewed the subject area model and performed initial mapping.

b. Both the model and the mapping were reviewed in a joint meeting with the data stewards (to resolve ambiguities, issues, etc.).

c. The mapping was approved by the appropriate data stewards.

3. Integration analysis was performed:

a. Identified data requirements, sources, targets

b. Designed a preliminary integration plan (ETL, messaging, Web services)

c. Received approval by the project

4. Information delivery requirements were finalized:

a. Identified information and end-use patterns

b. Designed the preliminary data mart and reporting plan

c. Received approval by the project

The benefits of this integration strategy have been significant. For example, the HR system went from 50 integration points with other applications across Good Energy down to 1. All the information that needs to be shared with other applications or for consolidated reporting is sent to the hub. Everyone, or every system, that needs HR data simply obtains it from the hub. This has resulted in a number of business benefits, such as increased performance of the HR system since it is not bogged down by reporting or other operational demands, and increased organizational agility since the HR system can evolve and needs to consider the impact of only 1 integration point rather than 50.

PART III

Implementation Practices

The thing that keeps a business ahead of the competition is excellence in execution.
Tom Peters

A successful integration team or practice is one that grows and thrives over time. Success is based on effective execution and not forced or mandated standards. Effective execution in turn is about being better, faster, and cheaper than the alternatives. The way one gets to be better, faster, and cheaper is by investing energy, time, and sometimes capital to improve processes. Simply wishing to be better is not enough—you need to *do something* to get better. And in order to continuously make process improvements, you need to become an expert in fact-based problem solving, measuring process effectiveness, and articulating the business value of investing in integration capabilities.

Part I of this book talked about strategy and vision. Part II talked about core principles and how to apply them. Part III is all about effective execution. After we wrote the first book on Integration Competency Centers in 2005, we received a tremendous amount of positive feedback but also many requests for more prescriptive practices around execution. This section of the book, we hope, addresses many of those requests.

Financial Management

Accounting is all about tangible assets. But given similar financial resources, these types of assets can be purchased by any company. Tangible assets provide organizations with a basic, off-the-shelf capability or platform for competing against other organizations. Intangible assets such as systems, software, processes, training programs, and research and development (R&D) represent investments that provide future value regardless of accounting reporting convention.

Joe Stenzel[1]

There are three reasons why this is the longest chapter in the book: The ability to secure funding is often one of the weakest skills among IT professionals; money is the universal language of business and therefore can serve as a unifying force to bring disparate groups together; and effectively managing financials, especially related to intangible assets such as data quality and future flexibility, is very hard.

By emphasizing commercial disciplines, we are seeking to ensure that the Lean Integration team (the Integration Competency Center) does not become isolated from the business environment that sustains it. Credibility is established by not only operating a successful ICC, but also being perceived as doing so as measured by the willingness of the parent organization to support the program financially.

---

1. Joe Stenzel, *Lean Accounting: Best Practices for Sustainable Integration* (John Wiley & Sons, 2007), Kindle loc. 2144–48.

This chapter addresses specific practices for making capital investments to drive continuous improvement, using financial metrics to enable cross-functional alignment and support, and using chargeback accounting to fund ongoing operations in a sustainable fashion.

In essence, running a shared-services function such as an Integration Factory or an ICC is very similar to running a business. The factory or ICC offers services to multiple internal customers and encourages adoption of standards by meeting customer needs through demonstrated value. The free-market economy offers an excellent example of how to build a vibrant, responsive, and sustainable business. While an internal business is not in it for the "profit" (at least not for itself), it can leverage many of the foundational elements that make the market economy work:

- **Contract law:** For an ICC, this translates into having well-defined services (e.g., written commitments) and keeping the promises that are made to internal customers.
- **Common currency:** An ICC implements this concept through internal chargeback accounting or transfer prices; while no real money changes hands, it nonetheless serves as the basis for measuring the ICC's value.
- **Regulatory environment:** The organizational equivalents are internal policies and standards; an ICC may be responsible for governing certain integration standards that apply across functional groups.

Table 11.1 provides an outline of four levels of financial management maturity as they relate to integration initiatives. This table can be used as a tool for assessing an organization's current level of maturity and for establishing a desired target maturity level.

Table 11.1 Financial Management Maturity Levels

Maturity Level	Financial Management Practices
Project	Integration projects above a given cost threshold follow a standard business case justification process that includes estimates for all project costs and benefits. Objective criteria are used to periodically assess the risks of large integration projects and to provide an early warning of threats to benefits realization.

Table 11.1   Financial Management Maturity Levels *(Continued)*

Maturity Level	Financial Management Practices
Program	Business case assumptions for large projects are incorporated into the budgets and performance targets of their business sponsors. Integration initiatives support cross-functional and multi-business-unit programs. Projects are linked to a well-defined value chain so that it is clear how the project is improving an end-to-end business process. The organization leverages economies of scale for purchasing and implementing shared integration infrastructures to reduce costs (e.g., an enterprise software license for a shared application system whose capital and operating costs are shared by more than one business unit).
Sustaining	A chargeback model is established with a product/service catalog that provides end users with plain English descriptions of integration services and their cost. The ICC operates as a self-funding model where all the costs of the group (including overhead) are recovered through service chargebacks (in other words, the customers of the integration services pay for 100 percent of ICC operations). Business cases for integration initiatives include the total cost of ownership, including the ongoing maintenance costs. Project budgets take into account the costs for replacing redundant systems slated for retirement.
Lean	The organization conducts post-implementation and ongoing reviews to measure the achievement of project benefits (this is the "Check" part of the PDCA Lean life cycle). Financial policies and practices are established to encourage refactoring of existing components to increase reuse across functions and business units and to proactively simplify the IT environment. The integration teams conduct periodic benchmarking of development and operational cost efficiency and invest continuously in automating manual tasks. Business cases include explicit factors that quantitatively weigh the degree of flexibility provided by the architecture for adapting to business changes and risks.

Challenges

Regardless of which economic model is used, an ICC that relies on shared IT infrastructure will need to make periodic investments to sustain the shared environment. To be clear, we are not referring to minor enhancements, ongoing maintenance, or minor process improvements, but rather to efforts that require a significant investment in human or financial capital in order to eliminate waste or reduce cycle times. Examples of significant investments include

- Metadata-driven tools to automatically generate or deploy integration solutions
- Factory dashboards to streamline information flows and reduce cycle time
- Rationalization of databases and establishment of an enterprise data warehouse
- Investment in data quality tools
- Major software upgrade of an existing shared-services environment
- Implementation of a high-availability grid computing infrastructure
- Technology refresh of a distributed integration system

These types of investments require funding that falls outside the day-to-day operations of an ICC. Although an ICC may operate for a year or more without requiring a major investment, eventually a significant investment is necessary. The questions that inevitably arise relate to how organizations should fund these efforts or even if and when they should undertake them in light of all of the other demands on limited capital resources.

Many ICC teams struggle with the issue of securing funding for infrastructure investments for which the need seems intuitively obvious to them. For a number of valid reasons it is difficult to create a business justification for a shared IT infrastructure. Some of the key challenges are outlined in this chapter.

It is also particularly crucial for ICCs to be able to change organizational behavior. A desired change may be simply to have certain activities performed by a shared-services function rather than individually by each enterprise silo; or it may involve aligning customer processes and business metrics across lines of business. In any event, while leading change in a large organization is not easy, it can be accomplished with an appropriate campaign. The following sections explore the underlying culture and forces in place that can cause roadblocks to change, and set the stage for how financial management practices and measures can break down those barriers.

Lack of Competition

The general opinion of a customer of an internal shared service is that external providers deliver better value as a natural outcome of competitive pressure. The perception is that internal providers either lack motivation or are resource-constrained and have little capacity for making process improvements. Standardization does allow a process to be well defined and executed, but it also introduces rigidity, which is the enemy of innovation.

So the first challenge to address is the danger that complacency will pervade the day-to-day operations of the ICC. From the moment of its inception, the ICC has to demonstrate that it is the most cost-effective option for delivering the required services.

Functional Silos

Enterprises are generally subdivided into a number of functional areas such as marketing, sales, distribution, finance, and human resources; these are commonly referred to as "silos" or "stovepipes." Deep knowledge of its own data and processes exists within each functional area, but little is known about other functions. Given the complexity and scale of the activities that are required for most enterprises to function, it is simply impossible for any one individual to understand all of the details. Yet the overall efficient operation of the enterprise requires a common understanding of data and seamless interaction across multiple functional teams.

The existence of functional silos and the absence of an end-to-end view are the root causes of the following types of issues:

- Production outages caused by unintended consequences of data/process mismatch
- Retrospective data cleanup efforts
- "Fire drills" to capture holistic snapshots for regulatory, compliance, or senior management reporting needs

ICC personnel need to free themselves from the "bunker mentality" and be proactive in the building and understanding of processes and functions throughout the enterprise. By definition, ICCs are chartered to optimize the whole; that means the staff will constantly face resistance from one functional area or another.

Supply and Demand Mismatch

Resources for a centralized function like an ICC tend to be budgeted on an annual basis, resulting in a capacity that is relatively stable and fixed. This conflicts with the demands of the project portfolio, which can fluctuate dramatically over the same period and therefore are difficult to predict in advance.

The resultant mismatch between supply and demand is the root cause of the perception that shared-services functions are unresponsive and inflexible.

For example, Figure 11.1 shows a flat line of about ten FTEs (full-time equivalent staff) representing the number of staff budgeted for the ICC for a one-year period. The wavy line shows the number of FTE resources that are required at various times throughout the year to respond to the demand for ICC services. In this example, the months of January through March are problematic since the ICC staff may be sitting idle. This could be a benefit for the ICC since staff may be able to use the excess capacity to perform some process improvement activities, but it could be a negative factor if senior management is looking for places to reduce head count. May and June are

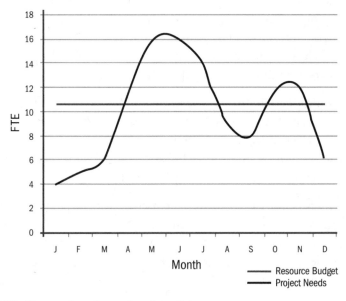

Figure 11.1 Demand and supply mismatch

also problematic since there is a demand for 60 percent more resources than are available. In this situation, the ICC director has only three options:

1. Refuse the additional work.
2. Lower quality on all of the work so that ten staff members can get it all done.
3. Make the staff work evenings and weekends to get all the work done.

None of these options is ideal, and all can have long-term negative consequences.

Conflict of Incentives

As described earlier, organizations are complex, so they are divided into functional silos. Each silo is rewarded and motivated to optimize its own operation; however, optimizing the whole may require sub-optimizing the parts.

Gaining the maximum benefit across an enterprise requires each silo to make trade-offs that may impact individual staff incentives and rewards. The conflict of interest (goals) between the silo perspective (trying to optimize the function) and the enterprise perspective (trying to optimize the whole) is the root cause of enterprise gridlock.

Diseconomies of Scale

One of the main reasons for centralization is to gain economies of scale. For example, multiple groups within an organization may perform similar activities but with varying degrees of efficiency and consistency. Centralizing the activities makes it easier to standardize and streamline the work, and thereby reduce the cost per unit of work, while improving quality and consistency. Centralization also allows scarce expertise to be consolidated.

Less well understood are the diseconomies of scale that can arise through centralization; for example, diseconomies of scale arise when the per-unit cost increases as the volume of work increases. The reasons for these diseconomies include factors such as

- The cost of communication between the central group and the rest of the organization
- Top-heavy management within the central group becoming isolated from the effects of their decisions
- Organization inertia and unwillingness to change entrenched processes
- Hidden costs of standardization (e.g., maintaining canonical models)

The fear of diseconomies of scale is the root cause of indecision about centralization/decentralization. ICC management must organize and guard against factors that drive diseconomies.

Change Is the Enemy of Operations

Business groups and IT groups have fundamentally conflicting objectives; whereas business is focused on the immediate competitive advantage, IT (especially the operations function) is focused on stability and "keeping the lights on." The business demands investments to drive innovation, which in turn drives change. To the IT group, change is the enemy of stability and is a problem to be controlled in order to safeguard daily operations.

The ICC has to be flexible enough not just to accommodate change but also to welcome it when an opportunity arises to improve operations. Indeed, the ideal position for a growing and dynamic organization is at "the edge of chaos"—maintaining control while in a state of constant rapid change. ICCs generally serve both constituents: business units that are driving investments in innovation, and operational units that are striving for stability. It is for this reason that ICC capabilities such as metadata repositories, architecture models, and configuration management databases are so critical. These capabilities provide the foundation for processes that support the effective management of change while controlling risks.

Inability to Communicate Value to Stakeholders

The value of a strategic investment such as an ICC needs to be communicated to the stakeholders (IT and/or business) so that they understand and appreciate it. IT personnel encounter a number of difficulties in communicating value to business leaders:

- The use of technical language that business people don't understand
- Inconsistent language across various lines of business (LOBs), making it hard for IT staff to understand business terminology
- The tendency of IT staff to describe their activities and how work is done rather than focus on the outcomes (what) and the benefits (why)
- The difficulty of translating "soft" benefits such as future flexibility of a given design into "hard," quantifiable business benefits

The inability to communicate IT value to business stakeholders is the root cause of reduced IT credibility. These communication difficulties are compounded by the use of synonyms and homonyms across the business and IT worlds. Different labels may be used for the same concept; and even more confusing, the same label may be used for quite different concepts.

Given that IT is delivering a service to the business, the onus is generally on ICC personnel to learn the business terminology.

Difficulty in Obtaining "Good" Data

The absence of data for metrics and quantified value propositions is the reason many proposals fail to secure approval. Yet such data is difficult to acquire for a number of reasons:

- Data may simply not be captured (e.g., the amount of time call center staff spends resolving customer data quality problems).
- Data may be captured inconsistently in different organizational groups (e.g., group A does staff time reporting by project phase but group B does it by staff activity).
- The data is not well defined and the people (or person) who know how to interpret it are too busy with other activities (e.g., the project manager who understands and could explain the staff time reports is totally consumed with getting the project completed).
- The owners of the data may be unwilling to share their information because it could be embarrassing or shine a light on some issues that they don't want highlighted.

There is no easy solution to the problem of acquiring the data that establishes the case for a Lean investment, and yet a full review of the available data is a prerequisite of the proposal. This should include metrics from the development and operation of existing integration applications. The key issue with metrics in demonstrating value to stakeholders is not their volume but their quality. "Low-level" measurable metrics (often activity-based) need to be aggregated to the more compelling outcome-based metrics.

Mismatch of Budget Horizon and Project Life Cycle

Many organizations establish their project investment portfolio on an annual basis and have little (or no) portfolio for multiyear initiatives; it is difficult to obtain funding for projects (or programs) that cut across budget-year boundaries or require several years to complete since they fall outside the "normal" project governance process.

Moreover, since corporate priorities and market pressures commonly shift from year to year, the original business case may no longer be relevant or compelling.

The mismatch of budget horizon and project cycle is the root cause of the project portfolio being focused on tactical short-term solutions that leave the tough problems unresolved. These are precisely the kinds of problems that a strategic resource such as a Lean practice is designed to address.

Organizational Support Diffusion

By definition, shared infrastructure programs require stable and broad-based organizational support. In the dynamic working conditions of the modern enterprise, this is difficult to secure.

For example, let's look at a typical integration initiative that requires ten teams (functional groups or application teams) to work together for one year. There are typically three levels of stakeholders on each team: area director, team manager, and front-line staff. Below the director level, often more than one individual is involved. Assuming that each of the ten teams has on average 5 people (a total of 50), after 12 months of promotions, transfers, and general churn, very few of the 50 will be in the same role. So there may well be few remaining in the core group who actually understand the need for the ICC and are prepared to support it.

Despite organizational changes, a Lean team must be able to build cross-functional support and sustain it indefinitely.

Activities

The financial management competency includes the following key activities:

1. **Developing business case justifications** for investments in the integration infrastructure of an organization and in the ICC itself. These efforts may be infrequent or relatively small in the case of incremental quick wins, or they may represent a major campaign in the case of a "making the wave" business case style. In any event, these efforts are periodic and don't follow a fixed schedule or pattern. Refer to the next section of this chapter on Business Case Development for additional details.

2. **Determining the chargeback accounting model** both for ongoing maintenance/operations services the ICC provides to the enterprise and for

project-based services. The choice of models available is often constrained by the internal accounting practices and policies of the financial organization. Nonetheless it is absolutely critical that the ICC director make it a top priority to

    a. Learn how the financial systems and processes in the organization operate

    b. Understand how organizational and individual behavior is influenced by the accounting practices

    c. Develop techniques to compensate for the negative effects of the chargeback model

    d. Challenge the status quo and encourage changes to the internal accounting controls

3. **Establishing key metrics and reporting** for an ongoing campaign to build and sustain broad-based management awareness of and support for the ICC. These metrics should definitely include financial ones, but they may also include other key economic indicators such as internal customer satisfaction, process improvement activities, and other quality and efficiency metrics.

Business Case Development

Establishing an ICC or shared infrastructure takes money, resources, and management attention. While most enterprises have requirements and defined standards for business case documents to justify projects that involve a financial expenditure or significant organizational change, integration initiatives present unique challenges that are associated with multifunctional cross-organizational initiatives.

Most IT personnel are quite capable of articulating the technical case for the degree of centralization that the ICC, standard technology, or shared integration system represents, but proving the business case is likely to be more challenging. As the technical case alone is unlikely to secure the required funding, it is important to identify the departments and individuals that are likely to benefit directly and indirectly from the implementation of the integration strategy.

These ideas provide a systematic approach to researching, documenting, and presenting the business justification for these sorts of complex integration initiatives.

The process to establish a business case for an ICC or shared infrastructure such as an enterprise data warehouse, ETL (extract, transform, load) hub, enterprise service bus (ESB), or data governance program (to name just a few) is fundamentally an exercise in analysis and persuasion. This process is demonstrated graphically in Figure 11.2.

Step 1: Clarify the Business Need

Integration investments should be part of a business strategy that must, in turn, be part of the overall corporate strategy. Mismatched IT investments will only move the organization in the wrong direction more quickly. Consequently, an investment in integration should (depending on the enterprise requirements) be based on requirements such as

- Improved data quality
- Reduction of future integration costs
- Reduction of system architecture complexity
- Increase in implementation speed for new systems
- Reduction of corporate costs
- Support for business priorities

The first step in the business case process, therefore, is to state the integration problem in such a way as to clearly define the circumstances leading to the consideration of the investment. This step is important because it identifies both the questions to be resolved by the analysis and the boundaries of the investigation. The problem statement identifies the need to be satisfied, the problem to be solved, or the opportunity to be exploited. The problem statement should address

- The corporate and program goals and other objectives affected by the proposed investment
- A description of the problem, need, or opportunity
- A general indication of the range of possible actions

Although the immediate concern may be to fulfill the needs of a specific integration opportunity, you must, nevertheless, consider the overall corporate goals. A business solution that does not take into account corporate priorities and business strategies may never deliver its expected benefits because of unanticipated changes within the organization or its processes.

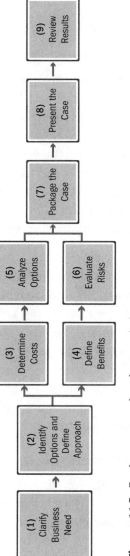

Figure 11.2 Business case development steps

There is a significant danger associated with unverified assumptions that can derail business case development at the outset of the process. It is imperative to be precise about the business need that the integration solution is designed to address; abandon preconceptions and get to the core of the requirements. Do not assume that the perceived benefits of a centralized service such as an ICC are so obvious that they do not need to be specifically stated.

In summary, key activities in step 1 include these:

- Define and agree on the problem, opportunity, or goals that will guide the development of the business case.
- Use brainstorming techniques to envision how you would describe the business need in a compelling way.
- Start with the end in mind based on what you know.
- Prepare a plan to gather the data and facts needed to justify the vision.
- Understand the organization's financial accounting methods and business case development standards.
- Understand the enterprise funding approval governance processes.

Note: It is important to review the core assumptions as the business case evolves and new information becomes available.

The key output from step 1 is a notional problem statement (with placeholders or "guesses" for key measures) and several graphical sketches representing a clearly defined problem/needs statement described in business terms. The MBF technique (see Appendix A) provides a template showing the basic structure of a problem statement with supporting facts and proposed resolution that can be summarized on a single PowerPoint slide. While the basic structure should be defined in step 1, the supporting details and action plans will emerge from the subsequent analysis steps.

Step 2: Identify Options and Define the Approach

The way in which you describe solutions or opportunities is likely to shape the analysis that follows. Do not focus on specific technologies, products, or methods, as this may exclude other options that might produce the same benefits but at a lower cost or with increased benefits for the same cost. Instead, try to identify all of the possible ways in which the organization can meet the business objectives described in the problem statement. This way, the options that are developed and analyzed will have a clear relationship to the organization's needs. Unless this relationship is clear, you may be accused of investing in technology for technology's sake.

Available options must include the base case, as well as a range of other potential solutions. The base case should show how an organization would perform if it did not pursue the integration investment proposal or otherwise change its method of operation. It is important to highlight any alternative solutions to the integration investment.

A description of what is meant by doing nothing is required here. It is not adequate to state the base case simply as the continuation of the current situation. It must account for future developments over a period long enough to serve as a basis of comparison for the proposed alternative solution. For example, an organization that keeps an aging integration technique may face increasing maintenance costs as the system gets older and the integrations become more complex. There may be more frequent system failures and changes causing longer periods of downtime. Maintenance costs may become prohibitive, service delays intolerable, or workloads unmanageable. Alternatively, demand for a business unit's services may ultimately decrease, permitting a reduction of costs without the need for an integration investment.

Be sure to examine all the options in both the short and long term:

- **Short term:** The document should highlight the immediate effect of doing nothing. For example, your competitors may already have implemented systems such as a customer integration hub or a data quality program and are able to offer more competitive services. Thus, the enterprise may already be losing market share because of its inability to change and react to market conditions. If there is significant market share loss, it should be presented in a way that emphasizes the need for something to be done.
- **Long term:** The base case should predict the long-term costs and benefits of maintaining the current method of operation, taking into account the known external pressures for change, such as predicted changes in demand for services, budgets, and staffing or business direction.

Problems can be solved in different ways and to different extents. In some cases, options are available that concentrate on making optimum use of existing systems or on altering current procedures. These options may require little or no new investment and should be considered.

A full-scale analysis of all options is neither achievable nor necessary. A screening process is the best way to ensure that the analysis proceeds with only the most promising options. Screening allows a wide range of initial options to be considered, while keeping the level of effort reasonable. Establishing a process for screening options has the added advantage of setting out in an evaluation framework the reasons for selecting, as well as rejecting, particular options.

Options should be ruled out as soon as it becomes clear that other choices are superior from a cost/benefit perspective. A comparative cost/benefit framework should quickly identify the key features likely to make a difference among options. Grouping options with similar key features can help identify differences associated with cost disadvantages or benefit advantages that would persist even if the options were subjected to more rigorous analysis.

Options may be ruled out on the basis that their success depends too heavily on unproven technology or that they just will not work. Take care not to confuse options that will not work with options that are merely less desirable. Options that are simply undesirable will drop out when you begin to measure the costs and benefits.

The objective is to subject options to an increasingly rigorous analysis. A good rule of thumb is that when in doubt about the economic merits of a particular option, the analyst should retain it for subsequent, more detailed rounds of estimation.

To secure funds in support of ICC infrastructure investments, a number of broad-based strategies and detailed methods can be used. The following are five primary strategies that address many of the funding challenges:

1. **Recurring quick wins:** This strategy involves making a series of small incremental investments as separate projects, each of which provides demonstrable evidence of progress. This strategy works best when the work can be segmented into small steps.

2. **React to a crisis:** While it may not be possible to predict when a crisis will occur, experienced integration staff are often able to see a pattern and anticipate in what areas a crisis is likely to emerge. By way of analogy, it may not be easy to predict when the next earthquake will occur, but we can be quite accurate about predicting *where* it is likely to occur based on past patterns. The advantage that can be leveraged in a crisis situation is that senior management attention is clearly focused on solving the problem. A

challenge, however, is that there is often a tendency to solve the problem quickly, which may not allow sufficient time for a business case that addresses the underlying structural issues and root causes of the problem. This strategy therefore requires that the ICC team perform some advance work, be prepared with a rough investment proposal for addressing structural issues, and be ready to quickly present it when the opportunity arises.

3. **Executive vision:** This strategy relies on ownership being driven by a top-level executive (e.g., CEO, CFO, CIO, VP, etc.) who has control over a certain amount of discretionary funding. In this scenario, a business case may not be required because the investment is being driven by a belief in core principles and a top-down vision. This is often the path of least resistance if you have the good fortune to have an executive with a vision that aligns with the Lean charter/mission. The downside is that if the executive leaves the organization or is promoted into another role, the momentum and any associated investment may fade away if sufficient cross-functional support has not been developed.

4. **Ride on a wave:** This strategy involves tying the infrastructure investment to a large project with definite ROI and implementing the foundational elements to serve future projects and the enterprise overall rather than just the large project's needs. Examples include purchasing the hardware and software for an enterprise integration hub in conjunction with a corporate merger/acquisition program, or building an enterprise hub as part of a large ERP system implementation. This strategy may make it easier to secure the funds for an infrastructure that is hard to justify on its own merits, but it has the risk of becoming too project-specific and not as reusable by the rest of the enterprise.

5. **Create the wave:** This strategy involves developing a clear business case with defined benefits and a revenue/cost-sharing model to which all stakeholders who will use the shared infrastructure agree in advance. This is one of the most difficult strategies to execute because it requires a substantial up-front investment in building the business case and gaining broad-based organizational support. But it can also be one of the most rewarding because all the hard work to build support and address the "political" issues is done early.

In summary, the activities in step 2 for identifying the options and developing the approach are these:

1. Assemble the evaluation team:

   a. Include a mix of resources if possible, including some change agents and change resisters.
   b. Use internal resources who "know their way around" the organization.
   c. Use external resources to ask the naive questions and sidestep internal politics.
   d. Prepare for evaluation, including understanding the organizational financial standards and internal accounting methods.

2. Define the options and a framework for structuring the investment decision:

   a. Identify the options (including the baseline "status quo" option).
   b. Screen the options based on short-term and long-term effects.

3. Determine the business case style.

The key deliverables resulting from step 2 are a list of options and a rough idea of the answers to the following questions for each of them:

- How does the solution relate to the enterprise objectives and priorities?
- What overall program performance results will the option achieve? What may happen if the option is not selected?
- What additional outcomes or benefits may ensue if this option is selected?
- Who are the stakeholders? What are their interests and responsibilities? What effect does the option have on them?
- What are the implications for the organization's human resources?
- What are the projected improvements in timeliness, productivity, cost savings, cost avoidance, quality, and service?
- How much will it cost to implement the integration solution?
- Does the solution involve the innovative use of technology? If so, what risks does that involve?

Step 3: Determine the Costs

It is necessary to define the costs associated with options that will influence the investment decision. Be sure to consider all the cost dimensions, which we describe here.

Fixed versus Variable and Direct versus Indirect Costs

The fixed costs are the costs that do not vary with the number of integration interfaces that are to be built. They can be costs that are incurred over a period of time but can be envisaged as one number at the end of that period. Examples are buildings, servers, and management overhead. Fixed costs typically do not change as the volume of output increases, although they may change in a step function such as when the building or server is fully utilized and another needs to be secured.

Variable costs are material and process costs that change with the volume of goods or services produced. In other words, each incremental unit output generates an incremental cost.

Direct costs are those that are unequivocally related to production outputs. For example, the cost of staff labor to program an interface is a direct cost. Indirect costs, on the other hand, may be considered fixed overhead costs or may be combined with direct costs on an allocation basis. For example, the cost of a desk and work space for a software developer may (based on the accounting policies of the enterprise) be considered as corporate overhead or may be added to staff labor costs along with other allocations, resulting in a "fully loaded" cost per hour.

Internal versus External Costs

External costs are sometimes referred to as "out of pocket" costs since they involve a direct expenditure of money, such as the purchase of a software license or hiring a consultant. Internal costs are generally for resources that have already been paid for and are being consumed by the investment project, such as using a server or software license that was purchased independently of the project or using employees to perform the work. It is usually easier to justify investment in a project that has primarily internal costs, unless the organization is severely resource-constrained, in which case it may be easier to obtain funding for incremental external resources.

Capital versus Operating Costs

Most enterprises have separate capital and operating budgets, as well as different governance processes for the two categories. Our recommendation is to keep both sources of funds in mind when preparing investment business cases and to develop a deep understanding of your enterprise processes and policies.

Aside from the formal processes, you should also seek to understand the informal processes and cultural dynamics. For example, in some organizations it is relatively easy to obtain approval for discretionary operating funds early in the fiscal year but it becomes increasingly difficult as the year progresses. Conversely, the same organization may maintain very stringent criteria for capital expenditures early in the fiscal year and ease up on constraints late in the year if the entire budget has not been consumed.

One-Time Costs versus Ongoing Costs

Up-front costs are the initial project development and implementation expenses. These can be substantial and should be carefully assessed. Fortunately, these costs are generally well documented and easily determined, except for projects that involve new technology or software applications. The main categories of one-time direct/fixed costs are

- Hardware and peripherals
- Packaged and customized software
- Initial data collection or conversion of archival data
- Data quality analysis and profiling
- Facilities upgrades, including site preparation and renovation
- Design and implementation
- Testing and prototyping
- Documentation
- Additional staffing requirements
- Initial user training
- Transition, such as costs of running parallel systems
- Quality assurance and post-implementation reviews

Ongoing costs are the expenses that occur over the life cycle of the investment. The costs to operate a facility, as well as to develop or implement an option, must be identified. The main categories of direct ongoing costs are

- Salaries for staff
- Software licenses, maintenance, and upgrades
- Computing equipment and maintenance
- User support
- Ongoing training
- Reviews and audits

Not all of these categories are included in every data integration implementation. It is important to pick the costs that reflect your implementation accurately.

The primary output from step 3 is a financial model (typically a spreadsheet) around the options with different views according to the interests of the main stakeholders.

Step 4: Define the Benefits

This step identifies and quantifies the potential benefits of a proposed integration investment. Both quantitative and qualitative benefits should be defined. Determine how improvements in productivity and service are defined as well as the methods for realizing the benefits.

- Identify direct (hard) and indirect (soft) benefits.
- Create a financial model of the benefits.
- Collect industry studies to complement internal analysis.
- Identify anecdotal examples to reinforce facts.
- Define how benefits will be measured.

To structure the evaluation, you will have to clearly identify and quantify the project's advantages. A structure is required to set a range within which the benefits of an integration implementation can be realized. Conservative, moderate, and optimistic values are used in the attempt to produce a final range, which realistically contains the benefits to the enterprise of an integration project but also reflects the difficulty of assigning precise values to some of the elements:

- **Conservative** values reflect the highest costs and lowest benefits possible.
- **Moderate** values reflect those you believe most accurately reflect the true value of the integration implementation.
- **Optimistic** estimates reflect values that are highly favorable but are also improbable.

Many of the greatest benefits of integration are realized months or even years after the project has been completed. These benefits should be estimated for each of the three to five years following the completion of the project. In order to account for the changing value of money over time, all future pretax costs and benefits are discounted at the internal rate of return.

Direct (Hard) Benefits

The enterprise will immediately notice a few direct benefits from improving data integration in its projects. These are mainly cost savings over traditional point-to-point integration in which interfaces and transformations between applications are hard-coded, and the cost savings the enterprise will realize because of the enhanced efficiency and automation made possible by improved integration approaches, tools, and artifacts. Key considerations include

- Cost savings
- Reduction in complexity
- Reduction in staff training
- Reduction in manual processes
- Incremental revenue linked directly to the project
- Governance and compliance controls that are directly linked

Indirect (Soft) Benefits

The greatest benefits from an integration project usually stem from the extended flexibility the system will have. For this reason, these benefits tend to be longer-term and indirect. Among them are

- Increase in market share
- Decrease in the cost of future application upgrades
- Improved data quality and reporting accuracy
- Decrease in the effort required for integration projects
- Improved quality of work for staff and reduced turnover
- Better management decisions
- Reduced waste and rework
- Ability to adopt a managed service strategy
- Increased scalability and performance
- Improved services to suppliers and customers
- Increase in transaction auditing capabilities
- Decreased time to market for mission-critical projects
- Increased security features
- Improved regulatory compliance

It is possible to turn indirect benefits into direct benefits by performing a detailed analysis and working with finance and management stakeholders to gain support. This may not always be necessary, but often it is essential (especially with a "make the wave" business case style). Since it can take a lot of time and effort to complete this analysis, the recommended best practice is to select only one indirect benefit as the target for a detailed analysis.

Figure 11.3 illustrates an example of a compelling exposition of ICC benefits. Note that the initial cost of integrations developed by the Integration Factory is greater than hand-coding, but after 100 integrations the factory cost is less than custom hand-coded solutions. In this example (which is based on a real-life case), the enterprise developed more than 300 integrations per year, which translated into a savings of $3 million per year.

It is also useful to identify the project beneficiaries and to understand their business roles and project participation. In many cases, the project sponsor can help to identify the beneficiaries and the various departments they represent. This information can then be summarized in an organization chart—a useful reference document that ensures that all project team members understand the corporate/business organization.

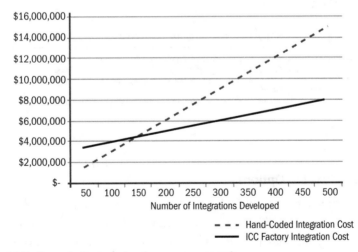

Figure 11.3 Sample factory business case graph

Leverage Industry Studies

Industry studies from research firms such as Gartner, Forrester, and AMR Research can be used to highlight the value of an integration approach. For example, all the percentages in Table 11.2 are available from various research reports. The example in the table is for a U.S.-based telecommunications company with annual revenue of $10 billion. The industry studies suggest that an ICC would save $30 million per year for an organization of this size.

Table 11.2   Industry Cost Benefits Metrics

Company revenue (telecommunications industry)		$ 10,000,000,000
Percent of revenue spent on IT*	5.0%	$ 500,000,000
Percent of IT budget spent on investments*	40.0%	$ 200,000,000
Percent of investment projects spent on integration†	35.0%	$ 70,000,000
Percent of integration project savings resulting from an ICC‡	30.0%	$ 21,000,000
Percent of IT budget spent on MOOSE§	60.0%	$ 300,000,000
Percent of MOOSE spent on maintenance (guesstimate—no study available)	15.0%	$ 45,000,000
Percent of integration savings on maintenance costs resulting from an ICC‡	20.0%	$ 9,000,000
Total potential annual savings resulting from an ICC		$ 30,000,000

* Forrester Research, "US IT Spending Benchmarks for 2007," November 13, 2007.
† Gartner Group, "Client Issues for Application Integration," November 6, 2003.
‡ Gartner Group, "Cost Cutting through the Use of an Integration Competency Center or SOA Center of Excellence," April 4, 2008.
§ MOOSE = maintain and operate the IT organization, systems, and equipment.

Step 5: Analyze the Options

After you have identified the options, the next step is to recommend one. Before selecting an option to recommend, you need to have a good understanding of the organization's goals, its business processes, and the business requirements that must be satisfied.

To evaluate investment options, select criteria that will allow measurement and comparison. The following list presents some possible analyses, starting with those that involve hard financial returns and progressing to those that are more strategic:

- **Analysis of cost effectiveness** demonstrates, in financial terms, improvements in performance or in service delivery and shows whether the benefits from the integration investment outweigh its costs.

- **Analysis of displaced or avoided costs** compares the proposed system's costs to those of the system it would displace or avoid; it may justify the proposal on a least-cost basis if it can be assumed that the new system will have as many benefits as the current system.

- **Work value analysis** requires an analysis of work patterns throughout the organization and of ways to readjust the number and types of skills required; it assumes that additional work needs to be done, that management allocates resources efficiently, and that workers allocate time efficiently.

- **Cost of quality analysis** estimates the savings to be gained by reducing the cost of quality assurance, such as the cost of preventing or repairing a product failure, and can consider savings that are internal and external to the organization, such as the enterprise's cost to return a product.

- **Option value analysis** estimates the value of future opportunities that the organization may now pursue because of the project; it uses decision trees and probability analysis and includes savings on future projects, portions of the benefits of future projects, and reductions in the risks associated with future projects.

- **Analysis of technical importance** justifies an infrastructure investment because a larger project that has already received approval could not proceed without it. This is likely when enterprises initiate integration programs as a consequence of a merger or acquisition and two large ERP systems need to communicate.

- **Alignment with business objectives** includes the concept of strategic alignment modeling, which is one way to examine the interaction between IT strategy and business strategy, and allows managers to put a value on the direct contribution of an investment to the strategic objectives of the organization.

- **Analysis of level-of-service improvements** estimates the benefits to enterprises of increases in the quantity, quality, or delivery of services and must be done from the enterprise's viewpoint.

▪ **Research and development (R&D)** is a variant of option value analysis, except that the decision on whether to invest in a large integration project depends on the outcome of a pilot project; this is most useful for high-risk projects, where R&D can assess the likelihood of failure and help managers decide whether to abort the project or better manage its risks. It requires that management accept the consequences of failure and that the pilot be a reasonable expense in determining the viability of an integration project.

After you have quantified the costs and benefits, it is essential to conduct a cost/benefit analysis of the various options. Showing the incremental benefits of each option relative to the base case requires less analysis, since the analyst does not have to evaluate the benefits and costs of an entire program or service. Some benefits may not be quantifiable. Nevertheless, these benefits should be included in the analysis, along with the benefits to individuals within and external to the organization. You have to look at the project from two perspectives: the organization's perspective as the supplier of products and services, and the enterprise's or public's perspective as the consumer of those services.

Hard cost savings come from dedicated resources (people and equipment), while more uncertain savings come from allocated costs such as overhead and workload. When estimating cost avoidance, keep these two types of savings separate. Assess how likely it is that the organization will realize savings from allocated resources, and estimate how long it will take to realize these savings.

Step 6: Evaluate Risks

Step 6 presents ways to help identify and evaluate the risks that an integration investment may face so that they can be included in the business case. It also includes how to plan to control or minimize the risk associated with implementing a data integration investment.

The purpose of risk assessment and management is to determine and resolve threats to the successful achievement of investment objectives and especially to the benefits identified in the business case. The assessment and management of risk are ongoing processes that continue throughout the duration of an integration implementation and are used to make decisions about the project implementation. The first decision about an integration investment option is whether to proceed. The better the risks are understood and planned for when this decision is made, the more reliable the decision and the better the chances of success.

The method underlying most risk assessment and management approaches can be summarized by the following five-step process:

1. Identify the risks facing the project.
2. Characterize the risks in terms of impact, likelihood of occurrence, and interdependence.
3. Prioritize the risks to determine which need the most immediate attention.
4. Devise an approach to assume, avoid, or control the risks.
5. Monitor the risks.

All but the last of these can and should be undertaken as part of the business case analysis conducted prior to the decision to proceed.

Not all risks are created equal. For each risk identified, characterize the degree of risk in terms of

- Its impact on the project (e.g., slight delay or showstopper)
- The probability of its occurrence (e.g., from very unlikely to very likely)
- Its relationship to other risks (e.g., poor data quality can lead to problems with integrating data)

Once the risks have been identified and characterized, they can be ranked in order of priority to determine which should be tackled first. Priority should be based on a combination of an event's impact, likelihood, and interdependence—for example, risks that have a severe impact and are very likely to occur. Therefore, they should be dealt with first to avoid having to deal with additional risks.

You can assign priorities to risk factors by assigning a weight to each risk for each of the three characteristics (impact, likelihood, and interdependence) and multiplying the three values to create a composite score. The risk with the highest score gets the highest priority. A general rule of thumb is to develop a risk mitigation plan only for the top five risks based on the rationale that there is no point in focusing on lower-priority risks if the major ones aren't addressed, and because of limited management attention it is not feasible to tackle too many at once. After you have mitigated some of the highest-priority risks, reevaluate the list on an ongoing basis and focus again on the top five.

Do not avoid or hide risks. The credibility of the business case will be enhanced by clearly identifying risks and developing a mitigation strategy to address them. Three main types of risks arise in IT projects:

1. **Lack of control:** Risks of this type arise from a project team's lack of control over the probability of occurrence of an event and/or its consequences. For example, the risks related to senior managers' decisions are often a result of the lack of control a project team has over senior managers.
2. **Lack of information:** Risks of this type arise from a project team's lack of information regarding the probability of occurrence of an event or its consequences. For example, risks related to the use of new technologies are often the result of a lack of information about the potential or performance of these technologies.
3. **Lack of time:** Risks of this type arise from a project team's inability to find the time to identify the risks associated with the project or a given course of action, or to assess the probability of occurrence of an event or the impact of its consequences.

There are three main types of responses to risk in data integration projects, and they are listed in ascending order of their potential to reduce risk:

1. **Assume:** A department accepts the risk and does not take action to prevent an event's occurrence or to mitigate its impact.
2. **Control:** A department takes no action to reduce the probability of occurrence of an event but upon its occurrence attempts to mitigate its impact.
3. **Avoid:** A department takes action prior to the occurrence of an event in order either to reduce its probability of occurrence or to mitigate its impact.

Selection of a type of response depends on the priority assigned to a risk, its nature (i.e., whether it is amenable to control or avoidance), and the resources available to the project. In general, the higher the priority of a risk, the more vigorous the type of response applied.

Step 7: Package the Case

Assemble the business case documentation and package it for consumption by the targeted stakeholders. Key activities in this step include the following:

- Identify the audience.
- Prepare the contents of the report.

- Package the case in different formats to make a compelling and engaging presentation, using
  - Descriptive graphics
  - Animation or simulation of process or data quality issues
  - Case studies and anecdotes
  - Comparative financial data
  - Customer testimonials

Step 8: Present the Case

The best analysis and documentation will be useless unless the decision makers buy in and give the necessary approvals. Step 8 provides suggestions to help ensure that your recommendations get a fair hearing. Use both formal and informal methods to present the proposal successfully. Key activities in this step include these:

- Find the right sponsor(s).
- Leverage individual and group presentations.
- Promote the proposal and obtain cross-functional buy-in.
- Model, pilot, and test-market the proposed solution.

Find a sponsor who can galvanize support for the business case, as well as for the subsequent implementation. The sponsor should be a person in a senior management position. Avoid starting a project without a sponsor.

The investment proposal will compete for the attention of decision makers and the organization as a whole. This attention is crucial, and information can be a vital element in helping enterprises to lobby the project decision makers throughout the life cycle of the decision process. Consequently, the proposal itself must be promoted, marketed, and sold. Market your proposal with an eye toward the enterprise culture and the target audience. Word of mouth is an important, but often overlooked, way of delivering limited information to a finite group.

A business case must convince decision makers that the analysis, conclusions, and recommendations are valid. To make this happen, use theoretical or practical models, pilot projects, and test marketing. Remember, seeing is believing, and a demonstration is worth a thousand pictures.

Furthermore, the model or pilot allows the assessment of any ongoing changes to the environment or to the assumptions. One can then answer the "what-if" scenarios that inevitably surface during the decision-making process. At the same time, there is a basis for reassessment and revision in the investments.

Step 9: Review the Results

Step 9 outlines a process for conducting ongoing reviews during the life cycle of the data integration project. Be realistic in your assessment of the feedback from the preceding stage. Whatever the difficulties encountered in the decision-making process, follow up after the decision to review the ongoing validity of the investment and reinforce support.

Reviews help to verify that the IT investment decision remains valid, and that all costs and benefits resulting from that decision are understood, controlled, and realized. The investment analysis contained in the business case defines the goals of the implementation project and serves as a standard against which to measure the project's prospects for success at review time.

The following types of reviews can be conducted:

- **Independent reviews:** These are conducted by an independent party at major checkpoints to identify environmental changes, overrun of time and cost targets, or other problems.
- **Internal peer reviews:** The objectives of the peer review are to verify that the project is still on course and to provide expert advice, counsel, and assistance to the project manager. In this way, the combined skills and experience of internal staff are applied to the project.
- **External peer reviews:** ICCs may also draw upon similar people in other departments or organizations to provide a different perspective and to bring a wide range of expertise to bear on project strategies, plans, and issues.
- **Project team sanity checks:** Another source of early warning for project problems is the project team members. These people are the most intimately aware of difficulties or planned activities that may pose particular challenges.
- **Oversight reviews:** These reviews, under a senior steering committee, should be planned to take place at each checkpoint to reconfirm that the project is aligned with ICC priorities and directions and to advise senior management on project progress.
- **Investment reviews:** The enterprise auditor can also review the performance of projects and, upon completion, the performance of the investment. At an investment review, the auditor reviews and verifies the effect of the investment to ascertain that the investment was justified.

The reviews should start as soon as money is spent on the investment. Major project reviews should be scheduled to coincide with the release of funds allocated to the project. In this approach, the project sponsor releases only the funds needed to reach the next scheduled review. The performance of the project is reviewed at each scheduled checkpoint or when the released funds run out. After review, departmental management can decide to proceed with the project as planned, modify the project or its funding, or even terminate the project, limiting the loss to the amount previously released.

Investment reviews can be scheduled to coincide with project reviews during investment implementation:

- The first investment review should be conducted no later than the midpoint of the project schedule, when the deliverables are under development.
- The second should be conducted after the end of the implementation project, when the deliverables have just started to be used in production.
- A final review should be conducted after the investment has been in production for between six months and a year.
- The exact dates for these reviews should ideally be determined by the timing of the investment deliverables. This timing should be clearly indicated in the investment plan.

The approved investment analysis should form the basis for criteria used in all reviews. The project schedule of deliverables, based on the investment analysis, establishes the timing criteria for project reviews.

After each review, the sponsor should say whether the investment will stop or continue. An investment may be stopped, even temporarily, for any of the following reasons:

- There is no agreement on how to conduct the review.
- The review shows that most of the expected results were not achieved.
- There were changes to the approved investment analysis, and it is not clear that the enterprise was made aware of the full implications of the changes.
- Changes to the approved investment analysis were accepted, but there is no additional funding for the changes or the enterprise has not accepted the new risks.

For the final investment review, the enterprise should demonstrate to the auditor that the investment achieved the expected results, and the auditor should report on the investment's level of success.

Case Study: A "Creating the Wave" Investment Strategy

A CIO was once heard to exclaim, "I have a billion-dollar budget and no money to spend." This wasn't the CIO of BIGCO (the pseudonym for the company in this case study), but it could have been. The problem at BIGCO was that an ever-increasing portion of the annual IT budget was being spent just to keep the lights on for items such as ongoing maintenance of applications, regulatory changes demanded by the federal government, disaster recovery capabilities mandated by the board, and ongoing operations.

One of the biggest perceived drivers of this trend was unnecessary complexity in the IT environment. Clearly, some amount of complexity is necessary in a modern IT environment because of the inherent intricacy of a multinational business operating in many legal jurisdictions, with millions of customers, 100,000-plus employees, hundreds of products, and dozens of channels where customers and suppliers interact. However, a tremendous amount of unnecessary complexity at BIGCO was self-imposed by past practices such as acquisition of companies without fully consolidating their systems; implementation of application systems in silos, resulting in duplicate and overlapping data and functions across the enterprise; lack of governance, resulting in incremental growth of systems to address only tactical needs; and integration as an afterthought without an enterprise standard framework.

No one at BIGCO disagreed with the problem, all the way from the CEO (who discussed it regularly in public forums) to the CIO to the software developers. Metaphorically, much of the low-hanging fruit had already been picked, but the really "juicy" fruit was still at the top of the tree. It was hard to pick because of the challenges mentioned earlier in this chapter.

This case explores how these challenges were addressed in a specific scenario: consolidating 30 legacy integration systems and transforming them into an efficient enterprise hub using the latest technologies. The 30 systems had been built incrementally over 15 years through thousands of projects without a master architectural blueprint. Each change was rational on its own, but resulted in multiple instances of middleware in a complex integration situation that clearly cost too much to maintain, was difficult to change, and was susceptible to chaotic behavior in day-to-day operations.

A lot of money was at stake in this case. The 30 systems had an annual run-rate operating cost of $50 million, and an initial back-of-the-envelope analysis showed that this amount could be cut in half. While there was some top-down executive support, much broader cross-organizational support was necessary, so the ICC team decided to use the "creating the wave" strategy. The first step was to build a business case. This turned out to be a six-month exercise involving a core team of four staff members, who engaged more than 100 stakeholders from multiple functions across the enterprise. They started out by gathering 18 months of historical cost information about each of the 30 systems. Some stakeholders didn't think 18 months was sufficient, so the team went to three years of history and for many of the systems eventually tracked down five years of history.

At the core of the business case, the ICC team wanted to show what would happen to the $50 million run-rate cost over the next three years under the status quo and compare it to the run-rate cost in a simplified environment. They used Microsoft Excel to construct the financial business model. It started as a couple of worksheets that grew over time. The final version was 13 megabytes in size and consisted of 48 worksheets showing five years of history and three years of projections for various scenarios, plus month-by-month project costs for two years. All of it was sliced and diced to show various views for different organizational groups.

What were the results of this case study? The final business model showed that an investment of $20 million would result in a net ongoing operational saving of $25 million per year. On the surface, this sounds like a solid business case—spend $20 million to save $25 million per year. There was, however, one major challenge that could have been a showstopper.

One of the 30 legacy systems, the largest one, was a mainframe-based application that consumed over 1,000 MIPS across mainframe servers in three data centers at an annual cost of $20 million. When the team visited the accounting staff to understand the allocation model so that they could determine how much could be included as "hard" dollar savings when the application was retired, the answer was $0. The accounting staff explained that "by shutting down the application, we are not able to shut down any of the mainframes because other applications are still reliant on them, we can't lay off any staff, and we won't save any floor space." In short, all of the costs that were represented by the $20 million were fixed costs allocated across the applications that used the shared services. The reality is that reducing capacity on mainframe servers by 1,000 MIPS had real value in an enterprise that was constantly increasing its computer workload. Specifically, the next project to come along that needed mainframe computing capacity would not have to pay $10 million or more to install a new mainframe or upgrade the existing systems. There were two problems with this benefit: First, the function that would benefit (the line of business) was different from the function that had to do the work to create the spare capacity (the IT organization); and second, the benefit would accrue at a future unknown date.

The team developing the business case could not resolve the issue since it was a corporate accounting and business case policy. But they could escalate it to senior management and request that they revisit the policy. Ultimately, the CIO and CEO met and agreed to change the policy to allow capacity that was freed up on a shareable resource to be considered as a hard-dollar benefit after an 18-month lag, regardless of which business unit might benefit from the savings. This was a very conservative ruling, but nonetheless it was sufficient to allow the business case to proceed.

Ultimately, the business case was approved, the project was completed successfully, the benefits were realized, and the organization is now using the same methodology (the one described in this chapter) to rationalize and simplify other infrastructure areas.

Case Study: Enterprise Data Warehouse Rationalization Business Case

The following is an example of a quantitative, fact-based analysis of a business problem and associated root cause, along with an action plan that could result from the application of the practices associated with this competency. The MBF technique (see Appendix A) is used to present the results.

Factual Statement of Problem, Performance Trends, and Objectives (Example)

As shown in the graphs in Figure 11.4, the enterprise data warehouse (EDW) storage capacity at BIGCO is doubling every 18 months, and production incidents have increased to an average of one severity level 1 or 2 outage every two days. The cost of the EDW was $22 million in 2008 and is increasing at a rate of 60 percent per year, despite lower storage costs. Implementing the EDW rationalization program would reduce the size of the EDW by 30 percent and simplify the environment, resulting in a drop in the annual cost increase from 60 to 20 percent (which would save BIGCO $84 million over the next three years).

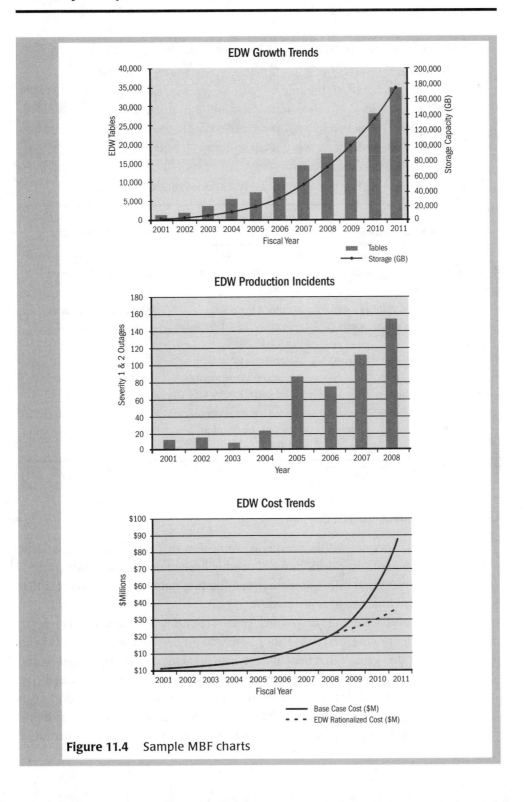

Figure 11.4   Sample MBF charts

Root Cause Analysis, Action Plan, and Expected Results

Based on the facts that BIGCO collected, the team put together an MBF action plan similar to the one in Table 11.3. Using this approach, they were able to concisely prioritize and describe the root causes behind the EDW challenges, the activities required to address the root causes, and the measurable facts that would result from addressing these root causes.

Table 11.3   MBF Action Plan for EDW Rationalization Project

Prioritization and Root Cause	Countermeasure and Activities	Impact Capability
Each LOB creates its own DB tables using its own standards.	Implement an ICC (John Smith, 120-day plan due by 4/1/09).	About half the goal to reduce growth trend.
There is no visibility into what data already exists in the EDW.	Acquire a metadata repository (Jane Doe, issue RFP by 3/15/09).	About half the goal to reduce growth trend.
Problems occur frequently because of poor understanding of interdependencies.	Establish an EDW configuration management board (Jane Doe, by 4/14/09).	Reduce production incidents by > 50 percent.
	Launch a data governance program (John Smith, 6/1/09).	Resolve all priority 1 and 2 audit findings by year end.

Chargeback Accounting

The ICC operates within a larger organization that needs to make periodic decisions about its priorities for allocating limited resources. In this context, an ICC needs not only to secure initial funding but also to demonstrate that continued investment is justified.

Chargeback accounting, which your accounting department may refer to as transfer pricing, describes the options and process for allocating costs in an ICC to other groups that benefit from its work. One of these options is to dispense with a chargeback mechanism and simply use a centrally funded cost center. Central funding, however, is generally considered to be a non-Lean practice since it disconnects the customer of the ICC from the funding source, which can lead to dysfunctional outcomes such as when the executive responsible for the ICC budget reduces the funding without a clear understanding of the impact on the ICC's customers. Another example of diseconomies is the supply and demand mismatch that was discussed earlier—having a fixed annual budget (and fixed staff) for a group that supports a variable workload.

Furthermore, there are additional benefits to a systematic approach to chargebacks, not the least of which is the psychological impact on consumers and providers of the service. It also encourages users to understand the internal financial accounting of the organization so that customers and management alike can work within the realm of its constraints and understand how it relates to the culture.

The goal of a Lean Integration practice should *always* be to implement a chargeback model and ultimately operate as a profit center rather than a cost center (which we also refer to as a self-funding model). This may not always be possible in the early stages of a Lean practice in some enterprises because of existing accounting practices and processes. In that case the ICC team needs to do two things: implement compensating processes to work around the limitations of a central funding model and avoid as many of the dysfunctional behaviors as possible, and mount a campaign to understand, and eventually change, the corporate accounting practices to support a chargeback model.

The campaign to change the accounting practices in an organization may take years, but nonetheless it is essential to pursue it. Stenzel, in *Lean Accounting*, provides some useful advice in this regard: "In order for accountants to fully participate in the lean process, they also need to adopt five lean accountant behaviors: (1) enable process ownership, (2) think sustainable growth first, (3) adopt a long-term view, (4) become a business partner to nonfinancial employees, and (5) adopt the enterprise view of lean."[2]

Economic Framework

As shown in Figure 11.5, the horizontal dimension of the economic framework is the *investment category* with strategic demands at one end of the spectrum and tactical demands at the other end. Strategic demands typically involve projects that drive business transformations or process changes and usually have a well-defined business case. Tactical demands are associated

---

2. Ibid., Kindle Loc. 2577–79.

with day-to-day operations or keeping the lights on. In the middle of the spectrum, some organizations have an additional category for "infrastructure investments"—that is, project-based funding, focused on technology refresh or mandatory compliance-related initiatives. These are projects that are generally considered nondiscretionary and hence appear to be maintenance.

The vertical dimension is the *funding source* and refers to who pays for the services: the consumer or the provider. In a free-market economy, money is exchanged for products or services. For internal shared-services organizations, rather than exchanging real money, accounting procedures are used to move costs between accounting units. Transferring costs from an internal service provider to the consumer of the service is generally referred to as a chargeback.

If we lay these two dimensions out along the *x*- and *y*-axes with a dividing line in the middle, we end up with these four quadrants:

1. **Demand-based sourcing:** This operating model responds to enterprise needs by scaling its delivery resource in response to fluctuating project

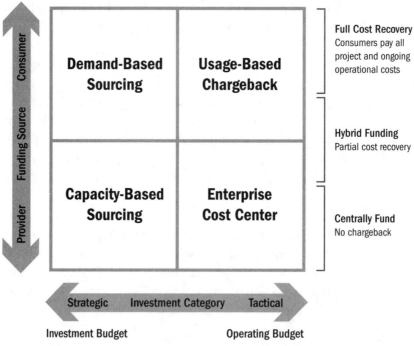

Figure 11.5 Economic framework

demands. It seeks to recover all costs through internal accounting alloca-tions to the projects it supports. The general premise is that the ICC can drive down costs and increase value by modeling itself after external ser-vice providers and operating as a competitive entity.

2. **Usage-based chargeback:** This operating model is similar to the demand-based sourcing model but generally focuses on providing ser-vices for ongoing IT operations rather than project work. Once again, the ICC in this model operates like a stand-alone business that is consumer-centric, market-driven, and constantly improving its processes to remain competitive. While the demand-based sourcing model may have a project-based pricing approach, the usage-based model uses utility-based pricing schemes.

3. **Enterprise cost center:** Typically, this operating model is a centrally funded function. This model views the ICC as a relatively stable support function with predictable costs and limited opportunities for process improvements.

4. **Capacity-based sourcing:** This operating model strives to support investment projects using a centrally funded project support function. Centrally funded ICCs that support projects are excellent models for implementing practices or changes that project teams may resist. Not charging project teams for central services is one way to encourage their use. The challenge with this model is to staff the group with adequate resources to handle peak workloads and to have enough non-project work to keep the staff busy during nonpeak periods.

In general, the ICCs that are funded by consumers and are more strategic in nature rely on usage-based chargeback mechanisms. ICCs that are provider-funded and tactical rely on capacity-based sourcing or cost center models.

Chargeback Models

The kind of chargeback model that is appropriate varies according to two fac-tors: what costs you want to charge and in what context, and the organiza-tional and individual behavior that you want to influence. This section focuses on specific recommendations related to the most common and rec-ommended patterns.

Figure 11.6 shows six of the most common chargeback models and a typ-ical application for each of them.

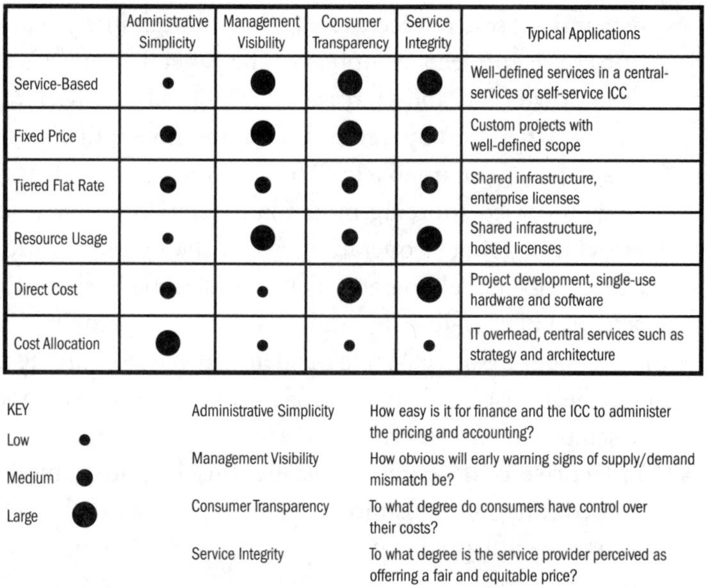

	Administrative Simplicity	Management Visibility	Consumer Transparency	Service Integrity	Typical Applications
Service-Based	•	●	●	●	Well-defined services in a central-services or self-service ICC
Fixed Price	•	●	●	●	Custom projects with well-defined scope
Tiered Flat Rate	•	•	•	•	Shared infrastructure, enterprise licenses
Resource Usage	•	●	•	●	Shared infrastructure, hosted licenses
Direct Cost	•	•	●	●	Project development, single-use hardware and software
Cost Allocation	●	•	•	•	IT overhead, central services such as strategy and architecture

KEY			Administrative Simplicity	How easy is it for finance and the ICC to administer the pricing and accounting?
Low	•		Management Visibility	How obvious will early warning signs of supply/demand mismatch be?
Medium	●		Consumer Transparency	To what degree do consumers have control over their costs?
Large	●		Service Integrity	To what degree is the service provider perceived as offerring a fair and equitable price?

Figure 11.6 Chargeback models

For example, the tiered flat rate model is recommended for charging individual projects or business units for their use of a portion of an enterprise license. Here is a scenario for how it could work: Let's say that the cost of a software license is $100,000 per server and that many projects that are part of an enterprise program could use the same software. A small project may use only a small fraction of the server, but since the license can be purchased from the vendor only in per-server increments, even a small project must pay $100,000. A medium-sized project needs the capacity of an entire server for itself, which would cost $100,000, and a large project might need three servers for a total of $300,000. The overall program will encompass six small projects, four medium, and two large. If each project purchased the license directly from the vendor, the total cost would be $1.6 million, as shown in Table 11.4.

An alternative approach is for the ICC to purchase an enterprise license and recover the costs through internal accounting transfers. Software vendors are motivated to sell enterprise licenses at a discount since doing so reduces their cost of sales and results in a larger up-front sale. In this scenario, we will assume that the enterprise license costs $1 million. Using our

Table 11.4 Project-Based Direct Purchase

Project Size	Number of Projects	License Cost per Project	Total License Cost
Small	6	$100,000	$600,000
Medium	4	$100,000	$400,000
Large	2	$300,000	$600,000
Total Cost:			$1,600,000

Table 11.5 Tiered Flat Rate Chargeback for Enterprise License Scenario

Project Size	Number of Projects	Chargeback Cost per Project	Total Recovered Cost
Small	6	$50,000	$300,000
Medium	4	$80,000	$320,000
Large	2	$200,000	$400,000
Total Recovered Cost:			$1,020,000

projected number of projects, we could allocate the cost of the license using a tiered flat rate: $50,000 for a small project, $80,000 for a medium project, and $200,000 for a large project, as shown in Table 11.5. Note that in this scenario, all projects pay less than they would have individually (which by itself is an incentive to use the standard software).

Note also that the total recovered cost is $20,000 greater than the purchase price of $1 million, which has some positive and negative aspects to it. The ICC may be able to use this $20,000 to fund other activities or to help pay for overhead costs. On the other hand, the $20,000 difference between the purchase price and the chargeback allocations may require a more complicated set of accounting transactions to ensure that all the accounts balance.

Service-Based and Fixed-Price Chargeback

These are the most sophisticated of the chargeback models and require that the ICC clearly define its service offerings and structure a pricing model based on defined service levels. Service-based pricing is used for ongoing service, whereas fixed pricing is used for incremental investment projects. In other words, both of them offer a fixed price for a defined service. This model is most suitable for a mature ICC that has well-defined service offerings and a good cost-estimating model.

Tiered Flat Rate Chargeback

The tiered flat rate is sometimes called a "utility pricing" model. In this model, the consumer pays a flat rate per unit of service, but the flat rate may vary based on the total number of units or some other measure. This model is based on the assumption that there are economies of scale associated with volume of usage and therefore the price should vary based on it.

Resource Usage Chargeback

In this model the "client" pays according to resource usage. Resources may be in one or more categories such as number of records processed, data volume transmitted, or CPU time used by the integration hub. Integration technology can support the collection of metrics for these and other types of resource usage.

Direct Cost Chargeback

Here the "client" pays the direct costs associated with a request that may include incrementally purchased hardware or software as well as a cost per hour or per day for developers or analysts. The development group provides an estimate (with assumptions) of the cost to deliver based on its understanding of the client's requirements.

Cost Allocation Chargeback

Costs can also be allocated on a more or less arbitrary basis irrespective of any actual resource usage. This method is typically used for ongoing operating costs but may also be used for project work. The general presumption with this method is that most IT costs are either fixed or shared and therefore should simply be "allocated" or spread across the various groups that use the services.

Organizational Behavior

In addition to the appropriate application or use of each of the six chargeback models, a second dimension is the organizational behavior that is influenced by the various models. Each of the chargeback models has a unique profile of simplicity, fairness, predictability, and controllability as perceived by the customers of the ICC and by other stakeholders. For example, the cost allocation model is perceived to be the simplest to administer (and hence may be the easiest for the accounting department to support), but it provides little useful information to management or the customer. Allocations are also perceived to have low integrity since, from a customer's perspective, the costs are not predictable (they may increase or decrease based on how the resource is shared by other groups), transparent (it is often hard to pinpoint exactly what costs are included in the allocation), or controllable (the customer has limited or no ability to impact the shared allocations).

The value of these organizational behavior aspects is reinforced by Stenzel in *Lean Accounting*: "Traditional accounting is compelled to allocate 100 percent of occupancy costs to products. Lean accounting allocates only the costs associated with the space utilized by enterprise value streams. This process highlights two key benefits. First, the value stream is motivated to continually reduce their footprint, including any idle inventory storage. Second, the space and the cost of unutilized resources are made visible to decision makers whose task it becomes to grow the business—either increase sales or develop new markets."[3]

For many of the reasons noted earlier, it is particularly important that the ICC be able to influence organizational silos and change organizational behavior. These objectives can include gaining support from silos to suboptimize their operations in the interests of the enterprise, or convincing groups to rely on a shared service rather than to do the work themselves. This is not easy but can be accomplished with an appropriate strategy. The most successful campaigns are sustained on three fronts: economic incentives, social pressures, and moral values. Here are some of the actions that an ICC can take along these three dimensions:

1. Economic incentives include the following recommendations or best practices:

    a. Optimize the delivery of services to be fast, inexpensive, and high-quality. For example, if you want everyone to use a common software solution rather than each group building or buying its own, make the

---

3. Ibid., Kindle Loc. 2528–32.

common solution so cheap, fast, and good that there is no economic motivation to deviate.

b. Make it easy for people to conform to standards. For example, if you want everyone to follow a certain data security standard, rather than publishing a large standards document that requires everyone to read, interpret, and design his or her own solution, simply offer a ready-to-deploy software solution that has the security standards embedded into it. Although it generally requires some investment to make difficult concepts "easy," the results in terms of acceptance are well worth the effort.

c. Offer financial subsidies to encourage behavior changes. For example, if a company is growing and needs a new building, don't charge the first group that moves into one floor of the building the cost of the entire building; instead, carry the cost of the empty floors in a central cost center so that there isn't an economic barrier to acceptance by the silos. As obvious as this is, in the IT arena it is often common practice to charge the full infrastructure cost of a new corporate direction to the first project that intends to use it.

d. Charge a risk reserve or operational premium for nonstandard solutions. For example, rather than mandate that everyone in the company use a certain database vendor, you could structure an IT pricing method that adds a project charge or operational charge for business units that choose to deviate.

2. Social pressure can also encourage compliance and collaboration. In some organizational cultures, these techniques can be more powerful than economic incentives:

a. Empower staff to escalate issues concerning nonconformance. This could include providing coverage for front-line staff who need to maintain a strong working relationship with business partners. For example, to encourage collaboration you could have a federated enterprise architecture function with some architects reporting in a solid-line relationship to business units. When one of these architects needs to take a position on an issue that will be unpopular with the business unit, have the central arm of the enterprise architecture function play the "bad cop" governance role.

b. Empower staff by making information available. For example, if you want to reduce the number of duplicate or redundant technologies or applications, shine a light on the problem by documenting and broadly communicating the portfolio.

    c. Ensure that the defined standards with which you want everyone to comply are in fact endorsed and communicated by a cross-functional management team.

    d. Measure conformance to desired standards by producing periodic reports that are public and visible. The groups or individuals that are not performing will be embarrassed by their peers for being out of compliance, which can be a powerful incentive.

    e. Reward compliance with standards and processes by publishing case studies, highlighting successes at team meetings, and recognizing positive behavior in public forums.

3. Moral values also play an important role in encouraging positive behavior:

    a. Encourage a commitment to the "greater good" by clearly communicating the value to the overall organization. Reinforcement messages include "We are all part of the same company; we all succeed or fail together" and "We are all serving the same customer. The customer is king."

    b. Publish integration principles and print them on posters (or mouse pads or coffee cups, for example) to keep them visible.

    c. Ensure fairness and an adequate level of transparency in decisions—especially those that may be unpopular. People will be much more supportive of unpopular directives if they are perceived to affect everyone equally.

To facilitate effective communications in support of these nonfinancial incentives, an ICC should consider establishing an internal "marketing" function. The role of internal marketing is to make the appropriate stakeholders within the organization aware of, interested in, and motivated to use the services of the ICC.

In summary, we recommend a hybrid approach of service-based, flat-rate, and measured resource usage methods of charging for services provided to internal clients:

- Direct cost for hardware and software procurement
- Fixed-price service-based for project implementation
- Measured resource usage for operations
- Tiered flat rate for support and maintenance

Chargeback Case Studies

This section provides two ICC chargeback case studies based on real-world examples. The name of the company and other facts have been disguised to allow us to be as specific as possible about the details.

Case Study: ETL COE Production Support Chargeback

A U.S.-based financial institution, LEAN-BANK, was looking for a way to reduce the cost of loading its Teradata-based data warehouse. The ETL process was mainframe-based and had an annual internal cost of more than $10 million, which was charged back to end users through an allocation process based on the percentage of data stored on the warehouse by each LOB. Load volume into the warehouse was averaging more than 650 GB/day, and demand for new loads was growing steadily. LEAN-BANK decided to implement a mid-range solution for all new ETL processes and eventually retire the more expensive mainframe-based solution.

Initial implementation costs of a highly scalable mid-range solution, including licensing, hardware, storage, and labor, were approximately $2.2 million annually. This solution consisted of an 11-node, grid-computing-based Sun system with a shared Oracle-RAC data repository. Three nodes were dedicated to production and two nodes each to development, system integration test, user acceptance test, and contingency. Estimated daily integration load capacity for this solution was greater than 40 TB/month.

Management wanted to implement the new solution using a self-funding mechanism, specifically a chargeback model whereby the projects and business units using the shared infrastructure would fund it. To achieve this goal, the cost recovery model had to be developed and it had to be compelling. Furthermore, given that the ETL capacity of the new mid-range environment exceeded the daily load volumes of the existing Teradata warehouse, there was significant opportunity for expanding how many applications could use the new infrastructure.

The initial thought was to use load volumes measured in gigabytes per month to determine chargeback costs based on the total monthly cost of the environment, including nonproduction elements. There would be an allocation to each LOB based upon data moved in support of a named application using the environment. Load volumes were measured daily using internal mid-range measurement tools, and costs were assigned based upon gigabytes per month moved. The problem with this approach was that early adopters would be penalized, so instead, a fixed-price cap was set on the cost per gigabyte per month. Initially, the cost cap for the first four consumers was set at $800 per gigabyte to find the right balance between covering much of the cost but at a price point that was still tolerable. The plan was to further reduce the cost per gigabyte as time went on and more groups used the new system.

After 18 months, with over 30 applications on board and loading more than 6 TB/month, the gigabyte-per-month cost was reduced to less than $50. Load volumes and the associated costs were tracked monthly. Every six months, the costs were adjusted based upon the previous six months' data and assigned to the appropriate named applications.

Over time, the chargeback methodology of gigabytes per month proved to be incomplete. Required labor was driven more by the number of load jobs per supported application and less by total volume. The chargeback model was adjusted to tie labor costs to the total number of jobs per application per month. Hardware and software costs remained tied to gigabytes loaded per month.

All in all, the chargeback approach was an effective way to use projects to fund a shared infrastructure. At the time of this writing, use of the new mid-range solution continues to grow. There is no set date when the legacy mainframe ETL jobs will be fully retired, but with all the new ETL work being deployed on the mid-range infrastructure, the legacy jobs will gradually shrink through attrition; eventually, it will be an easy decision to invest in migrating the remaining ones to the new environment.

Case Study: Self-Funding ICC Chargeback

Building further upon the case study at LEAN-BANK, funding for incremental production support personnel was identified as a risk in the early stages of deployment of the new shared infrastructure. The new integration environment and its associated processes were internally marketed as highly available and immediately ready for any application that needed the service. Over time, however, it became increasingly obvious that as more applications moved from project status to production status, incremental production support staff would be required. Forecasting that incremental production support labor and having the funds available to source the labor became increasingly challenging in an organization that planned base support budgets annually. In short, demand for production support resources was driven by projects, out of sync with the annual operating budget planning cycle.

As stated in the previous case study, the environment was self-funded by the applications using a fairly simple chargeback methodology. The chargeback methodology assumed that sufficient production support staff would be available to support all consuming applications. However, the data used to calculate a monthly application chargeback was based upon actual throughput metrics after several months in production. In other words, the metrics that showed that additional staff would be required became apparent months after the workload had already increased. When an application came aboard that required extensive support but did not have incremental labor forecast for it, the production support staff in place was forced to make heroic efforts to maintain the application. The resultant staff angst and internal customer dissatisfaction were significant.

To solve this issue, the concept of an operational surcharge to support the project before moving the application into production was instituted based upon estimated data and job volumes. Called Operational Capacity from New Initiatives (OCNI), this cost was added to the project estimate before initial funding was allocated to the project. Once the project was approved and funds were transferred between cost centers, the OCNI funds were pooled in a separate cost center (i.e., held in "escrow"), often from multiple projects, until the work volume in the environment exceeded prescribed limits (usually average hours worked by the production support staff during four weeks). When work volume limits were exceeded, incremental staff was sourced and paid for with the escrowed OCNI dollars. At the end of the budget year, the incremental staff were moved to the base operating budget and the cycle started over again with the new budget year. This allowed the flexibility to rapidly add production support staff as well as effectively plan for base staff in the following budget-year forecast.

The result was that operational support resources more closely aligned with the actual support workload. The operational staff were not as stressed, the internal consumers were happier because their costs were included up front in the planning cycle, the finance staff were pleased to make the model work within the constraints of the company's accounting rules, and IT management had increased confidence in making decisions related to the annual operating budget planning. In summary, it was a win-win for everyone.

CHAPTER TWELVE

Integration Methodology

Software entities are more complex for their size than perhaps any other human construct, because no two parts are alike. . . . If they are, we make the two similar parts into one, a subroutine, open or closed.

Frederick P. Brooks, Jr.[1]

A Lean Integration methodology cannot be "bought"—it must be cultivated and evolve from the ground up. When we talk about "buying" a methodology, we mean adopting a prescriptive collection of software development life-cycle techniques, tools, and templates. The issue is that the packaged "off the shelf" methods are virtually all project-based and don't address the issues of sustainability and continuous improvement that are the cornerstones of Lean Integration.

The Lean Integration methodology is concerned not just with building quality solutions, but also with establishing the processes to sustain solutions indefinitely in a production environment. Integration requires a specific methodology that is distinct from project management, software development, or application architecture methods. Integration does indeed leverage techniques from each of these and other disciplines, but it requires a unique collection of methods in order to achieve sustainable positive results.

---

1. Frederick P. Brooks, Jr., *The Mythical Man-Month: Essays on Software Engineering, Anniversary Edition* (Addison-Wesley, 1995), p. 182.

It certainly is possible, and highly encouraged, to adopt selected tools or techniques from the Open Source or supplier communities since there is little point in reinventing the wheel for basic activities or methods that have been proven to be effective. But much of the value of Lean, and the attribute that differentiates it from other methods, is the culture of continuous improvement and organizational learning, which demands that each organization develop its own approach.

This chapter provides an outline for how to establish a methodology for a specific organization. It also compares and contrasts Lean and agile methods and provides a case study in keeping standards as simple as possible. The chapter closes with a case study that shows how a consistent project methodology can be successfully adopted across independent business units in a highly distributed and diverse organization.

The scope for integration methodology is the enterprise system-of-systems, but this term can be applied at different levels. It usually refers to an entire corporate entity or government agency, but it could also refer to a subsidiary of a corporation or to a collection of entities operating as a supply chain within an industry. In any event, the significant point is that an integration methodology comes into play for multi-application integration efforts and not for single applications. Some large applications are themselves complex enough that they use middleware technologies to facilitate integration of the application components, but the process of integrating components within a system should not be confused with integration across systems.

Table 12.1 lists the levels of maturity in an organization with respect to the organization's commitment to the level of integration. As the level of maturity increases, the focus of design and corporate information flow becomes more vital to the lifeblood of the organization. As integration standards become ubiquitous and second nature to developers, information becomes more free-flowing and natural.

The primary challenges that an integration methodology must address are not only to deliver projects that implement integrated solutions, but also to ensure that multiple integration projects that may be in progress simultaneously do not conflict with each other, that different project approaches can be supported, and that the integrations will be sustained once the projects are over.

Table 12.1   Integration Methodology Maturity Model

Maturity Level	Integration Methodology
Project	Integration processes are ad hoc and success is dependent upon the efforts of competent and experienced individuals. Integration is generally viewed as a "project" activity and occurs during the development life cycle. Ad hoc maintenance is performed on integrations once in production. Few integration processes are defined formally. Limited change control is used as a gatekeeping function to production.
Program	Integration processes are defined to identify cross-functional and cross-system impacts of planned changes early in the project life cycle. Basic integration metrics around cost, schedule, and requirements are tracked, and the discipline is in place to repeat earlier successes on integration initiatives with similar characteristics. Change control has evolved into change management. A formal release process is defined that is integrated with change and configuration management and is used to control changes to applications.
Sustaining	Integration management processes for the full life cycle are standardized, documented, and universally applied across the enterprise. An ICC is established that has responsibility for managing and optimizing integration systems in production. Applications are designed with an integration layer as an essential prerequisite. Integration requirements carry more weight than functional requirements in terms of product selection.
Lean	Continuous improvement is enabled via quantitative feedback from processes and from piloting innovative technologies. Internal and external data and process definitions are unified, and common business functions support all channels. Non-development staff are able to define and implement new integrations within defined problem domains through self-service integration portals.

Many organizations tend to overlook the interdependencies between projects and ongoing management efforts. For example, once the integration team for a given project completes its work, it typically hands off each component of the integrated solution to the various functional teams which then maintain their individual pieces of the solution. Over time, the smoothly operating interdependencies between components (which existed at the time of initial deployment) begin to deteriorate. Independently managed elements change without clear end-to-end visibility of the impact.

Creating a sustainable model to build, coordinate, and maintain integrated solutions requires three main ingredients: a defined methodology for each integration project, governance checkpoints to ensure that projects conform to the standards and that they don't undermine or conflict with other integration projects, and a methodology to sustain the integration solution after the projects are completed. The rest of this chapter presents a collection of activities to guide an organization in developing and evolving a "custom fit" integration methodology.

Activities

As depicted in Figure 12.1, six steps are necessary to set up a sustainable integration methodology. Each step is explained in detail in the following sections. Note that we define here the steps to establish an umbrella integration methodology that still permits individual projects in the enterprise to use different methods.

The graphic implies that implementing an ICC is a waterfall, or strictly sequential, process, but it is more accurate to view it as a first-time-through series of activities. All of the activities must evolve over time and are subject to continuous improvement disciplines. Nonetheless, there is a more or less sequential nature to first establishing the integration methods:

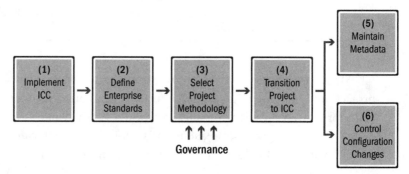

Figure 12.1 Integration methodology activities

1. **Implement the ICC:** An ICC is a prerequisite for a Lean Integration practice, so this is the first step.
2. **Define the enterprise standards:** Define the core standards for architecture, technology, and development that must be adhered to regardless of what project methodology is adopted.
3. **Select the project methodology:** Select a default or standard project integration methodology for the enterprise, and define governance checkpoints for each integration project, regardless of whether the standard project methodology is used or if an alternate methodology is adopted.
4. **Transition the project to the ICC:** Establish processes to transition integration accountability from the project team to the ICC for ongoing management of the integration dependencies.
5. **Maintain the metadata:** Maintaining metadata about integration dependencies and data lineage is one of the ongoing responsibilities of an ICC as applications and their dependencies change.
6. **Control configuration changes:** Establish an ongoing process to manage the changes in applications and their implications for or impacts on other applications.

Step 1: Implement the ICC

Implementing the ICC should be considered a project in its own right. In other words, define the requirements for the desired target state in terms of people, process, policy, and technology dimensions; develop a step-by-step plan to close the gap between the current state and future state; assign responsibility to a manager to implement the plan; and monitor and control the ICC launch implementation to ensure that it stays on track.

An ICC organization could be established quickly in as little as 90 to 120 days if there is a compelling case for rapid implementation such as a top-down directive or pending corporate merger. Alternatively, an ICC could evolve more gradually over a period of several years by moving through several organizational stages (best practices, technology standards, shared services, and central services), with each stage adding greater scope and responsibility.

Choosing the right ICC implementation requires answering questions about the services the ICC should offer and understanding the current organizational culture, financial accounting processes, and human resource allocation. Consider the benefits of an ICC implementation versus the costs and risks of a project silo approach. Choosing the right model is significant because a good ICC will grow in importance to the organization.

When choosing an ICC model, keep in mind that each type is applicable to a different set of business requirements. A company might well evolve through the various models. Some factors to consider include

- Organization size
- Business value/opportunity planning for an ICC implementation
- IT strategic alignment
- Urgency/bias for action

An ICC may be implemented quickly or it may evolve, but in either case a plan should be developed. Table 12.2 shows a sample 120-day plan with specific milestones for each 30-day period in four tracks that address the people, process, policy, and technology dimensions.

Step 2: Define the Enterprise Standards

Standards for implementation should fall into categories, for example, architecture, technology, and development. During the actual implementation, standards are developed for areas of integration development. As well, linkage to existing internal standards should be established.

There is a widespread problem of which many of us (including ourselves at various times over the years) are guilty: overengineering standards. We certainly see examples of overly complex specifications from the standards bodies, but even internal corporate standards can succumb to the same trap of developing overly complex and unimplementable standards.

A core Lean principle in regard to developing standards is to define the minimum number of things that must be the same so that everything else can be different. In the foreword to the book *RESTful Web Services* by Leonard Richardson and Sam Ruby, David Heinemeier Hansson admonishes against "what the merchants of complexity are trying to ram down everyone's throats."[2] It is not clear from his brief foreword who exactly Hansson (creator of Ruby on Rails) considers to be the "merchants" who are creating complexity. While there are indeed people and organizations that benefit from excessive

---

2. Leonard Richardson and Sam Ruby, *RESTful Web Services* (O'Reilly Media, Inc., 2007).

Table 12.2 Sample 120-Day ICC Implementation Plan

Milestone Category	Day 30	Day 60	Day 90	Day 120
People	▪ ICC director named ▪ Resource plan approved ▪ Sponsors and stakeholders identified	▪ Core team members on board ▪ Key partnerships with internal governance groups formalized ▪ Stakeholder communication plan documented	▪ Subcontractor and third-party agreements signed off ▪ Initial team training completed ▪ Enterprise training plan documented	▪ Staff competency evaluations and development plans documented
Process and policy	▪ ICC charter approved ▪ Early adopters and project opportunities identified	▪ ICC services defined ▪ Core integration standards or principles documented	▪ ICC service engagement and delivery process defined ▪ Internal communications and marketing plan documented ▪ Chargeback model approved	▪ Services discoverable and orderable by internal customers ▪ Regular metrics reporting in place ▪ Ongoing metadata management process in place
Technology	▪ Integration platform configured	▪ ICC tools selected ▪ SLA template established	▪ Operating procedures documented (availability management, fail-over, disaster recovery, backup, configuration management, etc.)	▪ Applications connected and using the integration platform ▪ SLA agreements signed off

complexity, we're not as cynical as Hansson and wouldn't give suppliers, standards bodies, or industry analysts as much credit for a premeditated complexity strategy that the term *merchant* suggests.

A number of forces create excessive complexity:

- The obsession with creating standards/protocols that are all-encompassing and deal with every possible situation
- The desire for consensus and harmony, resulting in the inclusion of everyone's point of view—even if some of them are not rational
- Weak discipline associated with the hard work of weeding out nonessential elements
- Poor reference architectures that don't provide a clear ME&C structure, thereby leaving lots of room for interpretation and overlap

None of these vulnerabilities is a unique attribute of the software vendor community or the standards bodies; these are human qualities to which everyone is subject.

As Samuel Johnson once said, "If I had more time I would have written more briefly." The fact is that the IT world is indeed complex, but it is the job of the Lean Integration team to do the hard work and take the time to make it simple for others.

The architecture of the Web, REST (which stands for "representational state transfer"), is a great example of the success of simplicity. While you might be able to get away with a more complex set of standards in your enterprise (especially if you have a strong central group that carries a big governance stick), any complex standard becomes increasingly harder to leverage effectively the bigger you get.

It is important to distinguish between "project standards," which are defined by the methodology selected in step 3, and "enterprise standards," to which all projects must conform. In addition to enterprise standards for technology, interfaces, information exchange protocols, and data definitions, the enterprise standards must also define the governance checkpoints that each project must follow. These checkpoints provide the mechanism to ensure that projects don't conflict with each other and that they conform to the enterprise standards.

Clearly documented enterprise standards are one of the best opportunities for establishing the ICC's value as a governance group. This will help in areas of resource utilization and service management and in reducing support costs.

Step 3: Select the Project Methodology

Building an ICC involves developing an ongoing discipline and support group around integration services and capabilities. This ongoing competency is independent of project methodologies and provides the support infrastructure for sustainable data and process integration.

Step 3 is the task of selecting a default or standard project integration methodology for the enterprise. Despite the fact that a standard may be defined, it is important to note that different integration projects may use different methods. For example, if you contract with a systems integration firm to serve as the prime contractor for a large project, that firm will almost surely insist that it use its own proprietary methodology since it is a key source of value.

Nonetheless, the ICC must be prepared not only to support the standard enterprise project methodology, but also to be flexible enough to support other projects that may be using other approaches. Step 3 involves defining governance checkpoints for each integration project, regardless of whether the standard project methodology is used or if an alternate methodology is adopted. Recommended checkpoints for waterfall-style projects include

- Completion of the project charter
- Approval of funding
- Identification and selection of the methodology for a given project
- Completion of high-level design, including the definition of all integration dependencies
- Completion of a detailed design and impact on shared technology components
- Start of integration testing
- Approval to migrate changes to production
- Post-implementation transition to ongoing support groups

Each of the defined checkpoints should specify who will perform the review and how (i.e., peer review, committee review, management review, etc.) and what documents or artifacts are required.

The approach for supporting projects that use agile or iterative methods is somewhat different. Agile methods focus less on documentation and formal handoffs and instead rely more on in-person communication and demonstrable results through frequent releases of incremental functionality.

See the following section on agile versus Lean methodology for a more detailed discussion of this topic.

Step 4: Transition the Project to the ICC

After each project is complete and ready to be transitioned, the solutions are turned over to the ICC for ongoing management of the integration dependencies. Items to transition include

- Project artifacts/drawings
- Data extraction and transformation rules
- Testing plans/results
- Reusable rules and objects
- Metadata sources
- End-to-end data flows and process dependencies

The ICC is responsible for identifying the actual transition deliverables and determining the timeline or phase of the project when specific items are due. The focus is not only to determine integration points, but also to manage ongoing maintenance.

Note that in addition to transitioning the "integration" dependencies to the ICC, the project team must also be prepared to transition ongoing responsibilities for the project to other IT groups (e.g., application maintenance, network, security, etc.).

Step 5: Maintain the Metadata

Maintaining metadata about integration dependencies and data lineage is typically one of the ongoing responsibilities of an ICC. As applications and their dependencies change, it is important to incorporate any changes that occur in various systems as a routine part of ongoing maintenance of the metadata that describes each of the components and their relationships.

More information on this topic can be found in Chapter 13, Metadata Management.

Step 6: Control Configuration Changes

Controlling configuration changes is also one of the key ongoing responsibilities of an ICC. A process must be in place to manage the changes in applications and their implications or impacts on other applications. The goal is to focus on the integration aspects of new changes as well as the configuration of the integration systems that support them.

More information on this topic can be found in Chapter 17, Integration Systems.

Summary

The Lean Integration methodology involves the process of selecting, developing, and sustaining an ICC model; coordinating and monitoring multiple projects as they are being executed; and sustaining the integrations once the projects are completed. The ICC model provides the integration governance over application systems as they are developed and progress through their life cycle.

Agile versus Lean Methodology

Agile principles and Lean principles have much in common. This section addresses the following questions:

1. Do agile methods complement or work against Lean Integration? In other words, what is the degree of alignment between agile principles and Lean Integration principles, and how would they work in an Integration Factory context?
2. Can Lean Integration support an agile project methodology? For example, an Integration Factory may be supporting multiple projects at any given time, some of which may be following a waterfall methodology and others an agile methodology. Is this a problem and should the factory have different processes for the two project types?

To begin, we need to provide a high-level overview of agile. Wikipedia defines it this way: "Agile software development refers to a group of software development methodologies based on iterative development, where requirements and solutions evolve through collaboration between self-organizing cross-functional teams. The term was coined in the year 2001 when the Agile Manifesto was formulated."[3]

---

3. Wikipedia, August 2009, http://en.wikipedia.org/wiki/Agile_software_development.

The Agile Manifesto makes the following value statements:

We value…

1. **Individuals and interactions** *over processes and tools*
2. **Working software** *over comprehensive documentation*
3. **Customer collaboration** *over contract negotiation*
4. **Responding to change** *over following a plan*

That is, while there is value in the items on the right, we value the items on the left more.[4]

Like many other methodologies, agile has its own unique language such as the "ScrumMaster," who maintains the processes in lieu of a project manager; a "sprint," which is typically a two- to four-week period during which the teams create a potentially shippable product increment; and the "daily scrum," which is a project status meeting that occurs every day and is time-boxed to usually 15 minutes. If we look past the buzzwords, we find many Lean concepts embedded in agile. Agile also uses some of the same techniques as Lean, including A4 problem solving and the "5 Whys."

Certainly there is more to integration than software development, but to the degree that integration does involve software development, there is a great deal of alignment between the respective methods, as summarized in Table 12.3. The left column shows the 12 agile principles from the Agile Manifesto. The right column shows the Lean principles that have many of the same objectives as the corresponding agile principles.

Table 12.3   Agile Principles Compared to Lean Principles

Agile Principles from www.agilemanifesto.org	Analogous Lean Principles/Concepts
1. Our highest priority is to satisfy the customer through early and continuous delivery of valuable software.	Focus on the customer Pull and flow Deliver fast
2. Welcome changing requirements, even late in development. Agile processes harness change for the customer's competitive advantage.	Plan for change Mass customization

---

4. www.agilemanifesto.org.

Table 12.3   Agile Principles Compared to Lean Principles *(Continued)*

Agile Principles from www.agilemanifesto.org	Analogous Lean Principles/Concepts
3. Deliver working software frequently, from a couple of weeks to a couple of months, with a preference to the shorter timescale.	Small batch sizes *Poka-yoke* (mistake-proofing)
4. Business people and developers must work together daily throughout the project.	Optimize the whole Empower the team
5. Build projects around motivated individuals. Give them the environment and support they need, and trust them to get the job done.	Empower the team
6. The most efficient and effective method of conveying information to and within a development team is face-to-face conversation.	*Gemba* (workplace) *Genchi genbutsu* (see for yourself) *Andon* (signaling light)
7. Working software is the primary measure of progress.	Eliminate waste
8. Agile processes promote sustainable development. The sponsors, developers, and users should be able to maintain a constant pace indefinitely.	Flow, Takt time, *heijunka* (production leveling), and other factory concepts
9. Continuous attention to technical excellence and good design enhances agility.	Build quality in
10. Simplicity—the art of maximizing the amount of work not done—is essential.	Eliminate waste
11. The best architectures, requirements, and designs emerge from self-organizing teams.	Empower the team
12. At regular intervals, the team reflects on how to become more effective, then tunes and adjusts its behavior accordingly.	Continuously improve
	Jidoka (autonomation) Automate processes Value stream optimization

Do Agile Methods Complement or Work against Lean Integration?

Several of the agile and Lean principles are very similar and don't need much clarification. A few of them, however, do deserve a few comments to highlight the unique qualities of one or the other.

One of the strongest themes in agile is iterative development, as indicated in principles 1 through 3, which even go so far as to prescribe the frequency of iterations. Lean doesn't prescribe an iterative approach nor does it put an arbitrary time frame on delivery, but it nonetheless aligns strongly with agile in the sense that Lean strives for small batch sizes (increments) and the fastest possible delivery in response to customer demand (pull). Lean also uses man-ufacturing techniques such as mass customization to achieve rapid delivery. Furthermore, one of the best ways to mistake-proof (*poka-yoke*) integration components is to build them incrementally and validate each iteration. As stated by Michael Levine in *A Tale of Two Systems*, "Continually ask this ques-tion: 'What is the minimum set of functions we can put into production and get business value?' Then do that. Then do it again."[5]

Agile principles 4, 5, 6, and 11 address team issues and also promote the idea of bottom-up empowerment, just as Lean does. Lean, however, does not prescribe the frequency of interactions (agile suggests daily meetings), nor does it insist on face-to-face conversations. Lean, however, does put a strong emphasis on visiting the *gemba* (the workplace where the work is being done), which accomplishes similar results. Business sponsors, users, and other stakeholders shouldn't sit in their offices and manage by reading status reports or participating remotely via conference call; they should *genchi genbutsu* ("go see for yourself"). Lean also relies heavily on pull sig-naling mechanisms such as *andon* lights; the equivalent in a software fac-tory may be an automated workflow tool that places a task on the integration team member's work queue. In short, Lean doesn't insist on face-to-face communications as long as the appropriate mechanisms are in place to ensure effective handoffs.

One way to achieve effective communications that doesn't necessarily require face-to-face interactions is the use of simulations, even in the early stages of a project before all the components of the end-to-end solution are available. Simulation tools have the benefit of forcing a degree of specificity that computer software demands; in other words, the act of programming a

---

5. Michael K. Levine, *A Tale of Two Systems: Lean and Agile Software Development for Business Leaders* (CRC Press, 2009), p. 291.

computer to produce a simulation forces you to be specific. And as explained by Levine, ". . . simulations [are] a mechanism of visual management, one of the key integrating events that helped teams collaborate effectively."[6]

Agile principles 1, 3, and 7 prescribe working software as the primary deliverable rather than specifications or documentation. Agile keeps much of the project documentation (such as requirements and user stories) on flip charts or whiteboards in the project room; these are discarded after the project is over. Lean is similar in that it focuses on what the customer values (working software) and eliminating waste such as unnecessary documentation that is not used after the project is over.

If agile and Lean are so similar, why couldn't one just use agile methods instead of Lean? There are several key concepts in Lean that agile does not address. Fundamentally, agile is a project methodology, whereas Lean is a sustaining methodology. Lean puts a strong emphasis on understanding, optimizing, and continuously improving the entire value stream, not just optimizing a given project. Agile does encourage team learning, but its focus is on staff development and not on institutionalizing end-to-end process improvements. Lean also applies manufacturing principles such as *jidoka* (autonomation) and mass customization to the software development process; agile is silent about these.

To answer the question in the header of this section, agile and Lean are generally very complementary when it comes to developing integration software components. Lean, however, goes further in providing sustainable practices. Our best advice to you is to select techniques from both practices and continuously learn and improve on them in your organization.

Can Lean Integration Support an Agile Project Methodology?

Another way to state this question is "Should an ICC, or Integration Factory, do anything different when supporting a project that is using a waterfall methodology versus a project that is supporting an agile methodology?" When the question is stated in this way, the answer is no, you shouldn't do anything different, for one simple reason: Focus on the customer and deliver what (s)he considers valuable. If the customer (the project being supported) desires rapid delivery of incremental integrations, the ICC should deliver that. If the customer desires formal delivery and signoffs

---

6. Ibid., p. 144.

of stage-gate deliverables, the ICC should deliver that. The beauty of the metadata-driven Integration Factory is that it can just as easily respond to both approaches since it views the factory information flows to be just as important as the material flows. The Lean disciplines involved in defining, optimizing, and automating both of these flows make it easy to tap into the metadata repository and extract formal reports and deliverables that the waterfall project requires or to focus on rapid delivery of small batches of functionality that the agile project demands.

An interesting observation that we have made over many years of experience in working on large, complex IT projects that follow a waterfall methodology is that they still require an agile integration approach. The reality is that the big requirements document that is produced in the early stages of the project never fully, or accurately, specifies the interfaces, data quality profile, or integration requirements. A common pattern we have observed is that the integration testing phase always takes longer than anticipated and involves multiple iterations of integration components as the "real" integration needs are uncovered. Once again the factory approach handles this situation elegantly by using a metadata-driven mass customization approach to rapidly deliver and redeliver integration components.

A question we have been asked on more than one occasion is "Which approach is better for a large-scale enterprise systems integration project or program: waterfall or agile?" We generally recommend agile methods, but there are times when it is challenging to do so. For example, there is often more than one customer or organization involved in a large-scale program, and everyone needs to buy into the agile approach for it to work effectively. Some customers (business sponsors) may demand certainty around project scope and cost, which often steers teams down a waterfall methodology path. It also may be difficult to replace a collection of tightly integrated legacy systems in an incremental fashion while also maintaining existing service levels, and hence a big-bang conversion may appear more feasible. Finally, integration teams may be separated geographically in large multinational firms, or the project may include vendor teams operating under different contractual terms, both of which make it difficult to apply agile principles of face-to-face communication.

To close the loop with the question at the header of this section: Yes, Lean Integration can indeed support agile projects just as effectively as it can support waterfall-style projects.

Case Study in Simplicity: The Architecture of the Web and REST versus SOA

One of the largest network-based computer applications in the world, if not the largest, is the World Wide Web. Specifically, it is a hypermedia application designed for publication of content and for consumption of information in a nonlinear fashion. The Web is massively scalable, consisting of millions of computers containing billions (10+ at last count) of pages of directly addressable content. The Web is fast and reliable, and its components interact seamlessly despite the anarchic environment; anyone can plug anything into the Web at any time without an overall coordinated plan.

This is no accident. The architecture of the Web is beautiful in its elegance and has allowed the World Wide Web to grow to the mind-boggling scale and tremendous diversity that exist today. The architecture of the Web is surprisingly simple with just a few constraints that are built on an efficient network infrastructure.

The architecture of the Web is commonly referred to as representational state transfer, or REST for short, as described by Roy Fielding in his doctoral dissertation "Architectural Styles and the Design of Network-Based Software Architectures."[7]

According to Fielding, "An architectural style is a named, coordinated set of architectural constraints." We suggest that all Lean organizations develop specific architectural styles for specific use cases and follow the patterns of success that have led the Web to be one of the most successful, and scalable, architectures in existence. The key design principles that give the Web its desirable properties include these:

- Application state and functionality are divided into **resources**.
- Every resource is uniquely addressable using a **universal syntax**.
- All resources share a **uniform interface** for the transfer of state between client and resource, consisting of a constrained set of **well-defined operations** and a constrained set of **content types** (including code on demand).
- The protocol is
  - Client/server
  - Stateless

7. Roy Fielding, "Architectural Styles and the Design of Network-Based Software Architectures" (PhD dissertation, University of California–Irvine, 2000).

- Cacheable
- Layered

The concept of a "service" in SOA and a "resource" in a Web-centric context are very similar. However, REST provides a few constraints that are left undefined in SOA and therefore open to interpretation. More specifically:

- In REST, resources are structured and designed so that they can be manipulated by a generic set of operations. In SOA, the operations and resources behind them are often tightly coupled. In both REST and SOA, the details of the resource are "hidden" behind the interface, but the REST approach of structuring the resources so that various representations of them can be produced and operated on by a generic set of operations seems to be a more natural way to resolve questions of service granularity and versioning, which in turn makes REST more reusable, flexible, and extendable.

- Each resource is uniquely addressable using a universal syntax. It is this syntax (the structure of the URI, or URL as it is more commonly known) that provides a simple yet effective way to manage the tremendously large and complex namespace. If we apply this concept to a typical company, every resource such as customer, account, order, employee, application, and so on could be further qualified by specific account numbers or other parameters and passed as part of the URI. The root names would be governed at the enterprise level (just like domain names on the Web), but qualifiers and extensions would be under the control of the application service provider.

- A useful way to think about resources and operations in REST is as nouns and verbs. There are many nouns (a virtually unlimited number), but there are very few (four to be exact: GET, POST, PUT, and DELETE) verbs or actions that can be performed on the resources. Proponents of REST maintain that *all* interaction needs can be satisfied by these four operations (the results on the Web demonstrate the validity of the assertion).

- The primary SOA protocol (SOAP, or Simple Object Access Protocol) and the primary REST protocol (HTTP) have a number of similarities but also some differences. Both adopt the client-server separation of concerns, which simplifies component implementation, reduces the complexity of interfaces, improves the effectiveness of performance tuning, and increases the scalability of pure server components. Furthermore, because messages are constrained to be self-descriptive, interaction is stateless between requests, thereby eliminating the need for centralized control, which could become a bottleneck. HTTP, however, is simpler than SOAP; whether one is "better" than the other is a matter of opinion and is one of the key areas for further analysis and validation.

Engagement Services Management

Because ICCs are, by definition, shared-services functions that support many and varied internal groups that are considered to be customers, it is essential that they operate as internal businesses with a portfolio of services that potential customers can easily find, understand, and order.

This section focuses on defining and developing the various services to be provided by the ICC. The number and type of different services provided (e.g., production operations, metadata management, and integration training) determine the initial size and scope of the ICC. Once the services have been defined and the appropriate capabilities established, the organization can consider sustaining the service(s) in an operational mode.

Services to be offered by an ICC should include the following attributes:

- Name of the service
- Description/narrative of the service
- Who the likely buyer or consumer of the service is
- Value proposition
- Cost of service
- Ordering mechanism and delivery process

Many people confuse service definitions with delivery processes. There is a natural tendency for individuals to describe what they do from their own perspective rather than from the perspective of the customer who is the consumer of the service. Lack of clarity on this distinction is a primary cause of failed adoption of an ICC. It is imperative, therefore, to internalize this distinction as a first step. Any attempt to develop a service portfolio or value proposition in advance of obtaining this insight is pointless, because the result will be an organization that is perceived to be internally rather than externally focused, a situation that undermines the success of an ICC.

The sequence of steps needed to fully define the portfolio of services is as follows:

1. Define the services, which in turn
2. Define the engagement and delivery processes, which in turn
3. Specify the capabilities and activities, which in turn
4. Drive the requirements for tools and skills

In summary, the first step is to define the services from the customer's perspective.

For example, consider a package-shipping company. If it defines its service and value proposition as guaranteed rapid delivery of packages from anywhere to anywhere in the world, it is likely to maximize processes such as an extensive network of local delivery vehicles, a fleet of airplanes, and sophisticated package-sorting and tracking systems.

If, on the other hand, it defines its service and value proposition as low-cost delivery of bulk goods to major U.S. cities, it is likely to maximize its network of truck and train delivery vehicles between major cities. Note that in this second scenario the customer is different (i.e., a smaller number of commercial customers instead of a large number of consumer customers) and the value proposition is also different (i.e., low cost versus speed and flexibility).

Thus, it is essential to begin with a description of the service based on a clear understanding of who the customer is and what the value proposition is from the customer's perspective. Once that has been established, you can begin to design the processes, including how the customer will discover and order the service.

After the process definitions are complete, the ICC can proceed to define the capabilities and activities necessary to deliver the service requests and also to determine the tools and staff skills required.

Note: Fulfillment elements such as capabilities, activities, and tools, while essential to maintain a competitive service delivery, are irrelevant to the customer and are non-value-added activities. For example, customers don't care how the delivery company knows about the current status of each package, as long as the organization can report the status to the customer.

Similarly for an ICC, the internal customers don't really care how the developer optimizes the performance of a given ETL transformation; they care only that it satisfies their functional and quality requirements.

There are two key tests for determining if the services have been defined at the appropriate level of detail:

1. The first is to list and count them. If you have identified more than ten ICC services, you have probably mistaken fulfillment elements for services.
2. The second is to apply a market-based price to the service. If an external organization with a comparable service description and a specific pricing model cannot be located, the service is probably defined at the wrong level.

Because defining services correctly is the foundation for a successful ICC operation, all automation, organization, and process engineering efforts should be postponed until misconceptions are resolved.

Service identification begins with the question "What need or want are we fulfilling?" In other words, "What is our market, who are our customers, and what do they require from us?" A service is defined in terms of explicit value to the customer and addresses items such as scope, depth, and breadth of services offered. For example, it should consider whether the service will be a one-size-fits-all offering, or whether gradations in service levels will be supported.

Individual services can then be aggregated into a service portfolio, which is the external representation of the ICC's mission, scope, and strategy. As such, it articulates the services that the ICC *chooses* to offer.

Two points are implied:

1. The ICC will consciously determine the services it offers based on perceived need and value. Simply performing a service "because we always have" isn't relevant.
2. No ICC can be world-class in everything. Just as an enterprise may develop strategic partnerships to outsource non-core competencies, so must the ICC. This means sourcing strategically for services that are non-core to ensure that the ICC is obtaining the best value possible across the entire service portfolio. Outsourcing for selected portions of the service delivery can have other benefits as well, such as the ability to scale up resources during periods of peak demand rather than hiring (and later laying off) employees.

A *value proposition* states the unique benefits of the service in terms the customer can relate to. It answers the questions "Why should I [i.e., the customer] buy this service?" and "Why should I buy it from the ICC?" ICCs are well positioned (because of their cross-functional charter) to understand the nuances of internal customer needs and to predict future direction and develop value propositions in a way that appeals to them.

Other Factors Affecting Service Offerings: Strategic versus Tactical Priorities

Another significant challenge of determining service offerings is the question of targeting offerings based on strategic initiatives or tactical projects. For example, if an ICC has a charter to directly support all strategic initiatives and provide support to tactical projects on an advisory basis, the service portfolio might include several comprehensive service offerings for strategic initiatives (e.g., end-to-end analysis, design, development, deployment, and ongoing maintenance of integrations) and offer a "best practices advisory" service for tactical projects.

A list of IT projects provided by the project management office for an organization can be scored on a 1-to-5 numerical scale or simply categorized as high, medium, or low, depending on the level of cross-functional integration that is required.

Once the projects are categorized and scored with regard to integration needs, the ICC could provide central services such as development management of strategic projects that have a high index of integration versus projects with low levels of cross-functionality (which could be supported with a best-practices ICC model).

The goal is to focus on ICC service offerings that are geared toward strategic integration initiatives and to provide minimal ICC services for tactical projects.

The key to a successful ICC is to offer a set of services that add value to the ICC team. Services can be very helpful in reducing project overhead for common functions in each data integration project. When such functions are removed from the project, the core integration effort can be reduced substantially.

Case Study: Integration Methodology in a Decentralized Enterprise

Case Study Context

We often hear IT leaders say, "We can't adopt a centralized integration methodology in our company—our business units are highly independent and won't accept a standard method that is dictated by head office. It just won't work in our culture."

The following case study challenges this perceptual roadblock by looking at how a global consumer products company, in a highly diversified culture with strongly independent operating groups, was able to adopt a standard integration methodology.

The enterprise we looked at is a 60-year-old consumer products company with over 100,000 employees worldwide. The company operates in 46 countries and 30 languages and prides itself on being successful by using a highly decentralized management structure where each of the 80-plus business units has a high degree of autonomy. The company's tremendous growth is attributed to its culture of "acting locally" while still being part of a global brand and striving to optimize the enterprise overall. The "glue" that keeps all these independent groups aligned is a set of management principles that have become part of the day-to-day culture of the company.

Despite the high degree of success that the company realized through its decentralization strategy, challenges began to emerge in the 1990s and became increasingly difficult after the turn of the century. Globalization combined with organic growth and acquisitions created an ever-increasing need for collaboration of business processes, applications, and data sharing across multiple operating companies. IT and business alignment was key to enabling and sustaining continued growth. Global visibility of information was becoming increasingly important for growth, quality, and cost effectiveness. In 2002 the company decided to implement an ICC to enable business units to continue with a successful decentralized management approach while simultaneously improving shared information management.

The Integration Challenge

The charter of the ICC was to create a strategy and platform for integrating business processes and applications. Previously, operating companies developed these services on their own. They were not using a common platform or a common process, and as a result they created systems that could not integrate easily with systems in other operating units. Each operating unit was creating its integration strategies using its own architecture, tools, and data standards. This approach prevented them from leveraging enterprise solutions deployed at other operating units and minimized knowledge sharing. The results were high maintenance costs and many disparate applications and business processes across the enterprise. There was often duplication of efforts that prevented the business from working efficiently.

The Solution: ICC and TPI

The ICC team strategy included the development of a global architecture and an integration methodology—total process integration or TPI for short. It served as a framework to allow the operating units to connect with each other and with their external business partners using a common approach. As a result, the separate units were better able to integrate information and use common processes and tools. The role of the ICC group was to provide services and support in the following areas:

- Global coordination and strategic planning
- Design consulting and consistency in the use of integration standards
- Centralized repository management
- Comprehensive education and training
- Production management and performance monitoring
- Deployment of flexible and open integration tools

The ICC was launched to develop a culture of sharing resources, solutions, and methodologies—including infrastructure and tools—to be leveraged across the enterprise.

The TPI methodology was a business-process-oriented approach used during the integration life cycle. It is a top-down approach that addresses the specific integration needs of the entire enterprise, not just individual applications or operating companies. The methodology uses standards, a process orientation, a common design approach, templates, and a philosophy of reuse to ensure an efficient and successful integration, and it covers the entire integration life cycle from project initiation to deployment.

As a result, the separate companies are better able to integrate information and use common processes and tools. Relying on an integration platform, the company has leveraged the TPI methodology in numerous projects to recognize substantial benefits that impact the bottom line.

Example: Procure to Pay

One of the early ICC successes was the "Procure to Pay" project, which benefited from the TPI methodology. The objective was to build reusable interfaces that integrated affiliate companies' ERP systems with the corporate procure-to-pay system (see Figure 12.2). The ICC team fostered communications across multiple organizational levels and multiple operating companies to build a consensus around the objectives, strategy, and goals for the

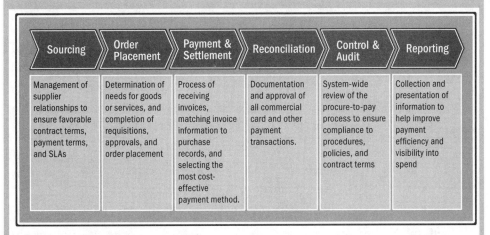

Figure 12.2 Procure-to-pay process

integrated solution as well as to build support for the adoption of the TPI methodology.

Sessions with internal customers (users) identified business process commonality and differences across business sectors. The TPI methodology guided the project's implementation. The project was deployed in the first year and made a powerful impact on end-to-end business operations. Information was orchestrated between Ariba (a Web-based procurement system) and multiple ERP instances (60 of them) using a standard integration platform.

Results

The ICC and the TPI methodology made three important contributions to the company's business: reduced costs, better decisions, and improved governance.

The ICC and TPI shared infrastructure generated cost avoidance savings of over $8 million in the first year, including

- $2 million saved from hardware consolidation
- $2.6 million saved from standardization on an integration platform
- $500,000 saved on shared education and training initiatives
- $3 million saved on shared code components, architecture, and design

Quality decisions depend on access to the right information at the right time. Highly decentralized organizations need to be able to share information and communicate easily between operating units and with external business partners. TPI supported this objective by leveraging consistent and accepted data definitions. This standardization improved production, manufacturing, inventory planning, and other business functions. As operating units improved communications and process integration, they realized

- Improved production, manufacturing, inventory planning, and other business functions
- Consolidation and elimination of redundant business processes
- Improved quality of data to get closer to "one version of the truth"

In subsequent years, the organization moved from decentralized IT toward common global and regional systems while continuing to support an extremely successful decentralized business model. IT teams were able to overcome the country and business group barriers to implement more enterprise-level applications because of the ICC's success. After five years, the enterprise enhanced TPI and adopted it as part of its governance process for SOX, security, and integration.

Key Lessons

There are many roadblocks to an ICC being accepted and thriving and growing in an organization with a highly decentralized operating model. The ICC in the case study was able to overcome the barriers through the following key attributes:

- The TPI methodology served as a rallying point for IT and business staff. The ICC followed an open process to gain input from disparate groups to enhance the methods, tools, and templates. It also put a significant amount of effort into internal marketing to build awareness and support for TPI.
- There was persistent leadership in the ICC group. There were many issues that the ICC needed to overcome; if it weren't for the determination of two key individuals in the group, the barriers would not have been overcome. The individuals were not "superstars"; they simply had a clear vision for the company and were determined to realize it.

- Frequent communications celebrated success. The internal marketing of successful projects made use of concrete measurable results, not just qualitative statements.
- There was bottom-up versus top-down support. The ICC did have senior management support, but it operated day to day in a way that built bottom-up support from staff across the organization.

CHAPTER THIRTEEN

Metadata Management

*A distributed system is one in which the failure of a computer you
didn't even know existed can render your own computer unusable.*

Leslie Lamport[1]

In a product factory, people can touch and see the goods being manufac-
tured. In the integration and data management world, however, humans cannot see and touch the assets directly; we can only see representations of bits
and bytes on computer screens, handheld devices, or paper printouts. Data
and software services are definitely real, but there must be a way of tracking
these ethereal objects to make up for the fact that we cannot see or touch
them directly.

Metadata provides the blueprint for data in an organization. Metadata is
also the information describing the data and data processes that enable efficient
factory operations and automation. The metadata management competency is
possibly the single most important technical requirement behind the success
and growth of Lean Integration and the Integration Factory concept. The
Integration Factory is possible only with the proper management of metadata
(data about data) in conjunction with appropriate technology and processes.

---

1. http://en.wikipedia.org/wiki/Leslie_Lamport.

Metadata is conceptually simple. It is documentation about data in terms of what it means; where it is located; when its definition was changed; how it is accessed, moved, and secured; who is responsible for it; who is allowed to use it; and so on.

Analogous to the blueprints that guide the construction of a building, metadata and the models and reports that are generated can be seen as the engineering blueprints of data for an enterprise. In fact, just as there are structural, electrical, and other blueprint views of a building, so do there need to be alternative views of metadata to support the different roles and uses in the business and IT functions.

However, there are several key differences between building blueprints and metadata repositories:

1. Blueprints represent the **target** architecture of a building, whereas data models (to be useful beyond the initial project) must reflect the changes made in the actual construction. For practical reasons, both buildings and IT systems may deviate from the target architecture during construction, but unlike a building, which is relatively static once completed, IT systems are dynamic and constantly changing. So it is critical that the data models be constantly updated to reflect the current state of production operations.

2. Blueprints are static models representing a point-in-time snapshot, whereas data models are dynamic and at the push of a button can be regenerated based upon the contents of the metadata repository. Maintaining a repository of structured data along with tools to generate models is a different discipline from working with hand-drawn models.

By capturing metadata, the IT organization has the ability to measure, manage, and improve its operations. Capturing metadata is critical to efficiently controlling change in enterprise systems, data, and services and the relationships among them. Metadata management provides the foundation to unraveling the complexity of the hairball. When all the integration points between enterprise applications are understood, managed, and controlled, the integration hairball is transformed into an integration system. Organizations that consider data to be an important asset commonly establish dedicated teams to manage metadata in order to ensure its quality and usefulness.

The metadata management maturity table (Table 13.1) provides a rough outline for four levels of metadata maturity. While there is a certain amount of subjectivity around some of the definitions, the outline is a useful tool for assessing an organization's current level of maturity and for establishing a desired target maturity level.

Table 13.1   Metadata Management Maturity Model

Maturity Level	Metadata Management
Project	Data is modeled for specific projects, often hand-drawn in static graphic tools such as PowerPoint or Visio, as required to aid in effective communications during the life of the project. The models may or may not be updated to reflect changes during construction and are stored in a document repository at the end of the project.
Program	Metadata management tools are used for sophisticated business models such as process models, event models, and data dictionaries in support of implementing new capabilities but are not generally considered a management tool for ongoing operations.
Sustaining	A system inventory is maintained in a central repository and serves as the "official" list of applications in the enterprise. Each system is given a unique identifier (name), which is used consistently across the enterprise. A metadata repository is in place that accurately reflects the data and integration dependencies between applications in the production environment. An enterprise reference model is used as a basis for common definitions of business functions and information subjects. There is a broad-based practice across the organization to capture data about IT elements (databases, servers, assets, incidents, etc.) and maintain it in a central repository. A metadata team collaborates with a configuration management database team to unify IT information.
Lean	A data governance program has been established, including a cross-functional committee consisting of senior business managers as well as data stewards. Metadata repositories are used to model future states and perform systematic impact analysis and risk assessment on the current environment state and changes to it. Scanning tools are used to automatically discover elements in production and changes to them. A unified (or federated) repository exists that serves as the equivalent of an ERP for IT databases; it contains relevant management information about IT processes, projects, systems, financials, assets, operations, services, and plans. Processes are in place to optimize the entire information life cycle from data capture through destruction in a controlled fashion.

Metadata Scope for Lean Integration

The potentially limitless scope of a metadata management competency is one of the first big problems to tackle. Metadata is yet another "boiling the ocean" problem—it's too big to tackle all at once, but if you select just a small, manageable scope, it may be too small to add value. Certainly, having a single enterprise metadata repository that contains all necessary information about all IT and business assets across the enterprise might seem like a valuable system, but many metadata initiatives collapse under this vast scope. For the purposes of Lean Integration, let us try to rein in the scope to something more manageable, achievable, and valuable.

In most IT departments, metadata is stored in proprietary repositories in many different tools such as the categories shown in Figure 13.1. The trick to making it useful for the business and IT is to pull the metadata together and determine how metadata in the different environments is related to other metadata.

Let's use an analogy with Google. In some ways, Google had it easy. Thanks to HTTP, HTML, and other standards, Google could create spider programs that crawl the highly homogeneous content of the World Wide Web and understand how pages are linked to each other. Google developed algorithms to score this information so that searching the content would provide highly useful results. In the metadata world of enterprise data, there are few standards yet that allow this kind of cross-vendor metadata crawling, but several companies have made good progress in starting to solve this problem, providing a way to understand and navigate the linkages between metadata objects that come from different vendors.

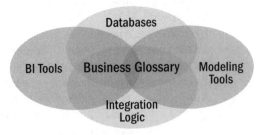

Figure 13.1 Metadata dimensions

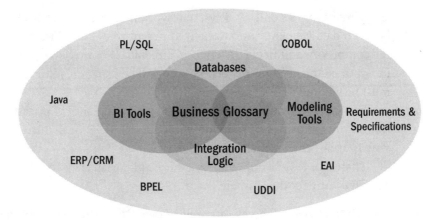

Figure 13.2 Metadata context diagram

Once these linkages are known, it is possible to begin crawling specific threads of the integration system, allowing people to understand where business terms can be found, how those business terms map to underlying databases, how changing one item might impact others, and so on.

To support a more mature Integration Factory, the metadata management capability can be extended so that the Venn diagram in Figure 13.2 includes other outlying and related metadata.

The outer ring in the figure presents additional challenges that can't all be tackled at once, but it is helpful to set the long-term vision for relevant metadata extensions after the core has been developed. The outer ring allows for an expansion of the factory to additional areas of the metadata management capability, in the priority order of cost and benefit as seen by the customers.

Metadata Management Framework

Our goal is to achieve a level of metadata management competency that allows different roles, working together as part of a Lean Integration team, to navigate the integration system in a manner appropriate to their roles in the organization. Analysts have a different perspective from developers, for instance. Business users are interested in business terms, metrics, reports, and such. Developers are interested in this information plus technical details such as primary or secondary keys, encryption, masking, and relationships between data elements. Additionally, different roles have different tolerances for complexity and detail. Therefore, a metadata management system must incorporate the needs of the people who will be using the information, and it must be tailored to their needs.

In order to navigate the integration system effectively, "metadata visualization" techniques need to be developed to the level of maturity that "data visualization" currently enjoys.

There are several different graphical, pictorial views of metadata that help to document the hairball:

- **"Data at rest":** This is our well-known phrase to describe how highly mature visualization capabilities like data models and schema diagrams help to show the way data elements, entities, and objects are related to each other.
- **"Data in motion":** This graphical view of metadata describes how data changes as it moves, either virtually or physically, from its source to its destination. We overload "data in motion" to include descriptions of services, processes, and other workflow-like documentation.

In Figure 13.3, physical metadata describing "data at rest" and "data in motion" is relevant to developers and administrators. As one moves up the layers, the metadata becomes more and more relevant to the business audience. At the top level is the most abstract business documentation, which describes how a company does business, defines its terms, and so forth.

We will be using this information architecture framework as we work through the competencies in the next several chapters to discuss the relationships that bind the competencies together through metadata. While we find this framework useful, we don't mean for this picture and its layers to be taken too literally. Concepts are missing from this diagram, and others may draw more layers or include a third dimension denoting the change in objects over time, for instance. This framework is intended to communicate the categories of metadata information and its potential to describe the complete hairball in a way that allows navigation and understanding of complex systems.

Metadata management is not just collecting the information; its value is that it allows analysts, architects, stewards, developers, and administrators to search, view, understand, change, and maintain the information that is relevant to their work. In other words, different roles should be able to quickly

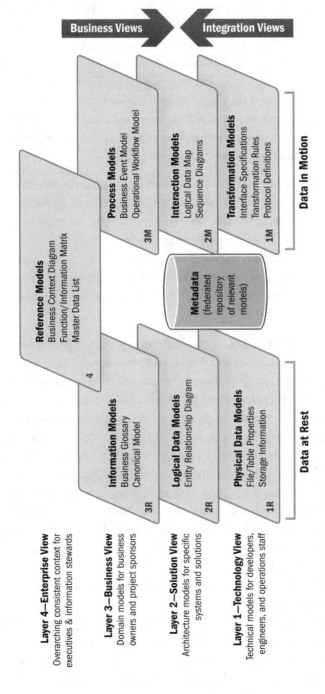

Figure 13.3 Information architecture framework

and easily navigate up, down, and across the stacks of the framework to understand data at rest and be able to link across to see how data is used in motion. All too often metadata projects have ended up creating a "metadata roach motel" where metadata comes in but no value comes out. In our view, to move up the maturity ladder requires giving the different roles the ability to get the information they need to do their jobs.

The framework features a four-layer architecture in which each layer focuses on a level of abstraction that is relevant to a particular category of stakeholders and the information they need:

- **Layer 4—enterprise view:** overarching context for information owners, governance committees, enterprise architects, and stewards
- **Layer 3—business view:** domain models for business owners, project sponsors, SMEs, and program managers
- **Layer 2—solution view:** architecture models for solution architects, designers, and analysts for specific systems and solutions
- **Layer 1—technology view:** technical models for developers, engineers, and operations staff

Layers 1 and 2 are typically created bottom-up (except when custom-developing applications), and layers 3 and 4 are created top-down.

Relevant information about the models is maintained in a metadata repository that is typically federated (i.e., having multiple repositories, each housing specific types of metadata models with common keys that can be used to link models to develop a consolidated view if required). Models are maintained for data at rest (i.e., data persisted and maintained by an application system) and data in motion (i.e., data exchanged and possibly transformed between applications). Sometimes the distinction is tricky, as with "view definitions" in a relational database. These definitions both define data at rest (the structure of the view name and fields as seen by someone accessing the view) as well as data in motion (the definition of the query that populates the view results that are returned).

Chapter 14 on Information Architecture provides a more complete description of all the model types.

There is an additional dimension to the diagram in Figure 13.3 that is critical to visualize. Behind all the objects implied, there is the historical knowledge of that object and how it has changed over time. For instance, to have a full view and understanding of a system, it can be useful to see the requirements documents and design specifications that were behind the original reasoning and development of systems. As discussed in Chapter 9, industry data models are purchasable to jump-start some data projects that appear at first glance to be valuable. Descriptions of data models without an understanding of the original requirements and business use cases can make it extremely challenging to figure out how to actually use these industry models.

Additionally, change histories of how metrics, services, or other objects have changed or grown over time are critical to know. Figure 13.3 should be seen only as the current-state picture for navigating the different layers of metadata and relationships between data at rest and data in motion. Keep in mind the third dimension (time) that associates the operational metadata behind the usage of objects, the original development of objects, and the continual change of those objects.

In other words, for metadata to become the active, live hypertext documentation for the integration environment, these views also need to show how IT systems and their dependencies change.

Challenges

While metadata is conceptually simple, there are a number of challenges associated with managing it in order to realize a business benefit.

Note: This competency does not focus on *project* challenges, but rather on challenges associated with sustaining a metadata practice in an ICC on an ongoing basis in support of either multiple projects or a broader data integration or data governance strategy.

Fully and accurately documenting the data in enterprise systems (and how data is accessed and moved) presents the following challenges:

- There are cost and risk concerns of an enterprise initiative versus a project initiative.
  - Enterprise initiatives are perceived to be more costly to implement and the business case or ROI may not be clear (refer to Chapter 11, Financial Management, for guidance).
  - Because of the inherent complexities associated with a cross-organizational program, enterprise initiatives are perceived as having a higher risk of failure (i.e., accomplishing a practical result).

- Robust process and information models are required but there are few generally accepted best practices. The general issues relate to
  - The need for a service-centric foundation (i.e., defining IT capabilities as services)
  - Logical to physical traceability
  - Dependency management
  - Modeling data at rest versus data in motion
- Metadata that is derived from a variety of sources and tools is often disparate, fragmented, and inconsistent and serves different purposes.
  - Various types of metadata come from sources such as RDBMS, XML, mainframes, and so on.
  - Descriptive (or business) metadata is used to describe the content of the metadata (e.g., zip code, bill of sale, sales data, etc.).
  - Administrative (or operational) metadata is used to manage the operations of the metadata (e.g., records read, time process, etc.).
  - Structural (or technical) metadata is used to describe the physical characteristics of the metadata (e.g., field name, data type, table name, table space, etc.).
- The value of metadata is largely underestimated and not necessarily a common development practice when constructing business applications.
  - In general, the value of documentation on a project is not high (except for very large projects) since the scope and complexity are generally small enough that more informal methods like model sketches, whiteboards, "quick and dirty" spreadsheets, or developers simply remembering it are often quite effective and efficient in the short term.
  - The following examples highlight how it is only after the project is over (or in the context of how the project impacts the broader enterprise) that the value of metadata becomes more evident:
    - Metadata can help with SOX compliance initiatives.
    - Metadata can provide stronger governance of when and where data is used, eliminating costly research and underestimated scope for new projects.
    - Metadata can provide better process control, much as pharmaceuticals use "lot numbers" for medicines and medical devices.
    - Metadata will lead to the development of best practices for data integration as a whole.

- Data governance and stewardship programs that could provide overall direction and guidance are not fully in place.
  - Having well-defined data stewards or owners is extremely important to the success of the use of metadata. (Refer to Chapter 14, Information Architecture, for guidance on how to do it and Chapter 11, Financial Management, for information on how to justify a broader program.)

Table 13.2 provides a high-level summary of common objections to a governance organization like an ICC and how the metadata management best practices can address these concerns.

Table 13.2   Objection Handling with Metadata Management

Common Objections to Metadata Management	Metadata Management Competency Response
Too expensive and time-consuming	Metadata appears to be an incremental cost, but if managed properly, it actually saves time and money because information that is frequently used is cataloged and indexed (much like a library with books). The need for regulatory compliance, enterprise governance, and efficient operations makes metadata management an essential enterprise competency. Use the financial management competency best practices to justify a program. Metadata management is crucial for eliminating waste and changing business systems with more agility.
Too complicated	Metadata may be complicated for those who need to manage and maintain it, but it shouldn't be complicated for others to use. It is for this very reason that an ICC is required since it is able to hide the complexity and make metadata simple and usable for business and IT users who need it. Once systems processes are in place and everyone understands the need to use these processes, the complexity is removed.
Too subjective and dependent on context	A hierarchy of different views of the metadata is needed to satisfy the needs of different stakeholders. A competent ICC with an appropriate enterprise architecture framework can provide the right level of detail in the proper context to make it useful. If suitable views/conceptual understandings are not presented to key stakeholders and implementation staff, either the project eventually does not happen or it is implemented incorrectly with costly outcomes.

Continues

Table 13.2 Objection Handling with Metadata Management *(Continued)*

Common Objections to Metadata Management	Metadata Management Competency Response
No end to metadata	Metadata is indeed a "boiling the ocean" problem. The ICC's role is to define a strategy with an appropriate scope that is manageable and delivers value. Some form of metadata analysis is always required on every project. If the metadata management function can be standardized and managed, project costs will be reduced.
Useless	There are many unsuccessful implementations of metadata that are indeed useless, but it is the implementation that failed, not the concept. There is a "right" way to manage metadata that is reflected in the best practices in this competency area.

Prerequisites

The primary prerequisite for the metadata management competency is to have a defined enterprise integration, data governance, SOA, Lean Integration, or similar strategy. In other words, metadata management is not an end unto itself. It should be viewed as an enabler for a broader cross-functional strategy and clearly be linked to that strategy.

A second prerequisite is to have clear ownership and accountability assigned for the metadata management activities. The accountability may be assigned to an ICC, a data warehouse team, an SOA Center of Excellence (COE), a business intelligence (BI) COE, or other similar group that is operating as a shared-services group supporting all of the applicable functional teams. The critical factor is that the assigned group has a clear enterprise-wide charter.

It is possible to leverage the metadata management practices without these prerequisites, but only in the context of a more narrowly defined scope for a single project/program or a single functional group. While a smaller scope does not offer an enterprise-wide benefit, it can be an excellent way to build expertise and begin a grassroots movement to generate awareness and interest in the broader enterprise.

Some of the other competency areas are not necessarily prerequisites, but they are often complementary practices that should be implemented in concert with a metadata management practice. The most important ones are

- Information architecture (for providing meaningful views for different stakeholders)
- Modeling management (for sustaining and evolving the models and their relationships)
- Financial management (for justifying the required infrastructure and structuring appropriate operational funding)

Industry Practices

Much has been written on metadata. Unfortunately, the most common definition thrown about, that metadata is "data about data," oversimplifies both what metadata is and how valuable it is. We describe metadata as "information about systems, processes, and information and how they work together that describes for the business and IT what they need to know to use, trust, change, and improve those systems, processes, and information."

Metadata elements focus upon the category of information (whether source, target, or transient), the context of data depending upon the role, the resource using the data, or the format in which the information is stored or displayed. For business intelligence usage of metadata, descriptions may also include items such as policy and security rules that relate to enterprise roles and governance issues regarding access, as well as the method for how data should be displayed (e.g., full, mask, or no display). Some of this relates to the classification of data as being for confidential, restricted, or unrestricted usage.

Our earlier book[2] contains a section on Advanced Concepts in Metadata. It defines the requirements for a scalable and predictable level of metadata service across the architect/design/build/deploy/operate/manage life cycle to include

- System-to-system data flow maps
- Detailed and searchable schemas for all data flows
- Middleware configuration management and how components interact with the integration infrastructure

---

2. John Schmidt and David Lyle, *Integration Competency Center: An Implementation Methodology* (Informatica Corporation, 2005), p. 134.

A metadata system is obligated to meet these requirements. Metadata is an established practice in many larger IT organizations. It began with basic "data dictionaries" that documented the business meaning of data elements and evolved into a general inventory of data, programs, and other IT assets. It has significant overlap with IT asset management and configuration management, and there is a general lack of consensus in the IT industry on the relative scope for these disciplines. Refer to section 8.6 of *ICC: An Implementation Methodology* [3] for further details and background.

The wide range of industry definitions highlights the fact that metadata management is still an emerging practice area. The reality is that metadata—in terms of both data about data and data about data processes—has been around for as long as the software industry has existed. In the past, metadata was an inherent element of any operational system or infrastructure. For example, a source code management system had metadata about the source code, an integration hub contained metadata about data transformations, and a messaging infrastructure contained metadata about how messages flowed from queue to queue.

The big shift in recent years is the idea that metadata should be managed as a separate and distinct entity, that is, that it has value in its own right and can benefit the enterprise if managed effectively. Furthermore, this added emphasis on metadata is based on the idea that metadata turns information into an asset that can be leveraged to generate additional business benefits for an organization. In other words, metadata is now seen as something that should be abstracted and managed independently from the underlying assets.

The idea of dealing with metadata as a separate entity has driven another major trend: the need for general-purpose metadata repositories and the need to federate or synchronize metadata across multiple domains and across a wide range of technology components. While there are some excellent tools on the market, as a general rule metadata repositories are still relatively immature. This does not mean that the tools are not useful; to the contrary, they are an essential element of a metadata management practice since it is impossible to manage a large, complex enterprise just with simple tools like spreadsheets.

As a result of the immaturity of the technology and standards, many organizations do not realize the potential benefits of a metadata strategy if they view it strictly as a technology solution. An effective strategy also requires organizational buy-in, training, and support for a wide range of stakeholders who need to update the repository, and policies and procedures to enforce and monitor usage.

---

3. Ibid.

Metadata Management Governance

Metadata management within a governance organization typically has scope where it relates to data functions described by the organization's charter. This organization has two considerations with metadata management: using automated middleware tools that contain metadata, and metadata found in custom code, custom dictionaries, spreadsheets, and other tools where metadata is manually entered. The recommended practice for capturing metadata is to load it automatically. Some tools lend themselves to automatic capture, while others require a custom development approach.

Each metadata attribute can be classified as either active or passive. Active metadata attributes are crucial to the operations of a particular software or integration component. For example, a connection to a database would be considered an active metadata object. Passive metadata attributes are more focused on documentation and classification of the metadata items.

Active metadata attributes should not be migrated on a bidirectional basis without understanding the full impact of such a change. Passive metadata attributes can be migrated bidirectionally without issues.

Activities

The key activities associated with implementing and operating a metadata management capability within the context of an ICC or data governance strategy are shown in Figure 13.4. The seven-step process is described in detail in the following sections.

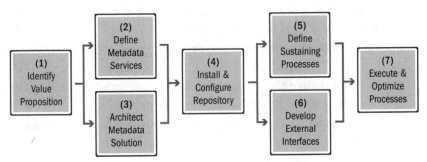

Figure 13.4   Metadata management implementation steps

Step 1: Identify the Value Proposition

The starting point for implementing a metadata management competency is to define the purpose and business value of maintaining it. This is a critical aspect of addressing the "boiling the ocean" problem. It is expensive and time-consuming to collect and maintain metadata, so it should be done only for those elements that have a clear linkage to the defined business need.

It is particularly critical to have a clearly defined scope for the metadata management practice, including what services are offered, who the users/consumers of the services are, what the purpose of the practice is, how it is linked to the enterprise strategy, and which organizational unit is accountable.

- Metadata sponsorship needs to have an enterprise view as opposed to a project view.
- Metadata can be sponsored through a data warehouse initiative to look at information at an enterprise level.
- A shared or centralized ICC service model has an opportunity to look at things from an enterprise level.
- All data storage and movement should be incorporated so that metadata can be captured.
- Funding for a metadata initiative has to be top-down through an enterprise type of view and sponsorship.

If a business case is required to justify the cost and organizational change implications of a metadata management capability, refer to the section on Business Case Development in Chapter 11 on Financial Management.

Step 2: Define the Metadata Services

This activity accepts the output from step 1 and defines the metadata management services that will be offered to the organization. Here is a list of some commonly offered internal services:

- **Project documentation:** a service for project teams to capture and maintain relevant metadata in a central repository
- **Compliance reporting:** a service for enterprise risk and compliance officers to report on conformance to defined policies
- **Data quality metrics:** a service for business leaders and data stewards to track conformance to defined data quality standards

- **Registration:** a service for federated (distributed) repository owners to register and catalog their content in a central registry
- **Synchronization and reporting:** a service for business and IT management to perform ongoing production reporting of centralized or federated (distributed) metadata
- **Discovery:** a service for business and IT management to perform metadata search, analysis, and reporting both on a one-time basis and for special projects
- **Cataloging and linking:** a service for all metadata owners and consumers to maintain the system of record for the enterprise keys

There is a strong interplay between the ICC organizational model (best practices, technology standards, shared services, and central services) and the metadata services that can be offered. For example, if the ICC model is a best-practices ICC, it will not have either the resources or the mandate to actually administer and operate a metadata management office (MMO). The shared-services or central-services ICC models are best suited for an MMO, particularly since they commonly include a production control function.

A data stewardship program is strongly recommended to help with the governance issues. Data stewards are those who know their subject areas and will help define the business rules so that they can be used consistently and have a defined accountability for data quality.

Step 3: Architect the Metadata Solution

This activity, which may take place in parallel with step 2, addresses the technical and solution architecture needs of the metadata management competency. Key considerations are these:

- For consistency, metadata should be captured using automated tools. Metadata that is manually entered is neither consistent nor complete.
- Repository interface standards and supported protocols should be defined.
- The security infrastructure should be defined early to ensure flexibility in supporting different access requirements.
- Performance and scalability should be considered with an eye toward an 18- to 24-month capacity projection.

- An operational or deployment architecture is needed, especially if a high volume of changes is expected in the number and variety of future metadata sources.
- Repository tools and information exchange standards should be selected.
- Tools that don't store metadata should be considered for replacement.
- Consider using industry standards where possible so that automatic tools can be purchased instead of homegrown.

Step 4: Install and Configure the Repository

This activity not only involves the physical installation and configuration of the repository hardware and software but also includes

- Reviewing and assessing metadata use cases
- Configuring out-of-the-box metadata access
- Determining meta-model extensions
- Inventorying metadata sources
- Defining requirements for custom interfaces

In summary, this activity is a key input for steps 5 and 6, which cannot effectively proceed without a clear definition of requirements and a development and test environment for the metadata repository.

Step 5: Define the Sustaining Processes

This activity is often one of the most complex tasks as it usually involves some amount of organization change and may impact how certain individuals perform their jobs. The specific activities will vary subject to the scope of the MMO and the details of the organizational changes that are needed. Following is a list of planning considerations:

- Metadata reports for business and technical users
  - There should be several governance checkpoints linked to project deliverables, especially early in the project life cycle. Determining whether the project is on track is a manual effort unless metadata reports can be used to accurately reflect the progress of the project.
- Governance considerations
  - Enforcement should occur early in the project life cycle to allow opportunity for correction.
  - Production control standards include provisions for capturing metadata.

- Project deliverables
  - Metadata capture should be part of each phase during project development.
  - Metadata requirements should be established for any signoff of any phase of the project.
  - The ICC should set guidelines and standards for what is required for each phase.
  - The rationale is that once a project is close to delivery, many metadata requirements could extend the project beyond expectation.
  - Enforcement of metadata standards should be tied to any production system requirements.
- Data stewardship
  - A data stewardship program is recommended to help with the governance issues.
  - Data stewards are those who know their subject area and will help define the business rules so that they can be used consistently.
  - The ICC should set guidelines on how data stewardship is implemented and maintained.
  - The ICC should set guidelines for the appropriate level of metadata required during the initial phases of metadata management.
  - Data stewards should be "close to the business" in determining data needs and system requirements.

Step 6: Develop External Interfaces

This activity calls for design, development, testing, and deployment of interfaces to metadata sources within the enterprise (or external to the enterprise).

Note: All interface code should be reviewed for reuse purposes. Most rules should be stored centrally, in either a reusable object or a database table, so that they can be published for use.

Step 7: Execute and Optimize the Processes

This final activity is one that never ends (unless the original business need for metadata is eliminated). It involves

- Executing the processes defined in step 5
- Supporting an integrated engagement and fulfillment process for the services defined in step 2
- Performing ongoing process improvements

- Communicating (marketing) the results and value of the MMO to the internal stakeholders
- Looping back through steps 5 and 6 any time a significant change is made to the centralized repository or back to step 3 if a major change is planned that requires a re-architected solution

Information Architecture

> *If a system is to succeed, it must satisfy a useful purpose at an afford-*
> *able cost for an acceptable period of time. Architecting therefore*
> *begins with, and is responsible for maintaining, the integrity of the*
> *system's utility or purpose.*
>
> Mark W. Maier and Eberhardt Rechtin[1]

Information architecture is a subset of enterprise architecture, and it is the discipline that turns data into information by adding context (semantics and metadata); addressing the structural design of shared information environments; and modeling integrated views of data at conceptual, logical, and physical levels. **Information architecture is an essential competency in support of enterprise data integration, process integration, and data governance strategies.** Architecture and integration are complementary enterprise practices. Architecture is about differentiating the whole and transforming the business. Integration is about assembling the parts into a cohesive, holistic system. One discipline takes a top-down approach while the other is more bottom-up; both are essential.

Lean can be associated with information architecture (or IA) from two perspectives: applying Lean practices to the *process* of IA, or using IA practices to achieve Lean Integration. IA methodologies involve a process that,

---

1. Mark W. Maier and Eberhardt Rechtin, *The Art of Systems Architecting* (CRC Press, 2000), p. 10.

like other processes, can be subjected to Lean principles. Applying Lean practices to the process of IA can make IA more effective and efficient. This book is not about architecture per se and so we shall leave it to others or to a future date to write about how Lean can be applied to architecture processes. However, a formal IA practice is a critical ingredient for achieving the benefits of Lean Integration. Limiting variation; architecting for change and reuse; fully documenting and continually improving the appropriate technologies, best practices, and processes—these all reflect Lean principles that benefit from a mature IA practice. We will discuss IA from this perspective.

While the focus in this book is on how integration practitioners can use IA, in Table 14.1 we offer our definition of IA maturity levels, the highest level being a "Lean architecture" practice. A Lean Integration practice can work with and take advantage of IA practices at all levels, but there are limitations on what integration teams can accomplish depending on the level of IA maturity. For example, if the IA maturity is at a level where a holistic inventory of application systems is not maintained (such as at the project or program levels), it will be very difficult for the Lean Integration team to eliminate certain kinds of waste such as redundant information in applications with overlapping functionality and duplicate integration points. In this context the Lean Integration team must either take on this task directly or simply focus on other aspects of Lean, such as standard interface definitions and rapid integration development using factory techniques to support project and program efforts.

Table 14.1   Information Architecture Maturity Model

Maturity Level	Information Architecture
Project	The architect role is in place and is actively practiced on projects. The effectiveness of a given architect is largely the result of the skill and experience of the individual and not of any systematic processes. Cross-system architectural issues are resolved through ad hoc and informal processes.
	Information architecture is mostly about analysis and design of the data stored by information systems, concentrating on entities, their attributes, and their interrelationships.

Table 14.1   Information Architecture Maturity Model *(Continued)*

Maturity Level	Information Architecture
Program	Architecture is practiced at the program level and involves a close working relationship between the architect and the sponsoring business unit from a planning perspective. Architecture artifacts are leveraged across projects and are considered an essential ingredient of achieving business benefits. Architecture practices are formally defined, and a distinction between logical and technical architectures is prevalent. A glossary of business-relevant data is maintained in specific business domains, including a list of business data elements with a corresponding description, validation rules, and other relevant metadata, and is used to identify system of record, quality metrics, ownership authority, and stewardship responsibility.
Sustaining	Architecture is viewed as a business transformation discipline and includes a formal business architecture in addition to a system, information, and technology architecture. A formal documented information architecture exists that includes the definition of a reference framework for information subjects and master data. Standard models are used to capture the information architecture in a repository, using information modeling tools. An enterprise-wide governance process is in place to ensure conformance to data standards. A "canonical data model" is applied to integration technologies as a definition for specific data passed between the systems of an enterprise. At a higher level of abstraction it may also refer to the definition of data stores.
Lean	The management of the "canonical data model" includes model-driven propagation of changes, quantification of impact analysis, test case generation, and integrated SLA management. Quantitative factors are used to measure the flexibility and adaptability of architectural designs. Future technology risks and changes are quantified and included in annual planning processes and in project business cases. "What-if" analyses of project approaches are evaluated as part of the development life cycle. Fuzzy matching of information architecture artifacts (i.e., metadata) aids in the identification of potential refactoring opportunities to continually reduce waste and complexity.

Challenges

In many organizations, there is a growing recognition that data has value not just for the group that captures it, but for the enterprise overall. This has driven the need for

- Data to be managed as a corporate asset
- Explicitly defined accountability for information, including data stewardship
- Data governance committees to facilitate cross-organizational needs
- Best practices for standard business glossaries, canonical data models, and conceptual business views, in addition to traditional logical/physical views
- Best practices for data quality

In short, data needs to be managed holistically and transparently from top to bottom in an organization. The business motivations for this growing trend include

- Application and data rationalization associated with mergers and acquisitions
- Master data management, a "single version of the truth" or a 360-degree view of customer, product, supplier, etc.
- Legacy data migrations in support of ERP or other cross-functional system implementations
- Regulatory compliance and enterprise risk management
- Operational business intelligence
- Information as a service (similar to SOA but with emphasis on data integration)
- Other needs such as supply chain optimization, customer experience improvements, or marketing effectiveness

A critical ingredient for addressing the business needs is an IA methodology that results in the following benefits:

- Helps business and IT groups work toward a common framework and road map
- Identifies redundancies
- Helps IT and the business make better-informed decisions
- Increases leverage with acquisitions and alliances

- Leverages knowledge management
- Generates cost savings by achieving alignment of capabilities
- Elevates the role of IA in business and operational planning
- Reduces risks through additional governance capabilities

While the industry trends, business needs, and business benefits paint a compelling picture of the need for and value of a mature information architecture program, there are a number of significant challenges associated with it:

- Lack of business involvement
- Creating a quantifiable business case
- Cross-functional complexity
- Gaining consensus on data definitions
- Determining an appropriate scope
- Funding for a "new" ongoing process
- Denial that data quality is the root cause of problems

For an IA practice to be effective, it must address each of these challenges. It is therefore critical to first explore each of the challenges in more detail in order to understand how the IA practice addresses them.

Lack of Business Involvement

As a quick check, ask yourself who in your enterprise is accountable for the effective use of

- **Human assets:** business lines or the HR function?
- **Capital assets:** business lines or the finance function?
- **Information assets:** business lines or the IT function?

In any organization the answer to the first two is obvious: Business lines manage and make decisions regarding human and capital assets. Although this is done with the help and support of the HR and finance functions that provide expertise in their respective disciplines, it is clear that it is the business leaders who decide when to hire/fire staff and whether or not to invest capital or cut costs.

However, when it comes to information assets, a common misperception among business leaders is that IT owns the data, since IT is responsible for the operation of the application systems. IT does indeed have a role in establishing processes, policies, standards, and technologies for information management (similar to the role HR and finance have for their respective assets), but without the active involvement of senior business leaders, most data governance programs never get off the ground.

Creating a Quantifiable Business Case

Several of the key challenges related to creating a business case for top-down IA are the following:

- Fear of claiming indirect benefits
  - Example: Investing in data quality technologies and a data integration program may be an *enabler*, but it is not the sole factor for driving an increase in revenue per customer. As a result, there is a fear of making a case for achieving business benefits that may be dependent on other factors outside the direct control of an ICC.
- Difficulty in quantifying ROI
  - Few internal metrics can directly justify an ICC, SOA, or data governance strategy.
  - Poor (or inconsistent) industry studies make competitive analysis difficult.
  - The analysis effort required to create a quantifiable business case may itself be large enough that it requires a business case.

Cross-Functional Complexity

There are several challenges related to data integration complexity:

- Inconsistent data models from package applications and legacy systems result in massive variation in data definitions, making it unclear where to start and which to use as a reference.
- A bottom-up approach has the risk of reinforcing and codifying legacy system data and process definitions that are not applicable in the current context.
- A top-down approach has the risk of "solving problems by whiteboard"—that is, eliminating details that are essential for understanding root cause.

Gaining Consensus on Data Definitions

Gaining consensus on definitions for a business glossary and/or business event model is a major challenge for several reasons:

- Rivalry between organizational groups and a history of distrust and non-communication can be barriers to collaboration.
- Transparent transformations are easy (e.g., dollars and euros), but semantic issues are difficult to resolve (e.g., system A has three genders defined but system B has five gender codes).

- The processes of different business domains may be sufficiently different that it is impossible to agree on anything other than the objective. For example, opening a credit card account may be so different from opening a mortgage account that the users see no similarity other than the end point.
- Users tend to remain steadfast in insisting that their definition is the right one (e.g., is a customer a consumer, prospect, person, or corporation?), thereby creating a barrier to collaboration.

Determining an Appropriate Scope

There are several challenges related to the scope of data analysis and governance:

- Creating data and process definitions for a medium to large organization is a "boiling the ocean" problem.
- It may not be clear where to start and what level of detail is required.
- There is a risk of becoming an "ivory tower" program (i.e., not connected with the real needs of business sponsors).
  - If the effort focus is just on projects, the bigger-picture implications may be missed.
  - If the effort focus is just on the big picture, it may be too theoretical and not address the needs of the projects.
- Grassroots efforts for a single functional area may provide value but pose a risk of undersizing the true effort and opportunity across the organization.

Funding for a "New" Ongoing Process

Even if the value of the IA practice and the initial investment to launch it are accepted, concerns about the ongoing costs to sustain the effort may become a showstopper:

- Enterprise models—whether they are enterprise architecture artifacts or metadata repositories—have an ongoing cost component.
  - If the ongoing cost is ignored (i.e., only the initial project efforts are funded), the models will become stale and ineffective.
  - If the ongoing cost is highlighted up front, the initiative may never be approved unless there is an overwhelming perceived benefit.
- There is little "good" guidance in the industry about how much effort is required to sustain these new processes.

Denial That Data Quality Is the Root Cause of Problems

A major challenge in many cases is that senior management simply does not believe that data inconsistencies are a serious concern:

- Individual business groups may not have visibility to enterprise issues such as
  - Inconsistent definitions of data that make it impossible to create an enterprise view
  - Redundant or duplicate information that creates inefficiencies and high costs to maintain
- Data quality issues may be "covered up" through manual efforts by front-line staff and managers and a culture of not escalating issues.
- When business leaders don't support a data governance program led by IT, business-based data capture, maintenance, and process flaws cannot be resolved—data quality issues reappear and reinforce the negative perception of IT.

Prerequisites

The major prerequisite for creating an enterprise IA is that it be established with a clear link to a broader enterprise strategy such as an ICC, SOA, or data governance program. In other words, IA is not an end unto itself. It should be viewed as an enabler for a broader cross-functional strategy and clearly be linked to that strategy.

It is possible to leverage the IA practice without this prerequisite, but only in the context of a more narrowly defined scope of a single project/program or a single functional group. While a smaller scope does not offer an enterprise-wide benefit, it can be an excellent way to build a grassroots movement to generate awareness and interest in a broader enterprise initiative.

Activities

Information architecture is the art and science of presenting and visually depicting concept models of complex information systems in a clear and simplified format for all of the various stakeholders and roles. Three key elements are crucial in growing the maturity of IA:

- **Methodology** for how to create and sustain the models
- **Framework** for organizing various model views
- **Repository** for storing models and their representations

Implementing these elements requires the following activities that help lay the groundwork for a good data governance program:

- Creating various views or models (i.e., levels of abstraction) for multiple stakeholders
- Adopting a shared modeling tool and repository that support easy access to information
- Keeping the models current as the plans and environment change
- Maintaining clear definitions of data, involved applications/systems, and process flow/dependencies
- Leveraging metadata for data governance processes (i.e., inquiry, impact analysis, change management, etc.)
- Clearly defining the integration and interfaces among the various platform tools and between platform tools with other repositories and other vendor tools

Methodology

The IA methodology is described here in the context of a broader data governance methodology, as shown in Figure 14.1. We define *data governance* as "the policies and processes that continually work to improve and ensure the availability, accessibility, quality, consistency, auditability, and security of data in a company or institution." Many of the activities and techniques are applicable in other contexts such as data migration programs or data rationalization in support of mergers and acquisitions. It is the task of the architect and program team to tailor the methodology for a given program or enterprise strategy or purpose.

The following list provides a high-level description of the ten steps of the data governance methodology. The IA methodology described here is most closely aligned with step 3 and steps 5 through 10.

1. **Organize a governance committee:** Identify the business and IT leaders who will serve as the decision-making group for the enterprise, define the committee charter and business motivation for its existence, and establish its operating model. Committee members need to understand why they are there, know the boundaries of the issues to be discussed, and have an idea of how they will go about the task at hand.

2. **Define the governance framework:** Define the "what, who, how, and when" of the governance process, and document the data policies, integration principles, and technology standards with which all programs must comply.

3. **Develop enterprise reference models:** Establish top-down conceptual reference models, including a target operating blueprint, a business function/information matrix, and a business component model.

4. **Assign organizational roles:** Identify data owners and stewards for information domains, responsible parties/owners of shared business functions in an SOA strategy, or compliance coordinators in a data governance program.

5. **Scope the program:** Leverage the enterprise models to clearly define the scope of a given program, and develop a plan for the road-mapping effort. Identify the high-level milestones required to complete the program, and provide a general description of what is to take place within each of the larger milestones identified.

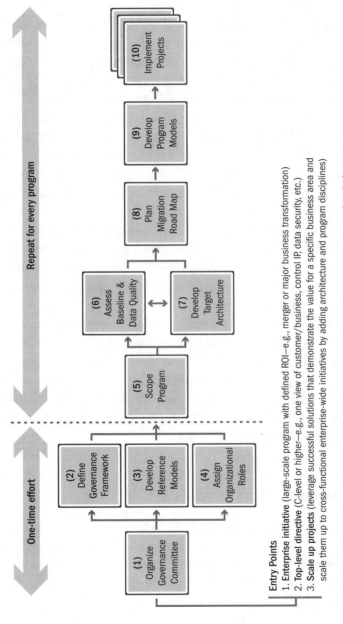

Entry Points
1. **Enterprise initiative** (large-scale program with defined ROI—e.g., merger or major business transformation)
2. **Top-level directive** (C-level or higher—e.g., one view of customer/business, control IP, data security, etc.)
3. **Scale up projects** (leverage successful solutions that demonstrate the value for a specific business area and scale them up to cross-functional enterprise-wide initiatives by adding architecture and program disciplines)

Figure 14.1 Information architecture within a data governance methodology

6. **Assess the baseline and data quality:** Leverage the enterprise models and the scope definition to complete a current-state architectural assessment, profile data quality, and identify the most important data as well as the business and technical opportunities.

7. **Develop the target architecture:** Develop a future-state data/systems/service architecture in an iterative fashion in conjunction with step 6. As additional business and technical opportunities become candidates for inclusion, the projected target architecture will also change.

8. **Plan the migration road map:** Develop the overall program implementation strategy and road map. From the efforts in step 5, identify and sequence the activities and deliverables within each of the larger milestones. This is a key part of the implementation strategy with the goal of developing a macro-managed road map that adheres to defined best practices. Identifying activities does not include technical tasks, which are covered in the next steps.

9. **Develop program models:** Create business data models and information exchange models for the defined program (i.e., logical and physical models are generally created by discrete projects within the program). The developed program models use functional specifications in conjunction with technical specifications.

10. **Implement projects:** This is a standard project and program management discipline with the difference that some data governance programs have no defined end. It may be necessary to loop back to step 5 periodically and/or provide input to steps 2, 3, or 4 to keep them current and relevant as needs change. As the projects are implemented, observe which aspects could have been more clearly defined and at which step an improvement should take place.

Information Architecture Models

The IA models are illustrated in Figure 14.2.

There are three reference models in the enterprise view (layer 4) of the IA framework but usually only one instance of these models for any given enterprise. These models are technology-neutral and implementation-independent.

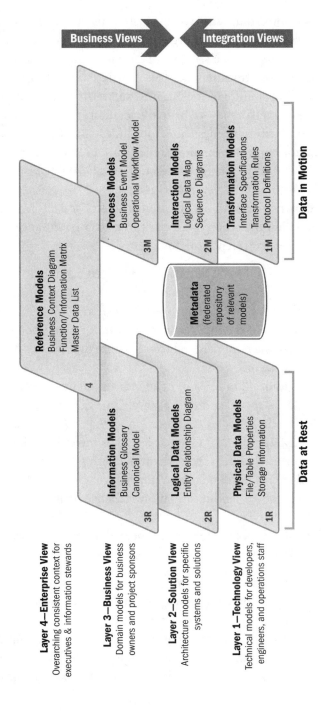

Figure 14.2 Information architecture models

313

- **Business context diagram:** The business context diagram for the enterprise shows key elements of organizational business units, brands, suppliers, customers, channels, regulatory agencies, and markets.
- **Function/information matrix:** This matrix is used to define essential operational capabilities of the business and related information subjects. The resultant matrix shows which information subjects are created by or used by the various business functions independently of how it is done. The functions and information subjects are used as a common framework to facilitate a consistent description of data at rest and data in motion in the business view models.
- **Master data list:** This is a list of business objects or data elements that are formally within the scope of an enterprise data governance program or master data management program.

Reference models may be purchased, developed from scratch, or adapted from vendor/industry models. A number of IT vendors and analyst firms offer various industry- or domain-specific reference models. The level of detail and usefulness of the models varies greatly. It is not in the scope of this chapter to evaluate such models, only to recognize that they exist and may be worthy of consideration.

There is a significant number of open industry standard reference models that also should be considered. For example, the Supply-Chain Operations Reference (SCOR) is a process reference model that has been developed and endorsed by the Supply Chain Council (SCC) as the cross-industry de facto standard diagnostic tool for supply chain management. Another example is the Mortgage Industry Standards Maintenance Organization (MISMO), which maintains process and information exchange definitions in the mortgage industry.

Some key advantages of buying a framework rather than developing one from scratch include these:

- **Minimizing internal company politics:** Since most internal groups within a company have their own terminology (i.e., domain-specific reference model), it is often a very contentious issue to rationalize differences between various internal models and decide which one to promote as the common enterprise model. A technique that is often attempted, but frequently fails, is to identify the most commonly used internal model and make it the enterprise model. This can alienate other functions that don't agree with the model and can in the long run undermine the data governance program and cause it to fail. An effective external model, however, can serve as a "rallying point" and bring different groups from the organization together rather than pitting them against each other or forcing long, drawn-out debates.

- **Avoid "paving the cow path":** The "cow path" is a metaphor for the legacy solutions that have evolved over time. An internally developed model often tends to reflect the current systems and processes (some of which may not be ideal) since there is a tendency to abstract away details from current processes. This in turn can entrench current practices, which may in fact not be ideal. An external model, almost by definition, is generic and does not include organization-specific implementation details.

- **Faster development:** It is generally quicker to purchase a model (and tailor it if necessary) than to develop a reference model from the ground up. The difference in time can be very significant. A rough rule of thumb is that adopting an external model takes roughly one to three months whereas developing a model can take one to three years. The reference model may involve some capital costs, but the often hidden costs of developing a reference model from scratch are much greater.

Regardless of whether you buy or build the reference models, in order for them to be effective and successful, they must have the following attributes:

- **Holistic:** The models must describe the entire enterprise and not just one part. Furthermore, the models must be hierarchical and support several levels of abstraction. The lowest level of the hierarchy must be mutually exclusive and comprehensive (ME&C), which means that each element in the model describes a unique and nonoverlapping portion of the enterprise while the collection of elements describes the entire enterprise. The ultimate mapping (discussed in the next chapters) to physical data may be much more complex because enterprise systems are not themselves ME&C.

  Note: It is critical to resist the urge to model only a portion of the enterprise. For example, if the data governance program focus is on customer data information, it may seem easier and more practical to model only customer-related functions and data. The issue is that without the context of a holistic model, the definition of functions and data will inherently be somewhat ambiguous and therefore will be an endless source of debate and disagreement.

- **Practical:** It is critical to establish the right level of granularity of the enterprise models. If they are too high-level, they will be too conceptual; if they are too low-level, the task of creating the enterprise models can become a "boiling the ocean" problem and consume a huge amount of time and resources. Both extremes—too little detail or too much detail— are impractical and the root cause of failure.

> **TIP**
>
> There are two "secrets" to achieving the right level of granularity. First, create a hierarchy of functions and information subjects. At the highest level it is common to have in the range of five to ten functions and information subjects that describe the entire enterprise. Second, at the lowest level in the hierarchy, stop modeling when you start getting into "how" rather than "what." A good way to recognize that you are into the realm of "how" is if you are getting into technology-specific or implementation details. A general rule of thumb is that an enterprise reference model at the greatest level of detail typically has between 100 and 200 functions and information subjects.

- **Stable:** Once developed, reference models should not change frequently unless the business itself changes. If the reference models did a good job separating the "what" from the "how," a business process change should not impact the reference models; but if the organization expands its product or service offerings into new areas, either through a business transformation initiative or a merger/acquisition, the reference model should change. Examples of scenarios that would cause the reference model to change include a retail organization transforming its business by manufacturing some of its own products or a credit card company acquiring a business that originates and services securitized car and boat loans.

Reference models, once created, serve several critical roles:

1. They define the scope of selected programs and activities. The holistic and ME&C nature of the reference models allows a clear definition of what is in scope and out of scope.
2. They use a common language and framework to describe and map the current-state enterprise architecture. The reference model is particularly useful for identifying overlapping or redundant applications and data.
3. They are particularly useful for identifying opportunities for different functional groups in the enterprise to work together on common solutions.
4. They provide tremendous insight into creating target architectures that reflect sound principles of well-defined but decoupled components.

Data at Rest

The data-at-rest pieces of the IA framework in Figure 14.3 provide a series of models at different levels of abstraction and with the information that is relevant to various audiences. Collectively, these models describe data as it is persisted in business systems or in integration systems (such as data warehouses or master data repositories).

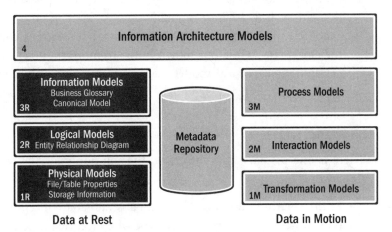

Figure 14.3 Data-at-rest models

Information Models (3R)

There are two information models on the business view (layer 3) of the IA framework. These are sometimes referred to as "semantic models" since there may be separate instances for different business domains.

- **Business glossary:** This is a list of business data elements with a corresponding description, enterprise-level or domain-specific synonyms, validation rules, and other relevant metadata. It is used to identify the source of a record, quality metrics, ownership authority, and stewardship responsibility.
- **Canonical model:** This is the definition of a standard organization view of a particular information subject. Specific uses include delivering enterprise-wide business intelligence (BI) or defining a common view within an SOA. In this book we define three canonical modeling techniques, each of which serves a specific purpose: canonical data modeling, canonical physical formats, and canonical interchange modeling.

  Note that while we show the canonical model at layer 3 in the framework, mature Lean Integration teams generally have canonical models at layers 2 and 4 as well. At layer 2, solution view, the canonical model represents common data definitions within the scope of two or more applications in a specific project or program. At layer 3, business view, the canonical model represents common data definitions within a business domain such as finance or marketing. At layer 4, enterprise view, the canonical model represents common data definitions or concepts across the enterprise. While not shown in the framework, it is possible to have yet another canonical model that represents common data definitions outside the enterprise as industry standard models within a supply chain.

Logical Data Models (2R)

There is one primary data model on the solution view (layer 2) of the IA framework:

- **Entity relation diagram:** This is an abstract and conceptual representation of data used to produce a type of conceptual schema or semantic data model of a system, often a relational database, and its requirements.

Physical Data Models (1R)

There are at least two primary physical data models on the technology view (layer 1) of the IA framework:

- **File/table properties:** The properties describe the structure and content of physical files, tables, interfaces, and other data objects used throughout the enterprise. These data objects could exist in relational databases, ERP or customer relationship management systems, message queues, mainframe systems, semistructured data coming from .pdf, .doc, .xls, or email files, or any other data source with a definable structure. Besides the structure and content properties, it is also crucial to track the relationships between these data objects as well as the change history of the data objects throughout the organization.
- **Storage information:** Particular files, tables, copybooks, message queues, or other information objects could have a single definition but have several physical instantiations throughout an organization. Keeping track of the access profiles and security characteristics as well as the storage characteristics of these objects is important for managing them.

The business glossary is implemented as a set of objects in a metadata repository to capture, navigate, and publish business terms. This model is typically implemented as custom extensions to the metadata repository rather than as Word or Excel documents (although these formats are acceptable for very simple glossaries in specific business domains).

The business glossary allows business users, data stewards, business analysts, and data analysts to create, edit, and delete business terms that describe key concepts of the business. While business terms are the main part of the model, it can also be used to describe related concepts like data stewards, synonyms, categories/classifications, rules, valid values, quality metrics, and other items.

Figure 14.4 shows some of the ways that different roles either create, modify, or collaborate on parts of the IA. Many of these steps could be optional, and this is obviously not intended to be the one and only "workflow" between these users. This picture represents some of the ways that different roles are continually working together to refine the information world for complex enterprises.

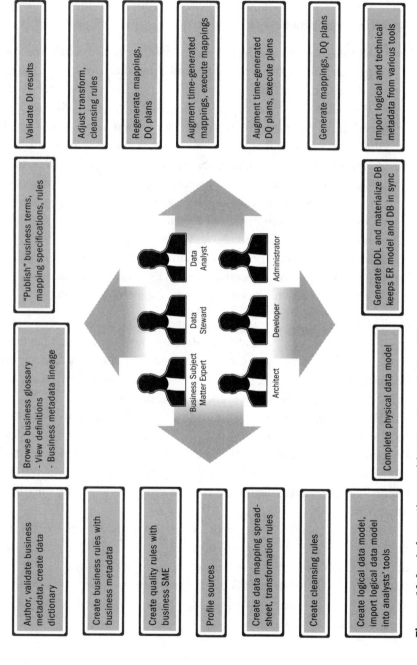

Figure 14.4 Information architecture team interactions

CHAPTER FIFTEEN

Business Process Management

Information on its own doesn't create business value; it is the systematic application of the information to the business issue that creates value.

Sinan Aral and Peter Weill[1]

Business process management (BPM) is a broad topic. We do not cover the full spectrum of BPM in this chapter; an entire book could be written about it. Nonetheless, a high-level discussion is essential in the context of Lean Integration. Data must be understood within the context of the many different business processes that exist across silos of complex organizations. Data outside this context runs the risk of being misinterpreted and misused, causing potential waste to the business and the ICC. Through this contextual understanding of information, reuse, agility, and loose coupling can be achieved by understanding how data fits in its various business process contexts.

A BPM COE is a special kind of competency center that provides a broad spectrum of services related to the full life cycle of BPM activities, including process modeling, simulation, execution, monitoring, and optimization.

---

1. Sinan Aral and Peter Weill, "IT Savvy Pays Off: How Top Performers Match IT Portfolios and Organizational Practices," MIT Sloan Center for Information Science Working Paper No. 353, May 2005.

From an ICC perspective, of primary interest are the *integration* aspects of BPM across the enterprise. To be more specific, this chapter focuses on

- Defining the most common models used to describe data in motion to different audiences, from low-level physical data exchanges to high-level business processes
- Describing five categories of BPM activities: design, modeling, execution, monitoring, and optimization
- Outlining architectural considerations in support of BPM

The chapter closes with a case from Wells Fargo and how that company applied the BEST architecture and Lean principles to achieve a highly efficient and continuously improving business process.

The business process maturity model shown in Table 15.1 is primarily related to the disciplines within the business areas and how consistently and formally the business process hierarchy is defined and managed across the enterprise. This is a critical factor in ensuring alignment between the IT organization and the business groups. A secondary factor of business process maturity is the degree of manual effort needed to keep the data in systems synchronized.

Table 15.1   Business Process Management Maturity

Maturity Level	Business Process
Project	Business processes are dynamic and may not be fully documented, and even routine activities are highly people-intensive.
	Replication of information across systems is either through batch processes or highly manual with the same information being entered into multiple systems.
	Process standards, even for similar processes, have not been defined and are performed differently by different functional teams.
Program	Business processes are documented and management processes are in place to monitor conformance and drive improvements within a functional area (but not necessarily cross-functionally).
	Replication of common information across systems is mostly automatic.
	Process modeling is done with standard language, stored in a repository, and monitored in production with basic BPM/monitoring tools.

Table 15.1 Business Process Management Maturity *(Continued)*

Maturity Level	Business Process
Sustaining	Business leaders are active participants in the integration life cycle and clearly see their role as part of the enterprise whole. Information is captured once at the source and flows to other systems in near real time. Information flow among applications and business units uses BPM and BAM (business activity monitoring) tools to automate common business decisions and notify business professionals of important events. Business processes are measured by process owners in terms of time, cost, and effectiveness and are controlled using quantitative data. The focus is on a cross-functional process view.
Lean	Business processes are optimized through scientific principles including controlled experimentation of new processes in production. Process simulation is practiced and BAM is used consistently regardless of implementation mechanics. A chief process officer or value stream manager has overall responsibility for continuous improvement of the enterprise and supply chain processes.

The challenges that the BPM competency and related Lean practices are intended to address include the following:

1. **Organizational agility:** Business processes are constantly changing as a result of competitive pressures, mergers and acquisitions, regulatory requirements, and new technology advancements. A methodology is needed from an integration perspective to enable rapid changes to business processes.

2. **Loose coupling:** When one step in a process changes for some reason, it is desirable to have an architecture and infrastructure that minimize the need to change downstream or upstream process steps.

3. **Common business definitions:** Multifunctional flow-through business processes have the challenge of maintaining consistent definitions of data. To make it even more challenging, the definitions of data can change depending on the process context. A common vocabulary is required for data and business processes in order to enable "one version of the truth." The key to process integration is data standardization. As

standardized data is made available, business owners can effectively integrate their processes.

4. **Channel integration:** Most organizations offer their customers more than one interaction channel. For example, retail organizations may have five or more (i.e., stores, call centers, Internet, mobile device, in-home service, third-party reseller, etc.). Business processes must therefore transcend multiple channels as seamlessly as possible. When this is done well, based on an integrated view of customer data and common processes, the systems can improve customer satisfaction and sales.

5. **Operational monitoring and support:** A major challenge in large, complex distributed computing environments is clearly understanding the implications of low-level technical events for higher-level business processes. Traceability among business processes and technical implementation is therefore critical.

Data-in-Motion Models

The prior chapter defined the models on the left side of the IA framework, the data-at-rest layers, so now we will take a closer look at the data-in-motion layers as highlighted in Figure 15.1. Like the data-at-rest layers, the data-in-motion layers also specify a series of models at different levels of abstraction with the information that is relevant to various roles. Collectively, these models describe how data moves between applications inside and outside the organization (such as supplier systems, customer systems, or cloud applications).

Process Models (3M)

There are at least two process models on the business view (layer 3) of the IA framework:

- **Business event model:** This is a common (canonical) description of business events including business process triggers, target subscribers, and payload descriptions (from elements in the business glossary). This model also fits into the classification of semantic models but in this case for data in motion rather than data at rest.

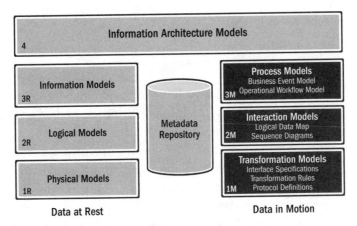

Figure 15.1 Data-in-motion models

- **Operational workflow model:** This model is a depiction of a sequence of operations, declared as the work of a person, a group, or a system. Workflow may be seen as any abstraction of real work at various levels of detail, thus serving as a virtual representation of actual work. The flow being described often refers to a document or information that is being transferred from one step to another or between a system and a person.

Interaction Models (2M)

There are two primary interaction models on the solution view (layer 2) of the IA framework:

- **Logical data map:** This describes the relationship between the extreme starting points and extreme ending points of information exchanges between applications. The logical data map also contains business rules concerning data filtering, cleansing, and transformations.
- **Sequence diagram:** The alternate representation of operational scenarios using UML techniques shows how process steps operate with one another and in what order. Individual operational process steps may have their own model representations, thereby creating a hierarchy of sequence diagrams at different levels of abstraction. Sequence diagrams are sometimes called "event-trace diagrams," "event scenarios," or "timing diagrams."

Transformation Models (1M)

There are three primary transformation models on the technology view (layer 1) of the IA framework:

- **Interface specifications:** Interface generally refers to an abstraction that a system provides of itself to enable access to data or process stems and separates the methods of external communication from internal operation. The specifications are the documented description of the data, operations, and protocol provided by or supported by the interface. Mature Lean Integration teams maintain integration specifications in structured metadata repositories.
- **Transformation rules:** These are the technical transformation rules and sequence of steps that implement the business rules defined in the logical data map.
- **Protocol definitions:** This is a set of rules used to communicate between application systems across a network. A protocol is a convention or standard that controls or enables the connection, communication, and data transfer between computing endpoints. In its simplest form, a *protocol* can be defined as "the rules governing the syntax, semantics, and synchronization of communication."

Activities

The activities that constitute BPM can be grouped into five categories: design, modeling, execution, monitoring, and optimization.

Business Process Design

Process design encompasses both identifying existing processes and designing the "to be" process. Areas of focus include representation of the process flow, the actors within it, alerts and notifications, escalations, standard operating procedures, SLAs, and task handover mechanisms.

Good design reduces the occurrence of problems over the lifetime of the process. Whether or not existing processes are considered, the aim of this step is to ensure that a correct and efficient theoretical design is prepared.

The proposed improvement can be in human-to-human, human-to-system, or system-to-system workflows and may target regulatory, market, or competitive challenges faced by the business.

Several common techniques and notations are available for business process mapping (or business process modeling), including Integration Definition (IDEF), BPWin, event-driven process chains, and BPMN.

Business Process Modeling

Modeling takes the theoretical design and introduces combinations of variables, for instance, changes in the cost of materials or increased rent, that determine how the process might operate under different circumstances.

It also involves running "what-if" analysis on the processes: "What if I have 75 percent of the resources to perform the same task?" "What if I want to do the same job for 80 percent of the current cost?"

A real-world analogy can be a wind-tunnel test of an airplane or test flights to determine how much fuel will be consumed and how many passengers can be carried.

Business Process Execution

One way to automate processes is to develop or purchase an application that executes the required steps of the process; however, in practice, these applications rarely execute all the steps of the process accurately or completely. Another approach is to use a combination of software and human intervention; however, this approach is more complex, making documenting the process difficult.

As a response to these problems, software has been developed that enables the full business process (as developed in the process design activity) to be defined in a computer language that can be directly executed by the computer. The system either uses services in connected applications to perform business operations (e.g., calculating a repayment plan for a loan) or, when a step is too complex to automate, sends a message to a human requesting input. Compared to either of the previous approaches, directly executing a process definition can be more straightforward and therefore easier to improve. However, automating a process definition requires flexible and comprehensive infrastructure, which typically rules out implementing these systems in a legacy IT environment.

The commercial BPM software market has focused on graphical process model development, rather than text-language-based process models, as a means to reduce the complexity of model development. Visual programming using graphical metaphors has increased productivity in a number of areas of computing and is well accepted by users.

Business rules have been used by systems to provide definitions for governing behavior, and a business rule engine can be used to drive process execution and resolution.

Business Process Monitoring

Monitoring encompasses tracking individual processes so that information on their state can be easily seen and statistics generated about their performance. An example of tracking is being able to determine the state of a customer order (e.g., ordered arrived, awaiting delivery, invoice paid) so that problems in the operation can be identified and corrected.

In addition, this information can be used to work with customers and suppliers to improve their connected processes. Examples of these statistics are the generation of measures on how quickly a customer order is processed or how many orders were processed in the last month. These measures tend to fit into three categories: cycle time, defect rate, and productivity.

The degree of monitoring depends on what information the business wants to evaluate and analyze and how the business wants it to be monitored, in real time or ad hoc. Here, business activity monitoring (BAM) extends and expands the monitoring tools generally provided by BPMS.

Process mining is a collection of methods and tools related to process monitoring. The aim of process mining is to analyze event logs extracted through process monitoring and to compare them with an a priori process model. Process mining allows process analysts to detect discrepancies between the actual process execution and the a priori model, as well as to analyze bottlenecks.

Business Process Optimization

Process optimization includes retrieving process performance information from modeling or monitoring and identifying the potential or actual bottlenecks and potential for cost savings or other improvements, and then applying those enhancements to the design of the process, thus continuing the value cycle of BPM.

Architecture

Figure 15.2 shows a typical high-level architecture that supports business process execution, monitoring, and optimization.

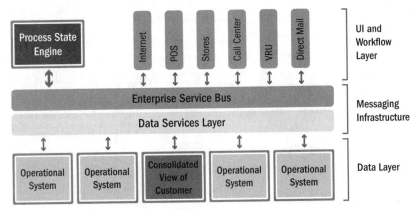

Figure 15.2   BPM architecture for channel integration or straight-through processing

The bottom layer of the graphic shows the business systems and integration systems that contain the data that is created, accessed, or updated as part of the business process. For simplicity, we refer to this as the data layer.

The messaging layer may be an enterprise service bus, or some combination of technologies that support real-time information exchanges between systems, event notifications, and publish/subscribe integration patterns.

The top layer of the architecture shows two key elements. The first is a process state engine that contains the business rules that define the process execution steps, the operational functions to monitor and control the processes, and the metrics and metadata that support process optimization. The process state engine may be a purchased application or an internally developed one, but in either case its primary purpose is to maintain information about the state of processes in execution independently of the underlying systems. In other words, the process state engine is an integration system that persists process state for cross-functional or long-running processes, whereas the other operational systems persist the business data. Long-running processes may be measured in minutes, hours, weeks, or even months. While it is possible for a process state engine to also control short-run processes (measured in seconds), these sorts of orchestrations are often handled in the service bus layer.

The second element on the top layer is the UI or user interface layer. This is a common architecture pattern for a multichannel integration scenario. The basic concept is to enable access to the data of record in the source system in real time from multiple channels such as the Internet, point of sale, or call center. Simple transactions are enabled by the enterprise service bus in a request/reply pattern. Longer-running processes may require the involvement of the process state engine in order to allow a process, such as opening an account, for example, to be started in one channel and finished in another channel without the user having to rekey all the data.

The net effect of this architecture is an extremely efficient (Lean) infrastructure that minimizes waste by providing a set of operational systems that are mutually exclusive and independent, yet provide users with a comprehensive and consistent view of the data regardless of which UI device they use to access it.

The following Post Closing case study is an exceptional example of a layered BPM architecture. This is the same case that was introduced earlier. Chapter 9 described the Lean principles that were used, and the following section completes the story with the integration architecture that enabled the impressive business outcomes.

Case Study: The Post Closing Systems Architecture

The Wells Fargo Home Mortgage Post Closing solution is an example of using the BEST architectural style. BEST stands for **b**usiness **e**vent **s**tate **t**ransition and defines the following coordinated set of architectural principles:

- **Straight-through processing (STP):** the process of seamlessly passing information to all parties involved in the transaction process without manual handling or redundant processing.
- **Event-driven architecture (EDA):** This software architecture pattern promotes the production, detection, and consumption of and reaction to events. BEST requires an explicitly defined business event model which defines notable things that happen inside or outside the organization from a business perspective. In this case, the team drew state transition diagrams (STDs) of the major entities as the critical part of the requirements and design phase and implemented the STDs in the process control engine. The STDs showed each state and the events/messages that caused a transition from state to state.
- **Exception-based processing (EBP):** This is an approach for enabling applications to automatically highlight particular events or results that

fall outside predetermined parameters. Exceptions that the system cannot handle automatically are placed in work queues for business operations staff to review and correct.

- **Service-oriented architecture (SOA):** This architecture is where the functions of internal and external transactional applications are exposed through standard interfaces and a messaging infrastructure. It is important to note that SOA doesn't equate to just "Web service" standards such as SOAP and Web Services Description Language (WSDL). The critical aspect of this architecture at Wells Fargo was asynchronous guaranteed messaging tied to the idea of system adapters. The project used a combination of files, database connections, Web service calls, and other means in order to get at the data and turn it into a message, and vice versa.
- A layered architecture includes
  - A user interface layer
  - A process management layer including a state engine
  - A messaging layer that supports publish/subscribe
  - A business service and application interface layer

The result of effectively applying these constraints is a scalable, reliable, and flexible architecture. For example, BEST supports extreme loose coupling and highly distributed application components. The great distribution emerges because events can be any notable thing that happens across the entire supply chain. The architecture is extremely loosely coupled because the event itself doesn't know about the consequences that it triggers; the source system relies on the messaging infrastructure to provide guaranteed delivery to all the downstream application systems that have subscribed to the event.

BEST achieves an ideal balance between two essential qualities in systems-of-systems: coupling and cohesion, which we discuss in more detail in the next chapter.

- **Coupling** is the degree to which each system component can change without affecting other components and is usually expressed as "loose coupling" or "tight coupling." Loosely coupled systems are a design goal and are considered useful when either the source or the destination computer systems are subject to frequent changes or are owned by different organizations. For example, the Wells Fargo Post Closing team determines the technical architecture of the systems it owns, whereas HUD, Fidelity, Shaw, and other external organizations independently determine their own architectures. Loosely coupled systems are essential in this context, and industry-standard message formats (such as MISMO) play a critical role in enabling efficient interactions between organizations.

- **Cohesion** is a measure of how strongly related and focused the various responsibilities of a system component are and is usually expressed as "high cohesion" or "low cohesion." In a highly cohesive environment, each component provides a set of functions that are unique and do not overlap with other components. Modules with high cohesion tend to be preferable because high cohesion is associated with several desirable traits of software, including robustness, reliability, reusability, and understandability, whereas low cohesion is associated with undesirable traits such as being difficult to maintain, difficult to test, difficult to reuse, and even difficult to understand.

The Post Closing solution is an excellent example of the value of maintaining the conceptual integrity of complementary architectural constraints. To be clear, other factors contributed to achieving success, including a clear vision, a great project team, effective partnerships inside and outside the company, an evolutionary approach, solid technical decisions, and strong executive sponsorship. But there is no question that the architecture was an essential enabler of the business outcomes.

CHAPTER SIXTEEN

Modeling Management

The complexity of software is an essential property, not an accidental one. Hence descriptions of a software entity that abstract away its complexity often abstract away its essence.

Frederick P. Brooks, Jr.[1]

One of the critical needs within all large corporations is to achieve efficient information exchange in a heterogeneous environment. The typical enterprise has hundreds of applications that serve as systems of record for information that, although developed independently and based on incompatible data models, must be shared efficiently and accurately in order to effectively support the business and create positive customer experiences.

The key issue is the scale and complexity that are not evident in smaller organizations. The problem arises when there are a large number of application interactions in a constantly changing application portfolio. If these interactions are not designed and managed effectively, they can result in production outages, poor performance, high maintenance costs, and especially a lack of business flexibility.

One of the primary methods for helping to meet integration needs is to make a complex system-of-systems easier to manage by presenting only the

---

1. Frederick P. Brooks, Jr., *The Mythical Man-Month: Essays on Software Engineering, Anniversary Edition* (Addison-Wesley, 1995), p. 183.

relevant information to different stakeholders to answer the questions they have. For this reason, abstraction and graphical visualizations are critical disciplines in an effective Lean Integration practice. Models are the primary language of integration and hence a critical dimension of an Integration Competency Center.

A model, which is an abstraction of a complex enterprise or system or other entity, is a useful and necessary tool to effectively communicate with all stakeholders, thereby helping to drive alignment across silos. We should always keep in mind the words of Brooks in the opening quote that models are not the same as the things they describe; models eliminate certain details in order to facilitate communication, but as we know from the fifth Law of Integration (Appendix B), "All details are relevant." The models themselves are entities that have a life cycle—they need to be developed, deployed, maintained, enhanced, and eventually retired or replaced with better models. Since modeling methods (if done properly) are repeatable processes, Lean techniques can be applied to them to improve productivity and reduce cycle times. In addition, the deliverables produced by the modeling processes are enablers for a Lean Integration organization because they help to eliminate waste (such as re-creating documentation or hunting for documents in the traditional paradigm), facilitate value stream mapping (by presenting a consistent picture and language to describe cross-functional processes and data), and support automation activities (i.e., interchange modeling can be thought of as a code generator for mapping rules).

There are many dimensions to modeling. In its broadest definition a model is a pattern, plan, representation, or description designed to show the main purpose or workings of an object, system, or concept. Some of the specialized disciplines that are relevant to a Lean organization include data modeling, business process modeling, computer systems modeling, and meta-modeling. That said, these modeling disciplines are broadly practiced in the industry with well-defined methods that are generally available through books and educational programs, so it would be redundant to include them here.

The primary focus of this chapter on modeling management is to support integration needs from two perspectives:

1. Provide some prescriptive guidance around canonical data modeling (for which there are few if any good practices available in the industry)

2. Offer some guidance and rules of thumb related to our experiences in creating and sustaining enterprise models and meta-models

Table 16.1 provides an outline of four levels of maturity. While there is a certain amount of subjectivity around some of the definitions, nonetheless it is a useful tool for assessing your organization's current level of maturity and for establishing a desired target maturity level.

Table 16.1   Modeling Management Maturity Model

Maturity Level	Modeling
Project	Models are used regularly but without a formal discipline. UML is used as a "sketching" language, and notation conventions are not strictly adhered to. Models are developed using free-form tools such as Word, Excel, PowerPoint, or Visio to document requirements/designs and are aligned through manual processes.
Program	Modeling notation and naming standards are defined and teams from different functions use similar tools. All staff know how to read UML (or equivalent) documents. Models are dynamic and stored as data in repositories rather than as static models. Multisystem interactions are routinely modeled.
Sustaining	Enterprise-wide reference models are in place for business processes/functions, application architecture, information architecture, business glossary, and information exchange or integration maps. While the models may be stored in separate tools or repositories, it is possible to combine or link them through common keys and strict adherence to naming conventions.
Lean	Models are used as "blueprints," and there is formal signoff on business process models and system design models before development begins. Transformation of models from one format to another is done automatically using leading-edge tools with a common semantic integration standard. MDA concepts are used in conjunction with code generation tools to directly generate software. Simulators are used to test requirements before design or development begins. Multiple future states are modeled and tools are used to identify and quantify impacts of planned changes.

Service-Oriented Architecture Can Create a New Hairball

SOA suggests an answer to the point-to-point integration problem through the creation of a service abstraction layer that hides the underlying data and system complexities from the builders of composite applications. Indeed, several years ago it would have been hard to find people worrying about data and integration problems during a discussion about SOA because people were worried about other problems (business/IT alignment, what ESB to use, how to monitor and manage the new system, etc.) and seemed to be under the impression that SOA would solve the data and integration problems.

Early practitioners quickly found that the data and integration problems were simply pushed down to another layer. In fact, because of the power of the new technologies to create services quickly, practitioners found that it was possible to create a new hairball in a fraction of the time it took to create the original hairball they were trying to fix. Figure 16.1 provides a visual description of how this new service layer creates a new hairball.

The bottom half of Figure 16.1 shows each service independently solving the problem of accessing and transforming data, typically through Java programs within the services. While the service abstraction layer certainly makes life easier for the *users* of the services in the top half of the figure, the *producers* of those services in the bottom half find that life gets worse. Because of the added layers of abstraction, it is now more difficult to determine the impact of a business or system change on the system. Additional modeling and data abstraction challenges are outlined in more detail in the next section, but the major takeaway here is that if abstraction is not added properly, with all important issues taken care of, it is best not to undertake SOA on a large scale.

So architects have begun to add a "data" service layer between the "business" service layer we see in the figure and the underlying physical systems, files, or interfaces that exist across the enterprise. Typically, this layer includes a logical, or canonical, model that attempts to model the data of the enterprise. In other words, a schema or model is presented that incorporates the critical enterprise data and relationships in a fashion that is entirely independent of the underlying applications, allowing business services to read and write these logical, canonical models using a variety of different delivery mechanisms, including Web services, SQL, XQuery, RSS, and others.

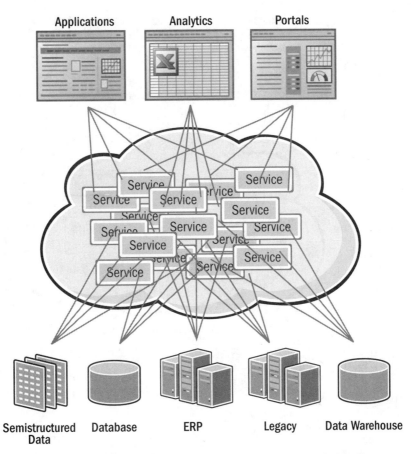

Figure 16.1   Services in an SOA creating a new integration hairball

In an ideal world, this logical schema and the underlying "data services" that read and write data to the physical systems would function like a typical relational database, except that as shown in Figure 16.2, the virtual database would span whatever information systems were necessary to satisfy the user's request. At design time, the canonical model and the necessary "read mappings" and "write mappings" that map and define the transformation rules between the logical canonical model and the underlying physical systems would provide the rules within which the optimizer would have to work. Business services or SQL requests coming into the canonical model would

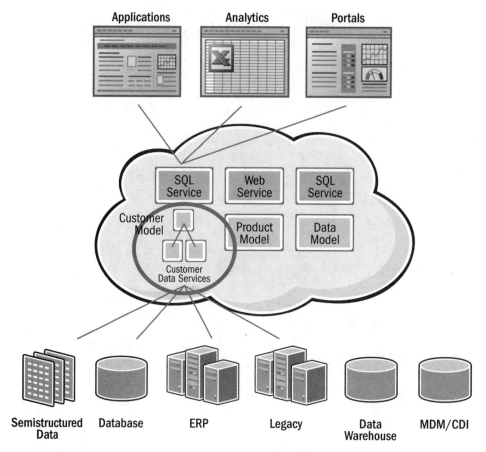

Figure 16.2   Canonical models and data services in an SOA

cause the optimizer to generate the appropriate run-time "data services" to fulfill the requests or commands.

In some ways, this describes how EII products work, except that for this to be helpful in facilitating the Lean principles of mass customization and planning for change (the benefit of a canonical layer), writing data would have to be handled with the same dexterity as reading data. Furthermore, access to *all* types of data (complex XML, ERP, mainframe, message queues, EDI, etc.), the ability to cleanse data or perform complex transformations en route, and the ability to provision data in multiple ways and monitor the SLAs of data access would all have to be supported in a high-speed, highly available fashion. Technology to meet these demands is just now becoming available.

Creating a canonical model is an extremely difficult exercise for reasons given in the next section. Failed enterprise data modeling exercises of past decades gave the canonical model concept a bad reputation. Certainly the difficulty of canonical models should not be minimized, but if the canonical model is actionable and useful, rather than just a static point-in-time model, it can provide significant business value in achieving the agility and business/IT alignment that SOA promises.

Challenges

The challenges that are addressed in this chapter are as follows:

- Communicating data semantics
- Achieving loosely coupled systems
- Sustaining enterprise models
- Maintaining efficiency and performance at run time

Communicating Data Semantics

Semantics (the meaning of data) is a complex issue in the world of computer software and comprises four categories:

- The syntax of the data element, which includes its type, length, format, valid values, and range limits
- The definition, which includes a name, prose description, source system of record, physical location, lineage (version), and other attributes, that is typically included in a metadata repository
- The process context, including business process state, update frequencies, access methods, legal limitations, domain of valid values, and their semantic meanings or business rules
- The relationship to other data elements or structures, including meta-metadata and other business rules or policies

In *ICC: An Implementation Methodology*, Integration Law #4 states, "Information adapts to meet local needs."

The Information Engineering movement of the early 1990's was based on the incorrect notion that an enterprise can have a single consistent data model without redundancy. A more accurate way to look at information is as follows:

Information = Data + Context

This formula says that the same data across different domains may have different meanings. For example, a simple attribute such as "Current Customer" can mean something different to the Marketing, Customer Service, and Legal departments. An extreme example is Gender, which you might think could only have two states: Male or Female—one particular enterprise has defined eight different genders. The same thing happens with natural languages (the various meanings that words adopt in different communities). The ICC must embrace informational diversity, recognizing that variations exist, and use techniques to compensate for them.[2]

A formal standard to communicate semantics is still a new and emerging field. The Semantic Web initiative shows promise, but it focuses primarily on human-computer interactions and not computer-computer interactions.

Achieving Loosely Coupled Systems

There is a widely held belief that canonical data models are a major enabler for loose coupling, which is an enabler for business flexibility. This is true only if the models are used properly. Improper use of canonical techniques actually couples systems more tightly and adds costs without offsetting benefits.

Conventional thinking suggests that a canonical data model, one that is independent of any specific application, is a best practice. When each application is required to produce and consume messages in this common format, components in an SOA are more loosely coupled. Here is what Gregor Hohpe has to say in his book *Enterprise Integration Patterns*: "The *Canonical Data Model* provides an additional level of indirection between applications' individual data formats. If a new application is added to the integration solution only transformation between the *Canonical Data Model* has to be created, independent from the number of applications that already participate."[3]

---

2. John Schmidt and David Lyle, *Integration Competency Center: An Implementation Methodology* (Informatica Corporation, 2005), p. 13.

3. Gregor Hohpe, *Enterprise Integration Patterns* (Addison-Wesley, 2003), p. 356.

The promised benefits of canonical modeling generally include increased independence of components, so that one can change without affecting other components, and simplified interactions, because all applications use common definitions for interactions. As a result, solutions are expected to be lower in cost to develop, easier to maintain, of higher quality in operation, and quicker to adapt to changing business needs.

The reality is that loose coupling requires much more than just canonical techniques. It must be part of a broader architecture strategy and development standards and encompass some or all of the items shown in Table 16.2.[4]

Table 16.2   Loose Coupling Practices and Their Cost Implications

Solution Dimension	Tight Coupling Practice	Loose Coupling Practice	Possible Price of Loose Coupling
Physical	Point-to-point	Intermediate broker	Third-party involvement and model maintenance
Communication style	Synchronous	Asynchronous	Late and unordered responses
Data model	Common complex types	Common basic types	Mapping and model maintenance
Type system	Strong	Weak	Run-time instead of compile-time errors
Interaction pattern	Navigate through complex object trees	Data-centric, self-contained message	Type system limitations
Control of process logic	Central control	Distributed control	Challenges finding out state of a process
Binding	Statically	Dynamically	Run-time instead of compile-time errors
Platform	Strong dependencies	Platform-independent	No platform-specific optimizations
Transactionality	2PC (two-phase commit)	Compensating transactions	Extended fault handling
Deployment	Simultaneous	At different times	Versioning, soft migration
Versioning	Explicit upgrades	Implicit upgrades	Many versions

---

4. Adapted from Nicolai M. Josuttis, *SOA in Practice: The Art of Distributed System Design* (O'Reilly Media, 2007).

While canonical modeling can indeed provide benefits if used appropriately, there is also a cost that must be addressed. The canonical model and interchanges themselves are incremental components that must be managed and maintained. Canonical data models and interchanges require effort to define, introduce a middleware layer (either at build time or run time, depending on which techniques are used), and incur ongoing maintenance costs. These costs can exceed the benefits that the canonical models provide unless care is taken to use the techniques in the right circumstances.

Sustaining Canonical Models

Once canonical models are developed, there are a number of challenges associated with maintaining them so that they retain their value and provide ongoing benefits:

- If canonical models are not sustained, they quickly lose their value and may in fact add complexity without associated benefits.
- Canonical models are sometimes linked to industry or standard models (to some degree) and require ongoing efforts to keep them current and relevant.
- The cost to sustain canonical models can be significant (e.g., a rule of thumb is that one FTE is needed for every 1,500 attributes or 200 entities/objects).
- Since canonical models are not directly linked to specific cost-justified projects, it may be difficult to justify the cost to sustain them.
- Unstructured tools (such as Microsoft Excel) are inadequate for anything other than the simplest canonical models.
- Specialized tools for effective management of complex models can be expensive and most likely need a business case.

Maintaining Efficiency and Performance at Run Time

Canonical techniques, if used improperly, can have serious negative implications on performance and operations. Here are some of the key challenges:

- **Nontransparent transformations:** Canonical formats are most effective when transformations from a component's internal data format to the canonical format are simple and direct with no semantic impedance mismatch. (But rarely are these format transformations simple.)

- **Indirection at run time:** While integration brokers (or ESBs) are a useful technique for loose coupling, they also add a level of indirection that complicates debugging and run-time problem resolution. The level of complexity can become almost paralyzing over time if process scenarios result in middleware calling middleware with multiple transformations in an end-to-end data flow. The benefits of loose coupling can be offset by the cost of administering the added abstraction layer over time.

- **Inadequate exception handling:** The beauty of a loosely coupled architecture is that components can change without impacting others. The danger is that in a large-scale distributed computing environment with many components changing dynamically, the overall system-of-systems can start to demonstrate chaotic (i.e., unexpected) behavior.

- **Performance degradation:** Middleware can add overhead (in comparison to point-to-point interfaces), especially if a given interaction involves multiple transformations to or from canonical formats.

Coupling and Cohesion Framework

This section represents work done by John Schmidt in several large corporate IT organizations over a five-year period. These efforts culminated in the formalization and publication of the BEST architecture while he served as the head of enterprise architecture at Wells Fargo Bank. The motivation was to provide practical "canonical" techniques and to clarify this typical IT industry buzzword—that is, an overloaded term with multiple meanings and no clear agreement on its definition. Schmidt's contribution to the industry in this effort was twofold:

- A coupling and cohesion framework that serves as a classification scheme for comparing canonical techniques (described in this section)
- Explicit definition of three distinct and complementary canonical modeling techniques, described in more detail in the following section:
  1. Canonical data modeling
  2. Canonical interchange modeling
  3. Canonical physical formats

The best architectural style in any given situation is the one that most closely addresses the functional and nonfunctional needs of the client. That said, there are two qualities that are highly desirable in any large distributed application environment: loose coupling and high cohesion. (We defined *coupling* and *cohesion* in the Wells Fargo case study at the end of Chapter 15.) These qualities fight each other. Techniques that result in loose coupling often result in low cohesion, and techniques that achieve high cohesion often result in tight coupling. An architectural style that finds an optimal balance between these two forces is the holy grail.

If we plot these two dimensions along the *x*- and *y*-axes and divide the resultant matrix in half, we end up with four quadrants as shown in Figure 16.3. The labels given to each of the four quadrants in the matrix are shorthand descriptions to characterize the kinds of solutions that are typically

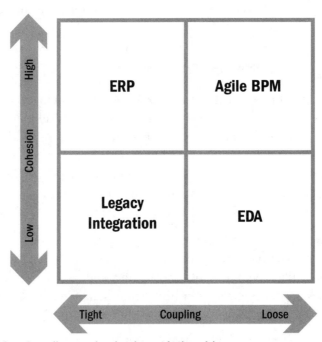

Figure 16.3   Coupling and cohesion relationship

found in each quadrant. The architectural style of each of the quadrants is outlined here:

- **Agile BPM (business process management):** Components are engineered around an ME&C enterprise-wide functional domain model. When implemented using loose coupling techniques, this is the holy grail of high reliability, low cost, and flexible business process solutions.
- **ERP (enterprise resource planning):** This architectural style is suitable for many needs but perceived as expensive to implement and inflexible to change. It is most effective in functional domains that are relatively stable.
- **EDA (event-driven architecture):** Typical applications are extremely loosely coupled one-to-many publish/subscribe processes or many-to-one event correlation solutions such as fraud detection or monitoring.
- **Legacy integration:** This is a portfolio of coarse-grained legacy systems that were acquired without a master reference architecture and were integrated using hard-coded point-to-point interfaces. This style is not desirable but it is a pragmatic reality in many organizations.

The "Agile BPM" quadrant is the most desirable, but also the hardest to achieve, and may never be fully realized since some techniques that result in high cohesion also result in tight coupling and vice versa. Furthermore, other factors such as the practical limitations related to modifying legacy systems, budget/time constraints, or infrastructure capabilities also can get in the way of achieving the nirvana environment.

Canonical Modeling Techniques

The importance of canonical data models grows as a system grows. Canonical data models reduce the number of transformations needed between systems and reduce the number of interfaces that a system supports. The need for this is usually not obvious when there are only one or two formats in an end-to-end system, but when the system reaches a critical mass in number of data formats supported (and in work required to integrate a new system, customer, or document type), having one or more canonical models becomes important.

B2B systems often grow organically over time to include systems that an organization builds or buys. For example, if a B2B system accepts 20 different inputs, passes that data to legacy systems, and generates 40 different outputs, it is apparent that unless the legacy system uses some shared canonical model, introducing a new input type requires modifications to the legacy systems, flow processes, and other areas. Put simply, if you have 20 different inputs and 40 different outputs, and all outputs can be produced from any input, you will need 800 different paths unless you take the approach of transforming all inputs to one or more canonical forms and transforming all responses from one or more forms to the 40 different outputs.

The cost of creating canonical models is that they often require design and maintenance involvement from staff on multiple teams.

This section describes three canonical techniques that can help to address the issues of data heterogeneity in an environment where application components must share information in order to provide effective business solutions:

1. Canonical data modeling
2. Canonical interchange modeling
3. Canonical physical formats

For a large-scale system-of-systems in a distributed computing environment, the most desirable scenario is to achieve loose coupling and high cohesion, resulting in a solution that is highly reliable, efficient, easy to maintain, and quick to adapt to changing business needs. Canonical techniques can play a significant role in achieving this ideal state.

Figure 16.4 illustrates how the three canonical techniques generally align with and enable the qualities in each of the four coupling/cohesion quadrants. There is some overlap between the techniques since there is no hard black-and-white definition of these techniques and their impact on a specific application.

Each of the three techniques has a "sweet spot"; that is, they can be applied in a way that is extremely effective and provides significant benefits. The application of these methods to a given implementation imparts architectural qualities to the solution. This approach does not attempt to prescribe which qualities are desirable or not since that is the responsibility of

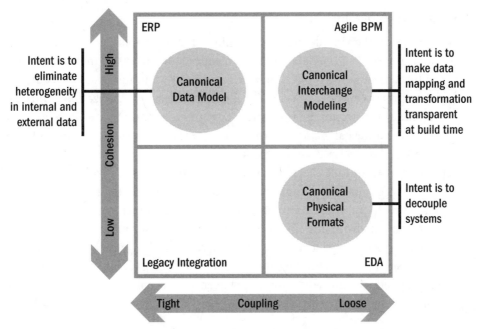

Figure 16.4 Canonical techniques in relation to the coupling-cohesion framework

the solutions architect to determine. For example, tight coupling could be a good thing or a bad thing depending on the needs and expectations of the customer. Tight coupling generally results in better response time and network performance in comparison to loose coupling, but it also can have a negative impact on the adaptability of components.

Furthermore, the three canonical approaches are generally not used in isolation; they are typically used in conjunction with other methods as part of an overall solutions methodology. As a result, it is possible to expand, shrink, or move the "sweet spot" subject to how it is used with other methods. This does not address the full spectrum of dependencies with other methods and their resultant implications, but it does attempt to identify some common pitfalls to be avoided.

When, and exactly how, to apply the canonical best practices should be a conscious, well-considered decision based on a keen understanding of the resulting implications.

Canonical Data Modeling

Canonical data modeling is a technique for developing and maintaining a logical model of the data required to support the needs of the business for a subject area. Some models may be relevant to an industry supply chain, the enterprise as a whole, or a specific line of business or organizational unit. The intent of this technique is to direct development and maintenance efforts so that the internal data structures of application systems conform to the canonical model as closely as possible.

This technique seeks to *eliminate heterogeneity* by aligning the internal data representation of applications with a common shared model. In an ideal scenario, there would be no need to perform any transformations at all when moving data from one component to another, but for practical reasons this is virtually impossible to achieve at an enterprise scale. Newly built components are easier to align with the common models, but legacy applications may also be aligned with the common model over time as enhancements and maintenance activities are carried out.

Common Pitfalls

- **Data model bottleneck:** A canonical data model is a centralization strategy that requires an adequate level of ongoing support to maintain and evolve. If the central support team is not staffed adequately, it will become a bottleneck for changes that could severely impact agility.
- **Heavyweight serialized objects:** There are two widely used techniques for exchanging data in a distributed computing environment: serialized objects and message transfer. The use of serialized objects can negate the positive benefits of high cohesion if they are used to pass around large, complex objects that are not stable and subject to frequent changes. The negative impacts include excessive processing capacity consumption, increased network latency, and higher project costs through extended integration test cycles.

Canonical Interchange Modeling

Canonical interchange modeling is a technique for analyzing and designing information exchanges between services that have incompatible underlying data models. This technique is particularly useful for modeling interactions between heterogeneous applications in a many-to-many scenario.

The intent of this technique is to *make data mapping and transformations transparent at build time.* This technique maps data from many components to a common canonical data model which thereby facilitates rapid mapping of data between individual components, since they all have a common reference model.

Common Pitfalls

- **Mapping with unstructured tools:** Mapping data interchanges for many enterprise business processes can be extremely complex. For example, Excel is not sophisticated enough to handle the details in environments with a large number of entities (typically over 500) and with more than two source or target applications. Without adequate metadata management tools, the level of manual effort needed to maintain the canonical models and the mappings to dependent applications in a highly dynamic environment can become a major resource drain that is not sustainable and is error-prone. Proper tools are needed for complex environments.

- **Indirection at run time:** Interchange modeling is a "design time" technique. Applying the same concept of an intermediate canonical format at run time results in extra overhead and a level of indirection that can significantly impact performance and reliability. The negative impacts can become even more severe when used in conjunction with a serialized object information exchange pattern, that is, large, complex objects that need to go through two (or more) conversions when being moved from application A to application B (this can become a showstopper for high-performance real-time applications when SOAP and XML are added to the equation).

Canonical Physical Format

The canonical physical format prescribes a specific run-time data format and structure for exchanging information. The prescribed generic format may be derived from the canonical data model or may simply be a standard message format that all applications are required to use for certain types of information.

The intent of this technique is to *eliminate heterogeneity for data in motion* by using standard data structures at run time for all information exchanges. The format is frequently independent of either the source or the target system and requires that all applications in a given interaction transform the data from their internal format to the generic format.

Common Pitfalls

- **Complex common objects:** Canonical physical formats are particularly useful when simple common objects are exchanged frequently between many service providers and many service consumers. Care should be taken not to use this technique for larger or more complex business objects since it tends to tightly couple systems, which can lead to longer time to market and increased maintenance costs.
- **Nontransparent transformations:** Canonical physical formats are most effective when the transformations from a component's internal data format to the canonical format are simple and direct with no semantic impedance mismatch. Care should be taken to avoid semantic transformations or multiple transformations in an end-to-end service flow. While integration brokers (or ESBs) are a useful technique for loose coupling, they also add a level of indirection that can complicate debugging and run-time problem resolution. The level of complexity can become paralyzing over time if service interactions result in middleware calling middleware with multiple transformations in an end-to-end data flow.
- **Inadequate exception handling:** The beauty of a loosely coupled architecture is that components can change without impacting others. The danger is that in a large-scale distributed computing environment with many components changing dynamically, the overall system-of-systems can assume chaotic (unexpected) behavior. One effective counter-strategy is to ensure that every system that accepts canonical physical formats also includes a manual work queue for any inputs that it can't interpret. The recommended approach is to make exception handling an integral part of the normal day-to-day operating procedure by pushing each message/object into a work queue for a human to review and deal with.

Navigating the Modeling Layers

The benefits of loose coupling can be undone if the cost of managing the complexity introduced by the additional layers of abstraction is not mitigated. The way to do this is to use the metadata management competency to tie everything together. Once again, one should not take the metadata framework diagram in Figure 16.5 too literally (there aren't necessarily just four layers, and what you really want in each layer is up to you), but the important concept is the need to see, down to a data element level, how information is accessed or changed from both the business and the IT perspectives. Regarding the management of canonical models, one needs the ability to see, among other things,

- How the canonical model has changed over time
- How the canonical model accesses underlying physical data
- Who uses the different canonical models and when

Different roles (architects, analysts, and developers) need to navigate the different layers of this model, up, down, and across, in a manner that is appropriate to their role and the questions they are trying to answer. Whether we're talking about structural metadata, business metadata, or operational metadata, all aspects need to be tied together through relationships within the metadata repository and reported on or displayed in a way that is appropriate to the different users.

Achieving the benefits of planning for change and mass customization is more a problem of people, process, and governance than of technology. For all the talk in this chapter about metadata, virtual databases, and SOA, we

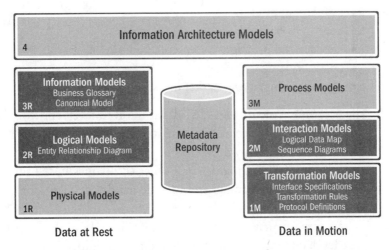

Figure 16.5   Modeling management required for data services support

recognize that business/IT alignment and business/business alignment regarding managing enterprise information is the harder problem. We address some of these issues in the next section.

Activities

Canonical models may be defined in any number of business functional or process domains at one of four levels:

1. **B2B:** external intercompany process and data exchange definitions
2. **Enterprise:** enterprise-wide data definitions (i.e., master data management programs)
3. **Business unit:** specific business area or functional group within the enterprise
4. **System:** a defined system or system-of-systems

For example, a supply chain canonical model in the mortgage industry is MISMO, which publishes an XML message architecture and a data dictionary for

- Underwriting
- Mortgage insurance applications
- Credit reporting
- Flood and title insurance
- Property appraisal
- Loan delivery
- Product and pricing
- Loan servicing
- Secondary mortgage market investor reporting

The MISMO standards are defined at the B2B level, and companies in this industry may choose to adopt these standards and participate in their evolution. Even if a company doesn't want to take an active role, it no doubt needs to understand the standards since other companies in the supply chain will send data in these formats and may demand that they receive information according to these standards.

A company may also choose to adopt the MISMO standard at the enterprise level, possibly with some extensions or modifications to suit its internal master data management initiative. Or one business unit such as the mortgage business within a financial institution may adopt the MISMO standards as its canonical information exchange model or data dictionary—again possibly with extensions or modifications. Finally, a specific application system, or collection of systems, may select the MISMO standards as its canonical model—also with some potential changes.

In one of the more complex scenarios, a given company may need to understand and manage an external B2B canonical model, an enterprise version of the canonical format, one or more business unit versions, and one or more system versions. Furthermore, all of the models are dynamic and change from time to time, which requires careful monitoring and version control. A change at one level may also have a ripple effect and drive changes in other levels (either up or down).

As shown in Figure 16.6, steps 1 through 5 are a one-time effort for each domain, whereas steps 6 through 11 are repeated for each project that intends to leverage the canonical models.

1. **Define the scope:** Determine the business motivation, functional or process domain, and level (i.e., supply chain, enterprise, business unit, or system) of the canonical modeling effort. Typical motivations include

   - Custom in-house development of a family of applications
   - Alignment with (and simplification of transformation with) industry or supply chain data/process models
   - Real-time ICC in support of flow-through processing or business event monitoring
   - Data standards in support of an SOA

2. **Select the tools and repository:** In small-scale or simple domains, tools such as Excel and a source code repository may be adequate. In complex environments with many groups/individuals involved, a more comprehensive structured metadata repository is likely to be needed along with a mechanism for access by a broad range of users.

3. **Identify the content administrator:** In small-scale or simple domains, the administration of the canonical models may be a part-time job for a data analyst, metadata administrator, process analyst, or developer. In large and complex environments, a separate administrator is often required for each level and each domain.

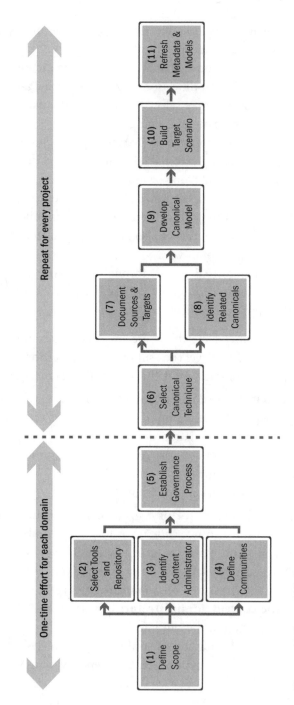

Figure 16.6 Modeling management 11-step process

4. **Define communities:** Each level and each domain should have a defined community of stakeholders. At the core of each community are the canonical administrator, data analysts, process analysts, and developers who are directly involved in developing and maintaining the canonical model. A second layer of stakeholders consists of the individuals who need to understand and apply the canonical models. A third and final layer of stakeholders is composed of individuals such as managers, architects, program managers, and business leaders who need to understand the benefits and constraints of canonical models.

5. **Establish the governance process:** Define how the canonical models will develop and change over time and the roles and authority of the individuals in the defined community. This step also defines the method of communication among individuals, frequency of meetings, versioning process, publishing methods, and approval process.

6. **Select the canonical technique:** Each project needs to decide which of the three techniques will be used: canonical data modeling, canonical interchange modeling, or canonical physical formats. This decision is generally made by the solution architect.

7. **Document sources and targets:** This step involves identifying existing documentation for the systems and information exchanges involved in the project. If the documentation doesn't exist, in most cases it must be reverse-engineered unless a given system is being retired.

8. **Identify related canonicals:** This step involves identifying relevant or related canonicals in other domains or at other levels that may already be defined in the enterprise. It is also often worth exploring data models of some of the large ERP systems vendors that are involved in the project, as well as researching which external industry standards may be applicable.

9. **Develop the canonical model:** This step involves an analysis effort, an agreement process to gain consensus across the defined community, and a documentation effort to capture the results. The canonical model may be developed either top-down, based on the expertise and understanding of domain experts; bottom-up, by rationalizing and normalizing definitions from various systems; or by adopting and tailoring existing canonical models.

10. **Build the target scenario:** This step is the project effort associated with leveraging the canonical model in the design, construction, or operation of the system components. Note that the canonical models may be used

only at design time, in the case of canonical interchange modeling, or also at construction and run time, in the case of the other two canonical techniques.

11. **Refresh the metadata and models:** This is a critical step to ensure that any extensions or modifications to the canonical models that were developed during the course of the specific project are documented and captured in the repository and that other enterprise domains that may exist are aware of the changes in the event that other models may be affected as well.

Summary

The key best practices are the following:

- Use **canonical data models** in business domains where there is a strong emphasis on building rather than buying application systems.
- Use **canonical interchange modeling** at build time to analyze and define information exchanges in a heterogeneous application environment.
- Use **canonical physical formats** at run time in many-to-many or publish/subscribe integration patterns, in particular in the context of a business event architecture.
- Plan for appropriate tools such as metadata management repositories to support architects, analysts, and developers.
- Develop a plan to maintain and evolve the canonical models as discrete enterprise components. The ongoing costs to maintain the canonical models can be significant and should be budgeted accordingly.

In summary, there are three defined canonical approaches among the five best practices, each of which has a distinct objective. Each method imparts specific qualities to the resultant implementation that can be compared using a coupling/cohesion matrix. It is the job of the architect and systems integrator to select the methods that are most appropriate in a given situation. The methods can be very effective, but they also come with a cost, so care should be taken to acquire appropriate tools and to plan for the ongoing maintenance and support of the canonical artifacts.

Case Study: European Interoperability Framework

The European Interoperability Framework for Pan-European Government Services is a useful case study and provides some context for effective practices. It defines three categories of interoperability:

1. **Technical interoperability** covers the technical issues of linking computer systems and services. It includes key aspects such as open interfaces, interconnection services, data integration and middleware, data presentation and exchange, accessibility, and security services.
2. **Semantic interoperability** is concerned with ensuring that the precise meaning of exchanged information is understandable by any other application that was not initially developed for this purpose. Semantic interoperability enables systems to combine received information with other information resources and to process it in a meaningful manner.
3. **Procedural interoperability** is concerned with defining business goals, modeling business processes, and bringing about the collaboration of administrations that wish to exchange information and may have different internal structures and processes. Moreover, procedural interoperability aims at addressing the requirements of the user community by making services available, easily identifiable, accessible, and user-oriented.

The European Interoperability Framework results in a three-layer architecture as shown in Figure 16.7:

1. **Protocol conversion:** Incompatible protocols, formats, or syntax requires technical conversion. That is, if you were to convert A to B and then convert B to A, you would end up with exactly what you started with. Protocol conversions are deterministic and mathematical in nature. A simple example is currency conversions or converting a two-letter state abbreviation into a numeric code based on a conversion table.
2. **Semantic transposition:** Incompatible data definitions require semantic transposition. This means that when you convert A to B and then B back to A, you end up with something similar but not identical. For example, if system A supports 20 product codes and system B supports

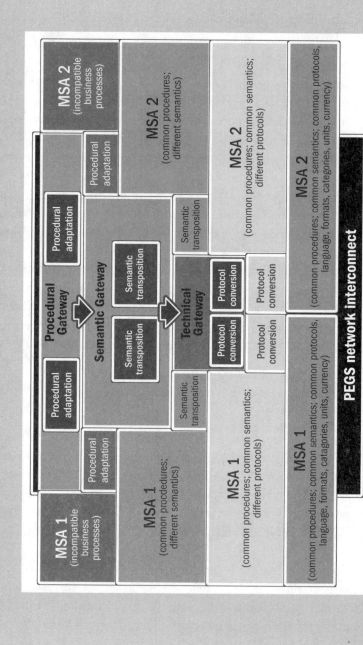

Figure 16.7 Graphical representation of the European Interoperability Framework

only 10 product codes, some of which are aggregates, a conversion from B back to A may not give exactly the same result. Another example is relational versus hierarchical data structures. System A has a relational model where two individuals in the same household point to the same address record; this is translated into system B where the address information is duplicated for each individual. The question, then, when converting B back to A, is whether the individuals are really in the same household or are independent individuals who happen to be living at the same address.

3. **Procedural adaptation:** Incompatible business processes require procedural adaptation. This level of transformation deals with more complex issues where the only thing that the two entities can agree upon is the goal. For example, the process of opening a credit card account may be so different from that of opening a mortgage account that only the end point (i.e., an opened account) can have a common definition.

Case Study: Object–Relational Mismatch

There are sometimes very subtle differences in the meaning of data that are hidden inside the applications and the databases that control them. One such example is the object-relational impedance mismatch that is caused by encapsulation and hidden representations, data type differences, structural and integrity differences, and transactional differences.

An example scenario is shown in Figure 16.8, demonstrating how a simple difference in structure between two applications sharing data can cause problems. The scenario looks at two ways that address information commonly associated with individuals.

Customer Servicing System

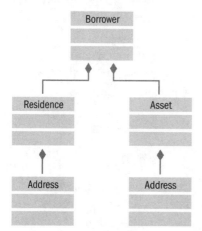

Mortgage Application System

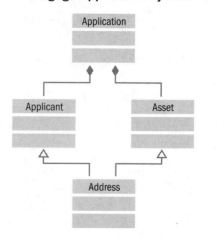

The Customer Servicing System (CSS) is an internally developed user interface system for call center staff to work with multiple back-end systems. It organizes data around individuals, including where they live and the assets they have borrowed against. Addresses are not normalized. When a customer (borrower) calls to update the home address, the change to the residence address does not automatically propagate to the asset address since they are separate instances.

The Mortgage Application System (MAS) is a vendor package that organizes customer and property information around applications. Addresses are normalized and only a single instance is stored physically if it is the same for the mortgage property, the applicant, and coapplicants. It is critical for certain tax calculations for the MAS system to know if the applicant is living in the home being financed.

Scenario:

A new application is initiated by CSS with a borrower, co-borrower, and asset where the asset is a residence where both borrowers live. The data is sent to MAS where a de-duping process results in one address object and three relationships.

Subsequently, the co-borrower phones the call center to change his address. CSS makes a real-time call to MAS to obtain the latest data and reestablishes the object hierarchy by cloning the address and attaching it in three places in the hierarchy along with the keys generated by MAS (i.e., the same object exists in three places in the CSS hierarchy with the same key). The co-borrower's residence address is updated in CSS, which now has three objects with the same key but one of them has different data.

Questions:

1. What rules can intelligently be applied to detect changes in duplicate objects with the same logical key?
2. Where should the data quality business rules be embedded: front-end CSS, back-end MAS, or somewhere else?
3. How could this issue be solved if both CSS and MAS are not easily modified?

Figure 16.8   Semantic example of object-relational impedance mismatch

CHAPTER SEVENTEEN

Integration Systems

Everything should be made as simple as possible, but not simpler.
Albert Einstein

The integration systems competency addresses the need for managing the life cycle of integration systems as a distinct class of systems that provide a sustainable operating infrastructure to support the free flow of information in an organization in an integrated manner. Here are some of the key characteristics of a functioning integration systems model:

- There is a shared infrastructure where applications can use and share integration components with relative ease.
- A common hardware/software infrastructure is in place that can be easily scaled.
- Development standards are in place to name objects in a standard format for easy identification.
- Operational SLAs exist where there is a specific availability that matches business requirements such as high availability or fail-over capabilities for 24/7 applications.

- Service definitions such as metadata availability, expert assistance, model management, and methodology can be expected as part of the support services.
- A migration and control function is defined for moving objects easily to production.
- Backout capabilities are in place should any migration fail.

Governance of these activities is usually managed by either an Integration Competency Center (ICC), Center of Excellence (COE), or another organization chartered with the responsibility to manage the environment over and above just production support. The concept of identifying, managing, and sustaining an integration system is key to achieving the benefits of reliable data integration.

In the context of Lean Integration, integration systems are in effect elements of the Integration Factory. Recall that the Integration Factory involves problem-solving tasks, information management tasks, and physical transformation tasks. The integration systems are the "machines" that perform the physical transformation tasks for day-to-day conversion of raw materials (source or unintegrated data) to finished product—meaningful, consistent, and integrated data in the hands of the customers or applications.

Integration systems also play a key role in the information management tasks by providing information about data processed, messages transmitted, failures encountered, service levels met, and so on. Some of this data may be of interest only to the operations staff who are operating the systems or to the ICC that is governing the overall environment and driving continuous improvements. Much of it is also of interest to the customers of the integration services, especially when something goes wrong and they want to understand what happened. The disciplines for managing, controlling, and operating integration systems are an essential competency for Lean Integration and the Integration Factory.

What Is an Integration System?

An integration system is a collection of components that are managed as a unit (usually by an ICC) for the purpose of data, application, or systems integration. Integration systems are separate from, and provide a service to, other systems within an enterprise. The services may include data migration, data consolidation, data synchronization, data cleansing, data replication, extract transformation and load for data warehousing, application synchronization and process orchestration, to name just a few. This contrasts with the traditional view of integration components that are managed as part of a business application (i.e., integrations managed as point-to-point elements with custom agreements between the cooperating applications) or are not managed at all (orphan integration components).

An integration system views the integration components from a holistic perspective. It defines clear boundaries around each business application and explicitly defines all the components that collectively represent the integration system and its functions—regardless of how distributed those components might be. A core rationale for managing integration components as systems is that it provides the ability to sustain integration across applications after initial projects are completed as they invariably change over time. Integration systems are characterized by the classification of components (i.e., transformation service, integration service, etc.), their function (i.e., message conversion, ETL, etc.), and the tools interface (i.e., design-time interface, run-time interface, etc.).

Figure 17.1 shows how information exchanges between two business applications are often depicted at the conceptual whiteboard level. At a conceptual level this makes sense, but the question is "What *is* the line in real life?" Figure 17.2 is a simple depiction of how integration systems can be isolated from application systems. This is how the information exchange might look at a real-life physical level. In the example, the "line" is really an integration hub that directly accesses the database associated with the source system and the target system.

In the next and more complex scenario in Figure 17.3, the simple "line" in the conceptual diagram is really a complex set of interactions between multiple components. There is a separate extract program that is associated with the sales system. The load program for the finance system has, by agreement, been assigned to be part of the integration system. Note that in this example, the queues that are part of the transport network as well as the security server have also been designated as part of the integration system.

Figure 17.1 Conceptual view of information exchange between business systems

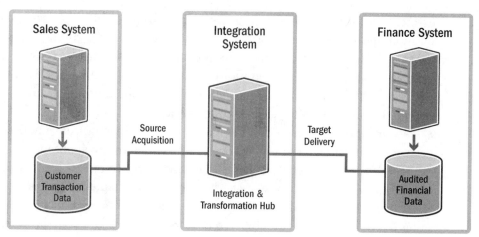

Figure 17.2   Example of a "simple" integration system

Questions that should be clarified in this example include these:

- Is the extract program part of the sales system or part of the integration system?
- Is the load program part of the finance system or part of the integration system?
- Are the queues part of the integration system (all of them or just some of them)?
- Is the security and encryption component part of the integration system?

Since a *system* is a purely abstract concept, there is no right or wrong answer to these questions. The important consideration is that there be an explicit definition and common agreement among the owners and those responsible for managing, operating, and sustaining each of the components. The key is to ensure that there is no ambiguity and to assign clear accountability for all components.

Integration Systems Taxonomy

Figure 17.4 further clarifies the term *integration systems* by showing a framework that contrasts integration systems with business systems. Business systems provide capabilities to support business functions such as accounting, marketing, manufacturing, sales, and so on. Integration systems provide capabilities to integrate the individual business systems into a cohesive whole

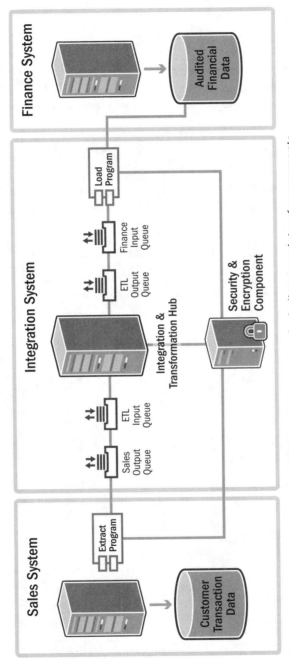

Figure 17.3 Example of a complex integration system including a variety of components

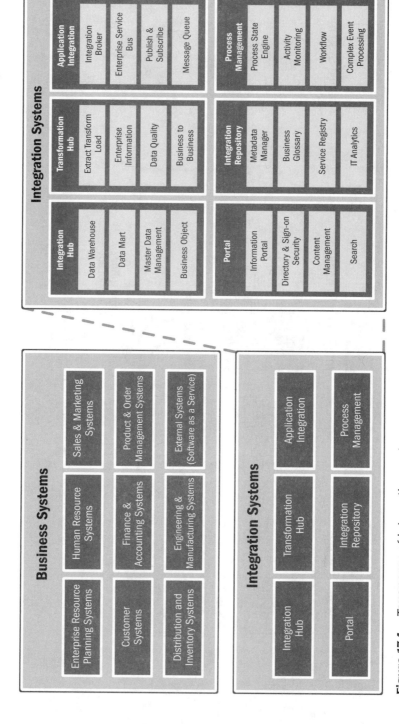

Figure 17.4 Taxonomy of integration systems

by consolidating, adapting, cleansing, and transforming data. Integration systems also control and monitor end-to-end business processes and provide an integrated experience to users or external customers. In other words, integrations between applications are viewed collectively as a "system" rather than as point-to-point appendages of the business applications.

The six integration systems shown in the reference model are in fact a high-level taxonomy referred to as "systems families." They in turn decompose to a more granular list of systems.

Note: There is not necessarily a one-to-one alignment between a given vendor product and one of these systems. Many off-the-shelf products provide functionality from more than one integration system category. This framework provides a common reference for classifying, comparing, rationalizing, and managing the various integration systems in an organization.

Some of the key ICC services that must be provided by the Lean team in support of the integration systems are

- Ongoing production support and SLAs for operational systems
- Migration processes that support the transition between development, system test, and production
- Data rationalization of new systems to reuse existing data and process components to achieve strong levels of integration
- Catalog services such as a business glossary of metadata for business, technical, and operational metadata
- Development and architectural support in scoping out new projects that will use the integration services platform

The goal is to manage the operations of the integration platform developed by the integration methodology competency and to sustain it as an efficient operating environment. Other items to consider include the availability of the integration platform, whether it is during business hours or 24/7 operations. As information flows naturally through an organization, the goal is to move the platform more toward a 24/7 operation.

Table 17.1 shows the integration systems maturity model adapted from *ICC: An Implementation Methodology.*[1] It provides a high-level framework for assessing an organization's current level of maturity in managing integration elements in a systematic fashion and for defining a future-state target. As the level of maturity increases, the focus of design and corporate information flow

---

1. John Schmidt and David Lyle, *Integration Competency Center: An Implementation Methodology* (Informatica Corporation, 2005), p. 38.

becomes more vital to the lifeblood of an organization. Application delivery, operational results/support, and metadata/data governance become parts of a mutual ecosystem rather than separate entities. One goal is to have its standards and disciplines become accepted community methods rather than enforced checkpoints.

Table 17.1   Integration Systems Maturity Model

Maturity Level	Integration Systems
Project	The most common interface pattern is hand-coded point-to-point interfaces. Integration work is done by direct collaboration between the systems being integrated, and the interfaces are considered to be extensions of the business applications rather than a separate system. Interface specifications are developed at a point in time during the project life cycle and stored along with project documentation.
Program	Applications are decoupled through an abstraction layer and middleware technology so that changing one minimizes the effect on others. XML message formats and canonical models are commonly used. Interface documentation is stored in a central location and shared by teams across the business unit. Portal technologies are used to provide end users with a common front end to most enterprise applications.
Sustaining	Applications are designed with an integration layer as an essential prerequisite. Integration requirements carry more weight than functional requirements in terms of product selection. Application interfaces are standardized across the enterprise. Integration systems for message, service, process, or data-related interfaces are designed and managed independently of individual applications. The integration systems have a defined life cycle, including ongoing operations, routine upgrades, and eventual retirement under the direction of a central governance team such as an ICC.
Lean	The integration systems, whether message-, service-, process-, or data-based, include a business layer that provides end users with the ability to directly monitor and control the operational interactions between systems. Users log in once and a role-based authorization mechanism allows them to access any application in the enterprise without having to log in again. Formal processes are defined for ongoing integration system portfolio rationalization and optimization.

Challenges

A number of the challenges associated with integration systems, such as funding and architectural alignment, are dealt with in other chapters. Here are several of the top challenges that are addressed explicitly in this chapter:

- **Shared infrastructure demands higher levels of service:** Consider these two scenarios: five separate and redundant integration hubs serving five different application teams, and one central and more efficient integration hub serving all five application teams. In the first scenario, if one integration hub is down, it impacts only one-fifth of the applications. In the second scenario it would impact all applications. Shared infrastructure requires more careful planning and sizing, increased availability, and so on than individual systems. On the other hand, consolidating systems into a shared environment often affords the organization the ability to implement high-availability and disaster recovery capabilities that should have been in place for each of the individual systems but may not have been cost-effective when considered separately.

- **Maintenance upgrades are a thankless job:** Maintaining a shared integration system at the latest revision level is critical, but many perceive maintenance activities as low-level, routine, and less rewarding—particularly in contrast to high-profile projects that often receive most of the management attention and accolades. Nonetheless, upgrading shared infrastructure is in many respects more demanding than project work and requires experienced and expert staff.

- **New product features often don't provide a compelling reason to upgrade:** Maintaining systems to keep them at the current software patch level and supported by the vendor can be expensive, but the hard benefits of new releases sometimes don't provide a compelling case to upgrade. Nonetheless, falling too far behind on upgrades is a risky practice and cannot be tolerated in a high-availability shared environment.

- **Portfolio rationalization:** The task of consolidating multiple independent integration systems (or hand-coded point-to-point integrations) into a consistent shared environment is not easy. The financial and organizational challenges that have already been mentioned are significant, but additional technical issues such as naming standards, security controls, and coordination across a complex portfolio of business systems that are constantly changing are also major challenges.

- **Evolving technologies (for example, EAI—enterprise application integration—and ETL product space):** The life cycle of new technologies is roughly 7 years; the past 30 years or so have demonstrated that most technologies are replaced by better, faster, and lower-cost technologies approximately every 7 years. This applies not just to integration systems but to the business systems they serve. Since it is not practical to replace all the business systems every 7 years, the net result is that integration systems must deal with a vast array of standards and must constantly stay current with the last technology that any given business system adopts.
- **Systems become "disintegrated" over time:** When a new integrated solution is first implemented, all the dependencies and information exchanges are well integrated (assuming the systems integrator did a good job on the project). But over time, as the individual and separate components evolve and change, the integrations can become fragile from an operational perspective and with reduced data quality. A governance organization must address the challenge of maintaining integration quality once the initial project implementation team has disbanded.

Industry Practices

With the advent of application-to-application middleware software, integration systems started to be recognized in the industry as a distinct class of systems in the 1990s. Some integration systems such as data warehouses were around much earlier, but it was the introduction of application-to-application middleware (also commonly referred to as EAI) that spurred the rapid growth in integration systems as a separate class of application systems. The general idea behind the industry trend is that custom-developed (hand-coded) point-to-point interfaces are not scalable, and at a certain level of complexity it becomes more efficient to treat the integration elements collectively as a system with its own life cycle that is independent of the business applications that are being integrated.

A related industry trend is the concept of managing systems as a service, that is, to describe the functions performed by a system as a set of value-added services and to formalize the operational commitment to provide the services in an SLA. One of the notable contributions to this idea was the work that originated in the UK known as the Information Technology Infrastructure Library (ITIL). ITIL is a set of concepts and techniques for managing information technology infrastructure, development, and operations. Of most relevance to the integration systems competency is the portion of ITIL that addresses infrastructure management. It recommends best practices for requirements analysis, planning, design, deployment, and ongoing operations management and support of technology infrastructure.

Another industry trend is the concept of ERP for IT. An ERP system is an automated solution supporting a major business process or functional area and is commonly seen in many major business functions such as finance, manufacturing, and distribution, to name just a few. The general idea is that IT also is a critical business function with complex processes associated with how it operates within the enterprise supply chain. As a result, IT should also have a formalized set of processes that are automated or semiautomated and enabled through application systems. Integration systems are a natural outcropping of this concept, which has been widely referred to as "ERP for IT."

Activities

Establishing an integration system capability involves a number of steps such as identifying the integration systems, establishing an ICC scope, and defining operational and rationalization procedures. The enterprise competencies are focused on preparing for the role of an ICC when applicable in an organization and building a sustaining operational model. Figure 17.5 shows the nine-step approach to achieving a Lean Integration systems capability.

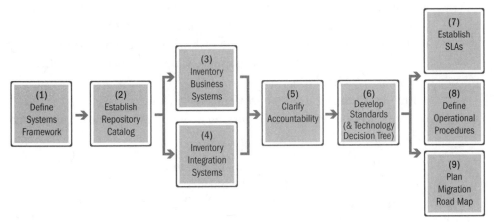

Figure 17.5   Steps to establish a sustaining integration systems capability

Step 1: Define the Systems Framework

When defining a systems framework, first build the taxonomy of business and integration systems much like what is shown in Figure 17.4. This taxonomy helps to differentiate between business applications and integration systems and provides a classification structure.

The framework shown in Figure 17.4 is a recommended starting point. The primary task in step 1 is simply to gain agreement across relevant stakeholders (i.e., the ones who will use the definitions) about exactly what name and description to give to each category. Note that this reference model does not describe either the current state or the future state of the enterprise integration systems. Rather, it is a reference or common dictionary used for the purposes of classifying and categorizing IT systems.

This step should be completed fairly quickly since the value is in applying the model (there is little value in having a well-defined framework that is not used). As a general rule, step 1 should not take more than one week and no more than one to two review meetings with the interested stakeholders.

Step 2: Establish a Repository Catalog

This step involves the definition of integration metadata that a governance group will need to capture and maintain in support of the systems inventory. Metadata is the key information that helps deliver value in an organization since it describes what kind of data about systems is relevant, what the attributes are, and what its uses are within the organization.

Some of the activities involved in this step are to

- Determine what metadata is being captured from each integration system (What level of detail is needed to support integration expertise?)
- Determine what is needed to relate each subject area and attribute (What type of subjects and services support each area? What are the attributes related to each subject area?)
- Buy/install the repository hardware and software
- Configure the repository (including extending the meta-model as necessary)

See Chapter 13, Metadata Management, for more details. Services provided include a glossary of metadata of the business as well as technical and operational metadata as part of the repository catalog service.

Steps 3 and 4: Inventory Business Systems and Integration Systems

The purpose of these steps is to identify business systems and integration systems and their associated stakeholders. Relevant metadata about each system should be captured so that a governance body has a record of its constituency.

The first part of this step is to identify all of the business application systems in the enterprise. Most organizations have one or more lists of systems, but they may not be complete or consistent. For example, there may be a complete list of all mainframe systems that is maintained separately from a list of applications on mid-range UNIX systems. Furthermore, there may be differences between naming conventions and the granularity of detail recorded for the systems. For example, a mainframe application may have a three-letter acronym as its name and consist of one COBOL program, in contrast to a Web application called "Customer Sales Portal" that consists of hundreds of software components distributed across dozens of servers. Finally, the existing lists of systems may be incomplete depending on how closely the information is controlled and how mature is the process of maintaining the list. Therefore, key steps are these:

1. Gather the existing lists of application systems.
2. Identify gaps and overlaps in the list and build a single common list.
3. Categorize the systems according to the taxonomy defined in step 1.
4. Normalize the list (for example, the mainframe COBOL program mentioned earlier may be part of a larger business application).
5. Capture relevant metadata about each system.
6. Load the data into the repository.

These steps are repeated for integration systems. The inventorying of integration systems and business systems can occur in parallel, but the two are shown as separate steps because the stakeholders involved are often different.

An optional (but recommended) activity is to also identify the technologies supporting the business and integration systems. This helps to identify gaps and overlaps in technology or function within an organization.

Step 5: Clarify Accountability

An ICC, or other appropriate Lean team, should have accountability for managing integration systems. In organizations that don't have an ICC, the responsibility may be assigned to other appropriate governing groups or to other business application support teams. The key is to ensure that there is clear accountability for business systems and integration systems in the organization.

Once the inventory of business and integration systems has been completed, there are two key sub-activities for step 5:

1. Determine which of the integration systems will be the responsibility of the ICC and which will be the responsibility of another group (such as an infrastructure group or application team). The ICC scope framework in Figure 17.6 provides a structure that can be helpful for gaining agreement across the organization.

2. Define the precise boundary between the integration system and the business systems it serves in terms of exactly which components are in scope (according to the taxonomy in Figure 17.4). This should include the definition of what is in a business system and what portion is the integration component. For example, some integration code embedded in an application may not be easily supported by the ICC. This step is a fairly detailed technical activity, and the results of the analysis should be captured in the repository catalog.

Figure 17.6 is a framework for defining the scope of an ICC. In its broadest context, a fully functioning, mature ICC is responsible for sustaining all internal and external integrations in terms of both initial project implementation

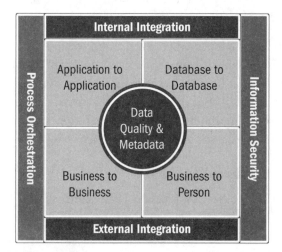

Figure 17.6   ICC functional scope framework

and ongoing maintenance, support, and operations. The ICC would have responsibility for these areas:

- **Application-to-application integration solutions**, where much of the real-time interactions between systems are managed
- **Database-to-database integration:** includes a range of solutions such as batch data migration, data synchronization, data consolidation, and business intelligence, to name a few
- **Business-to-business integration:** addresses the needs of extreme loose coupling with customer and supplier systems, adaptation to industry standard protocols, and handling of semistructured or unstructured documents
- **Business-to-person integration:** addresses "integration at the glass" by managing portal solutions, content management, presentation standards, and search capabilities
- **Process orchestration:** involves human workflow, management of long-running system-to-system flow-through processes, and coordination of processes across channels
- **Information security:** implements data encryption solutions, certificate management, authorization data, and single sign-on capabilities

Note that in the center are data quality and metadata. These are arguably the most important and critical aspects of an ICC, and they are positioned in the center because they impact all dimensions of data and process integration. Data quality should be addressed at all stages of a project's life cycle and in all types of integration solutions. In a real-time ICC it is particularly critical to establish policies and practices to ensure that data is accurate and complete at the point of entry. From a metadata perspective, this means managing data as an asset and documenting both "data about data" and "data about data processes." It maintains information about data at rest (application databases), data in motion (information exchanges between systems), data processes such as business usage (business glossary), and governance (policies and controls).

It is rare for an organization to have one ICC that is responsible for the full scope. A more common approach is to establish an ICC that focuses on an area that presents a specific opportunity or high-priority need for the business or to implement several ICCs, each with a different and nonoverlapping charter.

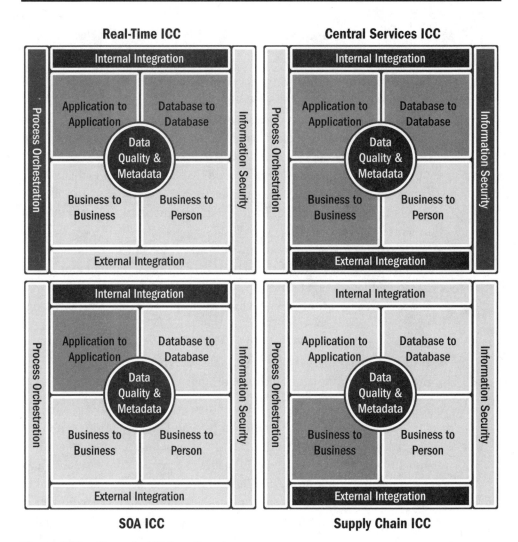

Figure 17.7   Example ICC functional scope

It is important that boundaries be clear regarding which group will support which component. Figure 17.7 shows some example frameworks for the ICC. Each scope definition framework helps to determine the scope of support for the ICC in terms of technology. Other methods for determining scope are more organizational in nature or based on application boundaries.

The scope of responsibility with which the ICC is chartered needs to be clearly defined. While each of the models in the figure can be implemented, they are simply examples of the ICC scope and definition that need to be determined when defining the initial charter.

Step 6: Develop Standards

After the inventory and ownership issues have been addressed, the next step is to apply common rules about when each technology and each system should be used. The recommended way to achieve this is to define usage standards and gain agreement across all relevant stakeholders. A technology decision tree is a useful way to capture the results of the agreement (refer to *ICC: An Implementation Methodology*[2] for details).

There are a number of checklists and standards activities related to the service. Chapter 12, Integration Methodology, describes several of the activities that are needed to set up a central-services organization. The following checklist shows key areas where we recommend that ICCs develop formal standards:

- Middleware technology selection (technology decision tree)
- Shared versus federated software configuration
- High availability and disaster recovery
- Development standards and naming conventions
- Migration control of development objects
- Data rationalization of new systems to reuse existing data and process components to achieve strong levels of integration
- Catalog services such as a business glossary of metadata of business, technical, and operational metadata
- Metadata management competency

Step 7: Establish Service Level Agreements

Step 7 is focused on establishing SLAs for the integration systems that have been assigned to the ICC for management and operational responsibility. SLA management includes discussion points around the following topics:

- Defining the SLA (or operation level agreement, OLA)
- Harmonizing the needs of diverse teams in a shared infrastructure

---

2. Ibid.

- Formality/informality of the SLA/OLA and expectations
- Impact on the organization of a missed SLA/OLA
- Design and build of systems that allow the SLA/OLA to be achieved
- Escalation path to resolve a missed or unachievable SLA/OLA
- Maintaining service levels and operation levels for growth

Each ICC technology should have a series of SLAs/OLAs as well as documented daily procedures for maintaining operations.

Step 8: Define Operational Procedures

Step 8 is focused on defining operational procedures for the integration systems that are within the ICC scope of responsibility. The operations manual should contain a high-level overview of the system (in order to familiarize the operations staff with new concepts) as well as the specific details necessary to successfully execute day-to-day operations. For data visualization, the operations manual should contain high-level explanations of reports, dashboards, and shared objects in order to familiarize the operations staff with those concepts.

Step 9: Plan the Migration Road Map

An objective of the ICC is to consolidate, centralize, and standardize (allowing for the reuse of objects and the simplification of development and operations). To achieve this goal, a decision must be made about which tool or set of tools and processes will be used and which others will be consolidated and/or retired. A further consolidation of servers and the reallocation of personnel may occur as part of the overall tool consolidation effort.

Step 9 builds upon the results defined for the target architecture in step 6 by looking at technology gaps and overlaps and developing a road map to address legacy integration systems that don't fit in the new target. The portfolio rationalization practice in the next section covers creating a process where technology meets the goals of the ICC so that the technology investment is efficiently leveraged both within and across data integration projects.

Portfolio Rationalization

Once the decision has been made to structure corporate integration activities into an ICC, an assessment of all software tools and their usage needs to be conducted. In this review, it may surface that the organization uses multiple tools, processes, servers, and human resources to perform similar tasks. An objective of the ICC is to consolidate, centralize, and standardize, allowing for reuse and simplifying development and operations. To achieve this goal, one must decide which tool or set of tools and processes will remain, and which will consolidate with the ones selected, and then be retired. In consolidating the portfolio of tools, there may also be consolidation of servers and reallocation of personnel. This section will cover the server and software tool consolidation efforts and in some cases refer to all these items as tools or tool sets.

There are a number of challenges regarding rationalizing this portfolio of integration tools, processes, and servers:

1. Selecting which tools and processes are a best fit for the organization
2. Retiring or managing the tools not selected
3. Migrating processing to the new tools and servers
4. Developer and end-user training

What Is Portfolio Rationalization?

Portfolio rationalization involves applying the principles of waste elimination and continuous improvement to the integration systems within an enterprise. It is applied as an ongoing process that allows the ICC to optimize the use of technologies and its features. Portfolio rationalization can be used to eliminate redundant technology or even to identify new technology gaps. The process of evaluating these tools, making the decisions on tool status, acting to migrate processing to the selected/standard tool set, managing the remaining and to-be-retired tools, and managing training on the selected tools is portfolio rationalization.

The business case for an ICC has already indicated the value of centralizing, standardizing, and consolidating integration activities. Similarly, consolidating the tool set adds to this value proposition with

1. Potential reduction in software license costs via bulk license agreements or a reduced number of total licenses
2. Reduced overhead for product training on a reduced number of software tools
3. Reduced complexity with a limited number of software tools and by standardizing on a common version of the software

4. Enabling resources to more readily provide coverage for each other, since standard methods and tools are common

5. Potential reduction in hardware maintenance costs with a reduced number of server footprints

Portfolio Rationalization Methodology

Based on the business drivers for portfolio rationalization, the ICC should initiate a process to evaluate the tools that are already part of the portfolio, as well as those that are candidates for future use. The process of inventorying the systems and tools and the selection process to define the target platform are part of the evaluation process. The same process is followed to resolve technology gaps as to select the standard tool used to consolidate the portfolio. Unused components can be retired or repurposed as they are no longer needed. This process is repeated continuously as new requirements surface and as market advances present opportunities to use newer technology.

Figure 17.8 shows the recommended seven-step process for achieving a Lean portfolio of integration systems in an enterprise.

Step 1: Clarify the Business Needs

Document the business needs or problems that drive adding new technology to the portfolio.

Step 2: Inventory the Systems and Tools

Evaluate both in-house tools and tools that are new to the organization. Determine the best fit in terms of features, compatibility, and future potential to meet the business needs. Follow the same process of evaluation to resolve tool gaps. Current systems and tools should be classified in one of the following categories:

- **Evaluation:** technology that is under evaluation for use
- **Selected:** technology that has been selected for use but not implemented

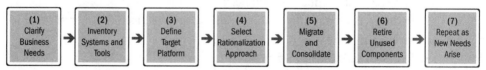

Figure 17.8   Seven-step portfolio rationalization methodology

- **Standard:** technology that is the recommended standard in the organization
- **Deprecated:** technology that is no longer standard in the organization but is still supported
- **Unsupported:** technology that is neither standard nor supported in the organization
- **Retired:** technology that has a defined exit strategy

Step 3: Define the Target Platform

Determine the classifications of the tool sets under consideration for new and existing tools, as well as tools to be replaced. Select the tool sets to use as the standards.

When technology gaps are recognized within the organization, begin an evaluation process for the tools to fill the gaps. Technology that can fill the gaps might already exist within the organization, or the resulting evaluation might require new software tools to be added to the portfolio. This situation is the simplest to manage with the ICC because consolidating or migrating the tools does not cause disruptions to existing systems.

If the ICC is mature, and the tools already exist as standards in the environment, use of these tools would merely be leveraging new functionality or capabilities. Possibly, licenses would be added to an existing contract. Perhaps the organization would leverage existing hardware, upgrade the existing hardware, or purchase new hardware. Capacity planning on the existing systems should leave room to add new applications and teams to the supported environment without reaching a capacity threshold.

If the technology you are adding is new to the organization, the infrastructure to support it within the ICC needs to be developed. Servers, processes, training, licensing, and standards will all need to developed and managed within the ICC framework. Starting from this fresh approach, new development can follow the standards and patterns put into place as the technology is introduced to developers and users.

Step 4: Select the Rationalization Approach

At this stage, tools have been evaluated, classified, and selected. Now it is time to decide how to move forward. The organization could take one of two approaches, described in more detail in Table 17.2:

1. **Rationalize by attrition:** Establish policies and procedures to contain any legacy components and simply build new (or modified) solutions on the target architecture. This could also be called the "self-funding" strategy.
2. **Conduct a rationalization project:** This is a proactive plan to shut down and migrate legacy components to the target architecture. This strategy generally requires a business case.

The attrition approach is less disruptive to the organization because human resources remain focused on other priorities, new user training is handled at a slower pace and involves fewer people at each iteration, and outages on existing systems do not occur. However, this method moves more slowly and does not realize the benefits of reduced license cost, reduced server overhead, and other benefits of consolidating the portfolio. In fact, adding the new, shared components for the desired target systems may increase these costs in the mid-term, until a significant portion of the legacy systems have been migrated and consolidated and can be retired.

Table 17.2 Application Rationalization Table

Strategy	Description	Benefit/Risk
Rationalization by attrition	Only new or modified tools move to new architecture and tools.	▪ Slow ▪ Does not disrupt status quo processing ▪ Continued infrastructure costs for maintaining multiple systems
Rationalization project	Develop a plan to move all similar processing to the new environment and tool set.	▪ Standardizes tool sets across the enterprise to leverage team capabilities and reduce complexity ▪ Reduces infrastructure costs as hardware is consolidated and old software is not renewed ▪ Enhanced object sharing capability ▪ Project team members not available for other work ▪ Outages during the migration and consolidation efforts may disrupt service

Step 5: Migrate and Consolidate

If the organization elects to conduct the rationalization project to consolidate and migrate the portfolio of tools, it needs to determine how best to do so.

Multiple versions of software tools may be in active use, and it is possible that each team has applied different standards. Bringing these disparate methodologies and systems together in a fashion that is logical and is least disruptive to the teams involved can be a challenge even when the same tool set has been used. An example of a road map that attempts to rationalize these issues is shown in Figure 17.9. End-user training, developer training, participation from the affected teams to test, and other logistics must be kept in mind.

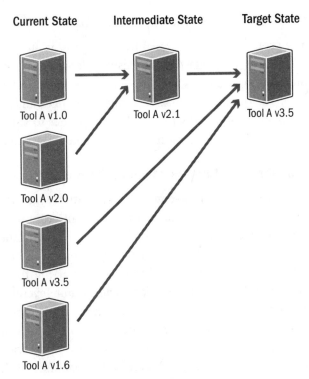

Figure 17.9 Infrastructure migration road map

There are various scenarios for migration and consolidation:

1. Hardware consolidation using a single version of the existing software tool set
2. Hardware consolidation using multiple versions of the existing software tool set
3. Hardware and software consolidation to the defined standard tool set

Step 6: Retire Unused Components

Retire or reallocate the architecture components no longer used, remove application processing from servers, and terminate contracts for unused software. The benefits of standardizing and consolidating integration systems are not realized until the old software and servers can be retired.

Step 7: Repeat as New Business Needs Arise

As new products become available, the organization may decide to move to new standards and reclassify the existing elements in the portfolio. Portfolio rationalization is an ongoing process to evaluate and implement the best tools for the organization. As technology changes and as the organization's needs change, continually review the approaches to software, hardware, and processing in the organization's portfolio, and make adjustments.

Portfolio Rationalization Using the Metadata Framework

The ability to query an inventory of integration systems in order to identify waste and monitor a continuous improvement program would be possible if the portfolio were modeled within layer 1 of the metadata framework, shown in Figure 13.3. The chapters in Part III of this book have walked down the metadata framework from top to bottom, starting from the business view and working down to the physical systems, but several highly mature ICCs work from the bottom up. These ICCs effectively began with an inventory of their integration systems and an identification of the duplication and waste that existed in their hairball. By eliminating integration duplication, they freed up system resources and increased the stability of their systems, particularly during times of peak load.

While this chapter has discussed rationalizing the portfolio of integration systems, one could follow the same methodology to rationalize the portfolio of information systems. A by-product of the inventory of integration systems happens to be the inventory of the information systems being integrated. Rationalizing information systems can have potentially even bigger cost benefits than the rationalization of integration systems, but sometimes this is stepping outside the bounds of the responsibilities of the ICC.

Lean Terminology

5S: A Lean methodology to create a productive and safe workplace. It consists of

- **Sort:** Keep only really necessary things.
- **Set in order:** Arrange and store everything to be easy to locate, access, and return to its storage place.
- **Shine:** Keep the entire work area clean and ready for production.
- **Standardize:** Create standard work documentation for tasks needed to keep work areas clean and orderly, with diagrams documenting where all tools and supplies are to be stored.
- **Sustain:** Ensure that workplaces are maintained as documented in standard work instructions through empowering operators to organize, maintain, and improve them; also include areas to be audited as a part of layered audit systems.

5 Whys: A method for identifying problem root causes by repetitively asking why, getting a response, and asking why again. The process continues until the identified cause can be linked back to the original problem and it is confirmed that removing or controlling the cause would eliminate the problem.

A3: Another Lean tool in common use; it is a persuasive one-page analysis and synthesis of a problem on A3-size paper (approximately 11 × 17 inches, hence the name), intended to get people involved and to act in ways they otherwise wouldn't. A3 is used effectively for a number of purposes, including annual plan goal deployment, project management, and problem solving. The content should

- Provide the background, context, and importance of the problem
- Assess current performance and the gap versus standard and perfection
- Determine specific goals and objectives of the project
- Analyze the problem to identify its root causes
- Recommend countermeasures that will eliminate defined root causes
- Define an action plan to implement recommended countermeasures
- Establish a measurement, risk mitigation, and review process and standardization plan

There are many benefits of organization-wide A3 use, among them:

- A3's standardized presentation format is understood across the organization so energy is focused on solving problems.
- There is increased speed of problem solving as repetitive use builds stronger problem-solving skills.
- A3s generate ideas from the entire organization as they are posted in areas accessible to everyone.
- They tell shop floor associates they are full team members with management.

Error-proofing—*poka-yoke*: A Lean set of practices intended to prevent the existence of conditions that can result in defects, or if it is not practical to prevent defects, to catch them as close to their source as possible.

***Jidoka*:** Providing machines and operators with the ability to detect when abnormal conditions have occurred and immediately stop work. *Jidoka* is sometimes called "autonomation," meaning automation with human intelligence.

Just-in-time (JIT) production: A production system of making and delivering just what is needed, just when it is needed, and in just the amount needed.

Kaizen: The continuous improvement of a value stream or an individual process to create more value with less waste. There are two levels of *kaizen*: System or flow *kaizen* focuses on the overall value stream, and process *kaizen* focuses on individual processes.

Kaizen **events:** A short-duration improvement project, normally one day to one week, completed by a team following a PDCA-based event methodology.

Kanban: *A* Japanese term for "sign" or "signboard." In Lean it is a signaling device giving authorization and instructions for producing or withdrawing (conveyance) items in a pull system.

Layered audit system: A system of auditing work areas involving operators and all levels of leadership. Shop floor operators audit their areas every day, team leaders may audit their areas weekly, area managers monthly, and plant managers maybe semiannually. Its purpose is compliance with standard work, coaching, and identification of future opportunities to improve.

Lean production system: A business system for organizing and managing product development, operations, suppliers, and customer relations that requires less human effort, less space, less capital, and less time to make products with fewer defects to precise customer desires, compared with the previous system of mass production. The term was coined by John Krafcik, a research assistant at MIT with the International Motor Vehicle Program in the late 1980s.

Level scheduling: A scheduling method of minimizing the effects of mix and volume variability. Work is released to production by pitch, a volume of product defined based on an increment of time to standardize small lot production. It functions in combination with shortening process setup times so smaller lots can be run efficiently. Production volume flexibility is created by using cell design and standard work to be able to quickly flex crew sizes based on Takt time.

Management by fact (MBF): A tool used in a number of methodologies including Six Sigma and CMM. It also has many similarities to the A3 problem-solving process. It is a concise summary of quantified problem statement, performance history, prioritized root causes, and corresponding countermeasures for the purpose of data-driven problem analysis and management. MBF uses "4 Whats" to help quantify the problem statement and the gap between actual and desired performance, and "5 Whys" to determine root causes. (See Figure A.1.)

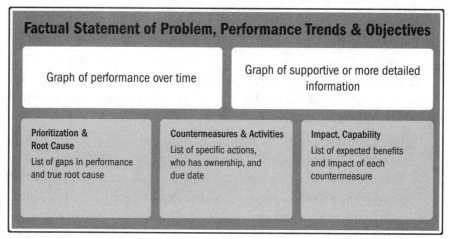

Figure A.1　MBF template

Obeya: *Obeya* in Japanese means simply "big room." It is a major project management tool used to enhance effective, timely communication and ensure project success by shortening the PDCA cycle. Similar in concept to traditional "war rooms," an *obeya* contains highly visual charts and graphs depicting program timing, milestones, and progress to date and countermeasures to existing timing or technical problems. Project leaders may have desks in the *obeya* to facilitate communication.

Pacemaker process: The production process nearest the customer, where products take on their definition. It sets the pace for a value stream. (The pacemaker process should not be confused with a bottleneck process, which necessarily constrains downstream processes because of a lack of capacity.)

PDCA (Plan, Do, Check, Act): An iterative four-step problem-solving process to:
- Identify the real problem, using the five whys, and define countermeasures to eliminate or control the root causes
- Implement the countermeasures
- Measure the new processes and compare against expected results
- Analyze the differences to determine their cause and repeat the problem-solving cycle if necessary

Process efficiency: The percent of total value stream lead time or throughput time that is value-added; it is calculated by dividing value-added time by total time from receipt of raw materials to shipment to customers.

Production lead time (throughput time and total product cycle time): The time required for a product to move all the way through a process from start to finish. At the plant level this is often termed *door-to-door time*. The concept can also be applied to the time required for a design to progress from start to finish in product development or for a product to proceed from raw materials all the way to the customer.

Source quality: A quality management approach to focus on defect prevention at it source or detection and correction as close to the generating process as possible. Defects are never allowed to be passed on to the next downstream process.

Supermarket: Lean term for an inventory buffer of raw materials, work in process, or finished goods, ensuring reliable supply to a downstream process; created to mitigate the consequences of supply variability, demand variability, and differences in the process times of two sequential processes. Withdrawal of material is authorized by a withdrawal *kanban* from the using process, and replenishment is authorized by a production *kanban* sent to the producing process.

Standard work for managers: Every team member has well-defined standardized work, which is critical to accountability, commitment, and achievement of results through waste elimination. Standardized work is defined for every level of management. Thus, managers must have structured time in their daily schedules for time on the shop floor. The daily schedule must be arranged so that managers review all operations over a defined period. The purposes are to

1. Audit standardized work
2. Coach team members in the Lean system and mentor continuous improvement
3. Follow up on previously identified deviations to ensure corrective action is being completed
4. Identify the next level of system improvement

This is a critical management activity required for sustaining Lean systems. A second standardized work activity for managers is leading policy deployment, or *hoshin kanri*, to ensure that operations are completely aligned with the annual business plan. The third manager's standardized work activity is conducting regular Lean operational reviews. Regular reviews are required to assure organizational accountability to fulfill operational plan goals.

Takt **time:** The increment of time, in seconds or minutes, required to produce one unit of product. It is calculated by dividing available production time by customer demand. For example, if a widget factory operates 480 minutes per day and customers demand 240 widgets per day, Takt time is 2 minutes. The purpose of Takt time is to precisely match production with demand. It provides the heartbeat of a Lean production system. The term is German for a precise interval of time such as a musical meter.

Toyota Production System (TPS): The production system developed by Toyota Motor Corporation to provide best quality, lowest cost, and shortest lead time through the elimination of waste. Development of TPS is credited to Taiichi Ohno, Toyota's chief of production in the post–World War II period.

TPM (total productive maintenance): A system for managing facility and machine maintenance focused on elimination of emergency maintenance through rigorous application of preventive and predictive maintenance practices.

Value stream: All of the actions, both value-creating and non-value-creating, required to bring a product from concept to launch and from order to delivery. These include actions to process information from the customer and actions to transform the product on its way to the customer.

Visual management: An important Lean principle and practice. As a principle it is the foundation of making the system transparent so that all can see and understand it, not just the experts. As a practice it means implementing practices, progress metric status, and project implementation status in simple standardized approaches that everyone in the organization can understand. For example, inventory in a supermarket should never fall outside defined minimum or maximum levels. Storage locations in supermarkets are designed to hold the maximum planned inventory. If inventory exceeds the maximum, it must be stored outside designated locations, creating a visible variation that will be caught during the daily audits. These obvious deviations are easily observed and demand immediate follow-up to understand root causes of system failures.

Work cell design: The process of organizing production process steps into logical groups, creating a layout to facilitate minimum materials handling and the most efficient use of operator time. The work at each workstation is balanced to minimize waste and improve flow, resulting in shorter cycle times and lower cost.

Waste: A resource-consuming activity that does not create customer value. In Lean there are seven specific types of waste: excess transportation, inventory, motion, waiting, overproduction, overprocessing, and defects.

Integration Laws[1]

Integration "laws" are ways of thinking about the fundamental drivers of integration. The laws reflect the reality of dealing with "systems-of-systems" (or complex systems) that are characteristic of enterprise integration. They represent the reality of "what is" rather than "what could be" and, just like the laws of physics, describe many characteristics of the real world.

An effective integration approach must not conflict with the integration laws. Although challenging them won't land you in jail, ignoring them will likely add to the list of failed integration projects. As you start down the path of your ICC implementation, remember these five laws.

Law #1: The Whole Is Greater than the Sum of Its Parts

The notion of "process decomposition" is deeply ingrained in most analysis techniques used in modern software development life-cycle methodologies. It is based on the presumption that there are natural boundaries along which

---

1. John G. Schmidt and David Lyle, *Integration Competency Center: An Implementation Methodology* (Informatica Corporation, 2005), pp. 12–14.

to divide a complex system into smaller components for integration. This approach comes from the reductionist perspective, dealing with one dimension of problem analysis.

While this approach helps with tackling relatively simple problems in short time frames, it fails as system complexity increases and natural boundaries disappear. All of the gains achieved by breaking down the big problem are lost as the cost of integrating the small solutions becomes untenable.

Most methodologies fail to realize that the essence of an end-to-end system cannot be captured by studying its individual components alone, and they fail to assign responsibility for the holistic solution. Or if accountability is clear for the initial *construction* of a solution, the solution can deteriorate if no one is responsible for sustaining the end-to-end processes on an ongoing basis.

Law #2: There Is No End State

Organizational entities split, merge, and morph into new structures. Political motivations and boundaries change. Technology evolves, and today's leading edge is tomorrow's legacy. An effective ICC approach must consider the full life cycle of a system and be based on best practices that recognize the adaptive nature of complex systems. From the start, we must plan for constant change.

Furthermore, ICCs must deal with legacy systems based on prior generations of technology. There have been many waves of application technology over the years that seem to move in regular seven-year cycles (e.g., mainframe to mini to microcomputers, monolithic to client/server to Web service applications, etc.). The shift from one wave to the next is neither instantaneous nor is it necessarily economically justified. In fact, a given technology usually lasts through several waves before it is fully replaced. Therefore, the ICC must deal with three to four generations of technology simultaneously.

Law #3: There Are No Universal Standards

Having too many software standards has the same effect as having no standards at all. Even successful standards (such as TCP/IP for the Internet) are not universal. When it comes to software standards such as COBOL or Java, interoperability and transportability come at the expense of vendor-specific extensions, forcing developers to use a less-than-ideal core set of "pure" language features.

The ICC should strive to define and adopt standards within the enterprise, but also work externally with standards organizations to gain agreement across the industry. That said, the ICC must deal with the reality that many forces—including competition, the "not invented here" syndrome, and evolving technologies—will result in many different standards for the foreseeable future.

Law #4: Information Adapts to Meet Local Needs

The information engineering movement of the early 1990s was based on the incorrect notion that an enterprise can have a single consistent data model without redundancy. A more accurate way to look at information is as follows:

$$Information = Data + Context$$

This formula says that the same data across different domains may have different meanings. For example, a simple attribute such as "Current Customer" can mean something different to the marketing, customer service, and legal departments. An extreme example is gender, which you might think could have only two states: male or female; but one particular enterprise has defined eight different genders. The same thing happens with natural languages (the various meanings that words adopt in different communities). The ICC must embrace informational diversity, recognizing that variations exist, and use techniques to compensate for them.

Law #5: All Details Are Relevant

Abstraction is the practice of representing a problem without all the details, developing a model solution based on the abstract problem, and then using the model to create the real-life solution. The success of this approach depends on our ability to build and use abstract models to manage and direct activities. But the effectiveness of an abstract model is inversely proportional to the complexity of the context, because no details can be safely ignored. The cost of developing and maintaining abstract models of the system and the project can become an economic black hole, consuming all benefits.

A successful ICC deals with this conundrum by decomposing the problem while maintaining a view of the entire picture. Although there is no easy solution, an effective ICC must strive to achieve *dynamic* models—models that are connected to the real world in such a way that when one changes, so does the other. Only then can we attain a truly sustainable integration infrastructure.

APPENDIX C

Glossary

This glossary is divided into two parts: common acronyms, and the most important integration and information technology terms used in this book. Note that this glossary will be maintained on the book's Web site, www.integrationfactory.com.

Note: Italicized acronyms are also included in the following definitions section.

Common Acronyms

API:	*Application program interface*
B2B:	Business to business
B2C:	Business to consumer
BI:	Business intelligence
BPEL:	Business Process Execution Language
BPM:	Business process management or business process modeling

BPMN:	Business Process Modeling Notation
CDC:	Changed data capture
CORBA:	Common Object Request Broker Architecture
DBMS:	Database management system
DI:	*Data integration*
EAI:	*Enterprise application integration*
EDA:	*Event-driven architecture*
EII:	Enterprise information integration
ESB:	*Enterprise service bus*
ETL:	Extract, transform, load
FTE:	Full-time equivalent (staff)
HTTP:	Hypertext Transfer Protocol
ICC:	*Integration Competency Center*
IS:	Information systems (organizational unit)
IT:	Information technology (organizational unit)
ME&C:	Mutually exclusive and comprehensive
MDM:	Master data management
MOM:	Message-oriented middleware
ODS:	*Operational data store*
POC:	Proof of concept
REST:	Representational state transfer
SLA:	*Service level agreement*
SOA:	*Service-oriented architecture*
SOAP:	Simple Object Access Protocol
SOR:	*System of record*
SQL:	Structured Query Language
UDDI:	Universal Description, Discovery, and Integration
XML:	eXtensible Markup Language

Definitions

Application: A deployed and operational IT system that supports business functions and services. Applications encapsulate data and are supported by multiple technology components. Applications may be logical or physical but are distinct from the technology components that are used to construct them.

Application program interface (API): A set of public programmatic interfaces that consists of a language and a message format to communicate with an operating system or other programmatic environment, such as databases, Web servers, and so forth. These messages typically call functions and methods available for application development.

Bus: An abstract software pattern used to transfer data between multiple systems. In contrast to the hub-and-spoke pattern, it uses a federation of components that all follow a common policy or protocol to send, route, and receive messages.

Business glossary: A list of business data elements with a corresponding description, enterprise-level or domain-specific synonyms, validation rules, and other relevant metadata. Used to identify the source of a record, quality metrics, ownership authority, and stewardship responsibility.

Business object: An encapsulated unit of application functionality closely aligned to data and data access considerations.

Business process: A structured description of the activities or tasks that have to be done to fulfill a certain business need. The activities or tasks might be manual steps (human interaction) or automated steps (IT steps). Business processes might be managed and implemented using modeling notations such as BPMN or EPC or execution languages such as BPEL. Some people differentiate between workflows and business processes by stating that business processes describe more generally what has to be done, whereas workflows describe how activities or tasks should be carried out.

Canonical: Reduced to the simplest and most significant form possible without loss of generality.

Canonical data model: The definition of a standard organization view of a particular information subject. To be practical, canonical data models include a mapping back to each application view of the same subject. The canonical data model is frequently implemented as an XML hierarchy. Specific uses include delivering enterprise-wide business intelligence (BI), defining a common view within a service-oriented architecture (SOA), and streamlining software interfaces.

Canonical model: A design pattern used to communicate between different data formats. The basic idea is that rather that writing translators between each and every format (with potential for a combinatorial explosion), it is sufficient just to write a translator between each format and the canonical format.

Capability: A thing that an organization, person, or system is able to do. Capabilities are typically very coarse-grained and may bring together a combination of people, processes, and technology.

Coupling: A dependency between two computer hardware or software elements or systems. Tight coupling is when the elements are strongly dependent on each other so that when one changes, the other is impacted. Loose coupling reduces dependencies between systems through techniques such as middleware abstraction layers, asynchronous communication, or compensating transactions rather than two-phase commit transactions to maintain consistency. In general, loose coupling leads to more complexity. For this reason, in a specific architectural style it is important find the right amount of loose coupling. Coupling is usually contrasted with cohesion. Low coupling often correlates with high cohesion, and vice versa.

Data entity: An encapsulation of data that is recognized by a business domain expert as a thing. Logical data entities can be tied to applications, repositories, and services and may be structured according to implementation considerations.

Data governance: The policies and processes that continually work to improve and ensure the availability, accessibility, quality, consistency, auditability, and security of data in a company or institution.

Data integration: Accessing data and functions from disparate systems to create a combined and consistent view of core information for use across the organization to improve business decisions and operations.

Data mart: A database structured for specific analysis and historical reporting needs.

Data warehouse: A subject-oriented, integrated, time-variant, and historical collection of summary and detailed data used to support the decision-making and other reporting and analysis needs that require historical, point-in-time information. Data, once captured within the warehouse, is nonvolatile and relevant to a point in time.

Enterprise application integration (EAI): An approach to integrating distributed systems so that they use a common infrastructure (middleware and/or protocol). With this approach, for each system it is enough to provide and maintain only one adapter to the infrastructure, instead of a specific adapter for each of the systems with which it communicates. The infrastructure might use a bus or hub-and-spoke approach.

Enterprise service bus (ESB): The infrastructure of an SOA landscape that enables the interoperability of services. Its core task is to provide connectivity, data transformations, and routing so that systems can communicate via services.

Event: A notification sent to a more or less well-known set of receivers (consumers). Usually, the receivers of an event have to subscribe to a certain type of event (sent by a certain system or component). Depending on the programming or system model, the systems sending the events (the providers) might or might not know and agree to send the events to the subscribing receivers.

Event-driven architecture (EDA): A software architecture pattern promoting the production, detection, consumption of, and reaction to events.

Governance: The discipline of tracking, managing, and steering an IS/IT landscape. Architectural governance is concerned with change processes (design governance). Operational governance looks at the operational performance of systems against contracted performance levels, the definition of operational performance levels, and the implementation of systems that ensure the effective operation of systems.

Hub and spoke: An abstract software pattern used to transfer data between multiple systems. In contrast to the bus pattern, it uses a central component that coordinates all communication between senders and receivers.

Information object model: A model used to provide traceability from the enterprise function and information subject models to the business glossary (i.e., an information object includes a list of data elements from the business glossary). Possibly used for assessing current information management capabilities (reflected in process and target systems models) or as a conceptual model for custom-developed application components.

Integration: (1) An infrastructure for enabling efficient data sharing across incompatible applications that evolve independently, in a coordinated manner, to serve the needs of the enterprise and its stakeholders. (2) The capability for efficient data sharing across applications in a coordinated manner to serve the needs of the enterprise and its stakeholders. The end result is a system-of-systems that supports sharing data and functions across incompatible applications to create a combined and consistent view of core information for use across the enterprise to improve business decisions and operations. (3) The capability to constructively face the tensions of incompatible business systems that need to interoperate and, rather than simply coupling them to satisfy a tactical need, generating a creative solution that contains elements of the individual systems but is superior to each—in other words, creating synergy where the whole is greater than the sum of the parts.

Integration Competency Center (ICC): A permanent cross-functional team operating as a shared-services function supporting multiple organizational units and sustaining integration in a coordinated manner. Alternate names include Business Intelligence Competency Center (BICC), Integration Center of Excellence (Integration COE), Data Quality Competency Center (DQCC), SOA Center of Expertise (SOA COE), Integration Solutions Group (ISG), Enterprise Data Management (EDM), and other variants.

Integration Factory: A cohesive integration technology platform that automates the flow of materials and information in the process of building and sustaining integration points. Examples of automation include requirements definition, code generation, testing, and migration of code objects.

Integration point: A data exchange or dependency between two business systems that provides discrete functionality and is designed and managed as a functional unit. An integration point may involve one or more interfaces with each of the systems involved and may involve any number of middleware elements, but it is still considered as one integration point. Conversely, if system A publishes the same data using the same interface to systems B and C, it is considered as two integration points (A–B and A–C). Furthermore, if data is combined from systems X and Y and then sent to system Z as a single message, it is also considered as two integration points (X–Z and Y–Z).

Interface: The externally visible definition of the operations permitted on an application component.

Interoperability: The ability of different systems to communicate with each other. Interoperability between different applications, platforms, and programming languages is a fundamental goal of integration.

Lean Integration: A management system that emphasizes creating value for end customers, continuous improvement, and eliminating waste as a sustainable data and process integration practice.

Measure: A quantitative performance indicator or success factor that can be traced on an ongoing basis to determine successful operation and progress toward objectives and goals.

Metadata: Data about data and data processes. Metadata is important because it aids in clarifying and finding the actual data.

Meta-model: A description of a model. A meta-model refers to the rules that define the structure a model can have. In other words, a meta-model defines the formal structure and elements of a model.

Methodology: A defined, repeatable approach to address a particular type of problem. A methodology typically centers on a defined process but may also include definition of content. May be used interchangeably with the term *method*.

Middleware: Computer software or hardware that connects other software components or systems. This technology evolved to provide for interoperability in support of the move to coherent distributed architectures, which are used most often to support complex distributed applications. It includes Web servers, application servers, and similar tools that support application development and delivery. Middleware is especially integral in managing and optimizing a system-of-systems at the enterprise level. Middleware sits "in the middle" between applications that may be working on different operating systems. It is similar to the middle layer of a three-tier single-system architecture, except that it is stretched across multiple systems or applications. Examples include EAI, ETL, EII, BPM, SOA, and MOM (message-oriented middleware).

Operational data store: A database that is subject-oriented, read-only to end users, current (non-historical), volatile, and integrated; is separate from and derived from one or more systems of record; and supports day-to-day business operations and real-time decision making.

Organization unit: A self-contained unit of resources with line management responsibility, goals, objectives, and measures. Organizations may include external parties and business partner organizations.

Pattern: A common combination of logic, interactions, and behaviors that form a consistent or characteristic arrangement. An important use of patterns is the idea of design templates that are general solutions to integration problems. They will not solve a specific problem, but they provide a sort of architectural outline that may be reused in order to speed up the development process.

Platform: A combination of technology infrastructure products and components on which various application programs can be designed to run.

Process integration: Automation of processes that cut across functional or application boundaries where process state needs to be maintained independently of the underlying application systems or where multiple data consumers or data providers need to be orchestrated as part of a business transaction.

Protocol: The rules governing the syntax, semantics, and synchronization of communication.

Publish/subscribe: A message exchange pattern where a service consumer subscribes to get a notification message from a service provider when a certain condition or state occurs or changes.

Road map: An abstracted plan for business or technology change, typically operating across multiple disciplines over multiple years.

Role: The characteristic and expected behaviors of an individual, derived from his or her responsibilities and preferences in providing value to the organization.

Service: In an organizational context, a set of benefits delivered by a service provider, mostly in close coordination with other service suppliers, commissioned according to the needs of the service consumer, and used by the requesting service consumer for supporting day-to-day business tasks. For example, an ICC provides services to internal consumers that may be other IT or business functions.

Service, information system: A service that is specifically provided by an automated IT-based solution. In an SOA, the IT realization of self-contained business functionality, sometimes also referred to as a Web service. Technically, a service is a description of one or more operations that use messages to exchange data between a provider and a consumer.

Service level agreement (SLA): A formal negotiated agreement between two parties that usually records the common understanding about priorities, responsibilities, and warranties, with the main purpose of agreeing on the quality of the service. For example, an SLA may specify the levels of availability, serviceability, performance, operation, or other attributes of the service (such as billing and even penalties in the case of violations of the SLA).

Service-oriented architecture (SOA): In its most general sense, an approach for architectures where the interfaces are services. In a more specific sense, it is an architectural style for dealing with business processes distributed over a large and heterogeneous landscape of existing and new systems that are under the control of different owners. The key concepts of SOA are services, interoperability, and loose coupling.

System: A set of interacting or interdependent computer hardware and software components forming an integrated unit. In this book, the terms *system* and *application* are often used interchangeably. A business system supports capabilities in a particular business domain (such as finance, marketing, manufacturing, sales, etc.), whereas an integration system supports capabilities in a particular integration discipline (such as data integration, process integration, data quality, business intelligence, etc.). See also the definition for **system-of-systems.**

System of record: The single authoritative, enterprise-designated source of operational data. It is the most current, accurate source of its data.

System-of-systems: The collection of interconnected systems in an enterprise. Modern systems that form systems-of-systems are not monolithic; rather they have five common characteristics: operational independence of the individual systems, managerial independence of the systems, geographical distribution, emergent behavior, and evolutionary development.

Transfer price: The price that one subunit (department or division) charges for a product or service supplied to another subunit of the same organization. Transfer pricing is the mechanism used by ICCs to charge for their services on either a market, cost-plus, or negotiated basis.

Web services: A set of standards that serves as one possible way of realizing an SOA infrastructure. Initially started with the core standards XML, HTTP, WSDL, SOAP, and UDDI, it now contains over 60 standards and profiles developed and maintained by standardization organizations, such as W3C, OASIS, and WS-I.

Workflow: Similar to a business process; a description of the activities or tasks that have to be done to fulfill a certain business need. Some people differentiate between workflows and business processes by stating that business processes describe more generally what has to be done, whereas workflows describe how activities or tasks should be carried out.

Index

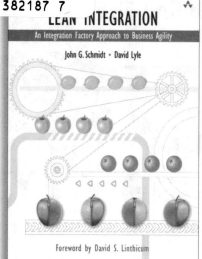